DATE DUE

SEP 2 7 2011			

Adolescent Encounters With Death, Bereavement, and Coping

David E. Balk, PhD, FT, is a Professor in the Department of Health and Nutrition Sciences at Brooklyn College of the City University of New York where he directs Graduate Studies in Thanatology. He is an associate editor of *Death Studies* and serves as that journal's Book Review Editor. His work in thanatology has focused primarily on adolescent bereavement. He wrote *Adolescent Development: Early Through Late Adolescence* (1995). With Carol Wogrin, Gordon Thornton, and David Meagher, he edited the *Handbook of Thanatology: The Essential Body of Knowledge for the Study of Death, Dying, and Bereavement* (2007). With Charles A. Corr, he edited the *Handbook of Adolescent Death and Bereavement* (Springer Publishing Company, 1996). He also serves on the Mental Health Advisory Board for the National Students of AMF Support Network, a program begun by bereaved college students to assist one another.

Charles A. Corr, PhD, CT, is Professor Emeritus, Southern Illinois University, Edwardsville, and a member of the Board of Directors of the Suncoast Institute, an affiliate of the Hospice of the Florida Suncoast (2000–present); the ChiPPS (Children's Project on Palliative/Hospice Services) Leadership Advisory Council of the National Hospice and Palliative Care Organization; the Executive Committee of the National Donor Family Council of the National Kidney Foundation (1992–2001 and 2006–present); and the International Work Group on Death, Dying, and Bereavement (1979–present; Chairperson, 1989–1993). His publications include more than 30 books and booklets, together with over 100 chapters and articles in professional journals on subjects such as death education, death-related issues involving children and adolescents, hospice principles and practice, and organ and tissue donation. His most recent book is the sixth edition of *Death and Dying, Life and Living* (2009), coauthored with Clyde M. Nabe and Donna M. Corr.

Adolescent Encounters With Death, Bereavement, and Coping

DAVID E. BALK, PhD, FT
CHARLES A. CORR, PhD, CT

Editors

New York

Springer Publishing Company, LLC
11 West 42nd Street
New York, NY 10036
www.springerpub.com

Acquisitions Editor: Sheri W. Sussman
Project Manager: Julia Rosen
Cover design: Mimi Flow
Composition: Apex CoVantage

09 10 11 / 5 4 3 2 1

Library of Congress Cataloging-in-Publication Data

Adolescent encounters with death, bereavement, and coping / David E. Balk, Charles A. Corr, editors.
p. cm.
Includes index.
ISBN 978-0-8261-1073-2 (alk. paper)
1. Teenagers and death. 2. Grief in adolescence. 3. Bereavement in adolescence. 4. Teenagers—Counseling of. I. Balk, David E., 1943– II. Corr, Charles A.

BF724.3.D43A37 2009
155.9'370835—dc22 2008050929

Printed in the United States of America by Hamilton Printing.

This book is dedicated to
Mary Ann Balk,
wife and best friend,
whose love and support,
wit, belief, and intelligence
make such a difference.

And to the memory of
Howard "Bud" Allen (1924–2008),
an eternal youth all his life,
full of fun and surprises,
always encouraging about our work,
and our very best neighbor ever.

Contents

Contributors

Donna Armstrong, MSW, CSW, is Daniel's Care Pediatric Coordinator at Hospice of the Bluegrass in Lexington, Kentucky.

David L. Bennett, AO, FRACP, FSAM, is Senior Staff Specialist, Department of Adolescent Medicine, and Head, New South Wales Centre for the Advancement of Adolescent Health, the Children's Hospital at Westmead, Sydney, New South Wales, Australia.

Michelle R. Brown, PhD, is Clinical Assistant Professor, Division of Child Psychiatry, Stanford University School of Medicine, and Pediatric Psychologist, Pediatric Psychiatry Consultation-Liaison Service, Lucile Packard Children's Hospital at Stanford in Stanford, California.

Alicia Skinner Cook, PhD, is Professor Emeritus, Department of Human Development and Family Studies, Colorado State University, Fort Collins, Colorado.

Vanessa Cook, D Clin Psych, is a pediatric clinical psychologist, currently working with children and young people for the National Health Service in Barnstaple, United Kingdom.

David A. Crenshaw, PhD, ABPP, is Director of the Rhinebeck Child and Family Center in Rhinebeck, New York.

Jana DeCristofaro, MSW, is the Coordinator of Children's Grief Services at The Dougy Center for Grieving Children in Portland, Oregon.

Craig Demmer, EdD, PhD, is Professor, Department of Health Sciences, Lehman College of the City University of New York.

Julie C. Dunsmore, AM, BSc (Psych) Hons, MPH, RN, is Director, Department of Health Promotion, Lower North Shore, Northern Sydney Central Coast Health, and Senior Clinical Psychologist, Trauma Recovery Coordinator NSW Health, the Royal North Shore Hospital, St. Leonards, Sydney, New South Wales, Australia.

Christopher W. Hall, MA, is a psychologist and Director, Australian Centre for Grief and Bereavement in Melbourne, Victoria, Australia.

Linda C. Hill, LCSW-R, FT, is a clinical social worker and grief therapist practicing in Poughkeepsie, New York.

Phyllis Kosminsky, PhD, is a clinical social worker in private practice in Westchester County, New York, and at the Center for Hope in Darien, Connecticut.

Deirdre Lewin, MA, is a Senior Director at Family Centers Inc. in Fairfield County, Connecticut, where she directs the Center for Hope and the Den for Grieving Kids, and is an adjunct faculty member in the Department of Psychology at Manhattanville College in Purchase, New York.

Jane Ribbens McCarthy, PhD, is Reader in Family Studies, Faculty of Social Sciences, Open University, Milton Keynes, United Kingdom.

Illene C. Noppe, PhD, is Professor of Human Development, Psychology, and Women's Studies in the Department of Human Development, University of Wisconsin-Green Bay, Green Bay, Wisconsin.

Lloyd D. Noppe, PhD, is Professor of Human Development, Department of Human Development, University of Wisconsin-Green Bay, Green Bay, Wisconsin.

Stacy F. Orloff, EdD, LCSW, is Vice President, Palliative Care and Community Programs, at The Hospice of the Florida Suncoast in Clearwater, Florida.

Lillian M. Range, PhD, is Professor of Psychology at Our Lady of Holy Cross College, New Orleans, Louisiana, and Professor Emeritus at the University of Southern Mississippi.

Catriona Reid, D Clin Psych, is a clinical psychologist currently working as Senior Practitioner at the Winston's Wish program in Cheltenham, United Kingdom.

Robyn A. Reid, BSW, is a social worker, Department of Education and Early Childhood Development, Victoria, Australia.

Stacy S. Remke, MSW, LICSW, is Coordinator, Children's Institute for Pain and Palliative Care, Children's Hospitals and Clinics of Minnesota, in Minneapolis, Minnesota.

Donna L. Schuurman, EdD, FT, is Executive Director, The Dougy Center for Grieving Children, in Portland, Oregon.

Heather L. Servaty-Seib, PhD, HSPP, is Associate Professor of Counseling and Development in the Department of Educational Studies, Purdue University, West Lafayette, Indiana.

Carla J. Sofka, PhD, MSW, is Associate Professor of Social Work at Siena College in Loudonville, New York.

Barbara Sourkes, PhD, is Associate Professor of Pediatrics and Psychiatry, Stanford University School of Medicine, and Kriewall-Haehl Director, Pediatric Palliative Care Program, Lucile Packard Children's Hospital at Stanford in Stanford, California.

Michael M. Stevens, AM, FRACP, is Senior Staff Specialist, Oncology Unit, the Children's Hospital at Westmead, Sydney, New South Wales, Australia.

Robert G. Stevenson, EdD, CT, is Assistant Professor of Counseling in the School of Social and Behavioral Sciences, Mercy College, New York City. He was a high school teacher and school counselor for 30 years and taught a high school death education course of his own design for 25 years in Bergen County, New Jersey.

Julie Stokes, MSc, OBE, is a clinical psychologist, founder, and Clinical Director of the Winston's Wish program in Cheltenham, United Kingdom.

Andrea C. Walker, PhD, LADC, is Associate Professor of Psychology, Oral Roberts University, Tulsa, Oklahoma.

Carol Wogrin, PsyD, RN, is Director, National Center for Death Education, Mount Ida College, in Newton, Massachusetts.

Andrew J. Young, PhD, is Chief Executive Officer, CanTeen—The Australian Organisation for Young People Living with Cancer, Sydney, New South Wales, Australia.

Foreword

It is difficult to top a classic work. Thirteen years ago, Charles Corr and David Balk edited a volume, the *Handbook of Adolescent Death and Bereavement*, which quickly became the standard text on adolescence and death. Few books matched either its breadth or its depth.

Yet, lightning does strike twice. In *Adolescent Encounters With Death, Bereavement, and Coping*, Balk and Corr again have edited a book that will set the direction of the field for yet another decade.

Adolescent Encounters With Death, Bereavement, and Coping breaks new ground in many ways. Some of these chapters highlight changes in adolescent experience since the first book was conceived. For example, Carla J. Sofka's chapter, "Adolescents, Technology, and the Internet: Coping With Loss in the Digital World," reflects on the wide-ranging use that adolescents now make of the Internet as they cope with loss and grief. Craig Demmer's chapter on HIV/AIDS encounters another, much more difficult reality, the number of adolescents throughout the world who have developed HIV infection, died of AIDS, or have been orphaned by the disease—the infected and affected.

Other chapters, among them chapters dealing with humor about death in adolescence, ethical issues, and therapy with adolescents experiencing prolonged grief, add new depth and insight on areas seldom explored as an aspect of adolescence. Taken together, all the chapters reaffirm another critical aspect of thanatology—the value of its multidisciplinary character. The authors here view adolescence and death from a variety of perspectives—including sociology, psychology, education, family studies, social work, nursing, philosophy, and anthropology—as well as from a number of different cultures. The result is a rich tapestry where every chapter makes a unique contribution while leaving the book as a whole strengthened by these varied voices.

Thematically the book makes some critical points. The first is that adolescents do encounter death in their journeys to adulthood. It is an inherent aspect of adolescence. Identity, independence, and intimacy are often considered the three *I*s of adolescent development. Yet, death is the ultimate challenge to each of these processes—the end of intimacy, the obliteration of identity, the demise of independence. If adolescence is the time during which one begins to recognize that one is unique, death becomes the ultimate threat. Mortality reminds one that the cost of uniqueness is finitude. While the very present orientation of adolescence and the invulnerability that arises from the emerging strength and mastery found in that period protect against the threat of death, it remains, emerging in the humor, song, games, films, and even books such as *The Outsiders,* which resonate with adolescence.

Death exists not only as a developmental recognition. It is an ongoing reality in the lives of adolescents. Parents and siblings sometimes die. Adolescents live with and sometimes die from life-threatening illnesses. Many of these deaths—by accidents, suicide, or homicide—are both sudden and deeply traumatic, complicating grief. Many adolescent losses, such as the deaths of friends and celebrities, can be disenfranchised, ignored by others. Death, these authors reaffirm, is not something just *out there* on the developmental horizon; it is also *in here*, a present, often unrecognized event that adolescents encounter.

While adolescents do encounter death, they cope with it using all their developmental strengths and resources. They find community with one another—even in an increasing digital world. Yet, the authors of these chapters, while acknowledging the adolescent's considerable assets, assert that caregivers have much that they can offer. Education, support groups, therapy, and grief camps can all add to the ability of adolescents to cope with loss. Camps and support groups, for example, build on the strong peer ties that are so critical to adolescents—creating communities where they can both take and offer support and solidarity.

The very nature of that support, as well as the inherent volatility and vitality of adolescence, takes a toll on the adult caregivers who so critically assist the adolescent coping with death. The editors were especially wise to end their work with a chapter focusing on caregiver fatigue.

Caregivers now have one more resource in their arsenal as they assist adolescents in coping with death, loss, grief, and bereavement. They now can count on this book, *Adolescent Encounters With Death, Bereavement, and Coping,* for insight and intervention.

Kenneth J. Doka, PhD
Professor, The Graduate School, The College of New Rochelle
Senior Consultant, The Hospice Foundation of America

Preface

Adolescent encounters with death and bereavement, as well as efforts by adolescents to cope with these encounters, frequently do not receive full-scale exploration. There are many reasons for this deficiency. All too often, these encounters are subsumed into examinations of childhood experiences, without taking into account the distinctive qualities of adolescent life. In addition, while many investigators have recognized that adolescence in general is a healthy time of life, one in which its members have escaped the problems of early childhood but have not lived long enough to face the problems of adulthood, they have incorrectly concluded that death-related encounters during adolescence occur only in small and insignificant numbers with little impact on the lives of the adolescents involved.

We believe there is need for a robust focus on death, bereavement, and coping during adolescence in its own right. Such a focus needs to include, but go beyond, investigations of familiar topics, such as suicide, HIV/AIDS, and parental or sibling bereavement during the adolescent years. We offer this book as part of a new effort to provide a broad resource to guide care providers, such as nurses, counselors, social workers, educators, and clergy, who seek to understand and help adolescents as they attempt to cope with death-related issues.

Writing separately and together, we have attempted over the years to contribute to the literature on these topics. One or both of us has also edited two prior books in this subject area. The first book devoted to a comprehensive survey of interactions between adolescents and death-related issues, *Adolescence and Death* (Springer Publishing Company, 1986), was edited by Charles A. Corr and Joan N. McNeil. Ten years later, that was followed by our coedited book, *Handbook of Adolescent Death and Bereavement* (Springer Publishing Company, 1996).

We agreed to undertake a third book in this field, the one you now hold in your hands, because we recognized that a great deal has transpired since the 1980s and 1990s in terms of theoretical understandings, research advances, and clinical management. For example, much has been learned about complicated bereavement in recent years. In addition, imaginative conceptual frameworks and models have appeared on the scene, such as the dual process model for understanding loss, ideas about assumptive worlds, debates about the benefits or potential harm of grief counseling with the normally bereaved, efforts to bridge the gap separating researchers and practitioners, and stimulating essays about recovery and resilience following bereavement.

The terrorist attacks on the World Trade Center and the Pentagon in September of 2001 changed the world in many ways. Compelling events of many types followed, such as conflicts in Afghanistan and Iraq; genocide and ethnic cleansing in Eastern Europe and Darfur; violent rites of passage into adulthood; epidemics of HIV infection among many third world adolescents and young adults; heightened environmental concerns about global warming and various forms of natural disasters; and the ongoing burdens of disease, poverty, and malnutrition on populations. There also has been the exponential spread of the Internet. We now live in Marshall McCluhan's worldwide media village, but with consequences that it is doubtful McCluhan had forecast.

Closer to home, the need for increased understanding of cultural diversity has become the norm within thanatological scholarship, as well as in the everyday practice of professionals (for instance, teachers, nurses, counselors, and other care providers) who come into contact with adolescents coping with death and bereavement.

We approached the best experts in their respective fields as contributors to this book. In so doing, we emphasized that their chapters should make every effort to synthesize contemporary scholarship and examine topics with more than mainstream American culture in mind. The contributing authors come from the United States, the United Kingdom, and Australia, as well as from multiple disciplinary perspectives, including sociology, psychology, education, family studies, social work, nursing, medicine, philosophy, and anthropology. Coverage includes a focus on differences in socioeconomic class, ethnic/racial identity, family composition, and the influence of coping with death and bereavement on adulthood sequelae.

As these contributors delivered their manuscripts to us, we were delighted to realize that we ourselves were learning new lessons about death, bereavement, and coping in the dynamic worlds of adolescents. New evidence, scholarly research, exciting interpretations, and practical insights came together in important ways. As a result, we believe *Adolescent Encounters With Death, Bereavement, and Coping* provides an overarching framework for understanding these topics, offers persuasive syntheses of specific areas of inquiry, and initiates scholarly discussion on subjects not previously examined. We trust you will share our judgment once you have had an opportunity to examine the contents of this book.

David E. Balk
Charles A. Corr

Background

PART I

The three chapters in part I provide essential background for all understandings of adolescent encounters with death, bereavement, and coping. In chapter 1, David Balk addresses the many changes occurring in early, middle, and late adolescence as individuals move from childhood to adulthood. In particular, these relate to the developmental challenges and tasks that are critical in each adolescent's quest to establish a distinct and stable identity, one that will serve the person well into his or her future. Balk brings out, on the one hand, the many dimensions of adolescent life—cognitive, emotional, behavioral, physical, interpersonal, and spiritual dimensions—and, on the other hand, the critical relationships through which adolescents engage with themselves, others, and the external world.

In chapter 2, Jane Ribbens McCarthy draws attention to processes involved in making meaning when adolescents encounter death and other types of major losses. These events do not merely "happen to" adolescents, as if that was all there was to it. In fact, finding or making meaning is central to the processes through which adolescents engage in "making sense of" or "finding a purpose through" their losses. Culture and context are key variables in these processes, which are affected by obvious material inequities and inequalities of power, as adolescents around the world "frame" or interpret their experiences.

Finally, in chapter 3 Alicia Skinner Cook examines ethical and methodological issues that arise when scholars and researchers seek to explore various aspects of bereavement and grief during the adolescent years. Cook shows why it is crucial to study adolescent grief experiences. She also recommends including adolescents in sound empirical research, even as she takes note of both the benefits and risks that must be faced in such explorations. Cook insists on attention to the unique circumstances of the adolescent's global situation and takes note of the emerging importance of the cyberworld in this type of research. That leads to the underlying key point in her argument: the need to avoid treating bereaved adolescents as subjects and to engage them, instead, as partners in describing and helping to understand their own experiences.

A basic lesson that reappears throughout these and subsequent chapters in this book is the need to listen actively and carefully to each adolescent as he or she shares descriptions and explanations of his or her experiences.

1 Adolescent Development: The Backstory to Adolescent Encounters With Death and Bereavement

DAVID E. BALK

Existential phenomenology has proposed that human existence involves relationships to oneself, to others, and to the external world (Attig, 1996; May, Angel, & Ellenberger, 1958). Separately, researchers into adolescence and proponents of the hospice philosophy have argued that being human involves cognitive, emotional, behavioral, physical, interpersonal, and spiritual dimensions (Balk, 2007; Corless & Nicholas, 2003; Corr, 2007). Both the three-fold schema from existential phenomenology and the holistic template informing hospice care provide important conceptual frameworks for understanding adolescence, death, and bereavement.

In this chapter, these two frameworks are the conceptual scaffolding for examining central topics in the lives of adolescents who encounter death and bereavement. The overarching perspective, is that the self, what Leighton (1959, p. 16) called "the acting of a person considered as a living, self-integrating unit," is the unifying and coherent assumption behind all these comments. Presented visually (see Figure 1.1), our argument has the holistic template nested within the three relationships from existential phenomenology and all of these ideas contained within the "living, self-integrating unit" of individuality we call the self.

EXISTENTIAL PHENOMENOLOGY AND THE RELATIONSHIP WITH ONESELF

A compelling task our society imposes on adolescents is to fashion stable, mature identities. According to Erikson (1968), the search for identity is the hallmark of adolescent psychosocial development. Forging a stable, mature identity cannot take place apart from expectations to master certain marks of maturity, sometimes called developmental transitions. Among these transitions are psychosocial expectations to gain increasing skill in maintaining intimate relationships and to decide on a career. It takes little imagination to see the connection between these transitions and the existential phenomenologists' emphasis on relationships with others and with the external world.

EXISTENTIAL PHENOMENOLOGY AND THE RELATIONSHIP TO OTHERS

Developmental phases within adolescence only accord with chronological age as broad and rough generalizations: Typically, it is thought that early adolescence begins with puberty (as early as age 10 in many

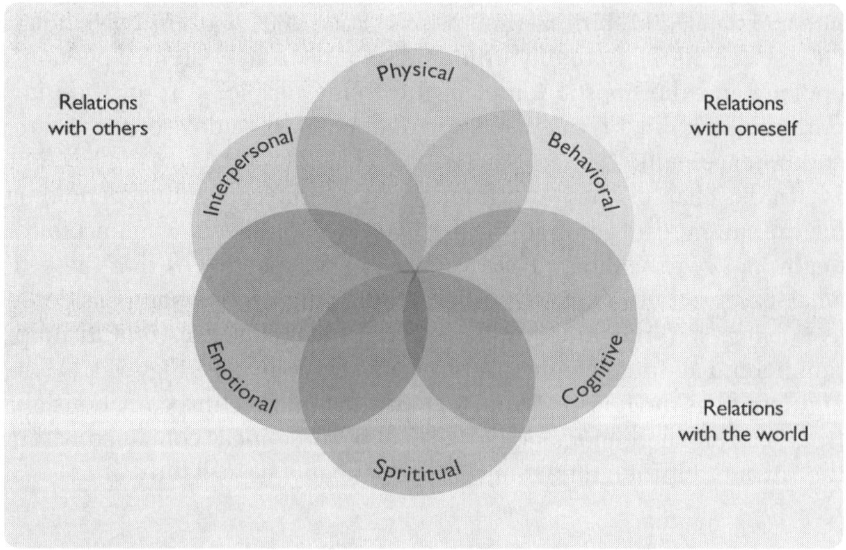

Figure 1.1 The self.

cases) and lasts until about age 14, middle adolescence lasts from ages 15–17, and late adolescence ranges from ages 18–23. In each of these phases, adolescents (at least those in westernized, developed countries) face distinctive tasks and conflicts (see Table 1.1) vis-à-vis other persons.

As individuals mature from early adolescence through later adolescence (Blos, 1979) they typically gain increasing skill in understanding the points of view of others. This growth in interpersonal maturity occurs in the midst of a maddening preoccupation with self that borders on solipsism in the early and middle adolescent years (Elkind, 1967): Adolescents seem convinced that they are the center of everyone else's thoughts, overreact to what others say or do, and consider that no one can understand how special they really are. An influence that alters this solipsistic preoccupation is relationships with peers, who can (a) disabuse each other of self-centeredness, (b) provide sources of support and understanding, and (c) foster empathy and love (Ladd, 2005; Parker & Gottman, 1989; Sullivan, 1953).

Table 1.1

TASKS AND CONFLICTS FOR ADOLESCENTS BY MATURATIONAL PHASE

Phase I	Age:	11–14
	Task:	Emotional separation from parents
	Conflict:	Separation versus reunion (abandonment vs. safety)
Phase II	Age:	14–17
	Task:	Competency/mastery/control
	Conflict:	Independence versus dependence
Phase III	Age:	17–21
	Task:	Intimacy and commitment
	Conflict:	Closeness versus distance

From "Helping Bereaved Adolescents: Needs and Responses," by S. J. Fleming & R. Adolph, 1986, in C. A. Corr & J. N. McNeil (Eds.), *Adolescence and Death* (p. 103), New York: Springer Publishing. Copyright © 1986 by Springer Publishing. Reprinted with permission.

EXISTENTIAL PHENOMENOLOGY AND THE RELATIONSHIP WITH THE EXTERNAL WORLD

Deciding what to do to earn a living is a major developmental transition imposed by society on adolescents. Persons in later adolescence who don't know what they want to do feel anxious. Some are simply late bloomers yet to have their imaginations captured by the appeal of a career or vocation. Some are adrift and remain so through their adult lives. There is a fundamental link between self-concept and occupational choice (Super, 1957), and later adolescents and young adults adrift about what career choices fit them provide clear examples of persons with marred relationships vis-à-vis self and the external world.

THE HOLISTIC TEMPLATE: COGNITIVE ASPECTS

The cognitive revolution in psychology, exemplified in such different approaches as Bandura's social learning theory and self-efficacy ideas (1977, 1997), Beck's cognitive therapy strategies with emotional disorders (Beck, 1976), Kelly's personal construct theory (Kelly, 1955), and the analysis of decision making by Janis and Mann (1977), set the stage in psychology for today's almost unquestioned acceptance of constructivism as the paradigm for explaining human learning and adaptation to stress. Neimeyer (e.g., 2001) is the major figure within thanatology who has championed constructivism.

For years scholars have accepted Piaget's (1929) description of cognitive development moving from preoperational to formal operational thinking. These notions still inform many within human development circles and within thanatology as well. While acknowledging the contributions that Piaget's model gave to considering the dynamism involved in an individual's forming increasingly complex comprehensions of reality, advances have been made that also need to be accommodated into our schemas of how our minds change over time.

According to Piaget, cognitive development culminates in formal operations. Clearly, evidence gained about lack of self-reflection suggests that concrete operations remain the norm for many into adulthood (Josselson, 1996; Shain & Farber, 1989). And yet there is striking verification gained in both longitudinal and cross-sectional studies of 18- to 23-year-old college students that the experience of a university education leads college seniors to think critically in ways that surpass how they reasoned when freshmen (Pascarella & Terenzini, 2005).

These gains in critical thinking are not restricted to college students. Skilled craftsmen (male and female) reason about their work in ways that clearly demonstrate abstract thinking: for example, in working on and designing engines, in imagining spatial relations, and in fabricating fine arts (Crawford, 2006). Shifts from concrete to formal operations have been invoked to explain the increasing realization within middle adolescence of the ambiguity of the social world (Adelson, 1971).

Two major advances in considering changes in cognition during adolescence involve (a) research on brain imaging and (b) research on subtle shifts in college students' reasoning. Magnetic resonance imaging has disclosed both structural and functional changes in the brains of adolescents (Giedd, 2004). These changes involve both neuroanatomy and neurophysiology and manifest themselves as "significant improvements in cognitive processing speed" and as vivid advances "in the development of executive functions including abstract thought, organization, decision making and planning, and response inhibition" (Yurgelun-Todd, 2007, p. 251; see also Whitford et al., 2006). These developments in brain structure and functioning become crucial in other aspects of adolescent growth, such as emotional understanding and interpersonal skill: As they mature cognitively, adolescents gain skills in metacognition, empathic understanding, and role taking.

A Harvard University educational psychologist gathered data from hundreds of students about how they reason (Perry, 1970). The picture that emerged is of movement from simplistic dualism through more complicated relativism to mature, committed relativism.

In their early years in college, students typically understand reality in terms of opposite values: right/wrong or good/bad, for instance. *Dualists* have a penchant for facts, and have trouble synthesizing competing points of view. Interested in facts, dualists do not consider that shades of meaning exist. They believe that facts are true or false and understand answers to be correct or incorrect. Rather than a changing, evolving body of understanding, knowledge for dualists is stable, unchanging, and true. Connections between ideas are difficult for dualists to comprehend; combining disparate information to form theories is beyond their capacity.

Relativists have reached more advanced intellectual development than dualists. Relativists engage in a more critical, skeptical approach to claims about truth and to claims based on authority. They expect that evidence will support claims. They appreciate that several sides can exist to a story and that alternative points of view compete for allegiance. Relativists appreciate that some ideas explain reality more adequately than other ideas. But they also accept that all ideas are open to revision. Relativists can synthesize information to form theories, and they do more than engage in rote memorization of unconnected facts. They apply and analyze the connections between ideas and facts. They see no basis for choosing one position over another. While convinced that relativism is correct, they can show the subtlety of arguments for and against an issue and can compare competing points of view. However, they make no commitment to a position other than relativism.

Committed relativists have achieved a level of cognitive development beyond that of relativism. They can compare competing points of view. They choose positions based upon evidence and reasoning. Unlike dualists, committed relativists see the ambiguity in knowledge and the need to remain open to new information. Unlike relativists, committed relativists weigh evidence and choose a position. They take provisional stands and remain open to revising their views should new information enter the picture.

THE HOLISTIC TEMPLATE: EMOTIONAL ASPECTS

Individuals typically gain increased emotional competence in their movement from early through later adolescence. In part these gains manifest themselves in self-referent attributions such as self-efficacy, shame, and pride (Reimer, 1996), and in other-directed responses such as sympathy and empathy (Barnett & McCoy, 1989). Increased emotional competence comes from the adolescent's mounting emotional lexicon, growing skill in managing emotional expressiveness, and responsiveness to the emotionality of others (Saarni, 2007). Again, the influence of brain changes allowing for metacognitions can be seen.

Emotional competence also occurs due to social influences, underscoring the interrelatedness of the holistic aspects illustrated in Figure 1.1. During adolescence the social context for emotional development expands increasingly beyond the family to include peers, teachers, school environments, and the media (radio, TV, the Internet, and films) (Balk, 1995; Cottrell, 2007; Larson & Richards, 1991).

Individual differences in temperament and character also contribute to the development of emotional competence. Attributions the adolescent makes about (a) the controllability of events, "the extent to which volitional control over an outcome could be exercised" (Reimer, 1996, p. 331), and about (b) the locus of causality, "factors within the person vs. factors within the environment" (Reimer, 1996, p. 331), provide significant influences for adolescents in parsing emotional understanding of and reactions to experiences.

THE HOLISTIC TEMPLATE: BEHAVIORAL ASPECTS

Adolescents engage increasingly in actions outside the supervision of parents, and this behavior signaling growing autonomy is fully expected: We count on adolescents to exercise increasing competency as reliable and trustworthy members of society. How would adolescents master the developmental tasks of forming autonomous identities and of entering into mutually satisfying, intimate relations if not allowed freedom to act beyond close parental supervision? Of course, the groundwork for such adolescent explorations has been established in early and ongoing parent–child relations whereby parents gradually shape independence and guide their children. Consider this example: One understands the anxiety of a parent whose 2-year-old daughter is missing in a large department store but also understands the full willingness of a parent to allow a 17-year-old daughter to shop on her own.

Whereas children's behaviors are marked primarily by physical activity, adolescents' behaviors show a distinct "decline in physical activity" (Hills, King, & Armstrong, 2007, p. 37). Evidence that sedentary behaviors are becoming pronounced during childhood has led to growing concerns that adolescent obesity will rise and become a continuing health risk, perhaps even contributing to a decline in life expectancy for whole generations.

Two categories of behavior have been employed traditionally to differentiate typical male and female adolescent behavior: externalizing versus internalizing behaviors. Externalizing behaviors are actions clearly visible and noticeable by others; internalizing behaviors are self-reflective thoughts known to the person thinking them and only to others if the person discloses them. How these two categories of behaviors are often applied is in differentiating girls' and boys' responses to distressing experiences: Boys act out in such ways as aggression and property destruction, while girls turn inward with self-accusatory thoughts (Newman, Lohman, & Newman, 2007).

This externalizing-internalizing dichotomy may be too neat and simple. There are many more opportunities these days for girls to engage in physical activities such as sports, and it is too simple to think that adolescent males are insensitive troglodytes who never engage in self-reflection. Surely in one arena (expression of emotions) the opposite of this externalizing-internalizing dichotomy seems the norm: Girls are much more likely to express their emotions publicly, whereas boys are much more likely to turn inward and be reflective. Yet on the whole it has been noted that bereaved males are more likely than females to do something active (externalizing behavior) (Martin & Doka, 2000).

THE HOLISTIC TEMPLATE: PHYSICAL ASPECTS

What principally demarcates adolescence from childhood are the physical changes of primary and secondary sexual characteristics. Primary sexual characteristics for females involve the ability to conceive, and for males the ability to impregnate a female. Secondary sexual characteristics are more or less physically noticeable: Breast development in girls and menstruation would be chief examples, as well as growth in height and in weight and in pubic hair development; growth in height, changes in voice timbre, facial and pubic hair development, and genital development would be the chief examples of secondary sexual characteristics in boys. A system for assessing sexual maturity divides levels of sexual maturity into five grades according to the extent to which secondary sexual characteristics have matured (Tanner, 1962).

Many studies have examined the short-term and long-term consequences for male and for female adolescents whose sexual maturation occurs on time, early, or late (Brooks-Gunn, 1987; Nishina, Ammon, Bellmore, & Graham, 2006; Peskin, 1967; Petersen, 1983; Tobin-Richards, Boxer, & Petersen, 1983). There have been some shifts in the cohort effects associated with the timing of sexual maturation. First, findings up into the 1990s will be covered.

Evidence into the middle 1990s indicated that early maturing boys gain a lasting psychological and social edge over on-time and later maturing peers in terms of self-confidence, independence, and attractiveness to others. On-time boys were seen as less attractive than early maturers and more attractive than late maturing boys. However, late maturing boys eventually demonstrated social and internal competencies such as willingness to explore options not seen in on-time or early maturing boys. Early maturing girls experienced considerable personal and social distress; their self-concepts suffered as the girls compared their increases in weight and body fat to the societal ideal of thin females. Early maturing girls looked older than their actual age, and older adolescent boys showed interest in them beyond the girls' social skill or emotional development. On-time girls had more positive body images and perceived they were more attractive to others than did early and late maturing girls. Late maturing girls were seen to be at the greatest social disadvantage: delays in puberty created barriers causing late maturing girls to lose social prestige and to adjust poorly. By the end of high school, early maturing girls were considered to be the most socially and intrapersonally advanced of all the girls: The early onset of puberty had forced them to find internal and social resources for dealing with adults and peers (Balk, 1995).

Recent research with an ethnically diverse sample of early adolescent boys and girls, as well as another study with early adolescent boys (Cohane & Pope, 2001; Nishina et al., 2006), found that early maturing boys were dissatisfied with their body images and had adjustment difficulties: many felt overweight and rather than being admired by peers were targets for social abuse. Furthermore, these early maturing boys engaged in activities to lose weight and develop muscle. Late maturing boys were concerned about being underweight and underdeveloped. In all cases, the issues of appearance mattered greatly, and given early adolescents' tendency toward the imaginary audience and the personal fable (Elkind, 1967), one can see the psychological difficulties for boys dissatisfied with their body image. Early maturing boys who actually were overweight and dissatisfied with their bodies were likely to be targeted by peers for teasing and bullying. It was not clear if the boys' self-consciousness gave off cues that elicited harassment from peers, and the researchers noted that peer aggravation of early maturing boys was "somewhat surprising because developing faster may have been expected to be protective for boys" (Nishina et al., 2006, p. 199).

Early maturing girls were still considered to experience the same short-term psychological disadvantages as had early maturing girls in previous cohorts. The social value of thinness in females presented stark contrast to the actual physical developments early maturing girls saw reflected in their bodies. However, because early maturing girls appeared older than they were, when moving from a middle school to a high school they were buffered from being victimized by older high school students (Nishina et al., 2006). Nothing was mentioned about social pressures from older boys and girls for which early maturing girls had not developed socioemotional competency. However, unlike what had been found in former research, physical development more mature than seen in same-aged peers protected the early maturing girl from being teased and bullied.

Outcomes of girls' dissatisfactions with their body images were the same regardless of the ethnic background of the girls: If dissatisfied, the girl felt depressed. African American females expressed more body satisfaction and more positive perceptions of their weight than did girls in other ethnic groups (White, Latina, and Asian). Across all the ethnic groups, there were more similarities than differences in boys' reactions to the onset of puberty (Nishina et al., 2006).

The hormonal changes that produce primary and secondary sexual characteristics traditionally are invoked to assert that adolescence is a time of conflict, storm, and stress (Hall, 1904). Depicting adolescence as a time of upheaval was furthered by psychoanalysts who maintained that abnormal psychology was so characteristic of adolescents that distinctions between normality and pathology in adolescence would be difficult to determine. Indeed, Anna Freud remarked that the one thing normal about adolescence is abnormality (Freud, 1971). This depiction of the impulsive and tumultuous adolescent has retained a strong staying power despite longitudinal and cross-sectional evidence that the great majority of adolescents experience their adolescent years as a time of relative calm and stability, and that only a minority of youths experience adolescence as a time of turmoil (Bandura, 1980; Offer, 1969; Offer, Ostrov, & Howard, 1977).

Developing a sexual identity is an important challenge for adolescents. This challenge is part of the overarching demand to form a stable sense of self, as well as to form lasting, intimate relationships. There is abundant anecdotal evidence that American culture (as well as most other cultures) holds forth heterosexual identity as the norm; empirical estimates indicate that same-sex orientation is the norm for approximately at least 10%–12% of the human population (Gonsiorek & Weinrich, 1991; Sell, Wells, & Wypij, 1995).

THE HOLISTIC TEMPLATE: INTERPERSONAL ASPECTS

Advances in social development occur during the adolescent years. Social development fits well with the developmental task of entering into and maintaining intimate friendships, as well as with existential phenomenology's emphasis on the centrality of relations with others.

Part of adolescent social development involves advances in reasoning about social situations. Such reasoning is an outgrowth of more nuanced perspective taking about social reality that marks adolescent cognitive development as well as increased opportunities during adolescence to engage in diverse experiences (Kohlberg, 1969).

Kohlberg (1971) analyzed 25 aspects he considered present in all societies as (a) how individuals reason about what is the moral thing to do when presented with a dilemma and (b) how to assess the stage of development of a person's moral reasoning. He developed criteria for determining which aspect(s) a person is using when reasoning about a situation. He said all the aspects reduce to principles about justice. To assess developments in reasoning about social situations, Kohlberg wrote vignettes with dilemmas and asked research participants what is the moral thing to do.

He analyzed answers to the moral dilemmas and said they fell into one of six stages of moral reasoning, with more advanced reasoning evident as one moved up the stages. Females produced answers that Kohlberg considered less advanced than answers from males, and at one point he concluded females could not reason beyond the middle stages in his model. A multiyear longitudinal study with males from various socioeconomic conditions produced results that Kohlberg said indicated gradual advances over time in moral reasoning so that by age 22 most participants were in or in transition to stage 4 of his moral reasoning scheme (Colby, Kohlberg, Gibbs, & Lieberman, 1983).

Gilligan (1977) challenged Kohlberg's approach because she said it presented hypothetical rather than real dilemmas. She also argued that the scoring criteria for determining stages of moral reasoning were fundamentally unfair to and inappropriate for assessing how females assess social situations. According to Gilligan (1982), females are much more inclined than are males to examine the interpersonal or relational aspects in a social situation, not the justice aspects. Gilligan maintained that Kohlberg's scheme is insensitive to the feminine perspective on moral reasoning and biased against them. There is no doubt that Gilligan's analysis struck a positive chord with many women.

Walker (1989) compared Kohlberg's and Gilligan's perspectives in a 2-year longitudinal study including 240 persons from 80 family triads (mother, father, child). The 80 children in the study varied in age from 6 to 16 at the start of the study, and 97% of the 240 participants stayed in the research for the full 2 years. Walker used three of Kohlberg's hypothetical dilemmas and asked all participants to select and review a dilemma from their own lives. When analyzing responses Walker used separate scoring schemes developed by Kohlberg and by Gilligan. Rather than there being a perspective favored by males and another perspective favored by females, Walker found that persons used both perspectives.

It would be a worthwhile project to examine the social reasoning of dying and of bereaved adolescents: devise social dilemmas involving death and bereavement, as well as ask the adolescents to select and review a dilemma of their own, and then examine responses in light of the scoring schemes devised by Kohlberg and by Gilligan. If done longitudinally with both bereaved and nonbereaved adolescents matched for age, gender, and other relevant social factors, and if valid measures of grief were obtained, one could assess whether over time bereaved adolescents' moral reasoning differs from the moral reasoning of nonaffected peers. One study of sibling death during adolescence that measured self-concept dimensions found that bereaved adolescents had responses about morals that were one standard deviation higher than the scores of the norm groups on which the measure had been standardized (Balk, 1983).

During adolescence individuals usually gain increasing skill in social perspective taking (sometimes called interpersonal understanding). A model of the growing complexity in social perspective taking presents five levels of qualitatively distinct and increasingly more intricate types of interpersonal understanding (Selman, 1980). This model has many features similar to Kohlberg's model of moral reasoning. The model allows researchers to understand what adolescents understand about such interpersonal issues as trust, jealousy, reciprocity, and conflict resolution.

Family relations and interactions play a significant part in the activity and the formation of the self. However, Harris (1995, 2002) challenged assertions about parental influence on children's development, asserting that parents exert minimal influence on the development of children and adolescents outside the home. Most research focus in human development has documented how parents do make a difference not only for children but also for adolescents (Collins, Maccoby, Steinberg, Hetherington, & Bornstein, 2000; Galambos, Barker, & Almeida, 2003).

Longitudinal studies of parentally bereaved children and adolescents (Haine, Wolchik, Sandler, Millsap, & Ayers, 2006; Sandler et al., 2003; Worden, 1996) have provided persuasive empirical evidence that the major difference in outcomes for children and adolescents is positive parenting. Caregiver warmth and consistent discipline characterize positive parenting: Attentive listening and emotional acceptance are indicators of a parent's caregiver warmth; setting and enforcing limits and being fair are indicators of consistent discipline. In a study of sibling bereavement during adolescence, a key aspect that differentiated emotional responses of the adolescents was the level of positive communication and the extent of emotional closeness between family members (Balk, 1983).

THE HOLISTIC TEMPLATE: SPIRITUAL ASPECTS

While recently there has been more attention paid to spirituality and adolescent development, contemporary literature reviews (Benson, Roehlkepartain, & Rude, 2003; Boyatzis, 2003) estimate that at most 1% of all scholarly articles have addressed the spiritual development of adolescents. Given the drive during adolescence for finding meaning, establishing relationships, and moving "beyond concrete childhood impressions of religion to reflect on issues and concepts that are embedded in existential and transcendental realms" (Markstrom, 1999, p. 205), this scholarly neglect is puzzling. One likely reason for the neglect is the embarrassment or awkwardness—in some cases, contempt and hostility—that empirical scientists feel toward spirituality and religion.

What is meant by the term *spirituality* is not an easy matter to settle. Bregman (2006) noted that the term is elusive, with numerous meanings described as "glow words" hiding a fundamental confusion. Bregman claimed to have found 92 definitions for spirituality. These 92 definitions have resulted from strains that secularism places on accepting religion: Spirituality is differentiated from religion, so that a person can speak of being spiritual without being religious. On the whole, these many definitions of spirituality refer to seeking meaning, connections with transcendence, and purpose.

Applied developmental scientists who have examined adolescence and spirituality consider that religion and spirituality interact with one another as complex, multidimensional constructs (Benson, 2004). They look for the social spheres within which religion and spirituality take shape for adolescents, and they consider simplistic definitions of the terms of no help in learning the impact they have on adolescents. As an example, one dissertation examined the spiritual development of modern Orthodox Jewish middle adolescent girls (Weiss, 2007); the author found each person influenced deeply by socially embedded themes, among them, music, tragedy in the lives of the Jews, and the State of Israel. As another example, a study of intimate conversations between later adolescents and their mothers examined "personal religious and spiritual beliefs and practices" (Brelsford & Mahoney, 2008, p. 62); attachment, relationship satisfaction, and disclosure in general between the adolescents and their mothers emerged in analysis of results, and the researchers noted that spiritual disclosure enriched the maternal-adolescent bonds.

Fowler (1981) produced a model of spiritual development over the life span. This model is based on the search for meaning and identity, a search considered at the core of human existence (Campbell, 1949; Erikson, 1968). Fowler acknowledges his indebtedness to three main figures who have impacted thinking about human development: Piaget, Erikson, and Kohlberg. Fowler's model of spiritual development, which he terms "stages of faith consciousness," is closely modeled on the stages of development found in the writings of these three men. Fowler proposed that faith consciousness moves from an undifferentiated impulse to establish meaning to an outcome of "universalizing faith" that few persons achieve (no one under the age of 60 in Fowler's research participants had reached this final stage of faith consciousness). The two stages of faith consciousness typical of adolescence are (a) "a synthetic-conventional faith" in which early adolescents encounter people from a variety of backgrounds and make accommodations to their understanding about what to believe and about what commitments are worthwhile, and (b) "an individuative-reflective faith" in which later adolescents engage in what Perry (1970) would call committed relativism—in this case, the adolescents make conscious, examined choices from alternatives and decide on roles and responsibilities to adopt in life. This movement in faith consciousness links both to Perry's views on cognitive development and to the developmental tasks of deciding on a career and forming an autonomous, stable identity.

SOME CONCLUDING COMMENTS

The three-fold relations fundamental to human existence and the multiple dimensions holism presents about human existence provide overarching frameworks for understanding adolescent encounters with death and bereavement. The conceptual scaffolding provided by existential phenomenology and by holism provides an organizing scheme for understanding the backstory to these encounters. The backstory is the expectation that adolescents will accomplish certain developmental tasks and make the transition to mature young adulthood.

Encounters with death and bereavement in adolescence, though more common than many persons realize, are not central to adolescence.

When such encounters do occur, they do so within the milieu of the individual's ongoing development. That milieu is the backstory influencing how adolescents respond to death and bereavement. Within the backstory are detailed means to gauge the cascading effects that death and bereavement have on adolescents. Within the backstory are foci for determining growth through crisis, resiliency in the face of misfortune, and problems in coping with the pressing life events that are part and parcel of an adolescent's encounter with death and bereavement.

REFERENCES

Adelson, J. (1971). The political imagination. In J. Kagan & R. Coles (Eds.), *Twelve to sixteen: Early adolescence* (pp. 106–143). New York: Norton.

Attig, T. (1996). *How we grieve: Relearning the world.* New York: Oxford University Press.

Balk, D. E. (1983). Adolescents' grief reactions and self concept perceptions following sibling death: A case study of 33 teenagers. *Journal of Youth and Adolescence, 12,* 137–161.

Balk, D. E. (1995). *Adolescent development: Early through late adolescence.* Pacific Grove, CA: Brooks/Cole.

Balk, D. E. (2007). Working with children and adolescents. In K. J. Doka (Ed.), *Living with grief: Before and after the death* (pp. 209–227). Washington, DC: Hospice Foundation of America.

Bandura, A. (1977). *Social learning theory.* Englewood Cliffs, NJ: Prentice Hall.

Bandura, A. (1980). The stormy decade: Fact or fiction? In R. E. Muuss (Ed.), *Adolescent behavior and society: A book of readings* (pp. 22–31). New York: Random House.

Bandura, A. (1997). *Self-efficacy: The exercise of control.* New York: W. H. Freeman.

Barnett, M. A., & McCoy, S. J. (1989). The relation of distressful childhood experiences and empathy in college undergraduates. *Journal of Genetic Psychology, 150,* 417–426.

Beck, A. T. (1976). *Cognitive therapy and the emotional disorders.* New York: International Universities Press.

Benson, P. L. (2004). Emerging themes in research on adolescent spiritual and religious development. *Applied Development Science, 8,* 47–50.

Benson, P. L., Roehlkepartain, E. C., & Rude, S. P. (2003). Spiritual development in childhood and adolescence: Toward a field of inquiry. *Applied Developmental Science, 7,* 204–212.

Blos, P. (1979). *The adolescent passage: Developmental issues.* New York: International Universities Press.

Boyatzis, C. J. (2003). Religious and spiritual development: An introduction. *Review of Religious Research, 44,* 213–219.

Bregman, L. (2006). Spirituality: A glowing and useful term in search of a meaning. *Omega, Journal of Death and Dying, 53,* 5–26.

Brelsford, G. M., & Mahoney, A. (2008). Spiritual disclosure between older adolescents and their mothers. *Journal of Family Psychology, 22,* 62–70.

Brooks-Gunn, J. (1987). Pubertal pressures: Their relevance for developmental research. In V. B. Van Hasselt & M. Hersen (Eds.), *Handbook of adolescent psychology* (pp. 111–130). New York: Pergamon Press.

Campbell, J. (1949). *The hero with a thousand faces.* New York: Pantheon Books.

Cohane, G. H., & Pope, H. G. (2001). Body image in boys: A review of the literature. *International Journal of Eating Disorders, 29,* 373–379.

Colby, A., Kohlberg, L., Gibbs, J., & Lieberman, M. (1983). A longitudinal study of moral judgment. *Monographs of the Society for Research in Child Development, 48,* 1–96.

Collins, W. A., Maccoby, E. E., Steinberg, L., Hetherington, E. M., & Bornstein, M. H. (2000). Contemporary research on parenting: The case for nature and nurture. *American Psychologist, 55,* 218–232.

Corless, I., &. Nicholas, P. (2003). Hospice and palliative care: A legacy in the making. In I. Corless, B. B. Germino, & M. A. Pittman (Eds.), *Dying, death, and bereavement: A challenge for living* (pp. 181–200). New York: Springer Publishing.

Corr, C. A. (2007). Hospice: Achievements, legacies, and challenges. *Omega, Journal of Death and Dying, 56,* 111–120.

Cottrell, L. M. (2007). *Attachment and risk taking among youth.* Unpublished doctoral dissertation, University of Wisconsin at Madison.

Crawford, M. B. (2006). Shop class as soulcraft. *The New Atlantis, 13,* 7–24.

Elkind, D. (1967). Egocentrism in adolescence. *Child Development, 38,* 1025–1034.

Erikson, E. H. (1968). *Identity: Youth and crisis.* New York: Norton.

Fleming, S. J., & Adolph, R. (1986). Helping bereaved adolescents: Needs and responses. In C. A. Corr & J. N. McNeil (Eds.), *Adolescence and death* (pp. 97–118). New York: Springer Publishing.

Fowler, J. W. (1981). *Stages of faith: The psychology of human development and the quest for meaning.* San Francisco: Harper & Row.

Freud, A. (1971). Adolescence as a developmental disturbance. In *The writings of Anna Freud* (Vol. VII, pp. 39–47). New York: International Universities Press.

Galambos, N. L., Barker, E. T., & Almeida, D. M. (2003). Parents *do* matter: Trajectories of change in externalizing and externalizing problems in early adolescence. *Child Development, 74,* 578–594.

Giedd, J. N. (2004). Structural magnetic resonance imaging of the adolescent brain. In R. E. Dahl & L. P. Spear (Eds.), *Adolescent brain development: Vulnerabilities and opportunities* (pp. 77–85). New York: New York Academy of Sciences.

Gilligan, C. (1977). In a different voice: Women's conceptions of self and of morality. *Harvard Educational Review, 47,* 481–517.

Gilligan, C. (1982). *In a different voice: Psychological theory and women's development.* Cambridge, MA: Harvard University Press.

Gonsiorek, J. C., & Weinrich, J. D. (1991). The definition and scope of sexual orientation. In J. C. Gonsiorek & J. D. Weinrich (Eds.), *Homosexuality: Research implications for public policy* (pp. 1–12). Newbury Park, CA: Sage.

Haine, R. A, Wolchik, S. A., Sandler, I. N., Millsap, R. M., & Ayers, T. S. (2006). Positive parenting as a protective resource for parentally bereaved children. *Death Studies, 30,* 1–28.

Hall, G. S. (1904). *Adolescence: Its psychology and its relations to physiology, anthropology, sociology, sex, crime, religion, and education* (Vol. 1). New York: D. Appleton.

Harris, J. R. (1995). Where is the child's environment? A group socialization theory. *Psychological Review, 102*, 458–489.

Harris, J. R. (2002). Beyond the nurture assumption: Testing hypotheses about the child's environment. In J. G. Borkowski, S. L. Ramey, & M. Bristol-Power (Eds.), *Parenting and the child's world: Influences in academic, intellectual, and social-emotional development* (pp. 3–20). Marwah, NJ: Lawrence Erlbaum.

Hills, A. P., King, N. A., & Armstrong, T. P. (2007). The contribution of physical activity and sedentary behaviours to the growth and development of children and adolescents: Implications for overweight and obesity. *Sports Medicine, 37*, 533–545.

Janis, I. L, & Mann, L. (1977). *Decision making: A psychological analysis of conflict, choice, and commitment.* New York: Free Press.

Josselson, R. (1996). *Revising herself: The story of women's identity from college to midlife.* New York: Oxford University Press.

Kelly, G. (1955). *Psychology of personal constructs.* New York: Norton.

Kohlberg, L. (1969). Stage and sequence: The cognitive-developmental approach to socialization. In D. Goslin (Ed.), *Handbook of socialization theory and research* (pp. 347–480). Chicago: Rand McNally.

Kohlberg, L. (1971). *Structure issue scoring manual.* Unpublished manuscript. Cambridge, MA: Center for Moral Development and Education, Harvard University.

Ladd, G. W. (2005). *Children's peer relations and social competence: A century of progress.* New Haven, CT: Yale University Press.

Larson, R. W., & Richards, M. H. (1991). Daily companionship in late childhood and early adolescence: Changing developmental contexts. *Child Development, 62*, 284–309.

Leighton, A. H. (1959). *My name is legion: Foundations for a theory of man in relation to culture.* New York: Basic Books.

Markstrom, C. A. (1999). Religious involvement and adolescent psychosocial development. *Journal of Adolescence, 22*, 205–221.

Martin, T. L. & Doka, K. J. (2000). *Men don't cry …women do: Transcending gender stereotypes of grief.* Philadelphia: Brunner/Mazel.

May, R., Angel, E., & Ellenberger, H. F. (1958). *Existence: A new dimension in psychiatry and psychology.* New York: Basic Books.

Neimeyer, R. A. (Ed.). (2001). *Meaning reconstruction and the experience of loss.* Washington, DC: American Psychological Association.

Newman, B. M., Lohman, B. J., & Newman, P. R. (2007). Peer group membership and a sense of belonging: Their relationship to adolescent behavior problems. *Adolescence, 42*, 241–263.

Nishina, A., Ammon, N. Y., Bellmore, A. D., & Graham, S. (2006). Body dissatisfaction and physical development among ethnic minority adolescents. *Journal of Youth and Adolescence, 35*, 189–201.

Offer, D. (1969). *The psychological world of the teenager.* New York: Basic Books.

Offer, D., Ostrov, E., & Howard, K. I. (1977). The self-image of adolescents: A study of four cultures. *Journal of Youth and Adolescence, 6*, 265–280.

Parker, J. G., & Gottman, J. M. (1989). Social and emotional development in a relational context: Friendship interaction for early childhood to adolescence. In T. J. Gerndt & G. W. Ladd (Eds.), *Peer relationships in child development* (pp. 95–131). New York: John Wiley & Sons.

Pascarella, E. T., & Terenzini, P. T. (2005). *How college affects students: A third decade of research* (2nd ed.). San Francisco: Jossey-Bass.

Perry, W. G. (1970). *Forms of intellectual and ethical development during the college years.* New York: Holt, Rinehart & Winston.

Peskin, H. (1967). Pubertal onset and ego functioning. *Journal of Abnormal Psychology, 72,* 1–15.

Petersen, A. C. (1983). Menarche: Meaning of measure and measuring meaning. In S. Golub (Ed.), *Menarche* (pp. 63–76). New York: Heath.

Piaget, J. (1929). *The child's conception of the world.* London: Routledge & Kegan Paul.

Reimer, M. S. (1996). "Sinking into the ground": The development and consequences of shame in adolescence. *Developmental Review, 16,* 321–363.

Saarni, C. (2007). The development of emotional competence: Pathways for helping children become emotionally intelligent. In R. Bar-On, J. G. Maree, & M. J. Elias (Eds.), *Educating people to be emotionally intelligent* (pp. 15–35). Westport, CT: Praeger.

Sandler, I. N., Ayers, T. S., Wolchik, S. A., Tein, J-Y., Kwok, O-M., Haine, R. A., et al. (2003). The Family Bereavement Program: Efficacy evaluation of a theory-based prevention program for parentally bereaved children and adolescents. *Journal of Consulting and Clinical Psychology, 71,* 587–600.

Sell, R. L., Wells, J. A., & Wypij, D. (1995). The prevalence of homosexual behavior and attraction in the United States, the United Kingdom and France: Results of national population-based samples. *Archives of Sexual Behavior, 24,* 235–248.

Selman, R. L. (1980). *The growth of interpersonal understanding: Developmental and clinical analyses.* New York: Academic Press.

Shain, L., & Farber, B. A. (1989). Female identity development and self-reflection in late adolescence. *Adolescence, 24,* 381–392.

Sullivan, H. S. (1953). *The interpersonal theory of psychiatry.* New York: Norton.

Super, D. (1957). *The psychology of careers.* New York: Harper & Row.

Tanner, J. M. (1962). *Growth in adolescence.* Oxford, UK: Blackwell Scientific Publications.

Tobin-Richards, M. H., Boxer, A. M., & Petersen, A. C. (1983). The psychological significance of pubertal change: Sex differences in perceptions of self during early adolescence. In J. Brooks-Gunn & A. C. Petersen (Eds.), *Girls at puberty: Biological and psychological perspectives* (pp. 127–154). New York: Plenum.

Walker, L. J. (1989). A longitudinal study of moral reasoning. *Child Development, 60,* 157–166.

Weiss, S. (2007). *Letting God in: The spiritual development of modern Orthodox high school girls.* Unpublished doctoral dissertation, New York, Yeshiva University.

Whitford, T. J., Rennie, C. J., Grieve, S. M., Clark, C. R., Gordon, E., & Williams, L. M. (2006). Brain maturation in adolescence: Concurrent changes in neuroanatomy and neurophysiology. *Human Brain Mapping, 28,* 228–237.

Worden, J. W. (1996). *Children and grief: When a parent dies.* New York: Guilford.

Yurgelun-Todd, D. (2007). Emotional and cognitive changes during adolescence. *Current Opinion in Neurobiology, 17,* 251–257.

2 Young People Making Meaning in Response to Death and Bereavement

JANE RIBBENS McCARTHY

Some things that happen, like small things, have made me who I am . . . my great grandfather died, it was about a couple of years ago and . . . like I knew him but like I went to Jamaica so I could get to know him more, but when he died I think it made me realize that I can't waste the time and seeing that the years are going by so quickly . . . I went to see him but I think that I could have got to know him a little bit more . . . since then I've like stayed around my family a bit more, more of a family person, that's probably what's made me so close to my family . . . I would like to practice law in Jamaica . . . I would like to make a difference . . . but I feel I would like to end up in Jamaica regardless. (Shirleen, interviewed between ages 13 and 17, living in London)[1]

Nobody knows exactly what happened [when a friend died in a car crash] . . . it was such a freak like, such a freak accident . . . That was when we thought it couldn't get any worse, and do you know, Brid's boyfriend, Owen, we were all friendly with, he committed suicide about 2 months after she died . . . We went to Owen's house then, the whole gang of us didn't leave each other for like 3 days . . . For the whole week we didn't stop crying . . . I think we overall coped well considering, like it's not something that is supposed to happen whenever you are 18 . . . I've got more serious, we all have, just got more serious and less light-hearted . . . I think it definitely changed us all, it has made us stronger, you can't go through something like that and not change. Especially at a time when everything is changing, when you're 17 a year's a long time. (Maeve, interviewed between ages 15 and 19, living in Northern Ireland)[1]

These quotations convey a powerful sense of young people constructing some sort of meaning as they consider these variable experiences of death in the overall narratives of their lives. In this chapter, I will consider key themes around young people and the ways in which they may seek to make meaning in response to such experiences. The discussion opens by considering how meaning making features within various social science and therapeutic traditions, including aspects of the meaning of *meaning*. This is followed by considering how meanings of death may be culturally and context specific—including the significance of inequalities of power and material contexts—taking up Klass's (1999) suggestion that we might usefully consider "responses to death" rather than "bereavement" as the key framework for understanding experiences of death, loss, and change across global contexts. Understandings of *the child* and *the adolescent* will also be considered for their culturally specific underpinnings, before considering the implications of meaning making for the existing evidence available on young people, death, and bereavement. The chapter concludes with some broad implications for professional practice.

MEANING MAKING

Across various social science disciplines, there is a strong tradition of placing meaning as central to any understanding of social life. This attention to meaning not only cuts across academic disciplines but is also found in a number of therapeutic approaches (Brewin & Power, 1997), including those concerned with bereavement (Neimeyer, 2000), and in writings on spirituality (Morgan, 2002). Such widespread agreement suggests that a focus on meaning making has much to offer as a framework for theorizing and researching young people's experiences of death and bereavement.

Within the social sciences, there are branches of psychology (e.g., Janoff-Bulman, 1992; Kelly, 1955), sociology (e.g., Weber, 1968), and anthropology (e.g., Geertz, 1973) that reflect strong intellectual (hermeneutic) traditions that emphasize the importance of seeing humans as meaning makers, such that we cannot understand social lives without paying attention to meanings. There are also others working within more scientific, perhaps positivist, frameworks who call for attention to meaning, such as Mackay (2003) in psychology or Rutter (2000) in the field of child psychiatry.

Within the hermeneutic approaches, meanings are recognized to be rooted in received cultures, even as they are recreated anew by people in various social and material contexts, structured by processes of power. Indeed, one of the key strengths of attending to meanings is that they can capture this sense of the duality of both cultures and individuality. Nevertheless, it is crucial to recognize the fluidity and contingency of *cultures*, as well as the culturally and socially located significance of *individuality*.

From these perspectives, meanings of death and bereavement will be significant in young people's lives, first in their consequences—since humans do not simply respond in any automatic way to external events but shape their actions by reference to the meanings that frame their understandings of the world. In this regard, even researchers who use quite structured, quantitative methods in the search for statistical patterns in human behavior may also stress the need to understand the meanings that young people give to situations in order to understand how they respond to them (Rutter, 2000). But second, meanings are significant because they are interchanged in social interactions, and systematized through institutions, in ways that help to create social realities in the first place. The social realities of death and bereavement for young people will vary significantly across time and place.

The Varying Meanings of *Meaning*

There are, however, some important differences of emphasis in the ways in which meanings are discussed in different fields and some key, but often unrecognized, variations in the meaning of *meaning*. These differences generally revolve around two main themes: meaning in terms of "making sense"—*I don't understand what you mean*—and meaning in terms of "finding a purpose"—*I didn't mean to cause such a problem* (Ribbens McCarthy, 2006). Some statements hover ambiguously between both these facets, as in the contention that *dreams have no real meaning*, which could be taken to mean that they make no real sense, or that they have no real purpose behind them—or maybe, both. This distinction is close to that of Janoff-Bulman and Frantz's concepts of meaning-as-comprehensibility and meaning-as-significance (discussed by Davis, Nolen-Hoeksema, & Larson, 1998), although the latter is more focused on value or worth rather than purpose. Davis and colleagues themselves distinguish meaning as sense making and as benefit finding. Nevertheless, operationalizing the concept of meaning for empirical research may be problematic (Davis, Wortman, Hehman, & Silver 2000) and can cause considerable confusion (Ribbens McCarthy, 2006).

In terms of meaning as "making sense," some writers stress the cognitive aspects of this sense making, while others would include emotion

(Carlsen, 1988), and others would question whether meanings are always necessarily expressed in linguistic form (Wetherell, 2001) and always consciously known. So meanings might be found not only in language but also in embodied actions, in symbols, and in objects themselves. In terms of meaning as "purpose," some might see this as part of the human quest for a response to the spiritual or existential challenges of life and death—as in, *Does life have any meaning?* Others might see it is a sign of mental well-being to be able to articulate a set of meanings around a particular experience in life, especially if it was a difficult or traumatic experience—as in, *Can I find any meaning in my friend's death?* A search for, or presence of, meaning in this sense can be regarded by some as something positive and desirable—a theme that is common in the literature on bereavement.

By contrast, a significant perspective within many social science disciplines that is less apparent in the bereavement literature (however, see Leming & Dickinson, 2007; Nadeau, 1990) suggests that meanings in terms of sense making are almost inevitably present in some minimal form in all social interactions, even if they are not articulated or consciously held—or social life would not be possible. Furthermore, from this view, meanings in terms of either sense making *or* purpose are not to be evaluated as such: They are not right or wrong, desirable or undesirable. Instead they are regarded as a key, intrinsic part of how social lives and interactions occur and underscore that for some (hermeneutic) branches of sociology, psychology, and anthropology, understanding these meanings is the central task for study. We can focus on how, and in what ways, young people *make sense* of their experiences of death. Whether this sense making gives them any belief of there being a *purpose* or meaningfulness in the death is an additional—although important—question. The primary intention, then, in such approaches is not to judge meanings or evaluate them as more or less helpful, healthy or unhealthy, functional or dysfunctional, worthy or reprehensible, but to study them and understand them.

Meanings in Context

But we also need to understand that young people do not create their meanings from nowhere; instead they draw creatively and actively on the meanings available to them in their cultural and social contexts. As meanings are interchanged in social lives, they may become more or less systematized over time. Such culturally systematic meanings may be drawn upon to enable people to make sense of their lives in ways that are fluid and pragmatic, according to the circumstances in which they are living, or they may be more forcefully or emphatically imposed on people according to the views and interests of other powerful social groups. Such culturally systematized meanings are not to be seen as right or wrong; rather, they need to be understood in terms of the ways in which people live out their lives in particular social, cultural, material, and historical contexts, as these are shaped by relationships of power. And very often, in considering young people's experiences of bereavement, both these cultural meanings and material contexts are taken for granted by researchers and professionals, and their crucial significance is overlooked. Certainly, when studying cultures with which we are very familiar, meanings can be very hard to identify because they tend to be deeply embedded in our own thought processes and our psyche, as well as in our wider contexts. Such assumptions can be very much taken for granted, sometimes framed in terms of what is "natural." This phenomenon can be seen, for example, when theories of child and adolescent development, which are central to much writing about young people and bereavement, are discussed as if they are unproblematically universal, rooted in biological maturational processes. Before we explore this issue further, however, we also need to consider how bereavement itself may be framed by particular cultural understandings and meanings.

YOUNG PEOPLE, DEATH, AND BEREAVEMENT IN GLOBAL CONTEXTS

Contemporary understandings of *bereavement* in the broad cultural contexts of industrialized societies are highly individualized and psychologized, having been hardly considered within sociology in such societies (with some notable exceptions, Walter, 1999), let alone examined cross-culturally. And, while death rituals have been studied by anthropologists, experiences of death have received little attention. Yet the concept intrinsically depends on the presence of a preexisting social bond or social reality that has been ruptured—hence the understanding of bereavement as loss. However, which particular deaths (or other ruptures) will be experienced as bereavement by the individual will depend on the meaning of the social bond or reality that is at stake. Even if we restrict the usage of bereavement to refer to experiences of death, can we know which categories of social bonds, or relationships, when ended by death, will constitute a bereavement and a loss, even if we restrict our discussion to contemporary industrialized societies? While the death of a stranger is not likely to be experienced as a loss, what of the death of a neighbor, a celebrity, an absent father, and so forth? But, while some categories of social relationships, such as mother, may be socially structured in ways that mean they are more significant generally for the individual's position in social life, any bereavement can only be understood in the context of the meanings of this particular relationship, as developed within the interactional dynamics between specific people over time and space. Bereavement always implicates both social and psychological aspects.

An emphasis on meaning needs to be oriented to material as well as psychic phenomena, including wider aspects of the relationships of power that may structure material and cultural phenomena in any given context. In parallel fashion, while we might expect some deaths to be more significant than others for young people living in particular social, historical, and material contexts, whether a particular death constitutes a bereavement for an individual will depend heavily on its meaning in both cultural and personal terms. Among young people living in the Central African Republic, for example, deaths of parents may not necessarily be included among those losses that individuals list as causing most grief (Hewlett, 2005).

These issues become all the more important when we seek to widen our view to think of deaths in contexts beyond those of contemporary Western industrialized societies. Yet such broadening of view may also enable new insights into the meanings by which deaths are understood in the cultures familiar to Western academics, framed as these are by specific cultural and material processes entailing what has been described as the sequestration of death (Craib, 1994; Giddens, 1990). Looking beyond the affluence and cultures of such Western societies suggests that the concept of *bereavement* itself needs to be re-thought and reconsidered, since it carries with it the assumptive framework of a particular psychologized, individualized notion of loss and bereavement, and associated models of grief. The existing literature on young people and bereavement is almost entirely based on such Western frameworks (Ribbens McCarthy, 2006), as is the broader literature on children's resilience (Ungar, 2008) and children's responses to traumatic adversities (Boyden, 2003). Klass (1999) suggests that it is more useful to conceptualize such experiences in terms of "responses to death," rather than to presume that the concept of bereavement is relevant across global contexts, and in relation to any specific death. And indeed Klass's important work (Klass, Silverman, & Nickman, 1996) on the significance of continuing bonds for bereaved individuals—challenging previously accepted Freudian views of the need for psychological detachment for grief resolution—itself draws upon a consideration of the ways in which ancestors continue to have key social significance in some non-Western societies such as Japan.

But thinking beyond bereavement may be a hard task for those of us from Western societies, since (a) the idea of the individual is so deeply rooted in post-Enlightenment, industrialized, liberal democratic cultures, and (b) Western theories of bereavement center on ideas of an individualized, internal emotional life, rooted in biology (Ribbens McCarthy, 2007b). In Western academic discussions of bereavement in cross-cultural contexts, we find a widespread view that grief is universal, such that its absence may implicitly be considered pathological (e.g., Stroebe & Schut, 1998), but, for example, there is no Hindi word for *depression*, only sorrow (Laungani, 2005), and similarly no Tibetan word for *guilt* (Terheggen, Stroebe, & Kleber, 2001). Furthermore, much of the existing research evidence outside Western contexts points to the implications of a significant death for somatic symptoms rather than for emotional responses (Stroebe & Schut, 1998; Terheggen et al., 2001). Indeed, Young-suck Moon (2005) suggests that individual "psychological space" may not be available in some societies.

All too often, then, writing on bereavement in global contexts starts, as with so much cross-cultural work, from Euro-American assumptions, such that, for example:

> Commonly made comparisons between Indian findings and Euro-American theories and findings imply—whether intended or not—that western human relationships provide the psychological standard against which to judge relationships in other cultures. (Gielen, 2003, p. xii)

In many societies, however, the death of one individual, such as the mother, may be contextualized by the fact that children's attachments may be quite dispersed among many caregivers, although, at the same time, the absence of *any* significant person to whom the child is attached can constitute a significant deprivation (Boyden & Mann, 2005). While Rosenblatt concludes that "grieving is malleable" (2001, p. 297), Klass (1999) critiques his work for being multicultural rather than cross-cultural, being still rooted in Western models of grief. Hence his call for a focus on "responses to death" rather than grief and bereavement, which leaves open what are the meanings of deaths in different contexts and whether these deaths constitute a loss and/or an intra-psychic emotional experience—or something else altogether. This conceptual shift opens up possibilities for understanding death through alternative frameworks, such as transition and change (Hockey, 2002).

Culturally based meanings are also, of course, significantly interwoven with material realities, and in this regard, the impact of material poverty leads some writers to suggest that grief may be a luxury for many in the world. Demmer (2007) made this conclusion in his study of 18 adults in South Africa who had been bereaved by AIDS, when "the constant struggle for survival took priority over grief" (p. 39). Consequently, despite a very clearly expressed concern for the plight of children orphaned through AIDS, Demmer comments that this emphasis on economics and survival seemed to extend to interviewees' discussion of children's needs too, such that "few mentioned the emotional impact of AIDS-related loss on children" (p. 46). And, indeed, the almost total absence of a literature on children's and young people's experiences of bereavement outside Western contexts is itself very striking (Ribbens McCarthy, 2007b).

One notable exception here is the study by Hewlett (2005) of young people living in two culturally distinct groups in central Africa—the Aka foragers and the Ngandu farmers. While young people from both groups had experienced high levels of loss through death (averaging 24 per person), they differed in terms of which deaths they regarded as most significant and how they described their responses. The culturally specific meanings of age, gender, and kinship thus shaped the significance of particular deaths in each group. Furthermore, among the Aka, with a nomadic lifestyle focused on foraging as a means of survival, relationships were understood primarily in emotional terms, and comfort for grieving young people was experienced mostly through physical contact. For the Ngandu young people, by contrast, the meanings of death were embedded in social structures that reflected a dependence on farming, and comfort was described primarily in terms of being given provisions to aid survival.

Material Inequalities

These examples draw our attention to the significance of material contexts for young people's experiences of death, in terms of structural inequalities, as well as cultural diversities, that may be found both within and between societies (Boyden, 2003). Such inequalities may impact in ways that are both obvious and also very deeply rooted in more personal experience. Marris, for example, discusses the importance of inequalities of power for being able to reduce the uncertainty we all experience as a "fundamental condition of human life" (1996, p. 1), with the result that "inequalities of power affect both vulnerability to bereavement and the ability to recover from it" (p. 118).

Such issues of inequalities are relevant, of course, within developed societies as much as anywhere else. Indeed, the likelihood of young people experiencing parental death in the UK, for example, is likely to vary significantly by social class and locality, since mortality rates are known to differ so strongly along these dimensions, and indeed such disparities have been increasing (Mitchell, Dorling, & Shaw, 2000). The more immediate effects (Worden & Silverman, 1996) and longer term outcomes of such deaths are also likely to vary with social class (Lutzke, Ayer, Sandler, & Barr, 1997), with deaths of fathers particularly likely to be significant for material well-being (e.g., Gersten, Beals, & Kallgren, 1991). Furthermore, material disadvantage is more likely to be associated with the experience of multiple deaths and difficult events in the lives of young people, and this compounding of difficult experiences is strongly associated with longer term unwelcome outcomes (Gerard & Beuhler, 2004; Gersten et al., 1991; Meltzer, Gatward, Goodman, & Ford, 2000).

But while these structural patterns draw our attention to the crucial importance of paying attention to the material contexts of young people's responses to death, they do not undermine the importance of meanings, which are also important in mediating the impact of such material contexts. The importance of the meanings that frame material inequalities has been encapsulated most obviously through the sociological notion of *relative deprivation,* but it can also be seen, for example, in the ways in which variations in parental coping styles—which are related to children's adjustment to parental death—themselves relate to structural inequalities, as mediated through such factors as household income, ill health, and housing (Ribbens McCarthy, 2006). As Boyden and Mann observe more generally:

> Meaning is a profoundly important mediating factor in children's experiences of adversity, and yet it has been largely ignored in the literature . . . how children respond to adversity cannot be understood without reference to the social, cultural, economic, and moral meanings given to such experiences in the contexts they inhabit (2005, p. 15).

Meanings of Childhood and Adolescence

Affluence may be associated not only with particular experiences of emotional life and bereavement but also with particular experiences of childhood (discussed by Montgomery, 2008). The increasing affluence of Western societies after industrialization was associated not only with particular cultural processes of the sequestration of death and the emergence of expert theories and models of grief, but also with the development of particular understandings of childhood and youth, underpinned by changing legal and institutional frameworks, and the emergence of expert theories of child development. In considering young people's experiences of death and bereavement, we find that it is not only theorizing of bereavement that has been strongly psychologized, but also the understanding of what it means to be a bereaved child or teenager, which has been largely underpinned by the developmental framework of adolescence. More sociological approaches based in the framework of youth, by contrast, have hardly touched upon issues of death and bereavement (Ribbens McCarthy, 2006, 2007a). So it is not only the meanings of bereavement that may need to be reconsidered when undertaking cross-cultural work, but the meanings of what it is to be a child or an adolescent. As Boyden (2003) discusses, Euro-American ideas of childhood have particularly stressed vulnerability and passivity, such that Western-based models of interventions maybe quite unhelpful outside such contexts if they are unable to see how children can be resilient and active agents.

Academic developments around childhood and youth studies (e.g., Kehily, 2007; Prout, 2004) have drawn our attention to young people as active meaning makers, but with historically and culturally variable inequalities of power and resources. These inequalities are related to institutionalized age status, which is associated with ideals and assumptions of what it means to be a young person, and also systematically related to other social patterns such as gender, social class, or ethnicity. In developed societies, then, not only are childhood and youth constructed through such features as child labor laws, and compulsory education, but also through ideals of the home as the proper place for childhood to take place, and all underpinned by models of child and adolescent development, which are themselves rooted in particular cultural and historical contexts (Burman, 2001). It is within these social and cultural contexts and discourses that existing research and knowledge of young people's experiences of death and bereavement have been constructed in Euro-American societies. But, while globalization—for better or worse—may be shaping and universalizing Western understandings and institutions of childhood and youth, through media and technology and such frameworks as the United Nations Convention on the Rights of the Child (Boyden, 1997), these understandings and institutions are always made meaningful through localized contexts, such as family, generation, religious ideas, legal frameworks, political and economic circumstances, and so forth (Woodhead, 1999). In such localized contexts, children have agency and they are meaning makers, even if this self-efficacy occurs within a world that is not of their own making.

Children's understandings of death constitute one small body of literature that exists in relation to children, young people, and death across global contexts. However, here too we find that the Western cognitive, linear developmental model predominates (Bluebond-Langner & DeCicco, 2006), and it is largely structured research instruments built on this model that are used in cross-cultural research. Even so, children's developmental understanding in these terms can be shown to be dependent on social class (Tallmer, Formanek, & Tallmer, 1974) and societal context (e.g., Schonfeld & Smilansky, 1989). And the use of an interpretive methodology with Japanese children enabled Sagara-Rosemeyer and Davies (2007) to undertake an open-ended exploration of their views of death in an abstract sense, finding that their beliefs of life, death, and reincarnation significantly challenged Western ideas of death as irreversible. Similarly, Hewlett (2005) found that ideas of reincarnation, which related to the age of the deceased, significantly shaped young people's responses to deaths in the groups she studied in the Central African Republic.

MAKING SENSE OF THE EVIDENCE ON YOUNG PEOPLE, DEATH, AND BEREAVEMENT

The meanings of death and bereavement for young people heavily depend on culture and context. As life events occur, including deaths, young people will make sense, of whatever kind, of their experiences, drawing on available systems of meanings structured by interpersonal, cultural, structural, and material contexts, including systematic differences of power associated with age status. It is important to see these various contexts, processes, and experiences as intimately interlinked, rather than as nested layers (as in Bronfenbrenner's, 1979, ecological model), because meanings run through all of them and none of them exist outside of meanings in social lives and in personal experience.

If we consider the broad range of possible experiences, a shift from the notion of adolescent bereavement to young people's responses to death may be a useful conceptual opening in considering varied contexts both between and within societies across the globe, raising new issues for research and for professional understandings. Young people's encounters with death in any society may be highly varied, but we may initially at least draw distinctions between *mediated deaths* that are encountered through the media (as in the deaths of celebrities they have never met) and *personalized deaths* that occur in their social networks or immediate face-to-face interactions. It may become apparent that we have very little research concerned with mediated deaths in young people's lives, and research into experiences of personalized deaths has been very largely confined to certain categories of death that are presumed to be significant in Euro-American societies, particularly deaths of parents, and, to a lesser extent, siblings, and perhaps friends. And yet, when British young people themselves are asked to describe deaths in their lives that have been significant, a much wider set of relationships will be included, such that the vast majority of young people state that they have experienced a significant bereavement (Harrison & Harrington, 2001). And, as we saw in the quotes at the start of this chapter, such significance may be felt by the young person through varied sets of meanings, which may not be well revealed through predominant psychological frameworks and structured research methodologies.

The existing—very predominantly Western-based—research evidence that we do have available has undoubtedly made important contributions to our understandings of bereavement in the lives of young people, and its usefulness must not be underestimated. But there are also considerable difficulties with this literature, from a number of different angles, not least its complexity and contradictory findings about the implications of bereavement for young people's lives in the shorter and longer term (Ribbens McCarthy, 2006). Within this situation, a focus on meaning may provide an important route forward, providing, as it does, a basis for dialogue across disciplines and a hinge between the experiential and the structural and cultural aspects of responses to death.

Conceptually, then, attention to meanings may be productive. Some writers indeed suggest that grief experiences can be crucially understood as a crisis of meaning, framed in terms of meaning reconstruction theory as a therapeutic process (Neimeyer, 2001). As discussed earlier, however, beyond this particular model, a conceptual framework of responses to death, and its relationship to concepts of bereavement and loss, all require attention to the meaning of the ruptured relationship or reality that underlies any experienced loss on the part of the individual. Additionally, concepts of transition and disruption are both widely used in relation to both bereavement and loss on the one hand, and the experiences of young people on the other (so that bereaved youths may constitute a sort of double jeopardy), and both these concepts crucially concern meanings—since meanings are a key aspect of what is disrupted or what is required for transition to occur.

Attention to meaning may also have a particular contribution to make to empirical and research issues, helping perhaps to disentangle some of the complexities in the existing evidence (Ribbens McCarthy, 2006). Contradictory implications of adolescent bereavement, for example, seem to arise for different individuals, families, and communities, with quite polarized responses being apparent around depression, self-esteem, educational attainment, sexual activity and partnering, family cohesiveness, and peer responses—giving rise to quite different patterns for different individuals, which are lost within aggregated statistical data.

> Such polarized and contradictory tendencies may perhaps reflect the ways in which the human spirit may respond to pain and suffering, through the different ways in which we may understand profound life events, leading to a new search for meaning, or to a profound disruption of meaning, in whatever sense we are using "meaning." (Ribbens McCarthy, 2006, p. 207)

An attention to meanings may be fruitfully explored through both qualitative methodologies, such as narrative approaches, as well as more structured quantitative approaches. Advances in statistical modeling in recent years have enabled researchers, concerned with the lives of children over time, to build sophisticated theoretical models encompassing intra- and interpsychic processes, individual characteristics, and life events, as well as aspects of social structure and social contexts. But understanding the patterns apparent in such data sets requires consideration of the ways in which all these different processes are mediated through the culturally based meanings they hold for people (Rutter, 2000), as these unfold over long periods of time in the lives of individuals.

Theoretically, too, an attention to meanings may enable us to recognize that a young person's response to a death may be significant without it necessarily constituting major bereavement as such. Such a possibility has received very little attention, either from researchers or from policy makers, who have focused heavily on bereavements in the lives of young people that might be expected to be particularly disruptive in the contexts of developed societies, failing to recognize that both death and bereavement may be mainstream issues in the lives of such young people, as they seek to make sense of the (changing and perhaps challenging) personal and social worlds in which they find themselves. Such a more open-ended, ethnographic approach might open up the area of "adolescent bereavement" not only to a much broader set of research questions but also to the potential contributions of different theoretical frameworks from other disciplines (Ribbens McCarthy, 2006).

CONCLUSIONS

Attention to meaning may be highly fruitful for the greater understanding of young people's experiences of death and bereavement, opening up possibilities of cross-cultural as well as cross-disciplinary dialogues, as well as drawing our attention to a much wider range of experiences than is currently considered in the literature. Yet the concept of meaning itself must always be carefully considered, if such dialogue is not to be undermined by misunderstandings of the meaning of *meaning*. And, at the same time, an attention to meanings need not—and indeed, must not—entail a neglect of material contexts and inequalities.

Concepts, such as loss and bereavement, are crucial for the ways in which everyday meanings can be highlighted, theorized, made visible, or marginalized in academic, professional, and expert research and discourses. Unless we—as individuals working from our own personal histories and cultural contexts—pay very close attention to our concepts, we risk imposing our own assumptions onto—in effect, "colonizing" (Ungar, 2008)—the experiences of others. The effect will be to limit our capacity to understand such experiences and, in the process, gain new insights and possibilities for understanding the significance of cultural and historical contexts for young people's meaning making in response to death and bereavement. At present the expert and research literature regarding young people, death, and bereavement are heavily framed, and limited, by particular models and concepts that highlight some meanings but obscure others.

If we return to the meanings expressed in the quotes from which we started this chapter, we can see how these young people framed their differing experiences of death through particular meanings. Some of these meanings are very subtle and contingent, but others appear recurrently through their interviews, as they narrate—and try to make sense of—their lives to the researchers over a period of years. And, arguably, these recurrent themes and meanings can only be discerned through close attention to such narratives over time. Thus the meaning of the death of Shirleen's great-grandfather in Jamaica is framed by reference to her family connections and her ethnic identity, both of which lead her to emphasize the importance of Jamaica for her overall orientation to life. Maeve's account of the deaths of two close friends is framed by the meanings it gives to her peer group friendships and, over time, by the meaning she gives to personal change in response to such significant events.

For people seeking to support such young people through their experiences of death and bereavement, there is an imperative to pay close attention to their individualized meanings. Such attention requires an exploration of the ways in which young people make sense of such events in terms of both their individual histories *and* the broader social, cultural, and material contexts in which their meanings are located. Such issues are crucial for understanding diversities across the great range of such contexts that occur within societies as well as between them.

Any such exploration requires that *we*—whether professionals or researchers—continuously reflect on our own meanings, including those that are taken for granted in our everyday lives, those that are encapsulated within our theoretical models and expert knowledge, and those that are expressed in our political stances and values. I have argued here that many social scientists, drawing on hermeneutic traditions, are interested in meanings as sense making, without wishing to advocate the need for meanings as purposefulness and without wanting to evaluate any particular meanings as more desirable and worthy than others. Nevertheless, this approach does not necessarily lead us into a position of cultural relativism. At some point we may decide that we want to assert the priority of some meanings over others on the basis of particular values we hold dear. The approach I have discussed here, however, would suggest that we need to be explicit about such prioritization of certain values, rather than implicitly incorporating our values and meanings into the theoretical and conceptual models that we adopt and that shape our research and our interventions. By being explicit, we can be ready to argue for our valued meanings in respectful dialogue, across disciplines, cultures, and social contexts, and hopefully, in the process, gain new insights into young people's responses to death in the diverse circumstances of their lives.

NOTE

1. These quotes are taken from five extended case studies analyzed with a general narrative approach and written up by Sue Sharpe, presented in Ribbens McCarthy (2006).

The larger longitudinal studies from which they were drawn involved repeated in-depth interviews with young people in a general project concerned with the lives of young people across contemporary Britain, and Sue Sharpe was a member of the original research team. I am indebted to London South Bank University for providing access to the materials. Further details of the study and associated publications can be found at http://www.sbu.ac.uk/fhss/ff/. The studies were funded by the Economic and Social Research Council.

REFERENCES

Bluebond-Langner, M., & DeCicco, A. (2006). Children's views of death. In A. Goldman, R. Hain, & S. Liben (Eds.), *Oxford textbook of palliative care for children* (pp. 85–94). Oxford: Oxford University Press.

Boyden, J. (1997). Childhood and the policy makers: A comparative perspective on the globalisation of childhood. In A. James & A. Prout (Eds.), *Constructing and reconstructing childhood: Contemporary issues in the sociological study of childhood* (pp. 184–215). Lewes: Falmer.

Boyden, J. (2003). Children under fire: Challenging assumptions about children's resilience. *Children, Youth and Environments, 13*(1). Retrieved January 25, 2007, from http://www.colorado.edu/journals/cye/13_1/Vol13_1Articles/CYE_CurrentIssue_Article_ChildrenUnderFire_Boyden.htm

Boyden, J., & Mann, G. (2005). Children's risk, resilience and coping in extreme situations. In M. Ungar (Ed.), *Handbook for working with children and youth: Pathways to resilience across cultures and contexts* (pp. 3–26). Thousand Oaks, CA: Sage.

Brewin, C. R., & Power, M. J. (1997). Meaning and psychological therapy: Overview and introduction. In M. J. Power & C. R. Brewin (Eds.), *The transformation of meaning in psychological therapies: Integrating theory and practice* (pp. 1–14). Chichester: John Wiley.

Bronfenbrenner, U. (1979). *The ecology of human development.* Cambridge, MA: Harvard University Press.

Burman, E. (2001). Beyond the baby and the bathwater: Postdualistic developmental psychologies for diverse childhoods. *European Early Childhood Education Research Journal,* 9(1), 5–22.

Carlsen, M. B. (1988). *Meaning making: Therapeutic processes in adult development.* New York: W.W. Norton.

Craib, I. (1994). *The importance of disappointment.* London: Routledge.

Davis, C. G., Nolen-Hoeksema, S., & Larson, J. (1998). Making sense of loss and benefitting from the experience: Two construals of meaning. *Journal of Personality and Social Psychology, 75*(2), 561–574.

Davis, C. G., Wortman, C. B., Hehman, D. R., & Silver, R. C. (2000). Searching for meaning in loss: Are clinical assumptions correct? *Death Studies, 24*(6), 497–542.

Demmer, C. (2007). Grief is a luxury: AIDS-related loss among the poor in South Africa. *Illness, Crisis and Loss, 15*(1), 39–51.

Geertz, C. (1973). *The interpretation of cultures.* New York: Basic Books.

Gerard, J. M., & Buehler, C. (2004). Cumulative environmental risk and youth maladjustment: The role of youth attributes. *Child Development, 75*(6), 1832–1849.

Gersten, J. C., Beals, J., & Kallgren, C. A. (1991). Epidemiology and preventive interventions: Parental death in childhood as an example. *American Journal of Community Psychiatry, 19,* 481–498.

Giddens, A. (1990). *The consequences of modernity.* Cambridge: Polity Press.

Gielen, U. P. (2003). Foreword. In D. Sharma (Ed.), *Childhood, family and sociocultural change in India* (pp. ix–xii). Oxford: Oxford University Press.

Harrison, L., & Harrington, R. (2001). Adolescents' bereavement experiences: Prevalence, association with depressive symptoms, and use of services. *Journal of Adolescence, 24*(2), 159–169.

Hewlett, B. L. (2005). Vulnerable lives: The experiences of death and loss among Aka and Nganda adolescents of the Central African Republic. In B. S. Hewlett & M. E. Lamb (Eds.) *Hunter-gatherer childhoods: Evolutionary, developmental and cultural perspectives* (pp. 322–342). New Brunswick, NJ: Transaction Publishers.

Hockey, J. (2002). The importance of being intuitive: Arnold Van Gennep's *The Rites of Passage. Mortality, 7*(2), 210–217.

Janoff-Bulman, R. (1992). *Shattered assumptions: Towards a psychology of trauma.* New York: The Free Press.

Kehily, M. J. (Ed.). (2007). *Understanding youth: Perspectives, identities and practices.* London: Sage/Open University.

Kelly, G. (1955). *The psychology of personal constructs.* New York: W. W. Norton.

Klass, D. (1999). Developing a cross-cultural model of grief: The state of the field. *Omega, Journal of Death and Dying, 39*(3), 153–178.

Klass, D., Silverman, P. R., & Nickman, S. L. (Eds.). (1996). *Continuing bonds: New understandings of grief.* London: Taylor & Francis.

Laungani, P. (2005). Cultural considerations in Hindu funerals in India and England. In J. D. Morgan & P. Laungani (Eds.), *Death and bereavement around the world: Vol. 4, Asia, Australia and New Zealand* (pp. 39–64). Amityville, NY: Baywood.

Leming, M. R. & Dickinson, G. E. (2007). *Understanding dying, death, and bereavement* (6th ed.). Belmont, CA: Thomson.

Lutzke, J. R., Ayers, T. S., Sandler, I. N., & Barr, A. (1997). Risks and interventions for the parentally bereaved child. In S. A. Wolchik & I. N. Sandler (Eds.), *Handbook of children's coping: Linking theory and intervention* (pp. 215–244). New York: Plenum Press.

Mackay, N. (2003). Psychotherapy and the idea of meaning. *Theory and Psychology, 13*(3), 359–386.

Marris, P. (1996). *The politics of uncertainty: Attachment in private and public life.* London: Routledge.

Meltzer, H., Gatward, R., Goodman, R., & Ford, T. (2000). *The mental health of children and adolescents in Great Britain.* London: The Stationery Office.

Mitchell, R., Dorling, D., & Shaw, M. (2000). *Inequalities in life and death: What if Britain were more equal?* Bristol: Policy Press/Joseph Rowntree Foundation.

Montgomery, H. (2008). *Small strangers: A cross-cultural introduction to childhood.* Oxford: Blackwell.

Morgan, J. D. (2002). Some concluding observations. In J. D. Morgan & P. Laungani (Eds.), *Death and bereavement around the world: Vol. 1, Major religious traditions* (pp. 193–196). Amityville, NY: Baywood.

Nadeau, J. W. (1990). *Families making sense of death.* London: Sage.

Neimeyer, R. A. (2000). Searching for the meaning of meaning: Grief therapy and the process of reconstruction. *Death Studies, 24*(6), 541–558.

Neimeyer, R. A. (Ed.). (2001). *Meaning reconstruction and the experience of loss.* Washington, DC: American Psychological Association.

Prout, A. (Ed.). (2004). *The future of childhood.* London: Routledge.

Ribbens McCarthy, J. (2006). *Young people's experiences of loss and bereavement: Towards an inter-disciplinary approach.* Buckingham: Open University Press.

Ribbens McCarthy, J. (2007a). "They all look as if they're coping, but I'm not": The relational power/lessness of "youth" in responding to experiences of bereavement. *Journal of Youth Studies, 10*(3), 285–304.

Ribbens McCarthy, J. (2007b, November 22–24). *The social and cultural contexts of children and young people's experiences of bereavement: Meanings of loss in globalized and localised worlds.* Paper presented at the Asian Youth and Childhoods, VIIIth International Conference of the Research Committee on Sociology of Youth and Research Committee on Sociology of Childhood, International Sociological Association, Lucknow, India.

Rosenblatt, P. C. (2001). A social constructionist perspective on cultural differences in grief. In M. Stroebe, W. Stroebe, R. Hansson, & H. Schut (Eds.), *Handbook of bereavement research: Consequences, coping, care* (pp. 285–300). Washington, DC: American Psychological Association.

Rutter, M. (2000). Psychosocial influences: Critiques, findings and research needs. *Development and Psychopathology, 12*(3), 375–405.

Sagara-Rosemeyer, M., & Davies, B. (2007). The integration of religious traditions in Japanese children's view of death and afterlife. *Death Studies, 31,* 223–247.

Schonfeld, D. J., & Smilansky, S. (1989). A cross-cultural comparison of Israeli and American children's death concepts. *Death Studies, 13,* 593–604.

Stroebe, M., & Schut, H. (1998). Culture and grief. *Bereavement Care, 17*(1), 7–11.

Tallmer, M., Formanek, R., & Tallmer, J. (1974). Factors influencing children's concepts of death. *Journal of Clinical Child Psychology,* 3(2), 17–19.

Terheggen, M. A., Stroebe, M. S., & Kleber, R. J. (2001). Western conceptualizations and Eastern experience: A cross-cultural study of traumatic stress reactions among Tibetan refugees in India. *Journal of Traumatic Stress, 14*(2), 391–403.

Ungar, M. (2008). Resilience across cultures. *British Journal of Social Work, 38*(2), 218–235.

Walter, T. (1999). *On bereavement: The culture of grief.* Buckingham: Open University Press.

Weber, M. (1968). *Economy and society: An outline of interpretive sociology* (G. Roth & G. Wittich, Trans.). New York: Bedminster Press.

Wetherell, M. (2001). Editor's introduction. In M. Wetherell, S. Taylor, & S. J. Yates (Eds.), *Discourse theory and practice: A reader* (pp. 9–13). London: Sage.

Woodhead, M. (1999). Reconstructing developmental psychology—some first steps. *Children and Society, 13,* 3–19.

Worden, J. W., & Silverman, P. R. (1996). Parental death and the adjustment of school age children. *Omega, Journal of Death and Dying,* 33(2), 91–102.

Young-suck Moon, S. (2005). The death system in Korean culture. In J. D. Morgan & P. Laungani (Eds.), *Death and bereavement around the world: Vol. 4, Asia, Australia, and New Zealand* (pp. 109–122). Amityville, NY: Baywood.

3

Ethics and Adolescent Grief Research: A Developmental Analysis

ALICIA SKINNER COOK

Although studies with bereaved populations have proliferated, the discussion of research ethics involving emotionally sensitive research has not kept pace. Ethics in bereavement research received little or no attention until the mid-1990s with the publication of a special issue of *Death Studies* that focused on this topic (Balk & Cook, 1995). This publication prompted closer examination of the unique issues faced by researchers studying bereaved individuals and families. A variety of articles and chapters followed, addressing such areas as ethics and investigator bias (Cook, 1997), the dynamics of ethical decision making (Cook, 2001), and ethics and methodological concerns (Stroebe, Stroebe, & Schut, 2003) when studying grief.

Other scholars have expanded the discussion of ethics and bereavement research to include diverse populations and situations. For example, Dyregrov, Dyregrov, and Raundalen (2000) studied how traumatized/bereaved refugee families perceived their participation in research. More recently, Meert and her colleagues (2008) examined ethical and logistical considerations of multicenter network research on parental bereavement research. This approach has the potential to recruit participants from diverse racial, ethnic, and geographic backgrounds, and significantly contribute to the understanding of the heterogeneity in bereavement.

Despite this expansion in the professional literature, virtually no attention has been given to the ethics of conducting research with bereaved adolescents. Considerable literature does exist on the ethics of research with adolescents in related areas (e.g., health research), and the findings of these studies will be extrapolated and applied to the context of bereavement in the present chapter. Other studies on ethics have used a broader age range, but a limitation of many of these articles is the use of the term *children* to refer to all nonadults. Combining young children and adolescents into one category obscures important developmental considerations. A few studies have examined findings by age group to yield useful information related specifically to adolescence.

WHY STUDY ADOLESCENTS AND GRIEF?

The Report on Bereavement and Grief Research (Center for the Advancement of Health, 2004) resulting from the *Grief Research: Gaps, Needs and Actions Project* concluded that improving care through the alignment of research and practice is an issue of critical concern in relation to bereavement care. The report underscores the need for empirically based grief interventions and recommends engaging both researchers and practitioners in considering ethical challenges. This need is particularly important with regard to adolescence and grief. Balk and Corr (2001) have observed that research on adolescent bereavement has had a short history, and the empirical literature on the effects of loss during this stage of development is limited.

The integration of the growing empirical knowledge on adolescent development and the professional literature on grief and bereavement with research ethics is crucial for those interested in protecting rights and interests of young people while advancing applied knowledge in the area of grief and bereavement. This chapter addresses ethical considerations in adolescent grief research from a developmental perspective. Specifically, the chapter will focus on the fundamental ethical concepts of the right to participation, informed and voluntary consent, and avoiding harm while maximizing benefits. Additionally, ethical issues will be explored with regard to the study of adolescent grief experiences and manifestations across cultures, as well as the expanding research contexts for studying this diversity.

THE RIGHT OF BEREAVED ADOLESCENTS TO PARTICIPATE IN RESEARCH

Stroebe et al. (2003) have asserted that the most basic ethical principle in research is the protection of the participants' rights, dignity, and well-being. With regard to the issue of rights, the right of adolescents to participate in research can itself be an ethical issue. Dibrell and Yamamoto (1988) have pointed out that adults have typically assumed that young people's assessment of the impact of life events on their physical and mental health is untrustworthy and, even if otherwise, would closely agree with the judgment of adults made on their behalf. These assumptions, however, have not received support when studied in a variety of cultural settings (Yamamoto, Soliman, Parsons, & Davis, 1987). Yamamoto and Felsenthal (1982) have observed that the lens through which adults perceive a situation is not the one that young people use; nor is it the same lens that is used to process, interpret, and cope with life experiences. With regard to perceptions of bereavement in particular, the findings from a study by Hogan and Balk (1990) of sibling loss raise serious questions about the accuracy and reliability of mothers' perceptions of the grief experienced by their adolescent children.

Atwool (2000) argues that the concept of subjectivity is central to postmodern theory and states that this conceptualization has particular importance when applied to youths who have experienced traumatic events. According to Atwool, applying postmodern theory to the understanding of the impact of trauma on young people's lives suggests that a useful starting point is the child/adolescent and the meanings that he or she attaches to the experience. An individual is not simply acted upon by the traumatic event or situation and the response of significant others, the community, and the larger culture; the child/adolescent is actively coping with the experience and its aftermath. By excluding young people as active participants in the research process, it can be argued that they are thus relegated to a minor role in their own experience. It is imperative that research on the effectiveness of intervention programs incorporates the voices of those affected, regardless of age.

Lansdown (1994) has divided the articles in the United Nations Convention on the Rights of the Child into the following three main types of rights: provision rights, protection rights, and participation rights. Participation rights include young people's rights to be heard, and their views respected and taken into account. Other scholars point out that although only a small number of social scientists participated in the formation of the Convention, they now have the opportunity to use their expertise to enhance the process of interpreting and implementing it (Wilcox & Naimark, 1992). The research arena is a key area in which participation rights can be applied.

In fact, social science researchers have stressed the importance of using participatory and interactive methods in HIV/AIDS research, and studies show that involving young people in the research process improves the relevance of the research (Obbo, 1998; Schoepf, 1991). The research agenda responds to the young peoples' own needs and problems and encourages them to contribute to intervention inputs. This approach attempts to develop a deeper understanding of all aspects of what is being studied in order to produce new knowledge that can better inform practice.

Hatgis, Dillon, and Bibrace (1999) note that psychology and various other disciplines within the human sciences have moved away from viewing those who are studied as subjects and reconceptualizing them as participants in the research process. By viewing adolescents as full research partners, researchers avoid losing sight of the implications and alternatives to their perspectives. The partnership model requires researchers to grapple with the interpretations that participants and others offer about the information that is gathered. Hatgis and her colleagues (1999) argue that a partnership model results in more comprehensive, and therefore better, science, thus increasing the opportunities for eliciting participant input on the research process and incorporating participant-generated questions. This approach allows researchers to more fully contextualize their research, more completely understand the impact of loss on adolescents, and provide more useful and relevant information to professionals and organizations that work on their behalf.

INFORMED CONSENT/ASSENT IN ADOLESCENT BEREAVEMENT RESEARCH

Federal regulations governing research with human subjects were first adopted in the United States in 1974. Soon thereafter the Belmont Report (NCPHS, 1979) identified the basic ethical principles that should be used in the conduct of research involving human participants and to develop guidelines to assure that research is conducted in accordance with the principles of respect for persons, beneficence, and justice. In 1983, additional regulations were added to govern research involving minors. Although adolescents are not specifically mentioned in the federal code, they are included with children as minors.

The federal regulations require parental consent, as well as child and adolescent assent, but do not stipulate a specific age at which assent must be sought. Assent is defined as the minor's affirmative agreement to participate in the research. The guidelines stipulate that mere failure to object should not be construed as assent. Wagener and colleagues (2004) note that although passive consent is not part of the federal regulations, it is a term commonly used in the research community. In the passive consent process, parents or guardians are provided with a letter discussing the nature and purpose of the research. If parents/guardians do not want their minor children to participate, they must return the letter; otherwise, passive consent is viewed as a waiver of parental consent.

In some circumstances, parental or guardian permission can be waived or modified, but only if this action is not inconsistent with state law. One example would be research in which subjects are so-called mature minors, and the procedures involve no more than minimal risk that the individuals might reasonably assume on their own. If parental permission is waived, then an appropriate mechanism for protecting the child (particularly younger ones) must be substituted (Areen, 1992).

In both law and ethics, minors have been presumed to be incapable of giving truly informed consent due to their immature cognitive skills, inadequate experience in a research context, and the actual and perceived power differential between children and adults (Thompson, 1990). Bruzzese and Fisher (2003) found that 7th graders, when compared to 10th graders, were still struggling to understand their veto power over adult permission, as well as their rights to be protected from harm and to be informed about research procedures and results. Overall, 10th graders' responses did not differ from those of adults. The findings underscore the ambivalent status of early adolescence when it comes to the capacity for self-determination decisions. These researchers suggest that assessing and enhancing minor research participants' understanding of their rights should be an ethical priority for developmental scientists. However, there has been limited scholarship on the understanding of adolescents' research rights and methods to enhance their assent capacity.

Caskey and Rosenthal (2005) note that research policies do often distinguish between children under the age of 12 and adolescents, but few policies account for the rapidly changing competencies of those from 12 to 20. Distinctions are made for older adolescents based on the fact that

18-year-olds are considered legal adults, yet such distinctions may not be supported by developmental theory. Development is a progression and does not occur suddenly when one reaches a certain age. Furthermore, there is much individual variation within an age group. While older adolescents may possess cognitive skills similar to those of adults, their ability to implement these skills may depend on the situation.

Adolescents have been shown to have clear notions about the role they should play in the decision about research participation and often feel they should have the prerogative to make the final decision. Empirical evidence suggests that most parents bring a style of decision making and negotiation that they use in their daily lives when interacting with their adolescents, and this style does not change markedly in the research context (Broome, Kodish, Geller, & Siminoff, 2003).

The ethical principle of respect for persons translates into the individual's right to autonomous decision making, but it is not clear how this principle can be applied to children and adolescents in a developmentally appropriate way. This issue continues to be a focus of debate within the bioethics community (Miller, Drotar, & Kodish, 2004), and much controversy still exists regarding the interpretation and applications governing research with minors. In a recent study of practices of institutional review boards (IRBs) regarding youth-focused research submissions, Wagener and her colleagues (2004) found much variability in how IRBs interpreted compliance with federal regulations, and substantial differences of opinion existed. One half of the 49 IRBs in this study indicated that they never granted parental waivers.

AN ANALYSIS OF RISKS AND BENEFITS IN DEVELOPMENTAL CONTEXT

Ethics is a vital part of the entire research enterprise. Ethical questions arise at every stage of the research process, especially in research with youths who typically have limited power and influence (Alderson, 2004). *Beneficence* is the ethical obligation to maximize benefits and minimize possible harms. Risk/benefit ratio is an inevitable equation at each stage of the research process from conception of the research question to dissemination of findings. While researchers must be concerned about the dangers of research, sensitivity to the risks should not obscure an equal sensitivity to the benefits that research may bring to those studied.

Benefits

Several empirical studies have examined perceived benefits of participating in bereavement research and found that adult participants valued the opportunity to "share their complete stories" from their own perspectives and talk about their loss. This research involvement is often perceived as helpful and can result in new insights, expanded meanings, and perceived strengths on the part of the participants. Individuals also often feel that they are making an important contribution in helping professionals better understand the grief process and helping other bereaved individuals better understand their own grief (Cook & Bosley, 1995; Dyregrov, 2004; Seamark, Gilbert, Lawrence, & Williams, 2000). Dyregrov, Dyregrov, and Raundalen (2000) point out that there have been many assumptions made about the potential risk of asking traumatized people to participate in research. In their own research with refugee families from Bosnia in an effort to broaden knowledge about the ethical dimension of conducting research on traumatized/bereaved populations, these investigators found that both refugee parents and their children (ages 6–19) in their small sample perceived the research experience as positive.

Cauce and Nobles (2006) conclude, based on their research with ethnic-minority, low-income, and homeless youths, that individuals from marginalized groups often welcome the opportunity to talk about themselves and painful incidents in their lives. A nonjudgmental interviewer can produce more comfort than distress and can validate the feelings of the young person through active listening.

To date, however, no studies have focused on the effects of participating in bereavement research on an adolescent sample. A first step could be modeled after a recent study by Beck and Konnert (2007) who surveyed the opinions of bereaved adults who had not previously participated in bereavement research to determine norms and variations in their judgments of acceptability regarding not only research participation but such variables as timing and recruitment methods. In this study, invitations to participate were posted to five grief support group message boards on the Internet; 316 individuals completed the first phase of the study, with 84 completing the second phase 1 year later. The individuals in this study felt overwhelmingly positive about the potential benefits of bereavement research, believing that it could be useful both to themselves and to others.

While some may question the ethics of involving bereaved adolescents in research, Holden (2003) demonstrated through the use of case studies the advantages of involving vulnerable individuals in research in terms of the benefits they themselves derive. The ideas and perspectives of vulnerable and marginalized individuals are often ignored. Their participation can be empowering both in psychological terms and through the resulting programs and policies that benefit from their input. It is equally important to identify the potential secondary benefits for research participants, such as the opportunity to inform the programs and policies by which they will be affected, the insights that are gained in the sharing of one's experiences, and the sense of competence and availability of support that can be reinforced through the research process.

Risks

Empirical studies have also asked bereaved adult participants about perceived risks or negatives associated with the research experience. While the positive statements have predominated, some individuals in these studies did report the experience to be stressful even though they were glad they had participated. Among bereaved individuals who had not actually participated in research, additional concerns included not being able to adequately express experiences or feelings and the fear of being misunderstood (Beck & Konnert, 2007).

The views (both negative and positive) of adults are important in adolescent bereavement research since they determine parents' consent for their adolescent children to participate in research, particularly younger ones. Bereavement research has some unique aspects that set it apart from other types of social science research (Cook, 1995). Societal and personal attitudes toward studying death-related topics influence the willingness of individuals to discuss loss-related topics in a research project and to allow their children to do so.

Federal guidelines dictate that if research involves more than minimal risk (a term that is not well defined but usually considered no greater than those encountered in everyday life or during the performance of routine physical or psychological tests), direct benefits to the individual participants should be anticipated. Provisions are also made for higher levels of risk with certain specified approval procedures. It is also suggested that studies involving more than minimal risk first be conducted on adults in order to better determine the level of risk involved. If this approach is not possible, research is to be conducted on older children before involving younger children (Areen, 1992).

Areen (1992) says that it may be wise to screen participants to exclude subjects who would be particularly at risk for psychological and/or emotional harm. Following this caution, a bereavement researcher might consider eliminating adolescent participants in a grief study who have a history of mental disorders or a low level of social support. However, adolescents who feel emotionally isolated and have little opportunity to talk about their loss may in fact be the ones most likely to benefit from participating in an interview study. It must be remembered that in assessing and consequently reducing risk to participants, research findings may be affected by the characteristics of the remaining participants. Consequently, limiting a study to adolescents who are adjusting well after a loss will have implications for the findings and conclusions drawn.

Developmental Considerations

The concern for beneficence is intensified when youths (rather than adults) are studied. Age-related changes exist with regard to research risks and benefits. One of the key ethical issues in behavioral research is related to privacy. Melton (1992) gives the example of the "Keep Out" sign on the doors of minors as a way of defining not only physical space but also psychological space and personal boundaries. Invasion of privacy is perceived as a personal violation in everyday life, and this view extends into the research arena. Few matters are as private as the complex feelings associated with loss and the relationship with a deceased loved one, and these feelings can hardly be avoided in grief research.

In his discussion of principles for the ethical consideration of privacy in research, Melton (1992) states that the privacy interests of children/adolescents and their families are serious matters deserving great weight in decisions about whether and how to conduct research. Also, as a general rule the more deeply private an experience or behavior is, the more careful researchers should be to protect it. Melton also maintains that participant consent should be contained before a zone of privacy is invaded and that research procedures should be no more intrusive than necessary. Thompson (1992) indicates that privacy interests and concerns increase and become more differentiated with maturation and broaden from an initial focus on privacy related to physical space and possessions in childhood to later including concerns with privacy related to information. Threats to confidentiality (e.g., parents wanting to know what an adolescent said in a grief interview) should be examined from the young person's perspective with respect for his or her boundaries.

Contrary to common wisdom, older youths can have more vulnerabilities in some areas than their younger counterparts. For example, youths may have better coping skills but be more susceptible to particular psychological harms from research, such as those involving threats to one's sense of self due to the importance of identity development during this life stage. (Within this age-related analysis, it is important to note that the concept of *self* has different meanings and progressions in different cultural contexts.) It is essential to examine risks and benefits within a developmental framework with emphasis on what is known regarding cognitive, emotional, and social development (Fisher & Tryon, 1990; Lindsay, 2000; Melton, 1992; Stanley & Sieber, 1992; Thompson, 1990).

Thompson's (1992) developmental formulation takes into account the fact that the older child and adolescent are more likely to have a larger repertoire of coping skills and thus greater adaptive functioning when dealing with a stressful situation. With increased maturity and cognitive skills, adolescents are better able to understand a range of feelings and emotional states and are therefore perhaps better able to express, interpret, and even accept the feelings elicited during a research session. These skills could be advantageous in mitigating the possible risks inherent in bereavement research while accentuating the potential benefits. By contrast, Thompson notes that social comparison information becomes a more significant mode of self-evaluation with increasing age. Peer influence and conformity are particularly strong during adolescence (Steinberg, 2007), and bereaved individuals during this life stage may be sensitive to appearing different from age mates in their reactions to loss or being different than peers because of the loss itself.

Adolescents also acquire the ability to make sophisticated psychological inferences of others' attitudes, motives, and feelings; this ability includes inferences regarding others' reactions to oneself (Thompson, 1992). Thus adolescents who participate in a research study on bereavement will be likely to gauge the reactions of the researchers to their responses and possibly search for verbal and nonverbal cues. If data are gathered in a group situation (e.g., grief support group or family interviews), the level of sharing by adolescents may be tempered by their perceptions of motives and the judgments others make of them in the research setting.

Unlike younger children, adolescents are less likely to be influenced by adults in their decision making, and their respect for authority is balanced by their understanding of individual rights and their quest for autonomy (Steinberg, 2007; Thompson, 1992). Hence, adolescents are less likely to be vulnerable to being coerced into participation in studies of their grief experience. Adolescence involves a gradual development of values and, with maturity, the increasing ability to make self-defining and autonomous choices. Schachter, Kleinman, and Harvey (2005) point out that adolescents may differ from adults in their perceptions and attitudes toward risks and benefits and may value these differently. In general, adolescents are more likely to engage in risk-taking behaviors and may place more value on the immediate situation rather than long-term consequences (Steinberg, 2007). This life stage is a time of movement toward increased independence from parents, but adolescents are still more dependent on parents for their well-being than are independent adults.

Caskey and Rosenthal (2005) advocate that researchers and institutional review boards use a developmentally based framework when making decisions regarding the implementation of research. According to these scholars, quality research will result from a thorough understanding of adolescent research participants and their unique needs. They conclude that:

> Our ability to use developmentally sensitive research practices will be enhanced by further understanding of issues associated with risk and benefit assessment by the adolescent, their parents, and institutional review boards, and by delineating ways to ensure that adolescent participants are adequately protected and have a developmentally affirming experience. (p. 61)

THE EXPANDED CYBERWORLD OF ADOLESCENTS: A NEW RESEARCH ARENA

Research methods must be appropriate for the age group being studied in order to elicit valid and reliable information (O'Kane, 2000). Many challenges exist in conducting research with bereaved adolescents that is both age appropriate and of relevance to their needs. Research methods and the ethics of research are always intricately linked (Jensen, Hoagwood, & Fisher, 1996).

Research using the Internet has recently increased because of access to a large and more diverse number of potential participants, as well as the ease of data collection and reduced time and costs. Rhodes,

Bowie, and Hergenrather (2003) predict that computer-mediated communications will play an ever-increasing role in the future of behavioral science research. This growing data collection method has challenged institutional review boards as they attempt to apply ethical guidelines and safeguard human research participants in an entirely new context. Rapid technological change and the increased mainstream use of information and communications technology has outpaced consideration of the associated ethical issues of analyzing Internet-based communications and collecting data from individuals online (Keller & Lee, 2003).

James, Oltjenbruns, and Whiting (2008) have highlighted the pervasive use of technology by today's adolescents; these authors conclude that cyberspace is one of the major contextual environments in which adolescents deal with grief. Their 24/7 cyberworld is part of their everyday lives as they keep in touch with friends through such means as instant messaging, text messaging via cell phone, personal Web pages and blogs, and participation on Internet sites such as MySpace and Facebook. For researchers interested in studying social support and adaptation to bereavement in adolescence, the expanding use of technology during adolescence for communication, social networking, and information gathering cannot be ignored. This new frontier of social interaction provides a rich and critical context for understanding the use of peer support during bereavement.

Keller and Lee (2003) have raised a number of ethical concerns associated with online research and emphasized that special care must be taken by online investigators with special attention paid to privacy, anonymity, confidentiality, informed consent, and potential harm. With technology changing so rapidly, security measures can quickly become obsolete and may increase risks associated with collection and storage of data. Further, Keller and Lee (2003) add that visual and auditory cues to distress cannot be perceived by investigators since online research participants cannot typically be seen. This obscuring of cues raises the question of how a psychological crisis might be handled over the Internet by those who conduct research on sensitive topics. It is important that participants have a way to contact the researchers after the study if they have questions or if access to mental health support is needed. Keller and Lee (2003) conclude that "the Internet can be fraught with ethical landmines, some of which are yet to be discovered" (p. 218), and the challenge for researchers is to find innovative ways of applying ethically responsible behaviors in this new research venue. They recommend that future deliberations over ethical issues surrounding the use of the Internet in human research include representatives from a variety of countries, cultures, and disciplines.

As stated, the prospect of conducting online research with bereaved adolescents raises additional ethical and practical issues. For example, the informed consent process can be confounded since the identity of the person giving consent cannot be verified. Since institutional review boards usually require parental consent for research participation of minors, how does a researcher go about obtaining this consent, and how does one know the actual identity and age of those clicking the "I consent" button? Furthermore, adolescents can also have a strong reaction to adults even logging on to MySpace and Facebook, considering it off-limits and often feeling at times like their space is being invaded when adults enter it. Before entering this new research terrain, investigators should carefully consider the risks, vulnerabilities, and trust issues that may arise. Increasingly, guidelines related to online research and ethics are provided in research methods texts and other specialized publications (Buchanan, 2004; Libutti, 1999; Mann & Stewart, 2000; McKee & DeVoss, 2007). This information can assist future researchers in conducting high-quality and ethical research in this important context of adolescent life. However, more scholarly work is needed that addresses the unique aspects of conducting socially and emotionally sensitive research with minors in this realm.

STUDYING BEREAVED ADOLESCENTS IN DIVERSE CULTURAL SETTINGS

Cook (2001) has emphasized that research ethics must be considered in context. As adolescent bereavement scholars attempt to expand our understanding of grief beyond White, middle-class America, they must remain cognizant of the link (and at times conflict) between ethics and cultural values and customs. Dyregrov, Dyregrov, and Raundalen (2000), in their study of the experience of refugee families in research participation, were reminded of the fact that research is always situated in a social, historical, and cultural context. In their study of Bosnian refugees and their children (aged 6 to 19) living in Norway, they found that the Bosnian parents decided important matters on behalf of their children and adolescents to a much greater extent than did Norwegians. The Bosnian parents in the study did not have a strong tradition of communicating with their children on difficult matters, and many parents consented to their children and adolescents participating in an earlier study without ever asking or informing them. While the majority of minors in retrospect indicated that they would have preferred to be asked directly by the researchers in the form of a letter, they also acknowledged the right of their parents to make decisions on behalf of the family. The study highlighted the cross-cultural challenges related to informed consent and the critical importance of preparing children and adolescents for the research process. Many of the children and adolescents in the study said they were worried and concerned about a foreigner coming to visit their family and talking with them. They reported feeling like they were preparing for an exam (except not really knowing what to prepare for) and being relieved afterward because they felt like they had "passed."

In their study, Dyregrov, Dyregrov, and Raundalen (2000) also found that participating parents thought it was "quite normal" that their children's versions of the experience were included since no one could provide this information other than the children themselves. The parents reported not having either fears or concerns regarding their children's participation and expressed trust of the professional qualifications of the researchers. This finding raises questions regarding cultural attitudes toward authority, status of refugees in a foreign country, and how these factors interact when agreeing to participate in a research study.

In some cultural circumstances, even the definition of what constitutes a child or adolescent poses issues, with chronological age perhaps not being the best indicator. Balk and Corr (2001) acknowledge that the age ranges associated with early, middle, and late adolescence are strongly influenced by Western cultural values. In the context of an African setting with research on AIDS orphans, it must be asked how development is altered by the social and economic environment (either accelerated or impeded) and the potential impact on ethical considerations in research. Indeed, the line between child/youth and adult can become easily blurred in this context. Nyambedha and Aagaard-Hansen (2003) indicate that their data suggest that the social positions occupied by orphaned children in the community may resemble those of adults in traditional society.

As adolescent bereavement research expands to include more experiences and cultural/ethnic groups, additional complexities in obtaining research approval can be expected. Research ethics committees (REC) in developing countries apply a variety of accepted international regulations when reviewing research, resulting in part from the fact that considerable research is conducted with international partners, but variation has been demonstrated when institutions apply human research regulations in different cultural contexts. Henderson, Corneli, Mahoney, Nelson, and Mwansambo (2007) conducted a study with members of the national REC in Malawi and found that international guidelines are interpreted in the context of local African conditions. Emphasis tended to be placed on examining the benefit to the community and ensuring that the informed consent process translates concepts in locally meaningful ways.

As addressed earlier in this chapter, online research holds significant potential for studying sources of information and support that bereaved adolescents seek and the dynamics of peer support following loss. Because of the ease of crossing geographical boundaries through the use of online methods, Internet-based cross-cultural investigations hold great potential for better understanding the ways culture influences adolescent coping styles. It is important, however, to differentiate culture from official governmental policies that might influence behavior and therefore research findings. Sturgill and Jongsuwanwattana (2007) point out, for example, that nations vary considerably on their privacy protections for citizens' Internet use. These authors explore a variety of other issues relevant to international researchers collecting data online and suggest caution in interpreting computer-mediated data.

CONCLUSION

If research on social and psychological issues for bereaved adolescents is conducted using ethical and methodologically sound approaches, numerous benefits can result for planning more effective education and intervention programs. However, more research on the ethics of conducting research on bereaved adolescents is needed. Sieber (2004) has been a strong advocate for empirical research on research ethics. In her view, ethical decision making by researchers and institutional review boards should be based on information gained through empirical research rather than on hunches regarding what potential research participants want to know, what they understand, and what they consider to be benefits and acceptable risks.

The majority of publications on the impact and other ethical implications of participation in bereavement research have addressed theoretical issues. Only a few notable exceptions have been quantitative or qualitative studies (Beck & Konnert, 2007; Cook & Bosley, 1995;

Dyregrov, 2004; Grinyer, 2004; Hynson, Aroni, Bauld, & Sawyer, 2006; Seamark et al., 2000; Williams, Woodby, Bailey, & Burgio, 2008), and these studies have largely focused on adults. As our understanding of how adolescents cope with grief expands, the field of adolescent bereavement needs well-designed and targeted research that will help us discover how best to achieve the dual aims of gaining important knowledge while respecting adolescent research participants. In this quest, Williams and her colleagues (2008) remind us to always honor the subjective and emotional nature of the grief experience, to attend to the affective state of the bereaved participant, and to "faithfully represent the voice of the informants" (p. 227).

REFERENCES

Alderson, P. (2004). Ethics. In S. Fraser, V. Lewis, S. Ding, M. Kellett, & C. Robinson (Eds.), *Doing research with children and young people* (pp. 97–112). London: Sage.

Areen, J. (1992). Legal constraints on social research on children. In B. Stanley & J. E. Sieber (Eds.), *Social research on children and adolescents: Ethical issues* (pp. 7–28). Newbury Park, CA: Sage.

Atwool, N. (2000). Trauma and children's rights. In A. B. Smith, M. Gollop, K. Marshall, & K. Nairn (Eds.), *International perspectives on children's rights* (pp. 19–31). Dunedin, New Zealand: University of Otago Press.

Balk, D. E., & Cook, A. S. (1995). Ethics and bereavement research [Special issue]. *Death Studies, 19*(2).

Balk, D. E., & Corr, C. A. (2001). Bereavement during adolescence: A review of research. In M. S. Stroebe, W. Stroebe, R. O. Hansson, & H. Schut (Eds.), *New handbook of bereavement: Consequences, coping, and care* (pp. 199–218). Washington, DC: American Psychological Association.

Beck, A. M., & Konnert, C. A. (2007). Ethical issues in the study of bereavement: The opinions of bereaved adults. *Death Studies, 31,* 783–799.

Broome, M. E., Kodish, E., Geller, G., & Siminoff, L. A. (2003). Children in research: New perspectives and practices for informed consent. *Ethics & Human Research Supplement,* September–October, S20–S25.

Bruzzese, J., & Fisher, C. B. (2003). Assessing and enhancing the research consent capacity of children and youth. *Applied Developmental Science, 7*(1), 13–26.

Buchanan, E. A. (Ed.). (2004). *Readings in virtual research ethics.* Hershey, PA: Information Science.

Caskey, J. D., & Rosenthal, S. L. (2005). Conducting research on sensitive topics with adolescents: Ethical and developmental considerations. *Developmental and Behavioral Pediatrics, 26*(1), 61–67.

Cauce, A. M., & Nobles, R. H. (2006). With all due respect: Ethical issues in the study of vulnerable adolescents. In J. E. Trimble & C. B. Fisher (Eds.), *The handbook of ethical research with ethnocultural populations & communities* (pp. 197–215). Thousand Oaks, CA: Sage.

Center for the Advancement of Health. (2004). Report on grief and bereavement research. *Death Studies, 28,* 491–575.

Cook, A. S. (1995). Ethical issues in bereavement research: An overview. *Death Studies, 19*(2), 103–122.

Cook, A. S. (1997). Investigator bias in bereavement research. *Canadian Journal of Nursing Research, 29*(4), 87–93.

Cook, A. S. (2001). The dynamics of ethical decision making in bereavement research. In M. S. Stroebe, W. Stroebe, R. O. Hansson, & H. Schut (Eds.), *New handbook of bereavement: Consequences, coping, and care* (pp. 119–142). Washington, DC: American Psychological Association.

Cook, A. S., & Bosley, G. M. (1995). The experience of participating in bereavement research: Stressful or therapeutic? *Death Studies, 19,* 157–170.

Dibrell, L. L., & Yamamoto, K. (1988). In their own words: Concerns of children. *Child Psychiatry and Human Development, 19*(1), 14–25.

Dyregrov, K. (2004). Bereaved parents' experience of research participation. *Social Science & Medicine, 58*(2), 391–400.

Dyregrov, K., Dyregrov, A., & Raundalen, M. (2000). Refugee families' experience of research participation. *Journal of Traumatic Stress, 13*(3), 413–426.

Fisher, C. B., & Tryon, W. W. (Eds.). (1990). *Ethics in applied developmental psychology: Emerging issues in an emerging field.* Norwood, NJ: Ablex.

Grinyer, A. (2004). The narrative correspondence method: What a follow-up study can tell us about the longer-term effect on participants in emotionally demanding research. *Qualitative Health Research, 14*(10), 1326–1341.

Hatgis, C., Dillon, J. J., & Bibrace, R. (1999). Psychology's subject(s): Moving toward the partnership model. In R. Bibace, J. J. Dillon, & B. N. Dowds (Eds.), *Partnerships in research, clinical, and educational settings* (pp. 15–26). Stamford, CT: Ablex.

Henderson, G. E., Corneli, A. L., Mahoney, D. B., Nelson, D. K., & Mwansambo, C. (2007). Applying research ethics guidelines: The view from a sub-Saharan research ethics committee. *Journal of Empirical Research on Human Research Ethics, 2*(2), 41–48.

Hogan, N. S., & Balk, D. E. (1990). Adolescent reactions to sibling death: Perceptions of mothers, fathers, and teenagers. *Nursing Research, 39,* 103–106.

Holden, S. (2003). *AIDS on the agenda: Adapting development and humanitarian programmes to meet the challenge of HIV/AIDS.* Oxford, UK: Oxfam Publishing.

Hynson, J. L., Aroni, R., Bauld, C., & Sawyer, S. M. (2006). Research with bereaved parents: A question of how not why. *Palliative Medicine, 20,* 805–811.

James, L., Oltjenbruns, K. A., & Whiting, P. (2008). Grieving adolescents: The paradox of using technology for support. In K. J. Doka & A. S. Tucci (Eds.), *Living with grief: Children and adolescents* (pp. 299–315). Washington, DC: Hospice Foundation of America.

Jensen, P., Hoagwood, K., & Fisher, C. B. (1996). Bridging scientific and ethical perspectives: Toward synthesis. In K. Hoagwood, P. S. Jensen, & C. B. Fisher (Eds.), *Ethical issues in mental health research with children and adolescents* (pp. 287–297). Mahwah, NJ: Lawrence Erlbaum Associates.

Keller, H. E., & Lee, S. (2003). Ethical issues surrounding human participants research using the Internet. *Ethics & Behavior, 13*(3), 211–219.

Lansdown, G. (1994). Children's rights. In B. Mayall (Ed.), *Children's childhoods: Observed and experienced* (pp. 33–44). London: Falmer Press.

Libutti, P. O. (1999). The Internet and qualitative research: Opportunities and constraints on analysis of cyberspace discourse. In M. Kopala & L. A. Suzuki (Eds.), *Using qualitative methods in psychology* (pp. 77–88). Thousand Oaks, CA: Sage.

Lindsay, G. (2000). Researching children's perspectives: Ethical issues. In A. Lewis & G. Lindsay (Eds.), *Researching children's perspectives* (pp. 1–20). Buckingham, UK: Open University Press.

Mann, C., & Stewart, F. (2000). *Internet communication and qualitative research: A handbook for researching online.* Thousand Oaks, CA: Sage.

McKee, H. A., & DeVoss, H. A. (2007). *Digital writing research: Technologies, methodologies, and ethical issues.* Cresskill, NJ: Hampton Press.

Meert, K. L., Eggly, S., Dean, J. M., Pollack, M., Zimmerman, J., Anand, K. J. S., Newth, C. J. L., Willson, D. F., & Nicholson, C. (2008). Ethical and logistical considerations of multicenter parental bereavement research. *Journal of Palliative Medicine, 11,* 444–450.

Melton, G. B. (1992). Respecting boundaries: Minors, privacy, and behavioral research. In B. Stanley & J. E. Sieber (Eds.), *Social research on children and adolescents: Ethical issues* (pp. 65–87). Newbury Park, CA: Sage.

Miller, V. A., Drotar, D., & Kodish, E. (2004). Children's competence for assent and consent: A review of the empirical findings. *Ethics & Behavior, 14*(3), 255–295.

National Commission for the Protection of Human Subjects of Biomedical and Behavioral Research (NCPHS). (1979). *The Belmont report.* Washington, DC: Government Printing Office.

Nyambedha, E. O., & Aagaard-Hansen, J. (2003). Changing place, changing position: Orphans' movements in a community with high HIV/AIDS prevalence in Western Kenya. In K. F. Olwig & E. Gullov (Eds.). *Children's places: Cross-cultural comparisons* (pp. 162–176). London: Routledge.

Obbo, C. (1998). Social science research: Understanding and action. In C. Becker, J. P. Dozon, C. Obbo, & M. Toure (Eds.), *Experiencing and understanding AIDS in Africa.* Dakar: Codesria, Karthala & IRD.

O'Kane, C. (2000). The development of participatory techniques: Facilitating children's views about decisions which affect them. In P. Christensen & A. James (Eds.), *Research with children: Perspectives and practices* (pp. 136–159). London: Falmer Press.

Rhodes, S. D., Bowie, D. A., & Hergenrather, K. C. (2003). Collecting behavioural data using the World Wide Web: Considerations for researchers. *Journal of Epidemiology & Community Health,* 57(1), 68–73.

Seamark, D. A., Gilbert, J., Lawrence, C. J., & Williams, S. (2000). Are postbereavement research interviews distressing to carers? Lessons learned from palliative care research. *Palliative Medicine, 14,* 55–56.

Schachter, D., Kleinman, I., & Harvey, W. (2005). Informed consent and adolescents. *Canadian Journal of Psychiatry, 50*(9), 534–540.

Schoepf, B. G. (1991). Ethical, methodological and political issues of AIDS research in central Africa. *Social Science & Medicine, 33*(7), 749–763.

Sieber, J. E. (2004). Empirical research on research ethics. *Ethics and Behavior, 14*(4), 397–412.

Stanley, B., & Sieber, J. E. (Eds.). (1992). *Social research on children and adolescents: Ethical issues.* Newbury Park, CA: Sage.

Steinberg, L. (2007). *Adolescence* (8th ed.). Boston, MA: McGraw Hill.

Stroebe, M. S., Stroebe, W., & Schut, H. (2003). Bereavement research: Methodological issues and ethical concerns. *Palliative Medicine, 17,* 235–240.

Sturgill, A., & Jongsuwanwattana, P. (2007). Legal and ethical concerns of collecting data online. In R. A. Reynolds, R. Woods, & J. D. Baker (Eds.), *Handbook of research on electronic surveys and measurements* (pp. 120–125). Hershey, PA: Idea Group.

Thompson, R. A. (1990). Vulnerability in research: A developmental perspective on research risk. *Child Development, 61,* 1374–1386.

Thompson, R. A. (1992). Developmental changes in research risk and benefit: A changing calculus of concerns. In B. Stanley & J. E. Sieber (Eds.), *Social research on children and adolescents: Ethical issues* (pp. 31–64). Newbury Park, CA: Sage.

Wagener, D. K., Sporer, A. K., Simmerling, M., Flome, J. L., An, C., & Curry, S. J. (2004). Human participants challenges in youth-focused research: Perspectives and practices of IRB administrators. *Ethics & Behavior, 14*(4), 335–349.

Wilcox, B. L., & Naimark, H. (1992). The rights of the child: Progress toward human dignity. In G. L. Abee, L. A. Bond, & T. V. C. Monsey (Eds.), *Improving children's lives: Global perspectives on prevention* (pp. 357–358). Newbury Park, CA: Sage.

Williams, B. R., Woodby, L. L., Bailey, F. A., & Burgio, K. L. (2008). Identifying and responding to ethical and methodological issues in after-death interviews with next-of-kin. *Death Studies, 32,* 197–236.

Yamamoto, K., & Felsenthal, H. M. (1982). Stressful experiences for children: Professional judgments. *Psychological Reports, 50,* 1087–1093.

Yamamoto, K., Soliman, A., Parsons, J., & Davis, O. L. (1987). Voices in unison: Stressful events in the lives of children in six countries. *Journal of Child Psychology and Psychiatry, 28,* 855–864.

PART II

Death

Adolescents have escaped the perils of infancy and childhood and have not lived long enough to succumb to the debilities of older adulthood. Still, adolescents are not wholly free from death-related perils. The six chapters in part II explore the leading causes of death and loss during the adolescent years, together with some of the major ways in which adolescents seek to cope with such challenges.

The first four of these chapters explore the principal causes of deaths during adolescence: accidents and homicide (chapter 4); suicide (chapter 5); HIV and AIDS (chapter 6); and life-threatening illnesses (chapter 7). The effects of these five causes of adolescent deaths are seen both in the United States and around the world. Some are preventable; all can be minimized. For these reasons, it is important to know how these causes of death operate during the adolescent years and what can be done about them.

Adolescents often respond to death-related encounters by using humor, the subject of chapter 8, or by turning to technology and the Internet, the subjects of chapter 9. Each of these resources—humor, technology, and the Internet—can be used by ill and bereaved adolescents in more or less constructive ways. That is why it is important for adults who are not so-called digital natives, as most adolescents these days are, to try to become familiar with these coping resources in order to be able to help adolescents more effectively.

4 Adolescents, Accidents, and Homicides

ILLENE C. NOPPE AND LLOYD D. NOPPE

Vehicular accidents and handgun homicides are the two most prevalent causes of adolescent deaths throughout the developed world. It is especially tragic that these are violent and often preventable occurrences in comparison to other forms of death. Despite the relative statistical unlikelihood of such adolescent deaths, the consequences of accidents and homicides for the bereaved are very profound. Furthermore, the publicity surrounding these events garners headlines that tend to disproportionately characterize a phase of the life span that already suffers from stereotyped mislabeling. A balance is required whereby these devastating premature losses are understood within the reality that the overwhelming majority of adolescents will not die in automobile crashes or school shootings. What we need to establish is how to better frame accidental and homicidal death in the context of adolescent development in the early part of the 21st century. The hope is to illuminate for thanatologists a window for exploring teenage accidents and homicides that is unique to this critical portion of human development.

DEVELOPMENTAL SYSTEMS THEORY

To set the stage for this discussion, we will introduce the perspective of developmental systems theory as exemplified by the work of

Bronfenbrenner, Lerner, and other developmental scientists (Lerner, Theokas, & Bobek, 2005). They have constructed five core principles that represent the most significant concepts of contemporary theorists. The first notion is that individual change takes place in the larger temporal progression of historical embeddedness, or that the events that occur across time influence personal development. Second, variations between and within individuals, interindividual and intraindividual differences, provide a wealth of diversity that affect developmental pathways. A third feature of the model is the emphasis on multiple levels of context, such that our ability to comprehend development requires the interactions among, for example, families, peer groups, schools, and communities. The fourth principle is to focus on issues of primary prevention and the optimization of healthy developmental trajectories, rather than to devote major attention to deficits and remediation. Finally, efforts are directed toward outreach scholarship or the bidirectional collaboration between developmental researchers and the communities in which the results may be usefully applied.

Beginning with the first principle of *historical embeddedness,* we can take a long-term view of how changes over time in the manner of adolescent accidents and homicides help us to recognize that such events are not recent developments. For example, adolescents are more likely to die in automobile accidents today than they were 50 years ago because they have much greater access to cars. By contrast, fewer teenagers now, at least in the United States, are likely to be killed by farm equipment or in factory accidents because of the decline of the family farm and stricter application of prohibitions against teen labor with dangerous machinery. School shootings and gang-related firearm homicides are no more tragic adolescent deaths than were duels, family revenge killings, border wars, or other acts that ended life so prematurely. However, compared to earlier in our history, compulsory school attendance has made this setting more central for many adolescent activities, positive and negative, while the easy availability of relatively inexpensive and highly potent weapons makes lethality more likely than with knives or fists, and media accessibility allows faster and more in-depth communication about teen deaths to be excessively publicized. Awareness of the temporal factor in adolescent death should not imply that we gloss over contemporary accident and homicide rates, but we do need to interpret how these particular statistics reflect historical trends.

The second principle of *individual differences* reminds us to take into account the many factors that might influence whether a particular adolescent is likely to be involved in an accidental or homicidal death. *Interindividual variables* such as ethnic background, immigrant status, gender, sexual orientation, socioeconomic status, and so forth, may reveal the reasons for varying probabilities of accidental or homicidal death. Developmental contextual theorists do not attempt to predict exact events because of the complexity of issues that lead to certain developmental trajectories; however, the likelihood of any given type of adolescent death may differ depending on whether the teenager is an African American male living in an urban ghetto or a White female from an upper middle-class suburb. *Intraindividual differences* are equally important to consider in exploring the probabilities for a particular teenager's involvement in an accident or a homicide. For instance, does the age of pubertal timing (i.e., earlier vs. later maturity) have some effect on risk-taking behavior that may lead to driving under the influence of alcohol, or does the level of an adolescent's cognitive development affect his or her decision making pertaining to weapon usage in dealing with anger? Answers to research questions of this nature may ultimately assist in creating improved prevention strategies.

Multiple and bidirectional relationships among various contextual levels of development is the critical third principle of developmental systems theory. We are charged with examining not merely an individual's personality, behavior, and development, but also how these factors interact with family members, friends, teachers, classmates, school settings, neighborhoods, community organizations, the media, religious groups, parental work environments and friendships, and other relatives. Numerous issues pertaining to adolescent accidents and homicides may be impacted by a clearer understanding of these and related variables. What kinds of role models are offered to the teenager for the use of guns to settle disputes? How effective are educational programs that deal with safe driving behaviors? Are the clergy providing appropriate guidance in their efforts to assist adolescent moral development? Does the impact of television programming, movies and videos, music on CDs and the radio, and Internet sources contribute to risk-taking activities? Beyond examining each of these influences individually, it is further incumbent on researchers to discover their interactions and grasp the reality that no one factor itself may be responsible for any specific accident or homicide. A more complex question might explore how teenage boys in single parent families, who have unstable friendships, are low achieving in school, and play violent video games frequently, are behaving in terms of road rage or being bullied?

The fourth principle of *optimizing healthy development and primary prevention* is derived from a greater understanding of the previous principles. Bolstering each teenager's developmental assets is the most appropriate means of inoculating them from the kinds of risky behaviors that lead to driving accidents or from choosing to alleviate frustrations with firearm homicides. The excessive use of alcohol, for example, can be viewed as instrumental in deaths resulting from incapacitated driving or lowered inhibitions to use guns. By combining the influences of parents, schools, churches, and other contextual levels, the hope would be to instill in adolescents what Lerner (2004) refers to as the "Five Cs" of positive individual development—competence, confidence, connection, character, and caring or compassion. This is a prevention model that would in the long term be cost effective in reducing accidental and homicidal adolescent deaths. In these cases, remediation is possible only for the bereaved. However, grief counseling is very challenging and does nothing to detract from the pointlessness of teenagers dying before really getting the chance to live a productive life.

Community collaborations that involve developmental researchers working directly with those on the front lines of adolescent nurturing and policy making provide the last of the five core principles. A greater effort to conduct *outreach scholarship in applied problems* such as accidents and homicides is surely a significant step in facilitating the fourth principle described above. Mental health professionals, teachers and school administrators, politicians and community leaders, as well as others who work on a regular basis with teenagers (e.g., pediatricians, coaches, scout masters, clergy) have many insights to offer on the issues relating to accidental and homicidal deaths. Fisher and Lerner (1994) state that developmental scientists "not only disseminate information about development to parents, professionals, and policy makers working to enhance the development of [adolescents], they also integrate the perspectives and experiences of these members of the community into the reformulation of theory and the design of research and interventions" (p. 7). Thus, our knowledge of accidental and homicidal deaths among teenagers will be greatly transformed and improved.

OVERVIEW AND STATISTICAL PORTRAIT

A truly global picture of the rates of adolescent accidents and homicides is difficult to obtain as a result of a myriad of factors. Of crucial importance is a definition that can be universally applied for these two causes of death. Such definitions, unfortunately, do not exist, although the International Classification of Diseases (IDC), created by the World Health Organization of the United Nations, does code causes of mortality (WHO, 2007). The IDC lists numerous causes of death involving *unintentional injuries,* which broadly characterize what are commonly understood as accidents. Although death in this manner is defined by its lack of intentionality, Kastenbaum (2004) astutely points out that intentionality often is difficult to assess, compounded by the observation that the death may actually result from the *responsibility* of another person, regardless of their intentionality. Thus, if a carload of adolescents dies in a motor vehicle accident, intentionality would most likely not be involved, but the driver would be responsible for this all too common tragedy.

The IDC system also codes the factors involved in death by homicide. *Homicide* occurs when a person takes the life of another and may either be intentional or unintentional. In many countries, accurate data are elusive because of factors such as a lack of resources for data collection, social stigma, war-torn trauma on a nation's infrastructure, or poverty. Even cultural perception of death plays an important role here, so that what may be viewed as an accidental injury in North America may take on a different meaning in countries in Africa or Asia. Resources may not necessarily be an issue in wealthy and developed countries, but the stigma associated with such sudden and frequently unanticipated deaths, and the social stratification that disenfranchises many youths who are not a part of the mainstream society, make it difficult to grasp the potential immensity of the problem. In addition, most statistics are based on information from adolescents passing through the juvenile justice system. However, these figures do not reflect the fact that many adolescent crimes are not reported, or in the case of homicide, the murderer is never found (Snyder & Sickmund, 2006). In such cases, if the offender is an adolescent, he or she will not be entered into the database. Regardless of the level of accuracy, the statistics do paint a picture that makes it hard to ignore the fact that young people, on the threshold of the most promising and productive years of their lives, are needlessly dying in ways that leave tragedy and sorrow in their wake.

In the United States, the latest data provided by the National Center for Health Statistics for 2004 and 2005 suggest that the leading cause of deaths in the 15- to 24-year-old age range is accidents, largely those from motor vehicles, intentional self-harm (suicide), and homicide, particularly by use of firearms (Kung, Hoyert, Xu, & Murphy, 2008). According to the U.S. Department of Health and Human Services (2006), in 2004, 49.8% of all deaths among 15- to 19-year-olds involved unintentional injury, and 14.1% of all deaths were the result of homicide.

Table 4.1 provides World Health Organization data of the death rates per 100,000 for accidents and homicides for the 15- to 24-year-old age group for 10 selected countries. The differences in these death rates are the consequences of economic, social, and cultural factors inherent in each country, as well as how the data are collected. Clear gender differences can also be seen across these countries. More recent data for the United States indicates that the death rate is 26.8 per 100,000 for motor vehicle accidents, 25.9 for other accidents, 0.5 for the accidental discharge of firearms, 13.0 for homicide, and 10.7 for assault by the use of firearms. These death rates are higher than for any other age group. Further parsing of the data indicates that these death rates are higher for males, particularly if they are Black or Hispanic (ChildStats.gov, 2008). In a delinquent population, these racial and gender inequities may be staggering. Templin, McClelland, Abram, and Mileusnic (2005) found that African American males had the highest mortality rate, resulting primarily from homicides, and more specifically, gunshot wounds.

These statistics portray only a snapshot of adolescent deaths resulting from accidents and homicide. Within each of these forms of death, a number of questions must be asked in order to better grasp why such deaths are prevalent in adolescent populations. Relating to the intraindividual differences dimension of developmental systems theory is the question of *intentionality*. Although counterintuitive to the word *accidents*, it is still of concern that some of these fatalities may have a deliberate component to them, either by the adolescent who died or by another who was somehow involved in the death, as in a drug overdose. Deaths by accident or homicide may pertain to the self or others. Thus, homicide typically is thought of as involving a perpetrator and a victim. However, deaths in motor vehicle accidents may leave the driver alive and his or her friends dead. The friends, relatives, and community survivors grieving over the sudden and traumatic loss of their youths must also be considered victims in these situations, many of whom are adolescents themselves. Finally, the demographic features of homicidal and accidental deaths, involving gender, ethnicity, socioeconomic status, education, and nationality, allude to the principle of interindividual differences of developmental systems theory that has so much to bear on understanding adolescent mortality from such causes.

Table 4.1

DEATH RATES PER 100,000 POPULATION FOR MALES AND FEMALES 15–24 YEARS OF AGE FOR SELECTED COUNTRIES

COUNTRY	YEAR OF MOST RECENT DATA	ACCIDENTS AND ADVERSE EFFECTS		MOTOR VEHICLE ACCIDENTS		OTHER TRANSPORT ACCIDENTS		ACCIDENTAL POISONING		FALLS		BY FIRE AND FLAMES		DROWNINGS AND SUBMERSION		MACHINERY		OTHER ACCIDENTS		HOMICIDE		OTHER VIOLENCE (OR OTHER EXTERNAL CAUSES)	
		M	F	M	F	M	F	M	F	M	F	M	F	M	F	M	F	M	F	M	F	M	F
Albania	2001	50.0;	9.2	10.5;	1.8	7.4;	0.7	5.9;	1.1	2.3;	0.4	0.8;	0.0	7.4;	0.4	4.3;	1.1	9.8;	2.6	13.7;	2.9	1.6;	0.7
Australia	2001	42.5;	10.6	27.8;	6.8	3.2;	0.5	5.1;	2.1	1.5;	0.4	0.2;	0.1	1.9;	0.2	0.4;	0.0	2.0;	0.4	2.2;	1.4	0.2;	0.2
Brazil	2000	51.8;	9.8	25.9;	5.7	4.9;	1.1	0.2;	0.1	1.5;	0.2	0.3;	0.2	8.6;	1.0	0.2;	0.0	9.5;	1.5	94.3;	6.9	13.1;	1.8
France	2000	42.6;	13.8	36.5;	10.7	0.8;	0.2	0.8;	0.5	1.6;	0.1	0.4;	0.2	1.5;	0.3	0.1;	0.1	5.9;	1.9	1.0;	0.5	0.9;	0.3
Israel	1999	23.1;	5.8	13.4;	3.8	1.8;	1.0	0.4;	0.2	0.4;	0.0	0.0;	0.2	1.7;	0.0	0.0;	0.0	4.6;	0.6	4.00;	0.6	6.1;	0.8
Kazakhstan	2002	70.3;	22.9	14.4;	5.6	5.3;	1.2	27.1;	10.2	2.1;	0.7	1.1;	0.4	12.7;	3.4	--	6.6;	1.3	15.6;	4.7	16.2;	3.8	
Mexico	2001	47.9;	10.2	16.5;	4.1	7.9;	1.6	1.1;	0.6	1.4;	0.2	0.6;	0.2	5.3;	0.7	0.4;	0.0	13.5;	2.6	21.4;	3.1	3.5;	0.9
Republic of Korea	2002	26.1;	7.7	19.6;	6.1	0.5;	0.1	0.3;	0.1	0.9;	0.2	0.5;	0.5	2.2;	0.4	0.1;	0.0	1.6;	0.2	1.0;	1.2	1.4;	0.8
Republic of Moldova	2002	51.1;	9.3	19.6;	6.0	2.6;	0.0	3.8;	1.5	1.8;	0.0	0.6;	0.6	7.9;	0.6	0.0;	0.0	14.9;	0.6	10.2;	4.2	5.3;	0.3
United States	2000	52.2;	19.2	36.5;	15.7	2.7;	0.6	4.6;	1.3	1.0;	0.2	0.6;	0.4	2.9;	0.3	0.3;	0.0	2.6;	0.5	20.9;	3.8	1.9;	0.5

From World Health Organization Statistical Information System, 2008, http://www.who.int/whosis/database/mort/table1.cfm.

ADOLESCENT DEATHS FROM UNINTENTIONAL INJURIES

Eaton and colleagues (2006) report that 31% of the deaths of 10- to 24-year-olds are caused by motor vehicle accidents and 14% by other unintentional injuries. Clearly, preventive efforts must first identify the reasons behind these high percentages. A major source is the risk-taking behavior of adolescents. Survey data point to lack of seat-belt use, failure to use helmets with bicycles or motorcycles, and riding or driving under the influence of alcohol as examples of behaviors that may result in accidents (Eaton et al., 2006). Such risk-taking behaviors are prevalent in other countries as well. For example, Sharma, Grover, and Chaturvedi (2007) found that 52.4% of adolescents aged 14–19 in south Delhi, India, reported not always wearing a seat belt, 23.3% never wearing a helmet, and 20% being a passenger in a car where the driver had been drinking. As in the United States, these rates were more prevalent for males than for females. Furthermore, Blum and Nelson-Mmari (2004) found that unintentional injury is the major cause of death for adolescents in all world regions, particularly in countries where industrialization has helped to lower the rates of death resulting from infectious diseases. Once again, the rates are substantially higher for males. In addition to deaths from motor vehicle accidents, World Health Organization data suggest that recreational and sports accidents are also significant causes of adolescent death (Blum & Nelson-Mmari, 2004). The neurological, cognitive, and emotional bases of risk-taking behavior certainly are implicated, but so, too, are the multiple contextual factors of industrialized countries that make extended dependence upon parents and high discretionary income, as well as changing expectations about adolescent behavior, contributors to these distressing outcomes. In developing nations, adolescent death caused by unintentional injury is more likely to be from burns, poisonings, falls, and drownings (Blum & Nelson-Mmari, 2004).

Many unintentional injuries are work related. In wealthier countries, adolescent employment is encouraged to develop vocational goals, to foster a sense of responsibility, and to generate spending money. In poorer nations, adolescents must work in order to support their families. Unfortunately, work-related hazards can lead to death. In the United States, the average number of adolescent deaths per year that are related to occupation is 70, a number that is believed to be underestimated (National Research Council and Institute of Medicine, 1999). Such deaths are most likely to occur in agriculture, retail trade, and construction and may be related to faulty supervision and training or placing adolescents in situations for which equipment and physical demands exceed their capacity. Adolescents also lack relevant work experience and their decision-making capacities may be hampered by immature cognitive and physical skills. Although there is concern at the national level, the rate of death arising from other factors, particularly homicide, overshadows work-related mortality statistics.

ADOLESCENTS AND HOMICIDE

The act of adolescent homicide is the product of a confluence of factors that need to be unpacked before such horrific behaviors can be understood and ultimately prevented. The homicides themselves are as varied as their underlying etiology. Adolescent homicides may be gang or drug related, enacted against family members in an extreme measure of domestic rage and frustration, for economic gain in robberies, a carefully plotted plan to seek vengeance in a school shooting, a seemingly random activity that terrorizes a neighborhood as cars and complete strangers are shot, involve the killing of a newborn by a distraught teenage mother, or related to warfare when youngsters are conscripted into rebel groups and forced to kill and maim. Such a menu of acts is set against a statistical picture from U.S. data that indicate that the murders, whether intentional or not, are caused by juveniles who typically are at least 15 years of age, use firearms, know their victims, tend to be of the same race, are overwhelmingly male, and are likely to be of African American descent (Moeller, 2001).

The United States is quite violent relative to other countries; homicidal rates are four times higher than those seen in other industrialized countries (Blum & Nelson-Mmari, 2004). But, it is clear that adolescent homicide also is a major global concern, as the figures are shockingly high and continue to increase, especially for adolescent males. Data compiled from the World Bank (1997) find homicide rates to be the highest in the Americas and the second leading cause of death of adolescent males in countries such as Columbia, Venezuela, and Brazil. For these countries, the leading basis is believed to be economic. Interestingly, homicide rates are not necessarily linked to poverty-stricken countries; rather, adolescent homicidal rates are highly related to being poor in a wealthy country—a function of income disparity leading to low social status (Pickett, Mookherjee, & Wilkinson, 2005). Mortality statistics, although frequently unreliable, show that assaults and homicide are rapidly becoming a fact of life in many developing nations (Blum & Nelson-Mmari, 2004). In cities in South Africa, for example, the media perpetuate the same fears as seen elsewhere of marauding gangs of teens. With regard to adolescent conscription into war, numerous reports from the United Nations and their aides working in war-torn regions such as Rwanda and Afghanistan (Heide, 1999) paint a picture of adolescents who are involved in armed conflict, killing others so as not to be killed themselves (Heide, 1999). The use of juveniles to maintain the front lines has become commonplace as war leaders have found that such child-soldiers are easy to manipulate and frighten into compliance, and as weaponry has become lighter and easier for youngsters to use (Blum & Nelson-Mmari, 2004).

When referring to homicide, a number of terms in the literature label an age group younger than 24 years. *Juveniles* is a term that the federal government of the United States tends to use for youths who are younger than 18 years of age, whereas the Federal Bureau of Investigation labels *juvenile arrests* as those that involve youths under age 17 (Heide, 1999). *Adolescence,* as a developmental term, has no well-established age boundaries, but generally is thought of as ranging from age 12 to 20. However, the most relevant adolescent mortality rates are found in columns labeled "15 to 24 years" in most statistical tables. Although anchored to the United States, the lessons that these data give are globally relevant. For example, Snyder and Sickmund (2006) deliver the good news that between 1994 and 2002 the number of murders by adolescents fell to record lows with their being implicated in 8% of all murders in 2002. Further, 2002 statistics reveal that 82% of adolescent murderers were male, 51% were White, 46% were Black, and 69% of them used a firearm to kill. The victims were apportioned as family members (16%), acquaintances (47%), or strangers (37%); between 1980 and 2002 most homicidal victims were 14 years of age (Synder & Sickmund, 2006).

We now turn to three specific examples that may, with the help of developmental systems theory, begin to shed light on these acts of violence.

Adolescent Familial Homicide (Parricide)

According to Moeller (2001), each year more than 300 parents are killed by their children, with adolescents (particularly sons) accounting for 15% of the deaths of their mothers and 25% of the deaths of their fathers. In addition, 30% of such deaths involve adolescents murdering their stepmothers, and 34% of the victims of adolescent homicide are stepfathers. A content analysis of parricide cases occurring worldwide found that out of 199 cases, 46% involved adolescents who were 17 years or younger, and the great majority were male (Boots & Heide, 2006). Heide (1992), who has written extensively about this serious problem, presents a profile of the factors contributing to adolescent parricide. Occasionally, adolescent parricide is committed by seriously cognitively disabled or mentally ill youths. However, Heide points out that such cases are small in number, and the most likely scenario involves a disturbing pattern that includes a history of family violence accompanied by child neglect, adolescent feelings of hopelessness, social isolation, inability for the adolescents to get help, parental drug abuse, and increased stress on the part of the adolescent ultimately leading to a lack of self-control. Poor attachment relationships, leading to an inability to feel empathy, sympathy, and caring on the part of the child also are a contributing factor (Horowitz, 2000). Emotional abuse seems to be more likely to be the cause of adolescent matricide. Also, sometimes one family member either covertly or overtly encourages the adolescent to kill the other parent (Ewing, 1990). Certainly the availability of firearms has contributed to parricide, although conditions of desperation can lead to homicide by other means, as in the case of a 16-year-old boy from Steubenville, Ohio, who killed his alcoholic mother with a bow and arrow after a history of abusive parenting (Heide, 1999). Even rarer are the cases where both parents are killed by their adolescent children, usually after a history of child abuse (Ewing, 1990), but sometimes for unfathomable reasons such as too restrictive parenting (Moeller, 2001). Despite the increased attention in the media, data assembled over a 24-year period by Heide and Petee (2007) show remarkably stable figures in the incidence of parricide by adolescent offenders.

Adolescent Female Murderers

Because most juvenile homicides are committed by males, adolescent female murderers have been largely ignored by the literature. A recent study of this targeted population provides useful comparisons to the male pattern of homicide (Roe-Sepowitz, 2007). Studying the extensive records of 29 female adolescents who were charged either with committing or attempting murder within the state of Florida, Roe-Sepowitz (2007) developed a statistical portrait of a female offender who is

16 years old, was most likely to use a car as the weapon, and knew her victim(s). Surprisingly, a large percentage of the murders (31%) resulted in multiple victims.

A special case of homicide by a female adolescent involves the killing of newborn infants (*neonaticide*) and seems to be more in the province of the female juvenile offender. The Child Trends Data Bank (2007) indicates that the greatest risk of infant homicide in the United States is within the first 24 hours of the infant's life. Such cases of neonaticide occur by young women from all racial backgrounds and socioeconomic levels. Many are enacted by adolescents living at home with their parents (Craig, 2004). These homicides are more likely to occur if the births occur outside of the hospital (Vallone & Hoffman, 2003). Reflecting the refrain of underestimated statistics, there are approximately 150 to 300 such homicides per year in the United States. Some have been well publicized, such as that of the so-called prom mom who went back to her high school prom after delivering a baby and placing it in the trash. These statistics are particularly unreliable because denial and/or concealment of the pregnancy seems to be a common factor leading to the death of the infant, and the longer the denial persists, the greater the chance that the homicidal act will occur. Furthermore, it appears that the homicides are not premeditated but rather caused by the panic and terror of immature girls who are dazed and confused (Vallone & Hoffman, 2003). Perhaps the failure to establish feelings of empathy with the newborn, along with being in a dissociative state, as well as the physical demands of labor and delivery, contribute to the likelihood of neonaticide. Unfortunately, information about neonaticide is not widely available from the international community, although the U.S. pattern seems to be replicated in Great Britain (Craig, 2004). In other countries, factors such as forcible rape of young adolescents, failure to obtain abortions, family shame, poverty, and giving birth to a female infant, are possible contributing factors.

School Shootings

On April 20, 1999, two students, Eric Harris and Dylan Klebold, began shooting at Columbine High School in Colorado. When the massacre was over, 12 students and a teacher were dead, the 2 murderers had committed suicide, and 23 others suffered from gunshot wounds. The Columbine school shootings represent the fourth deadliest school massacre in U.S. history and perpetuated belief that schools are not safe havens but places where metal detectors, suspicion of so-called loner and outsider students, and increased internal vigilance have become the norm. Media attention has no doubt led to concern that school violence is increasing, both in the United States and abroad. As a result, some students are afraid to go to school, many know of other adolescents who have brought a weapon with them to school, and students are wary of others in the classroom whom they think might be potentially violent (Kimmel & Mahler, 2003). Much effort within American education has been placed upon school safety procedures, curriculum changes, and activities designed to reduce gang involvement (Mulvey & Cauffman, 2001). In addition, efforts have been directed toward developing profiles of adolescents who are at risk for potential school shootings, leading to a proliferation of programs ranging from creating intensive support programs for students at risk to antibullying programs (Furlong, Kingery, & Bates, 2001).

Despite the increasing concern, school is still a relatively safe place for adolescents. Data from the 2003 Youth Risk Behavior Survey found that 6% of high school students reported carrying a weapon to school (Synder & Sickmund, 2006), a decrease from previous years. Furthermore, the most dangerous time period for adolescent homicide was just when school was over, between 3 P.M. and 4 P.M. Perhaps it is the destruction of the assumptive reality of school as an innocent place of intellectual development, the unpredictable quality of the massacres, the failures of rapid response to the trauma, and the seemingly contagious nature of the acts that make these relatively isolated incidents so profoundly terrifying.

RECAPITULATION OF FACTORS CONTRIBUTING TO ADOLESCENTS' DEATHS RESULTING FROM ACCIDENTS AND HOMICIDE: ECOLOGICAL SYSTEMS THEORY

The five core principles of developmental systems theory emerged from a general ecological approach created by Bronfenbrenner (1994), who posited that development was influenced by five systems that were ever widening in terms of their relevance and scope. The most proximal are labeled the *Microsystems,* which involve the individual and face-to-face situations, particularly the family, school, and peer group. Clearly, with respect to accidents and homicides, the unique biological characteristics of the developing adolescent, especially with respect to immature cognitive and neurological development, compounded by nonoptimal home environments, alienation from schools that fail to respond to the needs of such at-risk youths, and association with antisocial peers, lead to the potential for accidents and violence. The *Mesosystem*, representing the linkages between two or more Microsystems may also contribute to the problem, when there is a breakdown between what should be important linkages. Efforts at prevention of school massacres, for example, have implemented such programs as schools providing material and emotional support to families, as well as school-based work-release programs. Bronfenbrenner (1994) identified the *Exosystem* as the broader influences in which the adolescent is not so personally involved. Family social networks or the context of the neighborhood are examples of the Exosystem; impoverished urban neighborhoods regularly spawning violence, drugs, and homicides have consistently been identified as a high-risk factor both for accidents and homicides among adolescents. The *Macrosystem* pertains to the overall culture of a society, with its inherent belief systems, lifestyles, and opportunities. Herein lies the differential patterns of youthful accidents and violence that are seen globally. Whereas war and terrorism may be the root of adolescent death involving homicides and accidents in countries in the Middle East and Africa, in developed nations it may be perceived lack of opportunity to reach "the good life," drug abuse, and the availability of handguns that lead to adolescent mortality. Finally, the *Chronosystem,* linked to the principle of historical embeddedness, certainly plays a role, as we described at the beginning of this chapter. Figure 4.1 represents the multiple factors and systems involved in adolescent mortality resulting from accidents and homicides.

CONSEQUENCES FOR UNDERSTANDING ADOLESCENT DEATH AND BEREAVEMENT

The aftermath of death always creates ripple effects that reverberate across the multiple contexts of development discussed in this chapter. Family members, peers, neighbors, teachers, employers of adolescents, and the community at large, who mourn the wasted potential for society, are all bereft from an adolescent accident or homicide. Since adolescent grief, relative to other age groups, is characterized as particularly intense and emotional (Noppe & Noppe, 1996), youthful survivors of these deaths may, in addition to the normal grieving process, feel over-

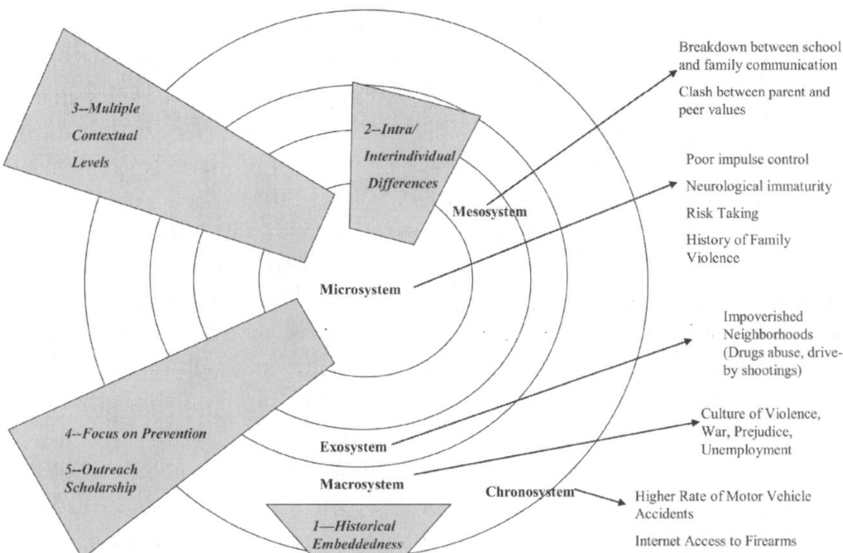

Figure 4.1 Developmental systems theory: Understanding adolescent accidents and homicide.[a]
[a] Core principles in boxes.

whelmed by their emotions, depressed, angry, and fearful of their own futures. Such effects are exacerbated by the fact that adolescent death resulting from accidents and homicides are sudden and traumatic. In addition, because in many societies there is an implicit belief that death is the province of the elderly, adolescent deaths may violate the fabric of a cultural assumptive world.

With regard to adolescent homicide, the youthful offender may enter the ranks of the grieving. Many adolescent homicides, borne out of impulsive acts of anger, peer pressure, or despair, can lead to years of remorse and mourning. For example, the psychological effects of neonaticide are not known—do young girls who kill their newborn infants spend a lifetime grieving over their dead child? Unfortunately, such forms of grief go unrecognized and unsupported by others; not having a "right" to cope with the task of their losses, they enter the unwanted fellowship of disenfranchised grievers (Doka, 2002).

Each form of accidental or homicidal death brings to bear its own set of complicating factors. With regard to accidents, survivors, especially parents, must deal with the guilt that accompanies the perception of preventability. Furthermore, depending upon the nature of the accident, the deceased may have lingered on life support, bringing with that scenario its own host of medical, ethical, and legal issues that are particularly contentious when the patient is young. The accident victim may have suffered an injury that led to body mutilation, which can further stress the coping responses of the survivors. With regard to homicides, the violent, usually intentional, nature of the act exacerbates the grief response on the part of the survivors. In such cases, risk for complicated grief is increased within a context of prior violence, when the offender and the victim were related, when the deaths are random, and when they are multiple, as in school shootings or in war. Each of these situations may find that the coping strategies of surviving family members are taxed, as they try to find meaning behind the deaths.

Contemporary responses to these deaths are evident in electronic forms of mourning and in approaches toward intervention. Both have lent their particular stamp on how such sudden and traumatic losses are experienced. The Internet, for example, offers many memorial sites, and these often appear when an adolescent accidentally dies or is murdered (see chapter 9 in this book). Popular group sharing sites, such as Facebook and MySpace, open opportunities for public mourning in a worldwide arena that is designed for adolescents. Popular music and music videos, from country to rap, offer a media icon's perspective on youthful deaths brought about by accidents and homicides. Such lyrics and images reflect the death-related attitudes of current adolescents and may also define the parameters of how such grief is to be experienced. Finally, such loss is the burden of a society as it tries to reduce the death rate with a myriad of intervention efforts. These efforts range from banning cell phones in cars, campaigns against drinking and driving, afterschool and work-release programs for juvenile offenders, and the efforts of United Nations workers who have brought grief counseling to the children and adolescents of war-torn countries such as Sierra Leone and Afghanistan (Gupta & Zimmer, 2008).

While specific educational and economic programs are necessary to drive the tragic statistics of accidents and homicide downward, there clearly is much more work that needs to be done for the psychosocial needs of the survivors of accidents and homicides. Such deaths are a global tragedy and a loss for us all. We do know, however, that in the face of grief, adolescents who are supported and understood are exceptionally resilient and positive (Noppe, Noppe, & Bartell, 2006). Thus, the future focus of intervention is to further understand the nature of adolescent grief and mourning associated with accidents and homicides, and to help foster adolescent resiliency by recognizing the multiple systems of their development.

REFERENCES

Blum, R. W., & Nelson-Mmari, K. (2004). Adolescent health from an international perspective. In R. M. Lerner & L. Steinberg, (Eds.), *Handbook of adolescent psychology* (2nd ed., pp. 553–586). Hoboken, NJ: John Wiley Press.

Boots, D. P. & Heide, K. M. (2006). Parricides in the media: A content analysis of available reports across cultures. *International Journal of Offender Therapy and Comparative Criminology, 50,* 418–445.

Bronfenbrenner, U. (1994) Ecological models of human development. In *International Encyclopedia of Education* (2nd ed., Vol. 3, pp. 1643–1647). Oxford, UK: Pergamon.

ChildStats.gov. (2008, June). America's children in brief: Key national indicators of well-being, 2006. Retrieved July 13, 2008, from http://www.childstats.gov/americaschildren06/hea9.asp

Child Trends Data Bank (2007, November). Retrieved July 13, 2008, from http://www.childtrendsdatabank.org

Craig, M. (2004). Perinatal risk factors for neonaticide and infant homicide: Can we identify those at risk? *Journal of the Royal Society of Medicine, 97,* 57–61.

Doka, K. J. (Ed.). (2002). *Disenfranchised grief: New directions, strategies, and challenges for practice.* Champaign, IL: Research Press.

Eaton, D. K., Kann, L., Kinchen, S., Ross, J., Hawkins, J., & Harris, W. A. (2006). Youth risk behavior surveillance—United States, 2005. *Journal of School Health, 76,* 353–372.

Ewing, C. P. (1990). *When children kill.* Lexington, MA: Lexington Books.

Fisher, C. B., & Lerner, R. M. (1994). Foundations of applied developmental psychology. In C. B. Fisher & R. M. Lerner (Eds.), *Applied developmental psychology* (pp. 3–20). New York: McGraw-Hill.

Furlong, M. J., Kingery, P. M., & Bates, M. P. (2001). Introduction to the special issue on the appraisal and prediction of school violence. *Psychology in the Schools, 38,* 89–91.

Gupta, L., & Zimmer, C. (2008). Psychosocial intervention for war-affected children in Sierra Leone. *The British Journal of Psychiatry, 192,* 212–216.

Heide, K. M. (1992). *Why kids kill parents.* Columbus, OH: Ohio State University Press.

Heide, K. M. (1999). *Young killers: The challenge of juvenile homicide.* Thousand Oaks, CA: Sage Publications.

Heide, K. M., & Petee, T. A. (2007). Parricide: An empirical analysis of 24 years of U.S. data. *Journal of Interpersonal Violence, 22,* 1382–1399.

Horowitz, M. A. (2000). Kids who kill: A critique of how the American legal system deals with juveniles who commit homicide. *Law and Contemporary Problems, 63,* 133–178. Retrieved July 10, 2008, from http://www.law.duke.edu/journals/63LCPHorowitz

Kastenbaum, R. (2004). *Death, society, and human experience* (8th ed.). Boston: Pearson.

Kimmel, M. S., & Mahler, M. (2003). Adolescent masculinity, homophobia, and violence: Random school shootings, 1982–2001. *American Behavioral Scientist, 46,* 1439–1458.

Kung, H., Hoyert, D. L., Xu, J., & Murphy, S. L. (2008). Deaths: Final data for 2005. *National Vital Statistics Reports, 56*(10). Hyattsville, MD: National Center for Health Statistics. Retrieved July 13, 2008, from http://www.cdc.gov/nchs/products/pubs/pubd/nvsr/nvsr.htm#vol56

Lerner, R. M. (2004). *Liberty: Thriving and civic engagement among America's youth.* Thousand Oaks, CA: Sage Publications.

Lerner, R. M., Theokas, C., & Bobek, D. I. (2005). Concepts and theories of human development: Historical and contemporary dimensions. In M. H. Bornstein & M. E. Lamb (Eds.), *Developmental science: An advanced textbook* (pp. 3–43). Mahwah, NJ: Lawrence Erlbaum Associates.

Moeller, T. G. (2001). *Youth, aggression, and violence: A psychological approach.* Mahwah, NJ: Lawrence Erlbaum Associates.

Mulvey, E. P., & Cauffman, E. (2001). The inherent limits of predicting school violence. *American Psychologist, 56,* 797–802.

National Research Council and Institute of Medicine (1999). Risks and opportunities, synthesis of studies on adolescence. Adolescents taking their place in the world. In M. D. Kipke (Ed.), *Forum on adolescence* (pp. 43–50). Washington, DC: National Academy Press.

Noppe, I. C., Noppe, L. D., & Bartell, D. (2006). Terrorism and resilience: Adolescents' and teachers' responses to September 11, 2001. *Death Studies, 30,* 41–60.

Noppe, L. D. & Noppe, I. C. (1996). Ambiguity in adolescent understandings of death. In C. A. Corr & D. E. Balk (Eds.), *Handbook of adolescent death and bereavement* (pp. 25–41). New York: Springer.

Pickett, K. E., Mookherjee, J., & Wilkinson, R. G. (2005). Adolescent birth rates, total homicides, and income inequality in rich countries. *American Journal of Public Health, 95,* 1181–1883.

Roe-Sepowitz, D. (2007). Adolescent female murderers: Characteristics and treatment implications. *American Journal of Orthopsychiatry, 77,* 489–496.

Sharma, R., Grover, V. L., & Chaturvedi, S. (2007). Health-risk behaviors related to road safety among adolescent students. *Indian Journal of Medical Science, 61,* 656–662.

Snyder, H. N., & Sickmund, M. (2006). *Juvenile offenders and victims: 2006 national report.* Washington, DC: U.S. Department of Justice, Office of Justice Programs, Office of Juvenile Justice and Delinquency Prevention.

Templin, L. A., McClelland, G. M., Abram, K. M., & Mileusnic, D. (2005). Early violent death among delinquent youth: A prospective longitudinal study. *Pediatrics, 115,* 1586–1593.

U.S. Department of Health and Human Services (2006). Child health USA 2006. Retrieved July 12, 2008, from http://www.mchb,hrsa.gov/chusa_06/healthstat/adoles cents/0326am.htm

Vallone, D. C., & Hoffman, L. M. (2003). Preventing the tragedy of neonaticide. *Holistic Nursing Practice, 17,* 223–228.

World Bank. (1997). *Crime and violence as development issues in Latin America and the Caribbean.* Paper prepared for the Conference on Urban Crime and Violence in Rio de Janeiro.

World Health Organization (WHO). (2007). *International Classification of Diseases Version 10.* Retrieved July 10, 2008, from http://www.who.int/classifications/apps/icd/icd10online/

5

Adolescents and Suicide

LILLIAN M. RANGE

Suicide is the third leading cause of death among adolescents in the United States (Centers for Disease Control and Prevention [CDC], 2007). In 2004, U.S. teens aged 15–19 had a suicide rate of 8.9 per 100,000, and young adults aged 20–24 had a suicide rate of 13.6. In comparison, all U.S. citizens had a rate of 10.93 (CDC, 2004). Thus, the rate of suicidal deaths increased steadily from ages 11 to 21 (Conner & Goldston, 2007).

The numbers of adolescents who consider or attempt suicide is alarming as well. The National Youth Risk Behavior Survey examined high school students who answered anonymously about the past 12 months. In 2005, among students in grades 9 through 12, 16.9% seriously considered suicide, 13% planned suicide, and 8.4% attempted suicide (CDC, 2006). Further, 20% to 30% of adolescents think about suicide, 19% in the past year (Evans, Hawton, & Rodham, 2005a). Suicidal thoughts and behaviors are common in adolescence.

In examining the problem of adolescent suicide, it is important to consider risk factors that may contribute to suicide rates, suicide prevention, interventions with suicidal adolescents, and responding after an adolescent's suicide (postvention). Information about adults is relevant, but the present focus is adolescents.

RISK/PROTECTIVE FACTORS

Factors associated with increased risk can be grouped in various ways. The American Psychiatric Association's (2003) comprehensive grouping guides this discussion.

Suicidal thoughts and behaviors in the past predict future behavior. More thoughts, plans, or attempts, as well as lethality and intent to die in previous attempts, increase the risk of death by suicide.

Psychiatric diagnoses, including major depression, bipolar disorder, schizophrenia, anorexia, alcohol use disorder, other substance use disorders, and personality disorders (particularly borderline), increase suicide risk. Among a representative sample of children and adolescents aged 9–16 from the southeastern United States interviewed several times from 1993 to 2000, suicide risk was greatest when the adolescent or preadolescent was depressed and anxious, or depressed and disruptive (e.g., oppositional-defiant disorder) (Foley, Goldston, Costello, & Angold, 2006). Among homeless individuals from England who recently contacted mental health services, suicide risk was greatest among young people who displayed schizophrenia, personality disorder, unemployment, and substance misuse (Bickley et al., 2006). Psychiatric diagnoses increase adolescents' suicide risk, and when disorders occur simultaneously, risk increases greatly.

Other psychological/psychosocial features associated with suicide include poor family relationships; recent lack of social support; drop in socioeconomic status; domestic violence; recent stressful events; and psychological features including hopelessness, inability to experience pleasure, psychic pain, anxiety, panic, shame, turmoil, decreased self-esteem, psychic vulnerability, impulsiveness, aggression, and agitation. Adolescents who attempt suicide are more likely than others to live apart from one or both parents at the time of the suicide, have lost a parent due to child placement or parental separation or death, live in a home where there is marital conflict, have poor parent–child relationships, and/or have a family history of antisocial personality disorder (Wagner, 1997). Among teens hospitalized because of suicide concerns, greater perceived peer rejection and lower close friendship support meant more severe suicidal ideation (Prinstein, Boergers, Spirito, Little, & Grapentine, 2000). With adolescents, romantic breakups are high risk. The ways youths perceive and think about stressors may be an important consideration in identifying those who are potentially suicidal (Nock & Kazdin, 2002).

These features are associated with suicide with or without the presence of psychiatric diagnoses.

Past abuse is associated with suicide. Adolescents who were physically or sexually abused are more likely than others to consider suicide (Evans, Hawton, Rodham, & Deeks, 2005b). Early childhood abuse and neglect present particularly potent risks (Brent & Mann, 2006).

Biological factors contribute to suicide. Many adolescents who attempt suicide are unable to regulate their mood or tolerate distress. The tendency toward such behavior runs in families, so it likely has a genetic component (Brent & Mann, 2006).

Cognitive features associated with suicide include negative automatic thoughts (Nock & Kazdin, 2002), loss of executive function, thought constriction (tunnel vision), polarized thinking, and rigidity. Adolescents develop self-defeating cognitions and behaviors that arise from low self-appraisal of their problem-solving ability (Yang & Clum, 1996). Reasons for living, in contrast, protect against suicide. In a 2-year follow-up of depressed inpatients, high reasons for living predicted fewer future suicide attempts in women but not men (Lizardi et al., 2007).

Demographic features can contribute to suicide risk. As with adults, suicide risk increases for boys, Native Americans, Whites, and sexual minorities. African American students report lower rates of seriously considering suicide and planning suicide than White and Latino students (CDC, 2006). Ethnic groups differ in the cultural context in which suicide occurs. For example, African Americans experience more perceived racism and discrimination and greater awareness of economic difficulties, but also more collaborative religious coping, social support, cultural cohesion, and extended family support. Native Americans experience more alcohol abuse, vulnerability to contagion, and intergenerational trauma, but also more traditional cultural values and spirituality. Latino and Asian American/Pacific Islander youths may have more interdependence and stereotyping that causes problems to be overlooked. Ethnic groups also differ in patterns of help seeking. African American, Asian American/Pacific Islander, and Latino youths are underrepresented in outpatient mental health services (Goldston et al., 2008). Lack of familiarity and language barriers can inhibit service utilization.

Alcohol use increases suicide risk. Alcohol abuse impairs judgment, reduces impulse control, and lowers mood. Over one third of adolescent suicide attempters consumed alcohol 6 hours before the attempt

(Hawton, Fagg, & McKeown, 1989). Depression combined with drug use is particularly potent in the suicide of adolescent boys.

Presence of firearms increases suicide risk, particularly when the gun is stored unsafely (Hardy, 2006). Up to 40% of children, and an even higher percentage of adolescents, have access to firearms at home. Children's (especially boys') well-documented fascination with guns appears resistant to intervention. Young children lack the cognitive maturity to generalize lessons about safety, while older children and adolescents believe they are invulnerable to injury. Firearms are the most common method of homicide and suicide (U.S. Department of Health and Human Services, 2005).

Many risk factors, such as hopelessness and psychiatric diagnoses, occur together. The three most useful indicators are presenting for treatment immediately after seriously attempting suicide, psychotic processes, and planning or intent (Shea, 1999).

PREVENTION

For adolescents, suicide prevention efforts typically occur either in schools or in the community. Adolescents themselves consider families, peers, and schools as more pertinent to preventing self-harm than external helping agencies (Fortune, Sinclair, & Hawton, 2008).

Thus, schools are a first line of defense against suicidal behaviors and can make a difference for students themselves and important gatekeepers. One prevention study randomly assigned suburban pre and early teens to one of three groups (Gillham et al., 2007). In a cognitive-behavioral/social problem-solving group, students learned to think flexibly and accurately about their problems, recognize and restructure pessimistic explanatory styles, challenge negativity, evaluate the accuracy of beliefs, and generate alternative interpretations. They practiced coping and problem-solving techniques (assertiveness, negotiation, decision making, and relaxation). In a life enhancement group, students role-played and discussed peer pressure, ethical dilemmas, trust and betrayal, communication, friendships, family conflict, goals, self-esteem, and body image. Groups (size 6 to 14), led by school teachers, school counselors, and trained graduate students, met 90 minutes after school for 12 weeks. Parents received $5 per session for each session their child attended and a $15 bonus if their child attended at least eight. A control group had assessment but no special training. Youths completed questionnaires at baseline, at 2 weeks postintervention, and every 6 months for 3 years. Results were mixed. In two schools, cognitive-behavioral and social problem-solving skills significantly reduced depression at the 2.5 year follow-up (Gillham et al., 2007). Benefits were strongest when group leaders were the intervention developers, research team members, or extensively trained and supervised graduate students. Effects were smaller when group leaders were school teachers, clinicians, or other researchers (Gillham, Hamilton, Freres, Patton, & Gallop, 2006).

Gatekeeper training for school staff aims to increase adults' knowledge of risk factors and warning signs of suicidal intentions (CDC, 1992). Gatekeeper training also typically includes strategies for questioning students about suicide and increasing awareness of referral protocols for suicidal students. In a randomized, controlled study, gatekeeper training raised school staff members' appraisals of their own preparation, efficacy, and access to suicide prevention services (Wyman et al., 2008).

Given the overlap of depression and suicidal thoughts and behaviors, it is reasonable to expect that cognitive-behavioral intervention reduces suicidal thinking and acts. Schools are a viable setting in which to teach depression prevention skills, particularly if school teachers and counselors are trained and supervised.

Communities are a second line of defense against suicidal behaviors. Crisis lines are important community mental health resources, especially for young women aged 16–18, who rate the crisis line as helpful (Meehan & Broom, 2007). By the end of the phone call, crisis line callers are less suicidal, improved in mental state (King, Nurcombe, Bickman, Hides, & Reid, 2003), more hopeful, and in less psychological pain (Gould, Kalafat, Munfakh, & Kleinman, 2007). Seriously suicidal adolescents reach out to telephone crisis services, and these services can help them.

Other community prevention strategies include screening for at-risk adolescents, educating primary care physicians, and educating the media (Gould, Greenberg, Velting, & Shaffer, 2003a). Because none of these approaches impact parents' gun ownership and safe storage practices, preventing firearm injuries and deaths among children and adolescents should be depoliticized and reframed as a public health issue (Hardy, 2006). When adolescents contact mental health services, helpful suicide prevention measures target schizophrenia, dual diagnosis, and loss of service contact (Bickley et al., 2006).

Prevention efforts to reduce youth suicide can start in the school or in the community. At school, students benefit from training in optimism, cognitive strategies, and problem solving, and gatekeepers benefit from training as well. In the community, recommendations include implementing crisis lines, screening, educating contact persons such as physicians and the media, and passing laws restricting guns.

INTERVENTION

Intervention includes assessment and treatment of suicidal adolescents. Assessment might involve clinical interviews, structured interviews, or questionnaires.

Assessment often starts with interviews containing open-ended questions about suicide. Because people communicate both verbally and nonverbally, interviews are very important. It is important to ask directly about suicide, using simple language (Shea, 1999). Unstructured interviews allow the interviewer to follow-up as needed and thereby provide in-depth information about potentially suicidal youths. Structured interviews can be quite informative as well. One structured interview designed specifically for adolescents contains 169 items in five modules on the presence, frequency, and characteristics of suicidal ideas, plans, gestures, and attempts (Nock, Holmberg, Photos, & Michel, 2007). This structured questionnaire has excellent interrater and strong test–retest reliability when used with adolescents, and strong parent–adolescent agreement.

Health professionals at times supplement interviews with suicide questionnaires. Many, such as the widely-used Scale for Suicide Ideation (Beck, Kovacs, & Weissman, 1979), are designed for adults, but a few target adolescents. Copyrighted questionnaires for adolescents are the widely used Suicide Probability Scale (Cull & Gill, 1982); the junior high and senior high versions of the Suicide Ideation Questionnaire (Reynolds, 1987); the Child-Adolescent Suicidal Potential Index (Pfeffer, Jiang, & Kakuma, 2000); and The Inventory of Suicide Ideation–30 (ISI-30; King & Kowalchuk, 1994), an outpatient screening tool.

Noncopyrighted questionnaires for adolescents include the Multi-Attitude Suicidal Tendency Scale (Orbach et al., 1991), which employs multiple-choice questions about attraction to life and death, and repulsion by life and death; the Juvenile Suicide Assessment (Galloucis & Francek, 2002), a structured interview for a juvenile justice setting; and the Reasons for Living for Young Adults (RFL-A; Gutierrez et al., 2002), which presents 32 reasons not to commit suicide. A comprehensive, well-organized assessment book is *Measuring Suicidal Behavior and Risk in*

Children and Adolescents (Goldston, 2003). All these instruments can be used in suicide assessment, and the RFL-A has unique positive focus.

Questionnaires about suicidal thoughts, intentions, and actions have advantages and disadvantages. Advantages include speed, ease, norms, and access to useful information that might be difficult to obtain in a face-to-face interview. Disadvantages include a temptation to view responses uncritically or believe that the suicidal state is static, and the danger that printed forms preempt a strong therapeutic relationship (Range, 2005a). Mental health professionals need to be aware of the interface of culture, adolescent suicidal behavior, and help seeking (Goldston et al., 2008), and they must exercise sound clinical judgment in assessing a potentially suicidal adolescent.

Assessment is the antecedent to treatment. Treatment typically involves some combination of therapy and or medical intervention.

Psychotherapy to reduce suicide risk may take the form of cognitive therapy, dialectical behavior therapy, or interpersonal psychotherapy. Therapy might also include outreach interventions, such as sending caring letters.

Cognitive-behavioral therapy (CBT) targets automatic thoughts and core beliefs that occurred just prior to the individual's suicide attempt. First, therapists teach specific cognitive and behavioral techniques with the goal of decreasing suicidal thoughts and preventing future suicide attempts. Then, therapists focus on cognitions and behavioral change, using techniques such as Socratic questioning, dysfunctional thought records, behavioral experiments, and role playing. Finally, therapists work on preventing relapse (Berk, Henriques, Warman, Brown, & Beck, 2004). CBT recognizes behavioral, affective, social, and environmental factors associated with suicide and reduces repeated suicide attempts (Van der Sande, Buskens, Allart, van der Graaf, & van Engeland, 1997). However, initial findings are mixed, the number of randomized trials is small, sample sizes are limited, treatment gains do not necessarily hold (Reinecke & Didie, 2005), and intervention efforts generally focus on adults not adolescents.

Dialectical behavior therapy (DBT), originally designed for older adolescents and young adults, has been modified for suicidal adolescents. The regimen includes individual therapy that aims for a balance between acceptance and change and uses diary cards on self-harm, suicidal thoughts and actions, alcohol and drug urges and use, medicine, cutting class, risky sex, and emotions; group therapy emphasizing mindfulness, emotional regulation, interpersonal effectiveness, distress tolerance, and balance; telephone consultation; family therapy; and a consultation team (Miller, Rathus, & Linehan, 2007). The length is 16 weeks, with an optional 16-week extension. DBT for adolescents simultaneously acknowledges that their actions make sense in their current lives, while at the same time challenging them to change their lives. DBT presents a hierarchy of treatment targets, starting with decreasing life-threatening behaviors and ending with finding freedom and joy. This approach offers enormous hope for suicidal adolescents.

Interpersonal therapy focuses on resolving problems in existing relationships and learning to form important new interpersonal relationships. The therapist expresses empathy and honors the client's self- and worldviews. The therapist provides choices and explains why, but avoids reassuring even when the teen seeks it. Interpersonal therapy for adolescents addresses issues unique to this developmental population such as disputes with parents and friends, difficulties with life transitions, initial experiences with grief, and stresses related to single-parent families (Mufson, Dorta, Olfson, Weissman, & Hoagwood, 2004). Overriding goals are identifying and correcting social skills deficits. Interpersonal therapy is highly structured, and usually lasts 15–20 sessions. Recent research comparing the results of cognitive therapy, interpersonal therapy, antidepressants, and control conditions indicated that psychological approaches and medicine are equally effective, and all treatments are more effective than control conditions.

An aspect of therapy with suicidal adolescents is life-maintenance agreements, also known as no-suicide contracts. The potentially suicidal adolescent agrees to refrain from any type of self-harm for a specified period of time and/or to seek help when in a suicidal state and unable to honor this agreement. The first published report of life-maintenance agreements described training 31 clinicians to make them (Drye, Goulding, & Goulding, 1973). Life-maintenance agreements are common therapeutic tools for psychologists (Motto, 1999), psychiatrists (Kroll, 2000), nurses (Farrow, 2002), crisis line workers (Mishara & Diagle, 1997), and other mental health professionals. Arguments for life-maintenance agreements are that they can strengthen the therapeutic alliance, instill hope, slow the suicidal crisis, and lower anxiety. Arguments against using life-maintenance agreements are that they can inhibit the therapeutic alliance, introduce coercion, and imply that the suicidal state is static or that the therapist is more interested in administrative details than in the client.

Recommendations for life-maintenance agreements are to use them within the context of an ongoing relationship, collaborate on the agreement, attend to the context, keep the wording simple, avoid the term *contract,* consult and document, and remember that alternatives are available (Range, 2005b). Most mental health practitioners are positive about life-maintenance agreements with adolescents when asked a general question (Davidson, Wagner, & Range, 1995), but some suicidal adolescents may be unwilling or unable to uphold their agreement.

Outreach interventions such as letters of concern may reduce suicide risk. One study of adults who refused ongoing care after being hospitalized for suicidality or depression randomly divided them into two groups: One group received personal letters four times per year for 5 years; one group received no further contact. Those in the contact group had a significantly lower suicide rate in the first 2 years (Motto & Bostrom, 2001). Designed for adults, this procedure could also be used with adolescents.

Another outreach intervention focused on social support for suicidal adolescents. Adolescents nominated up to four potential support persons, one of whom could be a peer. Support persons were trained and asked to contact the adolescents weekly to discuss concerns and encourage activities in support of treatment goals. Intervention specialists contacted support persons regularly. Compared to treatment as usual, girls (but not boys) reported fewer suicidal ideas and reduced mood-related impairment (King et al., 2006). Suicidal adolescent girls seem responsive to interventions that increase social support.

Medicines potentially helpful for suicidal adolescents include antidepressants, which may reduce suicide ideas if adolescents are depressed. From 1988 to 1994, antidepressant prescriptions for adolescents in the United States increased three- to five-fold (Zito et al., 2002). Antidepressants, however, are not necessarily given for suicide ideas or attempts. Meta-analyses indicate no significant excess of suicide, but excess nonfatal attempts and thoughts in children and adolescents who take antidepressants (Sakinofsky, 2007). A huge problem in research on antidepressants is that most studies are retrospective and not focused on suicide. Antidepressants may prevent suicide through their beneficial effect on depression, but controversy exists about whether they increase suicide risk.

Other medicines may also impact suicide rates. Lithium, an antimania drug, appears to reduce rates of suicide attempts and completions in people with bipolar disorder and recurrent depression (Sakinofsky, 2007). Antipsychotic drugs such as Haldol (haldoperidol) reduce suicide in persons with schizophrenia, particularly those who are highly agitated (American Psychiatric Association, 2003). Antianxiety agents such as

Valium (benzodiazepam) may reduce suicide by reducing anxiety but also lower inhibitions and enhance impulsivity (American Psychiatric Association, 2003). They are potentially lethal when combined with alcohol. Although medicines are readily available to adults, adolescents may not have access to them or realize that they might help.

Other medically focused interventions are sometimes used to treat suicidality. Electroconvulsive therapy is now a safe and reasonably effective treatment for severe depression that has resisted other treatment, and it may reduce suicide ideas in the short term (American Psychiatric Association, 2003). Further, adolescents who are severely depressed may not be able to wait 3–6 months to determine whether a drug or psychological treatment is working; so immediate electroconvulsive treatment may be appropriate. Hospitalization is often used when adolescents are suicidal. One study of psychiatrically hospitalized adolescents indicated that suicidal ideas abated for 6 months after discharge but increased between 9 and 18 months postdischarge (Prinstein et al., 2008).

Guidelines for medicine and medical procedures for suicidal adolescents include using adequate doses and maintaining them after initial symptoms have resolved or moderated, introducing medical procedures within the context of an empathic therapeutic relationship, and monitoring closely (Salzman, 1999). Medicine is not a cure for suicide but can be part of a comprehensive treatment program.

Controlled studies indicate that, as a whole, psychosocial treatments reduce risk of suicide attempts and completions (Comtois & Linehan, 2006). In one study with adolescents, the antidepressant Prozac plus cognitive-behavior therapy was more effective than Prozac alone in reducing adolescent depression (Emslie et al., 2006).

Interventions can reduce suicide risk, but there is no routine treatment. Rather, intervention should be tailored to specific adolescents, taking into account their cultural, religious, and family background.

POSTVENTION

Postvention is a term coined by Shneidman (1972) to describe appropriate and helpful acts that come after a dire event. After an adolescent's suicidal death, postvention can focus on friends and family or on the community at large who knew the teen only indirectly. Suicidal contagion is a particular concern.

Reactions to the suicide of a significant other may involve a wider repertoire of grief responses than those elicited after other modes of death (Ellenbogen & Gratton, 2001). Themes in grief following a suicidal death include questions of meaning, feelings of self-responsibility, and feelings of rejection or abandonment (Jordan, 2001). It is reasonable to conceptualize bereavement by suicide as a posttraumatic reaction (Callahan, 2000). In view of these possibilities, health professionals may need to offer help more proactively than is usual in most health care systems (De Groot, Keijser, & Neeleman, 2006). However, they should avoid naïve optimism or banal platitudes (Leenaars & Wenckstern, 1998) and use language that all can understand. Also, it would be helpful to encourage bereaved individuals to develop ways of coping with distressing flashbacks, visual images or other horrific sensations, and painful memories (Callahan, 2000). Specific interventions include group therapy, journaling, and narrative strategies.

Group approaches may be beneficial for those bereaved by suicide. In one adult study, two group interventions helped over time, regardless of the focus (Constantino, Sekula, & Rubinstein, 2001). These results suggest that the very process of interacting with a group of others who experienced the same thing helps, but research focusing on adolescents is needed.

Journaling may be helpful for those bereaved by the suicidal death of a loved young person. One Internet-based, twice-weekly journaling intervention focused on people suffering from complicated grief (Wagner, Knaevelsrud, & Maercker, 2006). Bereaved individuals, some bereaved from suicide, wrote 45 minutes twice per week for 5 weeks, focusing on exposure, intrusion, and recovery. Exposure included writing all their fears and thoughts about the event, and sensory perceptions, in as much detail as possible. They wrote with present tense and first person, without regard to grammar, style, or logic. Instructions encouraged reappraising the event; writing a supportive, encouraging letter to a hypothetical friend that reflected guilt, challenged dysfunctional automatic thinking and behavior, and corrected unrealistic assumptions; and developing rituals to remember the deceased, focusing on positive memories of the deceased, and using resources such as social contacts. The goal was to cope presently as well as in the future. Compared to waiting-list controls, those in the treatment condition reported significantly less intrusion and avoidance, and more adaptation. Journaling may help adolescents as well as adults.

Narrative strategies that promote meaning making regarding loss can mitigate bereavement complications (Neimeyer, 2002) and may be especially relevant after violent death. One research project involved adults who suffered from complicated grief telling and retelling the story of the loss in the context of reviewing and revisiting life goals (Shear, Frank, Houck, & Reynolds, 2005). They imagined conversing with the deceased, recalled (mostly) positive memories about the deceased, defined life goals, considered what they would like for themselves if their grief was less intense, identified ways to identify and recognize progress toward their goals, made concrete plans, and reengaged in meaningful relationships. Bereaved adults responded more strongly and quickly to this narrative strategy than to standard psychotherapy. This novel approach might be suitable for adolescents also.

After a suicidal death, contagion may occur. Contagion means that persons who learn of the suicide are influenced to attempt or commit suicide themselves. Vulnerable youths are susceptible to mass media reports of suicide, particularly news reports (Gould, Jamieson, & Romer, 2003b). Many countries including the United States, New Zealand, Sri Lanka, the United Kingdom, Australia, Canada, and Hong Kong have media guidelines for reporting suicide. These guidelines are similar, emphasizing that descriptions recognize the importance of role models; educate the public and offer help to vulnerable readers or viewers; and avoid glamorizing, sensationalizing, or providing explicit descriptions (Pirkis, Blood, Beautrais, Burgess, & Skehan, 2006).

After the death of Kurt Cobain, a well-known U.S. rock musician, public health and media officials worked together to prevent future suicides. Expecting the media to view a suicidal death as newsworthy, public health professionals worked with journalists to point out that suicide is a complex problem, Cobain was a talented musician but a disturbed individual, the death was far from romantic, and the grief of family members was intense. Media accounts specified how to identify high-risk persons, how depression plays a role in many suicides and can be treated, and how to contact agencies and resources for help (Jobes, Berman, O'Carroll, Eastgard, & Knickmeyer, 1996). There was no increase in the number of suicide deaths compared to before this suicide, although the number of suicide crisis calls increased (Jobes et al., 1996). These researchers concluded that cooperation with the media can actually reduce the likelihood of suicidal contagion.

Identifying risk factors, conducting prevention efforts at school and in the community, and actively intervening with suicidal adolescents can reduce suicidal thoughts and intentions in the long term. Suicidal adolescents can recover and go on to lead productive, happy lives. Postvention efforts after an adolescent's suicide can help bereaved individuals deal with their responses and discover some meaning from the tragedy.

REFERENCES

American Psychiatric Association. (2003). *Practice guideline for the assessment and treatment of patients with suicidal behaviors.* Washington, DC: Author. Retrieved February 21, 2008, from http://www.psych.org/psych_pract/treatg/quick_ref_guide/Suibehavs_QRG.pdf

Beck, A. T., Kovacs, M., & Weissman, A. (1979). Assessment of suicidal intention: The Scale for Suicidal Ideation. *Journal of Consulting and Clinical Psychology, 47,* 343–352.

Berk, M. S., Henriques, G. R., Warman, D. M., Brown, G. K., & Beck, A. T. (2004). A cognitive therapy intervention for suicide attempters: An overview of the treatment and case examples. *Cognitive and Behavioral Practice, 11,* 265–277.

Bickley, H., Kapur, N., Hunt, I. M., Robinson, J., Meehan, J., Parsons, R., et al. (2006). Suicide in the homeless within 12 months of contact with mental health services. *Social Psychiatry and Psychiatric Epidemiology, 41,* 686–691.

Brent, D. A., & Mann, J. J. (2006). Familial pathways to suicidal behavior: Understanding and preventing suicide among adolescents. *New England Journal of Medicine, 355,* 2719–2721.

Callahan, J. (2000). Predictors and correlates of bereavement in suicide support group participants. *Suicide and Life-Threatening Behavior, 30,* 104–124.

Centers for Disease Control and Prevention (CDC). (1992). *Youth suicide prevention programs: A resource guide.* Atlanta: National Center for Injury Prevention and Control.

Centers for Disease Control and Prevention (CDC). (2004). United States suicide injury deaths and rates per 100,000. Retrieved September 21, 2007, from http://webappa.cdc.gov/cgi-bin/broker.exe

Centers for Disease Control and Prevention (CDC). (2006). National youth risk behavior survey: 1991–2005. Retrieved October 1, 2007 from http://www.cdc.gov/HealthyYouth/YRBS/trends.htm

Centers for Disease Control and Prevention (CDC). (2007). Suicide trends among youths and young adults aged 10–24 years: United States, 1990–2004. *Morbidity and Mortality Weekly Reports, 56*(35), 905–908.

Comtois, K. A., & Linehan, M. M. (2006). Psychosocial treatments of suicidal behaviors: A practice-friendly review. *Journal of Clinical Psychology, 62,* 161–170.

Conner, K. R., & Goldston, D. B. (2007). Rates of suicide among males increase steadily from age 11 to 21: Developmental framework and outline for prevention. *Aggression and Violent Behavior, 12,* 193–207.

Constantino, R., Sekula, K., & Rubinstein, E. (2001). Group intervention for widowed survivors of suicide. *Suicide and Life-Threatening Behavior, 31,* 428–441.

Cull, J., & Gill, W. (1982). *Suicide Probability Scale manual.* Los Angeles: Western Psychological Services.

Davidson, M., Wagner, W., & Range, L. M. (1995). Clinicians' attitudes toward no-suicide agreements. *Suicide and Life-Threatening Behavior, 25,* 410–414.

De Groot, M. H., Keijser, J., & Neeleman, J. (2006). Grief shortly after suicide and natural death: A comparative study among spouses and first-degree relatives. *Suicide and Life-Threatening Behavior, 36,* 418–431.

Drye, R. C., Goulding, R. L., & Goulding, M. E. (1973). No-suicide decisions: Patient monitoring of suicidal risk. *American Journal of Psychiatry, 130,* 171–174.

Ellenbogen, S., & Gratton, F. (2001). Do they suffer more? Reflections on research comparing suicide survivors to other survivors. *Suicide and Life-Threatening Behavior, 31,* 83–90.

Emslie, G., Kratochvil, C., Vitiello, B., Silva, S., Mayes, T., McNulty, S., et al. (2006). Treatment for adolescents with depression study (TADS): Safety results. *Journal of the American Academy of Child & Adolescent Psychiatry, 45,* 1440–1455.

Evans, E., Hawton, K., & Rodham, K. (2005a). Suicidal phenomena and abuse in adolescents: A review of epidemiological studies. *Child Abuse and Neglect, 29,* 45–58.

Evans, E., Hawton, K., Rodham, K., & Deeks, J. (2005b). The prevalence of suicidal phenomena in adolescents: A systematic review of population-based studies. *Suicide and Life-Threatening Behavior, 35,* 239–250.

Farrow, T. L. (2002). Owning their expertise: Why nurses use 'no suicide contracts' rather than their own assessments. *International Journal of Mental Health Nursing, 11,* 214–219.

Foley, D. L., Goldston, D. B., Costello, E. J., & Angold, A. (2006). Proximal psychiatric risk factors for suicidality in youth: The Great Smoky Mountains Study. *Archives of General Psychiatry, 63,* 1017–1024.

Fortune, S., Sinclair, J., & Hawton, K. (2008). Adolescents' views on preventing self-harm: A large community study. *Social Psychiatry and Psychiatric Epidemiology, 43,* 96–104.

Galloucis, M., & Francek, H. (2002). The juvenile suicide assessment: An instrument for the assessment and management of suicide risk with incarcerated juveniles. *International Journal of Emergency Mental Health, 4,* 181–200.

Gillham, J. E., Hamilton, J., Freres, D. R., Patton, K., & Gallop, R. (2006). Preventing depression among early adolescents in the primary care setting: A randomized controlled study of the Penn Resiliency Program. *Journal of Abnormal Child Psychology, 34,* 195–211.

Gillham, J. E., Reivich, K. J., Freres, D. R., Chaplin, T., Shatte, A. J., Samuels, B., et al. (2007). School-based prevention of depressive symptoms: A randomized controlled study of the effectiveness and specificity of the Penn Resiliency Program. *Journal of Consulting and Clinical Psychology, 75,* 9–19.

Goldston, D. B. (2003). *Measuring suicidal behavior and risk in children and adolescents.* Washington, DC: American Psychological Association.

Goldston, D. B., Molock, S. D., Whitbeck, L. B., Murakami, J. L., Zayas, L. H., & Hall, G. C. N. (2008). Cultural considerations in adolescent suicide prevention and psychosocial treatment. *American Psychologist, 63,* 14–31.

Gould, M. S., Greenberg, T., Velting, D. M., & Shaffer, D. (2003a). Youth suicide risk and preventive interventions: A review of the past 10 years. *Journal of the American Academy of Child & Adolescent Psychiatry, 42,* 386–405.

Gould, M. S., Jamieson, P., & Romer, D. (2003b). Media contagion and suicide among the young. *American Behavioral Scientist, 46,* 1269–1294.

Gould, M. S., Kalafat, J., Munfakh, J., & Kleinman, M. (2007). An evaluation of crisis hotline outcomes: Part 2: Suicidal callers. *Suicide and Life-Threatening Behavior, 37,* 338–352.

Gutierrez, P., Osman, A., Barrios, F., Kopper, B., Baker, M., & Haraburda, C. (2002). Development of the Reasons for Living Inventory for Young Adults. *Journal of Clinical Psychology, 58,* 339–357.

Hardy, M. S. (2006). Keeping children safe around guns: Pitfalls and promises. *Aggression and Violent Behavior, 11,* 352–366.

Hawton, K., Fagg, J., & McKeown, S. P. (1989). Alcoholism, alcohol and attempted suicide. *Alcohol and Alcoholism, 24,* 3–9.

Jobes, D. A., Berman, A. L., O'Carroll, P. W., Eastgard, S., & Knickmeyer, S. (1996). The Kurt Cobain suicide crisis: Perspectives from research, public health and the news media. *Suicide and Life-Threatening Behavior, 26,* 260–271.

Jordan, J. R. (2001). Is suicide bereavement different? A reassessment of the literature. *Suicide and Life-Threatening Behavior, 31,* 91–102.

King, C., Kramer, A., Preuss, L., Kerr, D. C. R., Weisse, L., & Venkataraman, S. (2006). Youth-nominated support team for suicidal adolescents (Version 1): A randomized controlled trial. *Journal of Consulting and Clinical Psychology, 74,* 199–206.

King, J., & Kowalchuk, B. (1994). *Manual for Inventory of Suicide Ideation—30.* Minneapolis, MN: National Computer Systems.

King, R., Nurcombe, B., Bickman, L., Hides, L., & Reid, W. (2003). Telephone counseling for adolescent suicide prevention: Changes in suicidality and mental state from beginning to end of a counselling session. *Suicide and Life-Threatening Behavior, 33,* 400–411.

Kroll, J. (2000). Use of no-suicide contracts by psychiatrists in Minnesota. *American Journal of Psychiatry, 157,* 1684–1686.

Leenaars, A. A., & Wenckstern, S. (1998). Principles of postvention: Applications to suicide and trauma in schools. *Death Studies, 22,* 357–391.

Lizardi, D., Currier, D., Galfalvy, H., Sher, L., Burke, A., Mann, J., et al. (2007). Perceived reasons for living at index hospitalization and future suicide attempt. *Journal of Nervous and Mental Disease, 195,* 451–455.

Meehan, S., & Broom, Y. (2007). Analysis of a national toll free suicide crisis line in South Africa. *Suicide and Life-Threatening Behavior, 37,* 66–78.

Miller, A. L., Rathus, J. H., & Linehan, M. M. (2007). *Dialectical Behavior Therapy with suicidal adolescents.* New York: Guilford.

Mishara, B. L., & Daigle, M. S. (1997). Effects of different telephone intervention styles with suicidal callers at two suicide prevention centers: An empirical investigation. *American Journal of Community Psychology, 25,* 861–885.

Motto, J. A. (1999). Critical points in the assessment and management of suicide risk. In D. G. Jacobs (Ed.), *The Harvard Medical School guide to suicide assessment and intervention* (pp. 224–248). San Francisco: Jossey-Bass.

Motto, J. A., & Bostrom, A. G. (2001). A randomized controlled trial of postcrisis suicide prevention. *Psychiatric Services, 52,* 828–833.

Mufson, L. H., Dorta, K. P., Olfson, M., Weissman, M., & Hoagwood, K. (2004). Effectiveness research: Transporting interpersonal psychotherapy for depressed adolescents (IPT-A) from the lab to school-based health clinics. *Clinical Child and Family Psychology Review, 7,* 251–261.

Neimeyer, R. A. (2002). Traumatic loss and the reconstruction of meaning. *Journal of Palliative Medicine, 5,* 935–942.

Nock, M. K., Holmberg, E. B., Photos, V. I., & Michel, B D. (2007). Self-Injurious Thoughts and Behaviors Interview: Development, reliability, and validity in an adolescent sample. *Psychological Assessment, 19,* 309–317.

Nock, M. K., & Kazdin, A. E. (2002). Examination of affective, cognitive, and behavioral factors and suicide-related outcomes in children and young adolescents. *Journal of Clinical Child and Adolescent Psychology, 31,* 48–58.

Orbach, I., Milstein, I., Har-Even, D., Apter, A., Tiano, S., & Elizur, A. (1991). A Multi-Attitude Suicide Tendency Scale for Adolescents. *Journal of Consulting and Clinical Psychology, 3,* 389–404.

Pfeffer, C., Jiang, H., & Kakuma, T. (2000). Child-Adolescent Suicidal Potential Index (CASPI): A screen for risk for early onset suicidal behavior. *Psychological Assessment, 12,* 304–318.

Pirkis, J., Blood, R. W., Beautrais, A., Burgess, P., & Skehan, J. (2006). Media guidelines on the reporting of suicide. *Crisis, 27,* 82–87.

Prinstein, M. J., Boergers, J., Spirito, A., Little, T. D., & Grapentine, W. L. (2000). Peer functioning, family dysfunction, and psychological symptoms in a risk factor model for adolescent inpatients' suicidal ideation severity. *Journal of Clinical Child Psychology, 29,* 392–405.

Prinstein, M. J., Nock, M. K., Simon, V., Aikins, J. W., Cheah, C. S. L., & Spirito, A. (2008). Longitudinal trajectories and predictors of adolescent suicidal ideation and attempts following inpatient hospitalization. *Journal of Consulting and Clinical Psychology, 76,* 92–103.

Range, L. M. (2005a). The family of instruments that assess suicide risk. *Journal of Psychopathology and Behavioral Assessment, 27,* 133–140.

Range, L. M. (2005b). No-suicide contracts. In R. I. Yufit & D. Lester (Eds.), *Assessment, treatment, and prevention of suicidal behavior* (pp. 181–203). Hoboken, NJ: Wiley.

Reinecke, M. A., & Didie, E. R. (2005). Cognitive-behavioral therapy with suicidal patients. In R. I Yufit & D. Lester (Eds.), *Assessment, treatment and prevention of suicidal behavior* (pp. 205–234). Hoboken, NJ: Wiley.

Reynolds, W. (1987). *Suicide ideation questionnaire: Professional manual.* Odessa, FL: Psychological Assessment Resources.

Sakinofsky, I. (2007). Treating suicidality in depressive illness: Part 2: Does treatment cure or cause suicidality? *Canadian Journal of Psychiatry, 52*(Suppl. 1), 85S–101S.

Salzman, C. (1999). Treatment of the suicidal patient with psychotropic drugs and ECT. In D. G. Jacobs (Ed.), *The Harvard Medical School guide to suicide assessment and intervention* (pp. 372–382). San Francisco, CA: Jossey-Bass.

Shea, S. C. (1999). *The practical art of suicide assessment.* New York: Wiley.

Shear, K., Frank, E., Houck, P. R., & Reynolds, C. F. (2005). Treatment of complicated grief: A randomized controlled trial. *Journal of the American Medical Association, 293,* 2601–2608.

Shneidman, E. S. (1972). Foreword. In A. C. Cain (Ed.), *Survivors of suicide* (pp. ix–xi). Springfield, IL: Charles C Thomas.

U.S. Department of Health and Human Services. (2005). *Youth violence: A report of the Surgeon General.* Washington, DC: Author.

Van der Sande, R., Buskens, E., Allart, E., van der Graaf, Y., & van Engeland, H. (1997). Psychosocial intervention following suicide attempt: A systematic review of treatment interventions. *Acta Psychiatrica Scandinavica, 96,* 43–50.

Wagner, B. M. (1997). Family risk factors for child and adolescent suicidal behavior. *Psychological Bulletin, 121,* 246–298.

Wagner, B., Knaevelsrud, C., & Maercker, A. (2006). Internet-based cognitive-behavioral therapy for complicated grief: A randomized controlled trial. *Death Studies, 30,* 429–453.

Wyman, P. A., Brown, C. H., Inman, J., Cross, W., Schmeelk-Cone, K., Guo, J., et al. (2008). Randomized trial of a gatekeeper program for suicide prevention: 1-Year impact on secondary school staff. *Journal of Consulting and Clinical Psychology, 76,* 104–115.

Yang, B., & Clum, G. (1996). Effects of early negative life experiences on cognitive functioning and risk for suicide: A review. *Clinical Psychology Review, 16,* 177–185.

Zito, J. M., Safer, D. J., dosReis, S., Gardner, J. F., Soeken, K., Boles, M., et al. (2002). Prevalence of antidepressants among U.S. youths. *Pediatrics, 109,* 721–726.

6 Adolescents and HIV/AIDS

CRAIG DEMMER

Since 1981, over half a million people have died of AIDS in the United States (Centers for Disease Control and Prevention [CDC], 2007). While AIDS has predominantly affected men who have sex with men in the United States, increasing cases of AIDS among male, injecting drug users and their female partners have resulted in tens of thousands of children and adolescents who have lost one or both parents to the disease. Since the introduction of antiretroviral drugs in 1996, there has been a steady decline in the number of AIDS deaths in the United States. Still, people continue to die of AIDS in this country—an estimated 17,011 in 2005 (CDC, 2007). Between 2001 and 2005, 1,332 adolescents died of the disease in the United States (CDC, 2007). These numbers, however, pale in comparison to other regions of the world, particularly sub-Saharan Africa, where more than two thirds of all people with HIV live. There were an estimated 2.1 million AIDS deaths globally in 2007, and of these, 76% occurred in sub-Saharan Africa, making AIDS the leading cause of death in that region (UNAIDS, 2007). Other regions of the world that are also severely impacted by AIDS are South and Southeast Asia where there were an estimated 270,000 AIDS deaths in 2007, followed by Latin America (58,000 deaths) and Eastern Europe and central Asia (55,000 deaths) (UNAIDS, 2007).

It is roughly estimated that globally there are more than 15 million children (aged 0–17 years) who have lost one or both parents to AIDS, and over 11 million of these orphans live in sub-Saharan Africa (CDC, 2007). It is difficult to quantify how many children and adolescents have been impacted by the death of parents (not to mention the death of siblings and other family members) to AIDS. This matter is further complicated when researchers use different definitions of *orphan* (maternal orphan, paternal orphan, double orphan) or categorize them according to type of orphan (based on the HIV status of the child) or use different age cutoff points (children up to 15 years of age or those up to 18 years).

The focus of this chapter is on bereavement among adolescents resulting from an AIDS death, most typically the death of one or both parents from this disease. The chapter explores the socioeconomic and psychological impact of AIDS-related loss among adolescents. This chapter uses the latest UN definition of *orphanhood* as the loss of one or both parents (UNAIDS, 2004) and the World Health Organization definition of *adolescence* as being 10–19 years old (WHO, 2003). It should be pointed out that few empirical studies have been conducted on adolescents impacted by AIDS deaths. Rather, the trend has been to focus on children or to include children and adolescents and refer to them together as children. This chapter reviews empirical research that includes youths between 10 and 19 years of age. The lack of distinction between children and adolescents is an issue that needs to be addressed in future studies on this topic.

In the 1980s, the growing number of AIDS-related deaths in the gay community in the United States was described as resulting in "a secondary epidemic of AIDS-related bereavement" (Martin, 1988, p. 856). For each death, there are friends, family, and other loved ones who grieve that loss. As the AIDS epidemic has swept across the globe, affecting the poorest, most vulnerable members of society in each country, concerns have been expressed about the increasing numbers of young people orphaned by AIDS; their susceptibility to mental health problems; and whether they will likely turn to crime, violence, and other antisocial behaviors because of "a combination of poverty, no or very little moral education, poor educational levels and psychological instability" (Freeman, 2004, p. 153). Despite the duration and magnitude of the AIDS epidemic globally, it is only in the last few years that empirical research has been conducted on the impact of AIDS deaths on children and adolescents, and most of this research has focused on basic needs (Makame, Ani, & Grantham-McGregor, 2002). Remarkably few studies have dealt with the psychological impact of AIDS orphanhood (Bhargava, 2005; Cluver & Gardner, 2007a; Wild, 2001).

POVERTY

A number of studies worldwide have demonstrated the negative effects of AIDS-related illness and death on the household. For example, studies in South Africa (which has the largest number of people with HIV/AIDS in the world) have shown that households are often crippled financially as AIDS impacts the household over a long period of time, from when a family member becomes ill until long after his or her death (Gow & Desmond, 2002). In a study of poor, rural households in KwaZulu-Natal, Cross (2001) reported that the burden of incorporating youths orphaned by AIDS into the household, without additional support, typically pushes the household over the edge. The education costs of orphans, including school fees, transport to school, and school uniforms, are a particular drain on household finances. With few options for digging their way out of poverty, households fall into a downward spiral where spending for basic needs is drastically curtailed and little money is available for food. Many adolescents orphaned by AIDS must head households and take care of their siblings without help because if they are under 21 years of age they cannot qualify for grants as the primary caregiver (Walker, Reid, & Cornell, 2004).

There is growing evidence that the African tradition of strong extended family networks caring for orphans can no longer be taken for granted regardless of their willingness to help. There is deep concern that without major government and international support in sub-Saharan Africa to reduce the burden on households caring for youths impacted by AIDS, the long-term negative consequences for these households and youths will be incalculable (Miller, Gruskin, Subramanian, Rajaraman, & Heymann, 2006).

HEALTH AND SCHOOLING

Adolescents who have to care for parents who are sick with AIDS or those who have lost parents to AIDS may be at increased risk for poor health and are less likely to attend school than nonorphaned adolescents. A study of youths aged 6–14 years in Kenya showed that children of HIV-infected parents were more likely to be underweight and wasted, and less likely to receive appropriate medical care, than children of HIV-negative parents (Mishra, Arnold, Otieno, Cross, & Hong, 2007). But the evidence is not conclusive that there is a significant difference between

AIDS orphans and nonorphans on various physical health and nutritional measures. Among AIDS orphans and nonorphans under 18 years in Kampala, Uganda, Sarker, Neckermann, and Muller (2005) found that while AIDS orphans were more likely to be sick than nonorphans, there were no differences in levels of malnutrition between the two groups. Nevertheless, a study of households in Northern KwaZulu-Natal, South Africa, found that households that had adopted AIDS orphans were more likely to be "food-insecure" or to have less food, and it appeared that these households were using government grants that they received for being caregivers of orphans for other needs that the family had besides food (Schroeder & Nichola, 2006). It is unclear what effect this household decision may have on the nutritional status of these orphans.

The evidence seems to be clearer about the impact of AIDS orphanhood on access to schooling. A review of studies of children and adolescents orphaned by AIDS in sub-Saharan Africa (Andrews, Skinner, & Zuma, 2006) found strong evidence that they may be forced to withdraw from school at an earlier age than others, either to care for a parent dying of AIDS or because there is no money for school. Some must seek ways to earn money to support remaining family members. They may also have to withdraw from school because of the stigma attached to HIV/AIDS. Girls in households impacted by AIDS are more likely to be withdrawn from school earlier than boys (Bhargava, 2005). As the number of AIDS cases continues to rise in sub-Saharan Africa, more and more youths will be expected to shoulder the burden of caring directly for sick family members and being responsible for the household (Bennell, 2005).

FRAGMENTATION OF HOUSEHOLDS

Households may split up either before or after a parent dies of AIDS. When that happens, the adolescent is typically taken in by extended family regardless of the country. The transition is eased when the adolescent is adequately informed about the parent's illness, prepared emotionally for the parent's death, and consulted about a subsequent migration to a new household (Young & Ansell, 2003a). But this preparation does not always happen. In fact, it is rare that children and adolescents are involved in these discussions, and it usually becomes a matter of which relatives can afford to absorb these youths into their household (Young & Ansell, 2003b). Incorporation into a new household can be problematic not only for the extended family but for the adolescent as well. In a qualitative study of adolescents in Malawi and Lesotho who had moved to new household because of AIDS, Young and Ansell (2003b) reported that these adolescents were frequently treated differently from other youths in the household. For instance, especially when resources were scarce, they were not given the same food or provided with clothing. Some were beaten and given chores to earn their keep, while others were sent to work in order to support the household. Similar findings were reported in a qualitative study of youths orphaned by AIDS in Cape Town, South Africa (Cluver & Gardner, 2007b). Adolescents may become separated from siblings if they are split among relatives, thereby losing not only their parents but their siblings as well. They may also be forced to engage in multiple moves as the new caregiver gets sick and dies (Cluver & Gardner, 2007b; Young & Ansell, 2003b). As AIDS mortality continues to rise, it is likely that more youths will experience "residential instability" and migrate to new households (Ford & Hosegood, 2005). Because the displacement and migration of youths between households as a result of AIDS can be traumatic, the most effective policy intervention would be to provide more economic assistance to households, thus allowing youths to stay with relatives who really want them. This intervention would also reduce resentment among other youths in poor households and decrease multiple migrations (Ansell & Young, 2004).

YOUTH-HEADED HOUSEHOLDS

The loss of parents to AIDS has resulted in a rise in the number of youth-headed households, particularly in sub-Saharan Africa. Although this phenomenon has received a good deal of media attention, we still do not know much about the problem, nor do we have reliable statistics on the number of children living in youth-headed households. What is clear, though, is that youth-headed households are extremely vulnerable. Giese (2002) indicated that these youngsters are living on the margins of society, deprived of educational opportunities and recipients of few health and welfare services. Youngsters in affected households, especially girls, risk being sexually abused because they have no one to care for them (Bray, 2003). In a study by Thurman and colleagues (2006) of 692 youth heads of household aged 13–24 in Gikongoro, Rwanda, only 24% believed that relatives would help them, and 57% felt that the community would hurt them rather than help. Older youths (aged 19–24 years) were more likely to report a lack of support from relatives, and females had greater mistrust of community members due to their vulnerability. Overall, youths in this study expressed more confidence in the willingness of neighbors versus extended family to help them. The researchers concluded that interventions targeting the extended family as the first line of support for these youths may be misdirected at times and should instead involve unrelated community members who are better able and suited to support and protect these youths.

GUARDIANSHIP

In a survey of 1,400 current and prospective caregivers in three provinces of South Africa, Freeman and Nkomo (2006) reported that there was a high degree of willingness by extended family to provide a home to orphans and vulnerable youths, but the HIV status of these youths could be an obstacle to their placement in a home. Some adolescents will have no family or close friends to take them in. The willingness of strangers to care for these youths deserves more exploration; caution is urged, bearing in mind the potential for abuse (physical, sexual, and mental) by these strangers and the possibility that government grants and assistance intended for youths may be abused and used by the host family for their own needs. In a study of orphaned youths in Rwanda, Rose (2005) commented that family and community members may want to become guardians so that they can gain access to land and property that the youth inherited from his or her parents. Adolescents who do not have anyone caring for them are extremely vulnerable. Although there are legal protections for youths guaranteed within Rwanda's laws in terms of land rights, they usually lack the ability to defend these rights.

STIGMA AND SOCIAL SUPPORT

Probably the biggest factor that distinguishes AIDS-related bereavement from other types of bereavement is the social stigma that is attached to AIDS. Since the first cases were reported, AIDS has been regarded throughout the world as a highly stigmatized disease. For bereaved adolescents who have had a parent die of AIDS, the stigma can be manifested in several ways including silence, shame, denial, fear, anger, and violence. It is indeed sad that after nearly 3 decades of AIDS, such high levels of stigma still exist. In a study of high school students in the North West Province in South Africa, 64.1% believed that HIV-positive pupils should not be allowed in their school, 46.5% believed that AIDS was a punishment from God, and 42.3% were skeptical about having a meal with an HIV-infected person (Strydom, 2003). Even in countries like the United States, which has made enormous progress in HIV prevention education and treatment, HIV-related stigma is still rampant. Herek, Capitanio, and Widaman (2002) reported the following findings from their national household survey on HIV-related stigma in the United States: 12% believed that people with AIDS should be quarantined, 30.8% expressed anger or disgust toward people with AIDS, and 24.8% believed that people who got AIDS through sex or drug use have gotten what they deserve.

Individuals bereaved because of AIDS feel the "sting of stigmatization" through lack of social support (Nord, 1997). Social support means the availability of people who make these individuals feel that they care about them, love them, and value them (Sarason, Levine, & Basham, 1983). Without that support, persons are forced to keep the nature of the death secret and to hide their own grief. In essence they become "hidden grievers" (Dane & Miller, 1992). AIDS leads to "disenfranchised grief," which is defined as "the grief that persons experience when they incur a loss that is not or cannot be openly acknowledged, publicly mourned, or socially supported" (Doka, 1989, p. 4). Adolescents who lose a parent to AIDS are likely to receive less support and sympathy from family, friends, peers, and even teachers than if their parent had died of a more socially acceptable death such as cancer.

Relatively little is known about the influence of social support on distress among individuals who experience AIDS-related bereavement. In one of the few studies that have looked at the effect on social support on adolescents whose parent were infected with or died of HIV/AIDS, Lee, Detels, Rotheram-Borus, and Duan (2007) found that among their sample of adolescents in New York City those who had more social support providers reported significantly lower levels of depression and fewer conduct problems over a 2-year period. Adolescents who experienced the death of a parent to AIDS reported a significant increase in depression. Unfortunately, the protective effects of social support tended to decline over time. Nevertheless, the researchers suggested that future community programs focus on the effect of social support on reducing negative outcomes among adolescents and address the negative effects of AIDS-related parental deaths on adolescents.

Another study looking at the role of social support among adolescents who had lost a parent to AIDS indicated that those who had a greater number of people providing them with information and emotional support were more likely to use more coping strategies (probably because they were given more knowledge about specific coping strategies), and they were more likely to acknowledge a parent's cause of death as AIDS (Dillon & Brassard, 1999). Half of the sample named a relative who they said had helped them the most to cope with their parent's death. Of the 20 adolescents, 11 reported that they found comfort in talking with other adolescents about their grief. In resource-limited countries where high levels of AIDS-related stigma exist combined with low levels of support (formal and informal), it is likely that bereaved adolescents will be particularly vulnerable (Kalichman & Simbayi, 2004).

COPING WITH DYING PARENTS

Dealing with a seriously ill parent can be a potential threat to normal development and to physical and mental health among adolescents (Pedersen & Revenson, 2005). In a groundbreaking study, 414 adolescents in New York City living with parents with HIV/AIDS were followed for 6 years to assess their adjustment before and after a parent's death (Rotheram-Borus, Weiss, Alber, & Lester, 2005b). Not unexpectedly, adolescents reported more emotional distress and depressive symptoms soon after parental death than nonbereaved adolescents. The most significant finding was that adolescents experienced the most emotional distress more than 1 year prior to the death of the parent. Emotional distress declined immediately before the death possibly because adolescents and other family members experienced increases in social services support, medical care, and family support during the time shortly before the death. It also helped that many of the parents had custody plans in place and the new caregivers were already providing a stable home or making themselves available to the adolescent, thereby preparing the adolescent for the death and the transition to a new caregiver and a new life.

Because adolescents experience a variety of stresses before a parent with AIDS dies, it is important that interventions be introduced early on to help adolescents, parents, and other family members cope (Rotheram-Borus, Flannery, Rice, & Lester, 2005a). Adolescents have to deal with uncertainty and the fear of losing their parents; less physical and emotional availability of parents; anticipatory grief; changes in the household and daily life as a result of the parent's illness (e.g., hospitalizations, increased responsibilities and becoming a "miniadult," financial burdens on the family); fear of disclosing their parent's diagnosis to people outside the family and risking being ostracized because of the stigma associated with AIDS; loss of friends and changes in the support network; and changes in attitude, behavior, and/or grades at school (Woodring, Cancelli, Ponterotto, & Keitel, 2005).

The normal developmental challenges of adolescence are thrown into disarray for these adolescents who are trying to balance their need for freedom and independence, on the one hand, with their need for stability and dependence, on the other hand. They lack the emotional capacity at this developmental stage to confront serious life crises such as the illness and death of a parent (Reyland, Higgins-D'Alessandro, & McMahon, 2002; Woodring et al., 2005). However, studies have found no association between problem behaviors (externalizing symptoms) such as drug use, sexual risk, and conduct problems of adolescents and the health status of parents with HIV (Gardner & Preator, 1996; Rotheram-Borus & Stein, 1999). Adolescents are more likely to engage in problem behaviors because they are living in economically disadvantaged circumstances or when their parents are engaging in substance abuse. However, there is an association between a parent's health deteriorating and increased depression and anxiety (internalizing mental health symptoms) among such adolescents (Rotheram-Borus & Stein, 1999).

MULTIPLE LOSSES

Adolescents impacted by AIDS, particularly those living in developing countries, are likely to experience high numbers of AIDS-related deaths within their families and social networks. In communities devastated by AIDS, the "never-ending cycle of perpetual grieving" (Cho & Cassidy, 1994, p. 275) can lead to *bereavement overload,* a term coined by Kastenbaum (1977) to describe the experience of losing many loved ones in a relatively short period of time. The constant onslaught of AIDS-related deaths does not allow the bereaved individual enough time to grieve a loss before another death occurs. Each time a death occurs it reminds the individual of a previous loss, especially when previous losses are unresolved (Nord, 1997). As a result, bereaved individuals may become "emotionally overwhelmed, physically exhausted, or spiritually demoralized" (Mallinson, 1999, p. 167). Intuitively, one would expect that those who are confronted with multiple losses would be more at risk for complicated bereavement than those who report fewer losses. Unfortunately, there have been no studies to date that have directly explored the relationship between multiple AIDS-related losses and psychological distress among adolescents specifically, and studies of effects of multiple AIDS-related losses on adults have been inconclusive.

GRIEF AND HIV STATUS

A unique aspect of the AIDS epidemic is that many of those who are grieving an AIDS-related death are themselves HIV infected. This places an extra burden on them as they mourn (Goldblum & Erickson, 1999). Their grief may be intermingled with feelings about their own health and the prospect of dying (Kain, 1996). While coping with the loss of parents and others to AIDS, adolescents are confronted with their own mortality. So far it seems that HIV status will not automatically result in increased death anxiety, and Niemeyer and Stewart (1998) criticized the assumption that "death anxieties increase in a simple and linear fashion as individuals shift from being at-risk, to seropositive but asymptomatic, to symptomatic with AIDS" (p. 583). More research is also needed on what effects bereavement may have on the physical health status of HIV-infected adolescents. In the meantime, it is important that interventions be developed to help HIV-infected adolescents and their family members confront issues surrounding death and dying (Brown, Lourie, & Pao, 2000).

PSYCHOLOGICAL DISTRESS ASSOCIATED WITH PARENTAL DEATH FROM AIDS

It is well established that AIDS-related bereavement has the potential to be more problematic than bereavement from other types of death because of the stigma attached to AIDS, lack of social support for the bereaved, the nature of the illness and death, and the young age of those infected and affected (Dane & Miller, 1992). A number of cross-sectional and longitudinal studies over the years have indicated that individuals recently bereaved by AIDS exhibit intensified grief responses and higher prevalence of depression, anxiety, general psychiatric symptomatology, and suicidal ideation (Martin, 1988; Robinson, 2001;

Rosengard & Folkman, 1997; Summers et al., 2004). It is not unreasonable to assume that AIDS-related bereavement distress among adolescents, especially those living in resource-limited countries, is likely to be exacerbated by the multitude of stressors inherent in this context. To date, however, there has been limited research on the mental health of youths orphaned by AIDS. Cluver and Gardner (2007a) were only able to locate 24 quantitative studies on this subject worldwide, of which 5 were in the United States, and 19 in Africa. Most were conducted with youths who were not HIV infected. The pattern that emerged from their review of these studies was that youths orphaned by AIDS both in the United States and Africa experienced high levels of psychological distress. Most studies found internalizing problems; fewer found externalizing problems, meaning that these youths were more likely to experience depression and anxiety than conduct or behavior problems.

BEREAVEMENT INTERVENTIONS

In light of the limited amount of research on the psychological impact of AIDS orphanhood, it is not surprising that there is even less research on interventions to help youths cope with AIDS-related bereavement. Also, there are no efficacy studies of bereavement interventions for youths who have lost a sibling to AIDS or for parents who have lost a child to AIDS, and certainly no studies of interventions that target families that have lost a child to AIDS. Even among adults, there are only a handful of empirical studies of group interventions for those grieving the loss of other adults to AIDS, and they have all been conducted in the United States (Goodkin et al., 1999; Sikkema, Kalichman, Kelly, & Koob, 1995; Sikkema, Hansen, Kochman, Tate, & DiFranceisco, 2004). Rotheram-Borus, Stein, and Lin (2001) conducted an evaluation of an intervention in New York City that was designed for adolescents and parents who had AIDS, but the focus was on helping adolescents and parents cope with the impending death of the parent. The intervention consisted of group sessions for adolescents and their parents. For adolescents, topics included adapting to their parent's illness, dealing with the stigma, coping with their emotions, selecting a custodian, and reducing risk behaviors. Adolescents and parents were assessed over a 2-year follow-up period and compared to a control group of adolescents and parents with AIDS who did not receive the intervention. During the study period, 35% of the parents died. Children of deceased parents reported more emotional distress and problem behaviors 2 years later than nonbereaved youths. An important finding was that there was no difference in level of emotional distress among bereaved adolescents who had participated in the intervention and bereaved adolescents who had not. But bereaved adolescents were less likely to report problem behaviors (e.g., acting out) if they had participated in the coping skills intervention with the parents.

Richter, Manegold, and Pather (2004, p. 7) asserted that while there has been a proliferation of programs to assist youths impacted by AIDS in Africa, few of these programs have been evaluated, and hardly any have been subject to "rigorous experimental test." Since 2000, in community organizations throughout South Africa, memory-box projects have sprung up to help youths cope with anticipatory grief and death, as well as planning for the future (Smith, 2004). The concept of memory work has many forms and varies across contexts, but in a nutshell it involves youths working with a social worker, community caregiver, or so-called memory facilitator to collect various objects and place them in metal or wooden box (even a plastic soft drink container). Anything can be put in these boxes, including photographs, birth certificates, a letter from the parent, audiocassettes capturing stories and voices, drawings, and mementoes. Because of the scarcity of mental health resources in South Africa, this very inexpensive intervention has enormous appeal. The assumptions underlying memory-box work are that it is good for youths to know their family history, and that one way of gaining control over the situation during mourning is through remembering (Denis, 2004). It is believed that memory-box interventions can promote resilience among youths so that they will not be overwhelmed by the trauma of their parents' illness or death (Morgan, 2004). There is little empirical data, however, on the efficacy of this type of intervention.

CONCLUSION

While increased media attention has been devoted over the years to children and adolescents impacted by AIDS, especially those living in Africa, the response from both the scientific and the international assistance community has been slow. Reasons for this are not clear. According to a UNICEF report (2004), while the response to helping youngsters around the world who are orphaned by AIDS has been growing in recent years, "it lacks the necessary urgency and remains unfocused and limited in scope" (p. 6). What we do know for certain at this point is that children and adolescents who are orphaned by AIDS (not forgetting the countless others who may not have lost parents but who nevertheless have been affected by AIDS deaths of other family members, friends, and people in their communities) are vulnerable in many ways. UNICEF has prepared a comprehensive document consisting of principles and strategies that will hopefully mobilize and unite leaders worldwide around this important issue (UNICEF, 2004). For practitioners and researchers, there is a critical need for greater attention to be focused on understanding and addressing the needs of adolescents impacted by AIDS deaths on the individual, community, and national levels in those countries most affected by the HIV/AIDS epidemic.

REFERENCES

Andrews, G., Skinner, D., & Zuma, K. (2006). Epidemiology of health and vulnerability among children orphaned and made vulnerable by HIV/AIDS in sub-Saharan Africa. *AIDS Care, 18*(3), 269–276.

Ansell, N., & Young, L. (2004). Enabling households to support successful migration of AIDS orphans in Southern Africa. *AIDS Care, 16*(1), 3–10.

Bennell, P. (2005). The impact of the AIDS epidemic on the schooling of orphans and other directly affected children in sub-Saharan Africa. *The Journal of Development Studies, 41*(3), 467–488.

Bhargava, A. (2005). AIDS epidemic and the psychological well-being and school participation of Ethiopian orphans. *Psychology, Health & Medicine, 10*(3), 263–275.

Bray, R. (2003). Predicting the social consequences of orphanhood in South Africa. *African Journal of AIDS Research, 2*(1), 39–55.

Brown, L. K., Lourie, K. J., & Pao, M. (2000). Children and adolescents living with HIV and AIDS: A review. *Journal of Child Psychology and Psychiatry, 41*(1), 81–96.

Centers for Disease Control and Prevention (CDC). (2007, June). *HIV/AIDS surveillance report* (Vol. 17, Rev. ed.). Atlanta, GA: U.S. Department of Health and Human Services.

Cho, C., & Cassidy, D. F. (1994). Parallel processes for workers and their clients in chronic bereavement resulting from HIV. *Death Studies, 18,* 273–292.

Cluver, L., & Gardner, F. (2007a). The mental health of children orphaned by AIDS: A review of international and Southern African research. *Journal of Child and Adolescent Mental Health, 19*(1), 1–17.

Cluver, L., & Gardner, F. (2007b). Risk and protective factors for psychological well-being of children orphaned by AIDS in Cape Town: A qualitative study of children and caregivers' perspectives. *AIDS Care, 19*(3), 318–325.

Cross, C. (2001). Sinking deeper down: HIV/AIDS as an economic shock to rural households. *Society in Transition, 32*(1), 133–147.

Dane, B. O., & Miller, S. O. (1992). *AIDS: Intervening with hidden grievers.* Westport, CT: Auburn House.

Denis, P. (2004). Enhancing resilience in times of AIDS: The memory box programme of the University of KwaZulu-Natal. *AIDS Bulletin, 13*(4). Retrieved January 18, 2005, from http://www.mrc.ac.za/aids/june2004/aidsorphans.htm

Dillon, D. H., & Brassard, M. R. (1999). Adolescents and parental AIDS death: The role of social support. *Omega, Journal of Death and Dying, 39*(3), 179–195.

Doka, K. J. (1989). *Disenfranchised grief: Recognizing hidden sorrow.* Lexington, MA: Lexington Books.

Ford, K., & Hosegood, V. (2005). AIDS mortality and the mobility of children in KwaZulu-Natal, South Africa. *Demography, 42*(4), 757–768.

Freeman, M. (2004). HIV/AIDS in developing countries: Heading towards a mental health and consequent social disaster? *South African Journal of Psychology, 34*(1), 139–159.

Freeman, M., & Nkomo, N. (2006). Guardianship of orphans and vulnerable children. A survey of current and prospective South African caregivers. *AIDS Care, 18*(4), 302–310.

Gardner, W., & Preator, K. (1996). Children of seropositive mothers in the U.S. AIDS epidemic. *Journal of Social Issues, 52,* 177–195.

Giese, S. (2002). Health. In J. Gow & C. Desmond (Eds.), *Impacts and interventions: The HIV/AIDS epidemic and the children of South Africa* (pp. 59–77). Pietermaritzburg, South Africa: University of Natal Press.

Goldblum, P. B., & Erickson, S. (1999). *Working with AIDS bereavement: A comprehensive approach for mental health providers.* San Francisco: UCSF AIDS Health Project.

Goodkin, K., Blaney, N. T., Feaster, D. J., Baldewicz, T., Burkhalter, J. E., & Leeds, B. (1999). A randomized controlled clinical trial of a bereavement support group intervention in human immunodeficiency virus type 1-seropositive and—seronegative homosexual men. *Archives of General Psychiatry, 56,* 52–59.

Gow, J., & Desmond, C. (2002). Households. In J. Gow & C. Desmond (Eds.), *Impacts and interventions: The HIV/AIDS epidemic and the children of South Africa* (pp. 111–143). Pietermaritzburg, South Africa: University of Natal Press.

Herek, G. M., Capitanio, J. P., & Widaman, K. F. (2002). HIV-related stigma and knowledge in the United States: Prevalence and trends, 1991–1999. *American Journal of Public Health,* 92(3), 371–377.

Kain, C. D. (1996). *Positive HIV affirmative counseling.* Alexandria, VA: American Counseling Association.

Kalichman, S. C., & Simbayi, L. (2004). Traditional beliefs about the cause of AIDS and AIDS-related stigma in South Africa. *AIDS Care, 16*(5), 572–580.

Kastenbaum, R. (1977). Death and development through the lifespan. In H. Fiefel (Ed.), *New meanings of death* (pp. 18–45). New York: McGraw-Hill.

Lee, S. J., Detels, R., Rotheram-Borus, M. J., & Duan, N. (2007). The effect of social support on mental and behavioral outcomes among adolescents with parents with HIV/AIDS. *American Journal of Public Health,* 97(10), 1820–1826.

Makame, V., Ani, C., & Grantham-McGregor, S. (2002). Psychological well-being of orphans in Dar El Salaam, Tanzania. *Acta Paediatrica, 91,* 459–465.

Mallinson, R. K. (1999). The lived experience of AIDS-related multiple losses by HIV-negative gay men. *Journal of the Association of Nurses in AIDS Care, 10*(5), 22–31.

Martin, J. L. (1988). Psychological consequences of AIDS-related bereavement among gay men. *Journal of Consulting and Clinical Psychology, 56*(6), 856–862.

Miller, C. M., Gruskin, S., Subramanian, S. V., Rajaraman, D., & Heymann, S. J. (2006). Orphan care in Botswana's working households: Growing responsibilities in the absence of adequate support. *American Journal of Public Health, 96*(8), 1429–1435.

Mishra, V., Arnold, F., Otieno, F., Cross, A., & Hong, R. (2007). Education and nutritional status of orphans and children of HIV-infected parents in Kenya. *AIDS Education and Prevention, 19*(5), 383–395.

Morgan, J. (2004). The ten millions memory project. *AIDS Bulletin, 13*(4). Retrieved January 10, 2005, from http://mrc.ac.za/aids/june2004/aidsorphans.htm

Neimeyer, R. A., & Stewart, A. E. (1998). AIDS-related death anxiety: A review of the literature. In H. E. Gendelman, S. A. Lipton, L. Epstein, & S. Swindells (Eds.), *The neurology of AIDS* (pp. 582–595). New York: Chapman & Hall.

Nord, D. (1997). *Multiple AIDS-related loss: A handbook for understanding and surviving a perpetual fall.* Washington, DC: Taylor & Francis.

Pedersen, S., & Revenson, T. A. (2005). Parental illness, family functioning, and adolescent well-being: A family ecology framework to guide research. *Journal of Family Psychology, 19*(3), 404–409.

Reyland, S. A., Higgins-D'Alessandro, A., & McMahon, T. J. (2002). Tell them you love them because you never know when things could change: Voices of adolescents living with HIV-positive mothers. *AIDS Care, 14*(2), 285–294.

Richter, L., Manegold, J., & Pather, R. (2004). *Family and community interventions for children affected by AIDS.* Cape Town, South Africa: HSRC Publishers.

Robinson, L. A. (2001). Adult grief reactions following a sibling's death from AIDS. *Journal of the Association of Nurses in AIDS Care, 12*(2), 25–32.

Rose, L. L. (2005). Orphans' land rights in post-war Rwanda: The problem of guardianship. *Development and Change, 36*(5), 911–936.

Rosengard, C., & Folkman, S. (1997). Suicidal ideation, bereavement, HIV serostatus and psychosocial variables in partners of men with AIDS. *AIDS Care, 9*(4), 373–385.

Rotheram-Borus, M. J., Flannery, D., Rice, E., & Lester, P. (2005a). Families living with HIV. *AIDS Care, 17*(8), 978–987.

Rotheram-Borus, M. J., & Stein, J. A. (1999). Problem behavior of adolescents whose parents are living with AIDS. *American Journal of Orthopsychiatry, 69*(2), 228–239.

Rotheram-Borus, M. J., Stein, J. A., & Lin, Y. Y. (2001). Impact of parent death and an intervention on the adjustment of adolescents whose parents have HIV/AIDS. *Journal of Consulting and Clinical Psychology, 69*(5), 763–773.

Rotheram-Borus, M. J., Weiss, R., Alber, S., & Lester, P. (2005b). Adolescent adjustment before and after HIV-related parental death. *Journal of Consulting and Clinical Psychology, 73*(2), 221–228.

Sarason, I. G., Levine, H. M., & Basham, R. B. (1983). Assessing social support: The social support questionnaire. *Journal of Personality and Social Psychology, 44,* 127–139.

Sarker, M., Neckermann, C., & Muller, O. (2005). Assessing the health status of young AIDS and other orphans in Kampala, Uganda. *Tropical Medicine and International Health, 10*(3), 210–215.

Schroeder, E. A., & Nichola, T. (2006). The adoption of HIV/AIDS orphans and food security in rural Ingwavuma, South Africa. *International Journal of Technology Management and Sustainable Development, 5*(2), 173–187.

Sikkema, K. J., Hansen, N. B., Kochman, A., Tate, D. C., & DiFranceisco, W. (2004). Outcomes from a randomized controlled trial of a group intervention for HIV-positive men and women coping with AIDS-related loss and bereavement. *Death Studies, 28,* 187–209.

Sikkema, K. J., Kalichman, S. C., Kelly, J. A., & Koob, J. J. (1995). Group intervention to improve coping with AIDS-related bereavement: Model development and an illustrative clinical example. *AIDS Care,* 7(4), 463–475.

Smith, C. L. (2004). The memory book—and its close relations. *AIDS Bulletin, 13*(4). Retrieved January 17, 2005, from http://www.mrc.ac.za/aids/june2004/aidsorphans

Strydom, H. (2003). HIV/AIDS and South African adolescents: Attitudes and information needs. *Social Work/Maatskaplike Werk, 39*(1), 59–72.

Summers, J., Zisook, S., Sciolla, A. D., Patterson, T., Atkinson, J. H., & The HNRC Group. (2004). Gender, AIDS, and bereavement: A comparison of women and men living with HIV. *Death Studies, 28,* 225–241.

Thurman, T. R., Snider, L., Boris, N., Kalisa, E., Mugarira, E. K., Ntaganira, J., et al. (2006). Psychosocial support and marginalization of youth-headed households in Rwanda. *AIDS Care, 18*(3), 2220–229.

UNAIDS (2004). *Children on the brink 2004: A joint report of new orphan estimates and a framework for action.* New York: Author.

UNAIDS (2007). *AIDS epidemic update, December 2007.* Retrieved February 14, 2008, from http://www.UNAIDS.org

UNICEF (2004). *A framework of the protection, care and support of orphans and vulnerable children living in a world with HIV and AIDS.* Retrieved February 1, 2008, from http://www.synergyaids.com/documents/OVCFramework.pdf

Walker L., Reid, G., & Cornell, M. (2004). *Waiting to happen: HIV/AIDS in South Africa.* Cape Town, South Africa: Double Storey.

Wild, L. (2001). The psychosocial adjustment of children orphaned by AIDS. *South African Journal of Child and Adolescent Mental Health, 13*(1), 3–22.

Woodring, L. A., Cancelli, A. A., Ponterotto, J. G., & Keitel, M. A. (2005). A qualitative investigation of adolescent's experiences with paternal HIV/AIDS. *American Journal of Orthopsychiatry, 75*(4), 658–675.

World Health Organization (WHO). (2003). *Strategic directions for improving the health of children and adolescents.* Geneva: Author.

Young, L., & Ansell, N. (2003a). Young AIDS migrants in Southern Africa: Policy implications for empowering children. *AIDS Care, 15*(3), 337–345.

Young, L., & Ansell, N. (2003b). Fluid households, complex families: The impacts of children's migration as a response to HIV/AIDS in Southern Africa. *The Professional Geographer,* 55(4), 464–476.

7 Adolescents Living With Life-Threatening Illnesses

MICHAEL M. STEVENS, JULIE C. DUNSMORE, DAVID L. BENNETT, AND ANDREW J. YOUNG

This chapter describes the situation of adolescents who are living with life-threatening illnesses. Given that cancer remains the most common cause of death from disease in childhood and adolescence, despite advances in treatment (AIHW, 2007), this chapter will refer particularly to young people with cancer. However, many of the principles discussed and much of the practical advice offered can be applied to terminal illnesses and life-threatening conditions other than cancer, and some comments on three life-threatening conditions other than cancer are also provided.

HOW ADOLESCENTS REACT TO A CRISIS

Cognitive development involves the acquisition of formal thought processes and the ability to think in an abstract manner (Piaget & Inhelder, 1969). During adolescence, this process does not occur in a linear fashion. When a young person is in crisis or under threat, regression to a more concrete way of thinking often occurs. Frequently, adolescents are able to discuss complex issues beyond their years, yet behave in a very different manner. Interruption of developmental processes by illness may interfere with the adolescent's developing abilities to perceive the future and to understand the consequences of behavior. Because cognitive development is so influenced by psychosocial maturity, the choices adolescents make may not be easily understood by adults.

Neurobiological Factors

Recent advances in the study of brain development utilizing magnetic resonance imaging of the brain have determined that remarkable changes occur in the brain during the second decade of life (Giedd et al., 1999; National Institute of Mental Health, 2001). The understanding that adolescence is a time of profound brain growth and change is contrary to long-held ideas that the brain was mostly fully formed by the end of childhood. Between childhood and adulthood, the brain's so-called wiring diagram becomes more complex and more efficient, especially in the region of the prefrontal cortex, which is responsible for such skills as setting priorities, organizing plans and ideas, forming strategies, controlling impulses, and allocating attention. Hence, the ability to plan, adapt to the social environment, and imagine possible future consequences of action or appropriately gauge their emotional significance is still developing throughout adolescence. (It will come as no surprise to those living or working with adolescents to hear that it is now known that a teenager's brain is structurally different than an adult's.)

Building Resilience and Protective Factors

Responses of adults to stimuli tend to be intellectual in character, while those of teenagers are more often from the gut. This instinctive reaction suggests that while the changeability of the adolescent brain is well suited to meeting the demands of teenage life, guidance from adults remains essential while this decision-making circuitry is being formed, and that adolescents need to be surrounded by caring parents, adults, and institutions that help them learn specific skills and appropriate adult behavior (Weinberger, Elvevåg, & Giedd, 2005; Fuller, McGraw, & Goodyear, 2002). In times of crisis most adolescents require parental support to some extent but also sufficient freedom to be able to experiment with coping with the challenges by themselves. Their response, typically, is that they want to be loved and supported but not wrapped in cotton wool.

Adolescents with a life-threatening illness may welcome the support from parents developed during the crisis, yet feel confused as to how best to be a so-called normal adolescent when an opportunity arises to spend time away from their parents. Rather than confide in parents, they may prefer to confide in their peer group, particularly with peers who are in a similar situation, about their needs to experiment and for discussion of personal issues (Deem, 1986). A large school-based study of Australian adolescents called the Resilience Project investigated protective factors as they apply to young people (Fuller et al., 2002). Being well-connected to peers and having a good friendship group were rated jointly as the second most important protective factor when times were tough, after feeling loved by and connected to one's family. Young people faced with adversity have reported that peer connectedness and a sense of belonging are tied up with an identity related to a common life event. In CanTeen, the Australian Organization for Young People Living with Cancer (http://www.canteen.org.au), adolescents with cancer spoke of a "been there done that" connection (Dunsmore, 2002).

LOSSES MOURNED BY ADOLESCENTS WITH CANCER

Being an adolescent and living with a life-threatening illness involves significant grieving at the onset of the illness, during its course, and in its terminal phase. Not all of the losses are related to the process of having a chronic or debilitating illness.

Health

Young people describe losing the perception by others that as a healthy person, one is independent, in control, and not unreasonably vulnerable to physical harm or emotional upset. This altered perception results instead in their being regarded as precious. Some continue to experience avoidance by others, including friends and parents of friends, long after treatment is completed, because of irrational fears of contagion.

Prediagnosis Person

Adolescents with a serious illness often find themselves grieving for their former healthy selves. The onset of their illness prevents them from living in the style they enjoyed while well. The sick role makes them different because of feelings of weakness, lack of energy, and physical changes to their bodies. These physical changes can lower their standing within their peer group. One young person remarked, "People don't treat me like the person I used to be."

Prediagnosis Family

Following diagnosis of a life-threatening illness in a young person, family relationships may change. Life in the family is no longer the way it used to be. There is often a plea for life to return to the way it was. There is a common and erroneous perception that cancer leads to breakdown of families. Of 51 adolescents with cancer, 25 (49%) in a survey reported that they had become closer to their families; a further 21 (41%) reported no change (Dunsmore, 1992).

Body Image

Amputation, hair loss, weight gain, weight loss, and other side effects of treatment alter the young person's body image at a time when concerns about physical attractiveness and prowess are greatest. Loss of hair and related side effects may have an isolating effect on the adolescent, because of the resultant self-imposed restriction on socializing and, sometimes, rejection by peers. Use of cosmetic aids such as artificial limbs and wigs only superficially restores an adolescent's composure and confidence; the insult to body image is internal and cannot be restored properly by an external prosthesis.

Independence

The onset of a life-threatening illness during ages 12–18 makes it difficult for adolescents to become appropriately independent of parents and other authority figures and achieve a sense of personal autonomy. Ill adolescents are ambivalent about having to depend on parents for even their most basic care (e.g., changing of beds, toileting, washing, dressing, feeding). Considerable anger may be generated by the helplessness they experience over the loss of their independence. Matters are made worse if adolescents are unwittingly treated by staff of pediatric units in the same way as younger children.

Relationships With Parents

Ill adolescents are often attempting to deal with feelings of anger and ambivalence about their parents. There is now doubt that eventual independence from parents will be achieved. There are often concerns about the commitment of time and expense required of their parents, and about the demands placed on their own relationship. Roles within the family are often threatened. So-called protection rackets are common. Many adolescents attempt to hide their true feelings for fear of destroying their parent(s). Parents try to hide their pain from their child, for example, the father who wears sunglasses at night to hide his eyes, red from crying.

Relationships With Siblings

Siblings of ill adolescents may experience feelings of hostility and guilt. They may become resentful or even angry because of all the attention given to their brother or sister and the various resulting secondary gains. They may fear developing a similar illness. They may feel guilty, believing they have caused their brother or sister's disease because of some crisis that might have occurred at an earlier phase in their family's life. Other siblings report helplessness at not being able to make things right. As one young person said, "If only I could take his place, I would."

Relationships With Girlfriends/Boyfriends

Deterioration of the young person's appearance causes embarrassment. Ill adolescents frequently prefer to break off friendships, rather than risk causing their friends embarrassment or being abandoned by them. Their interest in sex appears to be similar to others their age (Dunsmore, 1992), although those in relapse have commented on missing out on sexual experiences because of their physical appearance and low energy levels. Lack of opportunity for sexual intimacy is often not addressed by parents or caregivers of adolescents with a terminal illness. Uncertainty about the future may adversely influence the development of a new relationship. The terminally ill young person may choose to break off a relationship to try to protect the partner from the pain of separation occasioned by death. Young people with a life-threatening illness do not want to be pitied. Their biggest fear is that someone may stay with them only because of pity.

School Life

Young people are upset by missing out on developmentally important milestones associated with day-to-day life at school, such as taking tests, dating, poking fun at authority figures, and participating in group experimentation with risky behavior (e.g., smoking or skipping school). Young men report their most disturbing losses are associated with loss of prowess, loss of energy, not being able to take part in sports, and being seen as wimps. Girls experience losses resulting from school absence most strongly in a social context, for example, isolation from their group, missing out on the latest gossip, and being unable to join in activities with best friends.

Indicators of the Future

A sense of worth in adolescence is linked to experiencing milestones along the journey to adulthood. If milestones and rites of passage such as examinations, graduations, school formals, and celebrations of significant birthdays are missed due to illness, a young person's sense of worth may deteriorate. Adolescents who have been given a poor prognosis may experience difficulty in resuming studies after completion of treatment, if they perceive the likely duration of their survival to be limited.

Certainty About the Future

Adolescents have a more mature concept of death and dying than do younger children, being able to see the permanence of death and the finality of separation that it involves. Thus, terminally ill adolescents mourn the loss of the future as well as of the past. It is in adolescence that life goals are becoming more strongly established in one's mind. Adolescents sense this loss when confronting the possibility of death. It is difficult to predict with certainty who will be cured. Adolescents with cancer are left in a limbo of uncertainty about the results of treatment, often for many years after diagnosis and commencement of therapy. "Living one day at a time" is a common motto of adolescents who are living with a life-threatening illness.

Hope

Frequently, young people who have been told that they may die soon report that people start to treat them as if they were already dead. As one 18-year-old said, "They treat me like a nonperson. It is as though I am in the coffin already and they are waiting to hammer in the final nails." Hope becomes an essential ingredient for living successfully for these young people. Their hopes may not necessarily be for a cure or magical recovery, but more often for joy and for success with the challenges of living. One can be very clear about the implications of one's life-threatening illness and still maintain hope. One adolescent had on her bedroom wall, "Be realistic. Plan for a miracle."

IMPLICATIONS OF LIFE-THREATENING ILLNESSES FOR EARLY, MIDDLE, AND LATE ADOLESCENCE

Adolescence has been divided into early, middle, and late phases. Although in practice the boundaries between these phases may be blurred, some differences between phases are evident in key issues, behaviors, relationships with peers, and in the effects of a life-threatening illness.

Early Adolescence

Early adolescence is a time of rapid physical growth and the onset of puberty. Early adolescents focus strongly on the development of their bodies. Membership in a peer group is important. Early adolescents with a life-threatening illness are most concerned about the effects of the illness on their physical appearance and mobility. Significant distress is common in adolescents with cancer if treatment results in weight gain, hair loss, scarring, or similar alterations to their physical appearance, which are perceived as drawing attention to their disability (Carr-Gregg & White, 1987). Because privacy is all-important to early adolescents, large ward rounds are often excruciatingly embarrassing (Dunsmore & Quine, 1995). Being less assertive than older adolescents, their concerns about such issues may go unrecognized.

Most early adolescents are still reliant on authority figures and are content to let parents act on their behalf (Levenson, Pfefferbaum, Copeland, & Silverberg, 1982). They do, however, wish to be involved in decisions and to have opportunities to talk with their doctor on their own (Carr-Gregg & White, 1987).

Because many early adolescents are disturbed by hospitals, the presence of familiar, friendly staff is all-important. Younger adolescents tend to rely on nursing or social work staff and parents to be their advocates, particularly with doctors. Younger adolescents also benefit (as do their older peers) by being grouped together in the hospital wherever possible (Towns, Sawyer, Stephens, Clarke, & Bennett, 2007). The use of symbolic language is common in this age group. The use of art, drama, song, music, writing, poetry, woodwork, photo montages, and collages all allow for external expression of young peoples' inner experiences. There is often no need for analysis of the process or for seeking meaning behind the expression.

Many young people are finding their voice on the Internet, on sites such as MySpace. Some young people have said that the Internet provides anonymity, so that they can explore the meaning of their experience without being labeled or held to account. The immediacy of the Internet is very appealing, and it also provides opportunity to increase their health literacy. Misinformation is a concern, prompting initiatives to develop youth-friendly but legitimate and professionally auspiced Web sites. Web counseling is becoming popular with youths. More research is needed in this area as to the efficacy and effects of such new technologies. Some health professionals are utilizing e-mail and text messaging to assist with communication and more timely responses to adolescents' concerns. The legal ramifications of such practices are only recently being explored.

Middle Adolescence

Middle adolescents most commonly focus on attracting a boyfriend or girlfriend, emancipation from parents and authority figures, and increasing interaction with peers. Middle adolescents with a life-threatening illness are most concerned about the effects the illness will have on their ability to attract a girlfriend or boyfriend, on their emancipation from parents and authority figures, and about being rejected by their peers. Time in hospital, and away from school, can interfere severely with social relationships and the acquisition of social skills (Katz, Rubinstein, Hubert, & Bleu, 1988).

Social standing within a peer group can be threatened. The ability to attract a boyfriend or girlfriend can be reduced if illness or treatment affects the way a young person looks. Being different within a peer group can signal disaster for an adolescent. Fear of rejection by peers can lead to many adjustment problems, including a lowering of self-esteem, withdrawal, depression, and acting-out behaviors (Bartholome, 1982; Bennett, 1985). Noncompliance with medical treatments and lifestyle changes is highest in this age group, requiring strategies other than merely exerting pressure or medical authority. Adapting regimens to young people's lives, for example, and helping them to see the advantages of self-care, can lead to improved compliance (Sawyer, Drew, Yeo, & Britto, 2007; Yeo & Sawyer, 2003). To young people in this age group, side effects of treatment may be more alarming than the threat of death. They understand the threat of death but often appear to make choices based on an unrealistic view of their invincibility.

With a life-threatening illness, middle adolescents often find themselves totally dependent on family again. This dependence and accompanying regression reduce self-esteem. A sense of personal autonomy is often compromised by hospitalizations and frequent trips to clinics and specialists involved in medical treatment. Many adolescents report frustration over loss of control of their life and a sense of being taken over by institutions and health professionals (CanTeen Focus Groups, 1991–1993). This loss of independence can be met with rebellion, noncompliance, or further regression. As control issues are so important in middle adolescence, informed consent and open communication with authority figures involved in management is vital.

Late Adolescence

Important issues for late adolescents include defining of careers, permanent relationships and lifestyles, increasing financial independence where this is possible, and separation from family. Late adolescents with a life-threatening illness are most concerned about the effects of the illness on their plans for career and relationships, and on their lifestyle. Time off work or away from study can interfere with work promotion and academic achievement (Chang, Nesbit, Youngren, & Robinson, 1987). This in turn can have ramifications on economic independence and self-esteem. Job discrimination has been widely reported, and life insurance and health insurance rejection are also common (Koocher & O'Malley, 1981). Illness and treatment can cause major social disruptions, increased dependence on parents, and consequent interference with the formation of intimate relationships. Some late adolescents with a life-threatening illness have to return home after having lived independently for a number of years.

Reproductive capabilities are reduced in some conditions, causing concern in this age group about intimate relationships and having children. Low energy or weakened physical capabilities can interfere with independence, economic security, and social flexibility. Questions from ill adolescents about fertility are common, even in the terminal stages of their illness. Sadness about possible loss of fertility, and thus loss of the chance to live on through their children, can displace sadness over the prospect of death.

Characteristics of adolescence and implications of a life-limiting illness in adolescence are summarized in Table 7.1.

Table 7.1

CHARACTERISTICS OF ADOLESCENCE AND IMPLICATIONS OF A LIFE-THREATENING ILLNESS IN ADOLESCENCE

Period/age	Early adolescence: 12–14 years (female); 13–15 years (male)	Middle adolescence: 14–16 years	Late adolescence: 17–24 years
Key issues and characteristics, focus	Focus on development of body; Most pubertal changes occur; Rapid physical growth; Acceptance by peers; Idealism; Mood swings, contrariness, stubbornness, temper tantrums; Day dreaming	Sexual awakening; Emancipation from parents and authority figures; Discovery of identity by testing limitations, boundaries; Role of peer group increases	Defining and understanding functional roles in life in terms of careers, relationships, lifestyles
Social/ relationships, behavior	Skills in abstract thinking improve; Foreseeing of consequences, planning for future; Physical mobility prominent; Energy levels high; Appetite increased; Social interaction mostly in groups; Membership in a peer group important	Relationships narcissistic; Risk-taking behavior increases; Intense peer interaction; Most vulnerable to psychological problems	Increasing financial independence; Planning for the future; Establishment of permanent relationships; Increasing time away from family
Relationships with adults	Parents and other authority figures still mostly respected; As part of adjustment to new "adult" bodies, may assert themselves as adults while still dependent on parents and caregivers; Some testing out (e.g., with time away from home)	Parental relationships strained; Separation from family begins; Some hero worship	Culmination of separation from family; Increasing financial independence; Sense of being equal to adults

(*Continued*)

Table 7.1

CHARACTERISTICS OF ADOLESCENCE AND IMPLICATIONS OF A LIFE-THREATENING ILLNESS IN ADOLESCENCE (*Continued*)

Relationship with peers	Peers used as standards for measurement of developmental progress and assessment of so-called normality; Comparisons of strength and prowess; Friendships with same sex generally more important	Interaction with peers increases; Questioning increases concerning who are one's friends and one's own identity and value; Sexuality and sexual preference of more concern	Increasing experimentation with intimacy outside family
Impact of life-threatening illness	Concerns about physical appearance and mobility; Privacy all-important; Possible interference with normal cognitive development and learning (school absence, mediation, pain, depression, fatigue); Comparison with peers hindered, making self-assessment of normality more difficult; Possible lack of acceptance by peers; Reliance on parents and other authorities in decision making; Hospitals perceived as disturbing	Illness particularly threatening and least well tolerated; Compromised sense of autonomy; Emancipation from parents and authority figures impeded; Interference with attraction of partner; Fear of rejection by peers; Limited interaction with peers may lead to social withdrawal; Dependence on family for companionship and social support; Hospitalization, school absences interfere with social relationships and acquisition of social skills; Noncompliance with treatment	Absences from work, study; Interference with plans for vocation and relationship; Difficulties in securing employment and promotion at work; Unemployment hinders achieving separation from family and financial independence; Discrimination in employment and health/life insurance; Loss of financial independence and self-esteem; Concerns about fertility and health of offspring

From "Adolescents who are Living with a life-threatening illness," by M. M. Stevens & J. C. Dunsmore, 1996a, in C. A. Corr & D. E. Balk (Eds.), *Handbook of adolescent death and bereavement* (pp. 107–135), New York: Springer Publishing. Copyright © 1996 by Springer Publishing. Adapted with permission.

JOURNEY THROUGH A LIFE-THREATENING ILLNESS: EXPERIENCES AND REACTIONS OF ADOLESCENTS WITH CANCER

There are common threads in the reactions experienced by young people living with cancer, as an example of a life-threatening illness. Knowledge of these reactions will assist those working with ill young people to be better aware of their needs. Any threat of death or disability is deemed by today's adolescents to be incongruent with the desirable lifestyle of a young person as portrayed by the media. Images of fit, healthy, beautiful, youthful individuals are visible everywhere. There is a mythological inference that the young can conquer all, including death. Adolescence is a time for experimentation, for expanding one's limits, for seeking new experiences. A sense of invulnerability is strong in adolescents. Only by experimentation can the boundaries of one's potential be learned. It is only through trial and error while learning how to manage conflict and deal with intimacy that a young person learns how to navigate successfully in the world of adults. The capacity to solve problems is predicted by the individual's exposure to multiple new experiences throughout the preadolescent and adolescent years (Inhelder & Piaget, 1958). The more restricted a young person's range of experiences, the fewer resources can be drawn on to solve problems.

At Diagnosis

When confronted with a diagnosis of cancer, young people so often respond with disbelief: "That happens to old people, I'm too young!" The adolescent and family often assume the worst, that the young person is going to die, and soon. They will be stunned, disbelieving, shocked. Soon afterward, feelings of anger, guilt, sadness, and depression set in. Reactions are similar to those seen in parents of younger children with cancer (Stevens, 2004). However, Dunsmore (1992) reported the great majority (96%) in a study of 51 adolescents with cancer considered that they were coping well; 62% perceived themselves as coping very well both with the diagnosis and subsequent treatment.

One of the goals in initial consultations is to readjust the adolescent's and parents' expectations to a more hopeful level, in keeping with the patient's actual prognosis. Adolescents prefer the conversation to be directed toward them rather than their parents. Suggestions for more effective communication with ill adolescents and their families are provided in Table 7.2.

Table 7.2

SUGGESTIONS FROM ADOLESCENTS TO GUIDE GOOD COMMUNICATION

COMMUNICATION	EXAMPLES GIVEN BY ADOLESCENTS	STRATEGIES FOR IMPROVED COMMUNICATION
What adolescents say ***inhibits*** *good communication*		
Impersonal detached manner	Sounding too textbookish Appearing uncaring Using intimidating tone or body language Excluding the patient Being stuffy	Avoid hiding behind the patient's chart Establish what both prefer to be called Be open to use of nicknames Talk to the adolescent, not about the adolescent
Use of authority behavior	Using medical terminology or jargon without explanation Conducting large ward rounds Treating adolescents as if they are unintelligent Limiting access to results of tests	Limit size of ward rounds; introduce strangers Inform patient of results promptly Provide opportunities for questions Assist understanding by seeking feedback (e.g., "This has been a lot of information to take in. Could you let me know in a nutshell what you have understood so far?")
Lack of time, haste	Not explaining time limitations Not appearing to listen (having one foot out the door) Delegating care to a more junior physician Not providing time for one-to-one discussions	Agree about time available for discussions Encourage adolescents to write down their questions Organize follow-up by appropriate staff members

(*Continued*)

Table 7.2

SUGGESTIONS FROM ADOLESCENTS TO GUIDE GOOD COMMUNICATION (*Continued*)

COMMUNICATION	EXAMPLES GIVEN BY ADOLESCENTS	STRATEGIES FOR IMPROVED COMMUNICATION
Generation gap	Appearing uncomfortable about spending time with patient	Be honest about issues of sex, fertility, relationships
	Embarrassment when discussing sensitive issues	Ask young person to explain further if not understood
	Showing frustration with adolescents	Maintain sense of humor and be prepared for some teasing about age
	Procrastinating over decisions	
	Trying too hard to relate at the young person's level	
*What adolescents say **facilitates** good communication*		
Interactive communication	Ability to listen	Choose an environment conducive to discussion
	Seeking feedback	Encourage discussion of alternatives and their consequences
	Allowing questions	Encourage discussion of fears or intense emotions by legitimizing these as being normal
Knowledge and professional expertise	Ability to make correct decisions	Provide a simple explanation for why decisions are made or information that supports a preferred course in treatment
	Demonstration of competent skills (e.g., inserting intravenous cannulas)	Provide access to written information
	Being able to explain reasons underlying decisions	Explain all procedures clearly
	Being confident	If unable to answer a question, acknowledge and be willing to research information required

(*Continued*)

Table 7.2

SUGGESTIONS FROM ADOLESCENTS TO GUIDE GOOD COMMUNICATION (*Continued*)

COMMUNICATION	EXAMPLES GIVEN BY ADOLESCENTS	STRATEGIES FOR IMPROVED COMMUNICATION
Honesty and a straight-forward approach	Providing an opportunity to discuss all related issues Not withholding information Not seeking to protect from the truth Not telling parents one thing and the patient another	Establish a direct style of communicating Adolescents benefit by receiving information about how communication may proceed (e.g., "I will be honest with you and not keep anything from you. Please ask if you think something is not being said.") Be willing to repeat information Be willing to review decisions
Professional friendship	Showing genuine concern for the adolescent as an individual, not just as a case or a disease Having a sense or humor Providing some self-disclosure Remembering small details about the patient Being there for support afterward	Respect the adolescent's privacy Maintain confidentiality Admit mistakes Treat adolescents as individuals Recognize that the adolescent's concerns and aspirations may change with time

From "Helping adolescents who are coping with a life-threatening illness, along with their siblings, parents, and peers," by M. M. Stevens & J. C. Dunsmore, 1996b, in C. A. Corr & D. E. Balk (Eds.), *Handbook of adolescent death and bereavement* (pp. 329–353), New York: Springer Publishing. Copyright ©1996 by Springer Publishing. Adapted with permission.

How Adolescents With a Life-Threatening Illness Feel Different From Healthy Peers

Young people with a life-threatening illness are often denied the opportunity to experiment. They are protected. Decisions are made for them. Disenfranchising adolescents in these ways leaves them feeling somewhat powerless and less able than their well peers to make experienced decisions.

The resilience observed in young people living with a life-threatening illness is often marveled at by those around them. The ability to bounce back from tough times, to deal with adversity, requires a range of individual characteristics such as social competence, problem-solving ability, autonomy, and a sense of purpose, as well as influential factors related to one's family, school, and community (Resnick, 2000). Most of these adolescents do not see themselves as being either extraordinary or brave, but rather as normal adolescents making the best of a difficult situation. They do, however, perceive themselves as being different from their well peers, as a result of coping successfully with what has happened to them. They perceive themselves as being more mature; more sensitive; more positive about life; less interested in the trivial; and less interested in worldly possessions, money, and power (Dunsmore, 1992).

Reactions When Completing Treatment

When planned treatment is completed and no further evidence of cancer can be detected, an adolescent may initially be euphoric, but later may be left with a lingering uncertainty about the future. On the one hand, there is hope for cure based on the promising response to treatment and the encouragement provided by the treatment team. On the other hand, there is fear based on awareness of a poor outcome for peers with a similar diagnosis, who frequently have become close friends during the course of treatment and follow-up.

Living With Uncertainty

The situation of survival being obtained at the cost of continuing danger has been described by way of a metaphor, the "Damocles Syndrome" (Koocher & O'Malley, 1981). Just as in the story of Damocles, adolescents with a life-threatening illness (e.g., cancer, cystic fibrosis, or HIV/AIDS) sit uneasily at the banquet of life, forever aware of the sword that hangs by a thin thread over their heads.

Confronting the Possibility of Death

Most adolescents with cancer will feel more in control if they have opportunities to discuss the what ifs and to evaluate their priorities in living. Some adolescents with a life-threatening illness will decline a proffered opportunity to consider the possibility of their own death. Others become more willing to consider the issue later in the course of their illness, especially when they have been restored to apparent health and are attempting to reshape their plans for the future.

Overprotection and Its Problems

Most adolescents living with a life-threatening illness describe their willingness to confront the illness directly. They speak of their belief that honesty is the best policy. In two surveys of CanTeen members, all participants in the surveys responded to the question on bad news. Ninety-six percent said categorically that they would want to be informed of adverse events in their management, such as failure of treatment or other setbacks, and, most important, if they were dying (Dunsmore & Quine, 1995). It is evident from these surveys and from responses provided within other discussion groups and workshops conducted regularly by CanTeen that young people who live with a life-threatening illness feel strongly about this issue.

Providing Bad News

When asked whom they would prefer to provide them with bad news, 48% of CanTeen members said that it should be the doctor, 35% their parents and their doctor together, and 12% their parents alone (Dunsmore & Quine, 1995). The manner in which such news is provided is vital if satisfactory relationships with the adolescent are to be maintained. Adolescents often comment on whether they think the news meant anything to the caregiver who provided it. As one said, "She really cared. She said she would continue to be my doctor, she would make sure I was looked after." Honesty, continuity of care, and feeling supported rather than abandoned, are important issues for those facing death. Continuity of care may be adversely affected both by the patient moving from pediatric or adolescent units to facilities caring for adults and by transfer into palliative care.

At Relapse

Contrary to their reactions at diagnosis, adolescents who had relapsed felt that having the cancer recur was more upsetting than the initial diagnosis, because of the poorer prognosis after relapse, the loss of hope entailed in relapse, and awareness and fear of what lay ahead. Young people with cancer who have experienced a recurrence of their disease will frequently speak of their fear of what lies ahead. As one 16-year-old said, "I sailed through treatment the first time. I always believed I would make it. This time it's more difficult. I see the pain and fear in the faces of my family. I see the pity in the eyes of my nurses and doctors."

Avoidance by Health Professionals

Avoidance is practiced not only by adolescents with a life-threatening illness, but also by their health professionals and parents (Foley & Whittam, 1990). The truth may be perceived as devastating by those surrounding the young person. Many health professionals have said they feel at a loss to know what best to do in these circumstances. When treatment goals are oriented toward cure, there may be a perception of having failed. The death of a young person is tragic and may provoke in a caregiver much sadness and reassessment of priorities, relationships, and of personal mortality.

Control of Visiting Rights

The terminally ill adolescent's family may seek to prevent visits by friends and peers in the belief that whatever time is left for their child deserves to be spent just with them. There may also be a conviction that this policy spares the friends from becoming upset. It is likely, however, that the adolescent does want special friends to be permitted to continue to visit. The young person's wishes should be respected.

Attempts to Mask Reality

The implications of the situation in which these young people find themselves cannot be concealed from them. For example, it is not uncommon for them to witness the death of a fellow patient while in hospital. Staff may attempt to disguise such an event by closing curtains around the bed, whisking away the deceased person's body, avoiding discussion about the deceased person, and ensuring that a new patient occupies the bed promptly. These ruses are described by young people as simply unrealistic. It is as if the young person who died vanished or, worse still, never existed. In group discussions, young people commonly describe in emotional terms how disposable they feel. Rather than vanish or cease to exist, they would prefer to be remembered and to be missed. They equate the manner in which they may be treated after death to their perceived worth and to the degree to which they were loved.

Privacy

Privacy is more significant for ill adolescents in comparison with older or younger patients because of their preoccupation with physical change, their awakening sexuality, and normal shyness. Further, young people fantasize about the potential for more intimate relationships with many other people with whom they come into routine contact, however little the potential may actually be for such relationships to develop. When caregivers are of similar age as the patient, these thoughts and feelings, and associated embarrassment, may be heightened.

Young people commonly have thoughts, feelings, and secrets that are not normally revealed to their families. That privilege may suffer after developing a life-threatening illness because of the perceived expectation that the patient with a serious illness must disclose all to the authority figures providing care. Recognition of the need for private time with a boyfriend or girlfriend is also important. Opportunities for physical closeness, for kissing and cuddling, are often denied during a life-threatening illness.

Caregivers should ensure that adolescents are not unduly or unnecessarily exposed during medical examinations and nursing procedures, by appropriate use of curtains and provision of garments providing privacy. Young people appreciate private discussions being removed to private areas, "away from prying ears." Young people should be asked what information they have provided can be disclosed to others and what they want kept confidential.

Terminally ill adolescents also value having some control over who can enter their personal space, whether at home or in the hospital. This control helps maintain a sense of privacy and dignity at a time when control over bodily functions may be failing.

Denial

Because well adolescents often behave as if personal death is unlikely, denial or avoidance are common strategies for coping with a life-threatening illness. The purpose of both denial and avoidance (Van Dongen-Melman, Pruyn, Van Zanen, & Sanders-Woudstra, 1986) is to ward off disruptive levels of anxiety and to allow, instead, for maintenance of normal functioning and self-image. Fluctuating episodes of denial and avoidance by adolescents with cancer have been observed both by the authors and others (Carr-Gregg & White, 1987). Young people who are terminally ill commonly use denial as a way of escaping temporarily from the brutal reality of their situation. Passing into and back out of denial assists them in adjusting bit by bit to their impending death. Further, they will not want to spend their whole time talking about death, preferring instead to talk about other nonthreatening subjects as a way of reducing their anxiety. This preference is often misinterpreted by caregivers as denial. One 17-year-old with osteogenic sarcoma of the pelvis said, "My life is short enough without having to spend all my waking hours talking about dying."

Sometimes what is being observed is not so much denial but the oscillation between two types of coping as described by Stroebe and Schut in their Dual Process model of coping (Stroebe & Schut, 1999; Stroebe, 2001). The young person moves between confronting and dwelling on the losses, and efforts to master or adapt to new realities. This pendulum at times swings from extremes of immersion in feelings and meaning making to practical and pragmatic doing and getting on with life. As one adolescent said, "I'm just over this cancer thing. I'm all griefed out."

In the Terminal Phase

The death of each adolescent is unique, because of differences in the natural history of each person's disease, differences in personalities of patients and families, the variety of preferences for style of care expressed by patients, and varying requirements for technical support related to their palliative care. Some adolescents will choose to die in denial. Some will request lots of noise; others want peace and quiet. Some will want their family around them, whereas others will not. Some will want to remain alert as much as possible to the end, even though in pain. Others will prefer to be heavily sedated.

It is the process of dying, especially loss of control, that adolescents fear most, rather than being dead. They fear becoming vegetative and totally dependent on others. They fear becoming dependent on others for their personal hygiene. They fear the embarrassment of becoming demented, helpless, and child-like. They express concerns that their pain may increase, that the truth will be withheld from them, and that they will not have an opportunity to achieve their goals in life. When in the hospital, many express concerns that they will not see their own room or their home again, or that they will not be able to say goodbye to their pets. Their greatest distress is for their loved ones. Young people have commonly worried excessively about the effect their dying was having on a sibling or a parent (Foley & Whittam, 1990). They also fear separation from their families and from their special friends. These concerns are more commonly expressed to carers or friends than parents, and even then only if the confidant is perceived as being willing to listen, honest, and trustworthy. Adolescents who are seriously or terminally ill commonly take steps to put their affairs in order. Young people who are dying may linger, close to death, for prolonged periods. They may simply need permission from their loved ones to die and will often die promptly when such permission is given.

LIFE-THREATENING CONDITIONS OTHER THAN CANCER

Many concerns of adolescents who are coping with cancer are experienced by young people with other life-threatening conditions. In this section, we note some modifications that apply to adolescents with cystic fibrosis, severe brain damage, and catastrophic illness with short life expectancy.

Cystic Fibrosis

A diagnosis of cystic fibrosis is commonly established in childhood. Thus, young people with cystic fibrosis learn at an early age that their life span is expected to be limited. Issues of dependency and of attaining goals in adolescence are experienced, as by young people with cancer. Denial is a common reaction in adolescents with cystic fibrosis, evidenced, for example, by noncompliance with physiotherapy, diet, and other important components of long-term therapy.

Severe Brain Damage

Issues affecting the family of an adolescent with severe brain damage may be more significant than those affecting the young person. Families of patients who are vegetative, apparently unresponsive, and totally dependent on them may exhaust their reserves of energy in caring for such young people. These families will benefit from the patient receiving periodic respite care, to assist them in recharging their spiritual batteries. Families of such adolescents should be encouraged to remember that the patient may still be able to hear despite being unable to respond and to continue talking to the young person at the bedside, even if about simple matters, such as what one is doing at that moment. These families may describe being in a dilemma of wanting the adolescent to die in order to be released, yet experiencing guilt over such feelings. Opportunities are required for these families to work through their anticipatory grieving.

Catastrophic Conditions With Short Life Expectancy

When a catastrophic illness or life-threatening condition (e.g., motor vehicle accident, acute cardiomyopathy, viral meningitis, or overwhelming sepsis) occurs in a previously well adolescent and death is imminent, issues of honesty with the young person become important. Young people in this situation are likely to suspect that they are about to die. They deserve honesty from their caregivers to ensure, for example, that something they want to say or have done can be accomplished. Families in this situation are often required to make urgent and painful decisions about treatment or organ donation. The aftercare of such families is as important as would have been the ongoing care of the young person, had he or she survived.

ISSUES ARISING

It is encouraging to remember that many children and young people with cancer survive their illness, complete planned treatment, and move on to new challenges associated with growing up as long-term survivors of previous cancer in childhood or youth. Similarly, many young people with cystic fibrosis and other chronic life-threatening illnesses besides cancer face similar challenges as they live on with a life-threatening illness into adulthood. A proportion of young people who have survived cancer unfortunately experience ongoing medical problems, for example, late recurrence of the original cancer or medical complications induced by treatment for the original illness. These young people will ultimately need transition to adult care.

The process of leaving a familiar pediatric service and effectively engaging in appropriate adult health care can be challenging and complex. The process often occurs when there are other significant transitions in a young person's life. Equity in health care, the ability to transfer complex patient information, consumer participation, and working with adult services to increase their capacity to respond in a developmentally appropriate manner are all important aspects of the process (Steinbeck, Brodie, & Towns, 2007).

In the current decade, the care of adolescents and young adults with cancer has become a concerning issue, certainly to pediatric oncologists in Australia, the United Kingdom, and the United States, because it has become obvious that improvement in overall survival of young adults with cancer is lagging well behind that of children and adults. There is also mounting evidence that young adults who develop late-onset childhood cancers survive in greater numbers if they are enrolled in appropriate childhood cancer trials rather than receiving generally less intensive therapy as commonly used for the same types of cancer in adults. These concerns are not, as yet, shared by many medical oncologists.

Numerous promising initiatives are currently underway in all three countries and elsewhere, seeking to improve survival and quality of life for adolescents and young adults with cancer. CanTeen, the Australian Organization for Young People Living with Cancer, was established in 1985. CanTeen's mission is to support, develop, and empower young people living with cancer by providing an Australia-wide peer support network for 12- to 24-year-olds including patients, siblings, offspring, and bereaved siblings and offspring. On behalf of young people with cancer, CanTeen is advocating for the establishment of adolescent and young adult cancer networks servicing each state and territory in Australia, headed by age-specific multidisciplinary centers of excellence for adolescents and young adults with cancer. The Australian federal government recently committed $15 million toward a proposed capital fund of $30 million for the construction of cancer centers for adolescents and young adults with cancer. CanTeen has committed to raising the additional $15 million.

CONCLUSION

Many imagine that caring for young people with cancer or other life-threatening illnesses must be depressing, stressful, and unrewarding. Undoubtedly this work is stressful at times, but those working in such fields will attest that they enjoy caring for their patients and families, and that the work is frequently rewarding and affirming. It is commonly described as a significant privilege to be afforded the opportunity of working with young people and their families, because of the opportunity provided, by caring, to experience enriching friendships and human contacts, and to witness the transformations that occur in empowered young people living with life-threatening illnesses. In confronting the possibility of death, and in dying, they teach us with humor and with love, about the preciousness of life and living.

REFERENCES

Australian Institute of Health and Welfare (AIHW). (2007). *Young Australians, their health and wellbeing* (AIHW cat. no. PHE 87). Canberra: AIHW. Retrieved May, 26, 2008, from http://www.aihw.gov.au/publications/index.cfm/title/10451 (pp. 19–20).

Bartholome, W. G. (1982). Good intentions become imperfect in an imperfect world. In J. Van Eys (Ed.) *Children with cancer: Mainstreaming and reintegration* (pp. 17–33). Lancaster, England: MTP Press.

Bennett, D. L. (1985). Young people and their health needs: A global perspective. *Seminars in Adolescent Medicine, 1,* 1–14.

CanTeen Focus Groups. (1991–1993). *Archival videotapes.* St. Pauls, New South Wales, Australia: CanTeen.

Carr-Gregg, M., & White, L. (1987). The adolescent with cancer: A psychological overview. *The Medical Journal of Australia, 147,* 496–501.

Chang, P-N., Nesbit, M., Youngren, N., & Robinson, L. (1987). Personality characteristics and psychosocial adjustment of long-term survivors of childhood cancer. *Journal of Psychosocial Oncology* 5(4), 43–58.

Deem, R. (1986). *All work and no play? A study of women and leisure.* Milton Keynes, England: Open University Press.

Dunsmore, J. C. (1992). *Too much too young? Adolescents with cancer: An exploration of their needs and perceptions of how cancer has made them different from others their age* [Treatise]. University of Sydney, Australia.

Dunsmore, J. C. (2002). The laughter and the tears: Getting behind the mask in adolescent grief. *Grief Matters: The Australian Journal of Grief and Bereavement,* 5(2), 26–30.

Dunsmore, J. C., & Quine, S. (1995). Information, support, and decision-making needs and preferences of adolescents with cancer: Implications for health professionals. *Journal of Psychosocial Oncology, 13*(4), 39–56.

Foley, G. V., & Whittam, E. H. (1990). Care of the child dying of cancer: 1. *CA: A Cancer Journal for Clinicians, 40,* 327–354.

Fuller, A., McGraw, K., & Goodyear, M. (2002). Bungy jumping through life: A developmental framework for the promotion of resilience. In L. Rowling, G. Martin, & L. Walker (Eds.), *Mental health promotion and young people: Concepts and practice* (pp. 84–96). Sydney: McGraw-Hill.

Giedd, J. N., Blumenthal J., Jeffries, N. O., Castellanos, F., Liu, H., Zijdenbos, A., Paul, T., Evans, A., & Rapoport, J. L. (1999). Brain development during childhood and adolescence: A longitudinal MRI study. *Nature Neuroscience, 2*(10), 861–863.

Inhelder, B., & Piaget, J. (1958). *The growth of logical thinking: From childhood to adolescence.* New York: Basic Books.

Katz, E. R., Rubinstein, C. L., Hubert, N. C., & Bleu, A. (1988). School and social reintegration of children with cancer. *Journal of Psychosocial Oncology, 6*(3/4), 123–140.

Koocher, G. P., & O'Malley, J. E. (1981). *The Damocles syndrome: Psychosocial consequences of surviving childhood cancer.* New York: McGraw-Hill.

Levenson, P., Pfefferbaum, B., Copeland, D., & Silverberg, Y. (1982). Information preferences of cancer patients aged 11–20 years. *Journal of Adolescent Health Care, 3,* 9–13.

National Institute of Mental Health (2001). *Teenage brain: A work in progress.* Retrieved May 26, 2008, from http://www.nimh.nih.gov/health/publications/teenage-brain-a-work-in-progress.shtml

Piaget, J., & Inhelder, B. (1969). *The psychology of the child.* London: Routledge & Kegan Paul.

Resnick, M. D. (2000). Protective factors, resiliency, and healthy youth development. *Adolescent Medicine: State of the Art Reviews, 11*(1), 157–164.

Sawyer, S. M., Drew, S., Yeo, M. S., & Britto, M. T. (2007). Adolescents with a chronic condition: Challenges living, challenges treating. *Lancet, 369,* 1481.

Steinbeck, K. S., Brodie, L., & Towns, S. J. (2007). Transition care for young people with chronic illness. *International Journal of Adolescent Medicine & Health, 19*(3), 295–303.

Stevens, M. M. (2004). Care of the dying child and adolescent: Family adjustment and support. In D. Doyle, G. Hanks, N. I. Cherny, & K. Calman (Eds.), *Oxford textbook of palliative medicine* (3rd ed., pp. 806–822). Oxford, UK: Oxford University Press.

Stevens, M. M., & Dunsmore, J. C. (1996a). Adolescents who are living with a life-threatening illness. In C. A. Corr & D. E. Balk (Eds.), *Handbook of adolescent death and bereavement* (pp. 107–135). New York: Springer Publishing.

Stevens, M. M., & Dunsmore, J. C. (1996b). Helping adolescents who are coping with a life-threatening illness, along with their siblings, parents, and peers. In C. A. Corr & D. E. Balk (Eds.), *Handbook of adolescent death and bereavement* (pp. 329–353). New York: Springer Publishing.

Stroebe, M. S. (2001). Bereavement research and theory: Retrospective and prospective. *American Behavioral Scientist, 44*(5), 854–865.

Stroebe, M. S., & Schut, H. A. (1999). The dual process of coping with bereavement: Rationale and description. *Death Studies, 23*(3), 29–31.

Towns, S. J., Sawyer, S. M., Stephens, L., Clarke, S. D., & Bennett, D. L. (2007). Hospital based care of young people in Australia. *International Journal of Adolescent Medicine & Health, 19,* 317–23.

Van Dongen-Melman, J. E., Pruyn, J. F., Van Zanen, G. E., & Sanders-Woudstra, J. (1986). Coping with childhood cancer: A conceptual view. *Journal of Psychosocial Oncology*, *4*(1/2), 147–161.

Weinberger, D. R., Elvevåg, B., & Giedd, J. N. (2005). *The adolescent brain: A work in progress.* Paper for the National Campaign to Prevent Teen Pregnancy. Retrieved May 26, 2008, from http://www.alateenpregnancy.com/reports/BRAIN.pdf

Yeo, M., & Sawyer, S. M. (2003). Strategies to promote better outcomes in young people with chronic illnesses. *Annals of Academic Medicine Singapore*, *32*, 36–42.

8 Adolescents, Humor, and Death

DONNA L. SCHUURMAN AND JANA DeCRISTOFARO

"A funny thing happened on the way to the cemetery," 16-year-old Aaron shared in his teen grief support group at The Dougy Center for Grieving Children & Families in Portland, Oregon. "My dad was into hunting, and on the drive to the cemetery we passed a big black-and-white sign near a field that said, 'No target shooting,' and it was just riddled with bullet holes. He would have laughed at that, and I did too, and it made me feel like he was with me in some way, even then." The other teens nodded and smiled, opening a half hour discussion about ways they felt their deceased parent or sibling still "showed up" in their lives. Many of the examples included humor.

Numerous examples discussed later in this chapter look at how humor evolves in adolescents, the kinds of humor they find relevant, differences between boys and girls, benefits of laughter, and the role humor plays in the adolescent social setting. But despite the important role humor plays in the lives of teens, the subject of humor in the specific population of teens grieving a death has received minimal attention in the professional literature.

Several studies have explored how teens use humor and how it contributes to their social relationships, including how it facilitates learning and coping with adverse life events (Erickson & Feldstein, 2007; Lyons, 2005; Sanford & Eder, 1984). Others discuss the cognitive development of the brain and how that impacts children's ability to understand different types of humor (Glenwright, 2007; McGhee, 1989; Washington University, 2007). And while there is some literature about the use of humor in counseling and other mental health settings, including considerations for working with culturally diverse populations, the research on humor and adolescents grieving a death is sparse. (Jones, 2004; Maples et al., 2001; Vereen, Butler, Williams, Darg, & Downing, 2006).

WHAT IS HUMOR?

Humor is a funny thing, its intended success dependent on a range of variables, including developmental age, social background, culture, timing, and context. What one person finds funny may appall another, and what a person finds humorous is relative to his or her circumstances, state of mind, and present situation. And intended humor may sometimes fall flat.

According to the *Merriam-Webster's Student Dictionary* (2007), humor is "a changeable state of mind often influenced by circumstances," and "the power to see or tell about the amusing or comic side of things." Its origin from the Middle Ages ties into the belief that a person's health and disposition were the result of a balance or imbalance of fluids in the body called *humors,* from the Latin word meaning *moisture.* These four fluids—blood, phlegm, yellow bile, and black bile—were thought to regulate a person's disposition, as cheerful, sluggish, gloomy, or melancholy, respectively.

WHAT KINDS OF HUMOR ARE THERE?

Some studies classify humor as positive or negative, and affiliative or aggressive, particularly within friendships and close relationships (De Konig & Weiss, 2002; Erickson & Feldstein, 2007). In a study of married couples, De Konig & Weiss (2002) found that some couples use positive humor as a way to reconnect or enhance closeness, while others utilized humor as a way to change the subject if tension arose. Some couples used negative humor as a way to express dissatisfaction, irritation, and anger in an ambiguous way. Erickson and Feldstein studied teen participants and identified affiliative humor as a means to strengthen relationships. This humor includes telling funny stories, laughing with others, and making jokes. Seen as "positive," this use of humor also "moderates the effects of stress through more positive appraisals and more realistic cognitive processing of environmental information" (Erickson & Feldstein, 2007, p. 257). In their study, affiliative humor was associated with approach coping, a method of engaging as a way to face challenges in life. It was also positively correlated with personal adjustment and negatively correlated with depressive symptoms.

Aggressive humor was identified as a way to enhance oneself at the expense of others and their relationships. This type of humor involved excessive self-defeating, sarcastic, and self-disparaging remarks. The researchers labeled this humor as avoidance coping. Aggressive or so-called negative humor was positively associated with increased depression, anxiety, and aggression, and negatively correlated with self-esteem and psychological well-being. Self-defeating humor was "uniquely predictive of depressive symptoms above and beyond coping and defense contributions" (Erickson & Feldstein, 2007, p. 268). Further, self-defeating humor "involves enhancing one's relationship with others to the detriment of the self," indicating that this humor is particularly common during adolescence as children work to create strong bonds with their peers (Erickson & Feldstein, 2007, p. 268).

A common sentiment about humor of whatever type is that the setting and timing color whether it is received as affiliative or aggressive. This influence is particularly evident in humor commonly referred to as *dark* or *gallows.* Defined as "humor that makes fun of a life-threatening, disastrous, or terrifying situation" (Merriam-Webster's online dictionary, http://www.mw4.m-w.com), its recipients may find it humorous under extremely specialized conditions and offensive under others.

Specific types of humor include *blue humor,* common among teenagers, which is based on easily offensive subjects like sex, body parts, and bodily functions. *Blunder humor* is wit based on a person who makes a mistake, which makes them appear foolish, also a common form of amusement among adolescents. *Wisecrack humor* revolves around clever remarks about a particular person or thing, including quick wordplays about a person or event. *Repartee humor* includes clever replies and retorts, with the most common form being the insult. The form of humor known as *sarcasm,* which Dostoevsky (1961) called "the last refuge of shy pure persons against those who rudely and insistently try to break into their hearts," (p. 167) characteristically cuts down a person, group of people, or event in a way that is often received as biting. *Satire* is sarcasm that makes fun of something, but in order for it to be understood, there must be a shared or understood context for the satire (Audrieth, 1998).

"Satire, parody, and cartoons have a way of delivering a very real message without actually coming out and saying what they mean. These elements are the 'gray areas' of language and communication. Sometimes we laugh so that we don't cry" (Parker, 2007).

We laugh "because the answer is so unexpected and shocking. You see, there has to be that element of surprise and shock in every joke—the thing that's called the twist, or the gimmick, or the punch, or the topper, or the tag-line, or the gag line; but whatever you call it, it's got to be a surprise, a shock, and that's what makes you laugh. There are so many different kinds of humor: there's wit, satire, parody, caricature, burlesque, and just plain clowning around" (Bernstein, n.d.).

In this sense, death itself is the ultimate joke because there's nothing more unexpected for a teenager than having a parent or a sibling or even a friend die. It's out of order and the opposite of what's supposed to happen. While it's not a laughing matter when someone dies, the shock and surprise explains a piece of what many teens encounter when first telling someone about the death. Many teens talk about peers who responded to the news with "what, you're joking, no way," which many of them found hurtful. They're upset that anyone would think they could joke about that, and it's uncomfortable to have to defend their story—to prove that the person died.

WHAT DO WE (THINK WE) KNOW ABOUT TEENS AND HUMOR?

Understanding humor "is a result of resolving incongruities—resolving the conflict between the expected and the actual, which requires a combination of cognitive skills" (Washington University, 2007). It requires abstract reasoning, short-term memory, and cognitive flexibility, which are "complex, higher mental functions believed to be associated with the frontal lobes" (Baycrest Center for Geriatric Care, 2003). Frontal lobe development in adolescents is ongoing, and a full discussion is beyond the scope of this topic, though most adolescents are capable of understanding a full range of humor, dependent again on the context, their experience, and cognitive reasoning.

Sanford and Eder (1984) studied teenagers during lunch periods and identified four types of humor commonly used by students: (a) memorized jokes, (b) practical jokes, (c) funny stories, and, (d) humorous behavior. They found that memorized jokes were often a means for teens to talk about sex and sexual topics. Jokes were a safe way for them to address this topic without "being held accountable for precise meanings or details" (p. 237). Teens used jokes about adult matters as a way to prove to their peers that they were mature or worthy of being with older students. Jokes were a way to demonstrate their knowledge about subjects that are generally considered taboo or off-limits. Memorized jokes were also most often shared with new acquaintances.

Practical jokes appeared to serve opposing purposes—either to strengthen friendships or to make fun of people outside the accepted circle of friends. Funny stories were reserved for established friends and, rather than focus on taboo subjects, were grounded in the details of teens' everyday lives, incorporating events from school, friendships, family, sports, and daily life.

Humorous behavior was expressed both verbally and nonverbally; often it was behavior used to act out off-limits concepts that teens are curious about like sexual development, drugs, and bodily functions. Humor allows teens to delve into unknown topics in an ambiguous way. They can joke about ideas and opinions without having to take responsibility for any part. "Humor was found to play an important role in peer interactions. Its indirect nature allowed adolescents to discuss sensitive topics and convey feelings towards others without being held accountable" (Sanford & Eder, 1984, p. 243).

Some teens specialize in self-disparaging humor, sarcasm, and verbal put-downs. According to the University of Manitoba's Melanie Glenwright, "sarcasm is something we don't 'get' until a certain point in our childhood stage of development, late in our primary years." In studies over a 6-year period, Glenwright "found that children tend to be literal thinkers and their ability to perceive and process sarcasm is developed over time." She hypothesizes that although children are able to detect sarcasm at about age six, they don't understand the intended humor behind it until at least age 10 (Glenwright, 2007).

Another study by Professor Sam Shuster points to a gender difference in humor. After spending a year unicycling around towns in England, Shuster found that 75% of the male spectators responded with snide or combative remarks, as opposed to 5% of females who responded similarly. His findings also indicate that humor changes with age as boys responded with curiosity in early childhood but switched to more aggressive words and physical actions when they entered adolescence. With females, Shuster noted that as children and young teenagers, girls were almost nonreactive. When they reached adulthood, most women responded with praise, encouragement, or concern (*British Medical Journal*, 2007).

THE BENEFITS OF HUMOR

Numerous studies have demonstrated benefits of humor: it assists us physically, cognitively, emotionally, and behaviorally. When we laugh or are amused, our bodies feel more at ease and energized. Cognitively, we are able to take on a larger perspective when humor is introduced, and this effect decreases rigid or automatic thought patterns. Emotionally, it is difficult for two emotional states to occur at exactly the same time so someone can't laugh and feel depressed in the exact same moment.

Humor Has Physical Benefits

Current research focuses on the physical and emotional benefits of humor. A number of studies in the medical and nursing field support the idea that humor and laughter are integral components of health and healing (Balick & Lee, 2003; Canisius College, 2008; Maples et al., 2001; Richman, 2006; Schwartz, 2007; Sultanoff, 1997; Texas A&M University, 2005). Laughter has been shown to create a eustress state, which produces healthy emotions and supports the immune system by increasing b-cells, t-cells, the antibody IgA, which fights upper respiratory infections, and gamma-interferon, a disease fighting protein. It also decreases the release of stress hormones that can lead to high blood pressure, heart disease, and weight gain (Beck, Felten, Tan, Bittman, & Westengard, 2001).

Some studies show that "laughter reduces high blood pressure, increases optimism and hope, and reduces stress" (Schwartz, 2007). Other evidence that laughter is good for the physical body is illustrated in a study of patients who viewed a 60-minute comedy, after which they showed a decrease in dopamine, epinephrine, and cortisol levels, which normally increase during stressful situations (Balick & Lee, 2003).

Sultanoff (1997) identifies how accumulated stressors tax our immune systems, leaving us vulnerable to physical illnesses and emotional wear and tear. This accumulated stress can affect an adolescent's ability to attend school, complete assignments, form healthy friendships, and successfully renegotiate ever-changing relationships with the adults in his or her life. Laughter and humor stimulate the production of immunoglobulin A, an immune booster, which helps to protect a teen's physical well being. Laughter and humor also work to increase emotional resilience, allowing for the possibility for perceiving options about how to respond to new stressful situations.

Humor Helps Us Connect With Others

One of the tenets of successful humor is the ability to understand the intended funniness in it. Researchers have found that humor may be used as a tool to develop social connections and strengthen relationships (affiliative) or to create distance from others (aggressive, negative humor) (De Konig & Weiss, 2002; Erickson & Feldstein, 2007; Sanford & Eder, 1984).

When used affiliatively, "humor has been found to increase group cohesion, reduce stress, and offer therapeutic opportunities" (Maples et al., 2001). It "helps us connect with others" (Association for Applied and Therapeutic Humor, 2008).

Humor Gives Us a Different Perspective and Shifts the Way We Think

A number of studies and anecdotal information confirm humor's ability to help people see themselves and their life challenges in a new way (Clarke, 2003; Jones, 2004; McGhee, 1989). Humor can open people up and help them relax enough to tune into what they already understand or don't understand about themselves. Laughter and the accompanying ability to see circumstances with a sense of humor and perspective can lessen anxiety. It's difficult to laugh and be worried at the exact same moment. Humor can help to lengthen the times in between intense sadness or fear. Since humor is based on twisting the expected into an unexpected outcome, perhaps that enables people to think creatively and see their situations in new, flexible ways. "Humor in counseling provides students with the 'reality check' necessary to realize that their experiences and feelings are natural and not uncommon" (Maples et al., 2001, p. 59).

Humor Can Serve as a Coping Mechanism

From a counseling perspective, a sense of humor is a protective factor, allowing people to put their life struggles and insecurities in a context bigger than themselves (Corey, 1996; Jones, 2004; Vereen et al., 2006). Humor can be a way to generate some space between a person and his or her pain, introducing the buffering effect of acknowledging a common experience as well as the physiological improvements from laughter. A 1996 study by the Association for Applied and Therapeutic Humor (2008) found that "happiness is directly related to humor, not merely life circumstances." Regardless of what tragedies befell people, their attitude and access to humor and laughter acted as buffers (Clarke, 2003).

Humor is a way to express oneself in difficult, heartbreaking conditions without having to be direct or serious. It may help diffuse difficult or potentially embarrassing situations and reduce the stress or anxiety often inherent in highly charged emotional circumstances. "Research in using cognitive behavioral interventions in a range of situations has suggested that humor can be a very effective mechanism for coping with acute stress" (Jones, 2004, p. 33).

Humor Can Increase Hope

Because "humor replaces distressing emotions with pleasurable emotions" (Association for Applied and Therapeutic Humor, 2008) it can act as a destressor to help us regain emotional control over a situation. It may help us step outside of ourselves, so to speak, in order to see the world, and our place in it, from a different vantage point. In so doing, it may open us up to multiple options for coping with difficulties, and increase the sense of hope, even in difficult circumstances.

ADOLESCENTS GRIEVING A DEATH AND HUMOR

Aside from the obvious difficulty of facing the death of someone in their lives, multiple additional factors may interfere with, shift, and adjust an adolescent's perspective regarding humor. Joking around may be harder to do because the teen doesn't want to be judged by others as not caring. He or she may believe it's not okay to laugh or joke because it could be perceived as an affront to the memory of the deceased. Some teens may resist humor because they are attached to their current feeling state: "Don't make me laugh; I want to be angry, depressed, and sad right now." Additionally, because friendships often shift and change after a death, they may not have as many (or the same) friends to joke and bond with.

On the flip side, because of humor, bereaved adolescents certainly have more material to work with, and humor among grieving teens often veers to the weird, odd, or unusual things people do or say following a death. As McGhee (1989) points out, after a death, they are immersed in a new world of hospitals, emergency response personnel, funeral directors, funeral items, grief rituals, and common social responses. Adolescents get to know the theme of grief and loss and then have a new realm of associations to find humor in.

For example, a teen theater troupe at the Dougy Center wrote and performed a skit about a cooking show, with a famous chef doing so-called grief food. They poked fun at the idea that food can heal the hurt, that people tend to bring the same items (like casseroles, perhaps because they're easy to freeze), and that some people use food as a way to avoid talking to grievers. A skit includes this line from "Chef Smith": "Now, the best way to deliver the 'grief casserole' is to tiptoe up to the front door, put the casserole on the welcome mat, ring the doorbell, and then run like hell back to your car before you actually have to talk to the grieving person."

DeSpelder and Strickland (2004) describe three ways humor is connected to death:

1. It brings a taboo subject into the conversation, allowing us to talk about it freely.
2. It provides an alternative, if only momentarily, to the gripping sadness, and a chance to release some physical and emotional tension.
3. Humor is an equalizer, bringing people together over shared experiences, increasing a sense of commonality and "in it together"-ness.

Humor "aids us in confronting our fears and gaining a sense of mastery over the unknown" (DeSpelder & Strickland, 2004, p.17).

Grieving teens who have peers to identify with, either in formal support groups or through more informal networks, may develop new friendships with those who can identify with the experience of loss. "Situations that might not seem funny to us, as outside observers, provoke laughter, smiles, and joking among certain cultures . . .[humor is] a device for passing along lessons and traditions through storytelling" (Balick & Lee, 2003, p. 88). If we believe grieving teens constitute a separate cultural group, then it follows that they would have stories and humorous anecdotes that "outsiders" wouldn't be able to relate to in the same way. Part of what draws grievers together is this ability to share the darkly comedic moments with others who will understand what they are talking about and not judge them as unfeeling, cold, or twisted. It is with other grievers that teens who are dealing with a significant death can talk freely about the thoughts and interactions that are funny in the context of grief. Sharing these stories with each other helps to build a sense of community and mutual understanding that lessens the isolating impacts of grief.

Many grieving teens will relay humorous stories about different aspects of the death that outsiders might not find funny. One teen spoke of going to the funeral home and looking through the caskets and urns when she came across a locket used to hold a portion of cremated remains. Her family ended up laughing about the locket saying, "Why in the world would you want to split up the ashes into a locket? You could end up with a nose or the big toe!" Another teen talked about returning home with her mother's cremated remains. When she went through security at the airport and was asked about the box contents, she replied, "It's mom, we're taking her home," which prompted a series of strange looks from the security staff.

Other teens talk about using funny comments or one-liners to defuse potentially stressful, uncomfortable, or deeply emotional moments. On Thanksgiving, Marla's family gathered at the grave of her mother who had died from a heart attack that summer: "It was freezing cold and muddy so we huddled together to keep warm. My sister said 'look at this, mom managed to get us all together for Thanksgiving.'" Another teen's family took his dad's favorite lemon pie to the grave on Memorial Day. Once there, they decided it would be a waste to leave it and that their dad would want them to eat it. They didn't have any forks or spoons so they just dug in with their hands, getting pie all over their faces: "We were sure Dad was getting a good laugh at us."

Another teen theater troupe at the Dougy Center wrote and performed a skit where each member picked a different metaphor for what grief felt like to him or her and acted that out with noise and movement. The examples were a curious combination of serious emotional content and humorous delivery. Fifteen-year-old Adam spoke of feeling as though Godzilla had tromped through his life, destroying everything in his path. This heavy and sad image was turned into something funny as the troupe members stomped around, exaggerating the sounds and movements of Godzilla. It seemed to be a way to talk about the enormous impact the deaths had on their lives, emotionally and physically, without being solemn or somber in describing how they were affected.

Many teens describe having difficulty accessing humor and laughter in the wake of the loss. "It's hard to be lighthearted now; I can't relax enough to find anything funny. I used to laugh all of the time, but since my dad died I'm so serious," says Claudia, 14, whose dad died from cancer less than a year ago. Another teen, whose mom died from pancreatic cancer 6 months ago, talked about how her sense of humor changed dramatically after the death: "Things that I used to think were funny like TV shows and movies just aren't anymore; now I just think they're stupid and they don't make me laugh." This shifting sense of humor also played out in her family system. "This year at Christmas we didn't have the same funny family jokes because my mom was always part of them and without her there no one wanted to say anything," she says. Another teen, Linda, described a similar situation where what she once found funny in the company of her mother has lost its humorous element. Linda is a competitive ice skater, and her mom used to be at every show, helping her to laugh and be silly about the things that went wrong. "It's hard to find the humor now; when I do something wrong I just beat myself up when before my mom would've helped me to laugh about it," says Linda.

On the other end of the spectrum are the teens who turn to humor as a way to cope with the death. "These days I'm excessively sarcastic—I try to make everything around me funny," says Nick, 17, whose mom died a year ago. Mary, whose older brother died in a car crash, had this to say: "On bad days I laugh at everything. It's like half of my brain is sad and the other half is jittery and really awake so I get all hyper. It makes me feel better and since his death, I'm even more this way."

When asked about how the death has changed their sense of humor, almost every teen talked about the "your mother" jokes that are so prevalent in their peer groups. For those teens that have had a mother die, these comments provoke a wide range of strong emotions from rage to sadness. Some teens' reactions are so strong they end up in physical fights with the person making the comments. While some teens will reply "my mom's dead," others become too upset to say anything, relying on friends to come to their defense and explain the situation. Even teens that have had a father or sibling die have similar negative reactions to these jokes.

CULTURAL CONSIDERATIONS

A full discussion of the role of humor in different cultural groups and settings is beyond the scope of this chapter, but it is an important consideration to be mindful of. Regardless of the cultural group, it is important to remember that what might be funny for one culture or cultural subgroup may not translate that way to another. "What is considered to be humor between two people in one situation can be interpreted in another situation as ridicule or wearing a mask if trust and a sense of connection . . . are absent" (Maples et al., 2001, p. 55). Grieving teens represent a cultural subgrouping with their own set of humorous topics. Establishing a common language and atmosphere of mutual respect will set the stage for everyone to use humor in an appropriate way.

SUMMARY AND FURTHER RESEARCH

Not surprisingly, adolescents' experience of humor recalibrates after the death of a family member or friend. While some may find it hard to see humor in anything, others are comforted by the wry and ironic aspects of coping with loss. More research on the role of humor in grieving teens' lives may shed light on how humor may serve as a protective factor following a loss through death.

REFERENCES

Association for Applied and Therapeutic Humor. (2008). Retrieved July 28, 2008, from http://www.aath.org

Audrieth, A. L. (1998). The art of using humor in public speaking. Retrieved July 28, 2008, from http://www.squaresail.com/auh.html#types

Balick, M., & Lee, R. (2003). The role of laughter in traditional medicine and its relevance to the clinical setting: Healing with ha! *Alternative Therapies*, 9(4), 88–91.

Baycrest Center for Geriatric Care. (2003, August 25). Appreciation of humor doesn't change with age. *ScienceDaily*. Retrieved August 2, 2008, from http://www.sciencedaily.com/releases/2003/08/03082507356.htm

Beck, L. S., Felten, D. L., Tan, S. A., Bittman, B. B., & Westengard, J. (2001). Modulation of neuroimmune parameters during the eustress of humor-associated mirthful laughter. *Alternative Therapies*, 7(2), 62–76.

Bernstein, L. (n.d.) *Young people's concerts.* New York, NY: Amberson Holdings LLC. Retrieved August 4, 2008, from http://www.leonardbernstein.com/studio/element2.asp?id=388

British Medical Journal. (2007, December 23). Humor develops from aggression caused by male hormones, professor says. *ScienceDaily*. Retrieved August 2, 2008, from http://www.sciencedaily.com/releases/2007/12/071220195636.htm

Canisius College. (2008, January 26). Laughter is the best medicine. *ScienceDaily*. Retrieved August 2, 2008, from http://www.sciencedaily.com/releases/2008/01/080124200913.htm

Clarke, C. V. (2003, May). The healing power of laughter: Liberal doses of humor are a proven prescription for wellness. *Black Enterprise.* Retrieved July 28, 2008, from http://findarticles.com/p/articles/mi_m1365

Corey, G. (1996). *Theory and practice of counseling and psychotherapy.* Pacific Grove, CA: Brooks/Cole.

De Konig, E., & Weiss, R. L. (2002). The relational humor inventory: Functions of humor in close relationships. *The American Journal of Family Therapy, 30,* 1–18.

DeSpelder, L. A., & Strickland, A. L. (2004). *The last dance: Encountering death and dying* (7th ed.). New York: McGraw Hill.

Dostoevsky, F. M. (1961). *Notes from the underground.* New York: Signet. (Original work published 1864)

Erickson, S. J., & Feldstein, S. W. (2007). Adolescent humor and its relationship to coping, defense strategies, psychological distress, and well-being. *Child Psychiatry Human Development, 37,* 255–271.

Glenwright, M. (2007, August 9). Getting sarcastic with kids. *Science Daily.* Retrieved August 2, 2008, from http://www.sciencedaily.com/releases/2007/08/070803141811.htm

Jones, C. P. (2004). Humor in the therapy room. *Counselling & Psychotherapy Journal, 15*(10), 32–33.

Lyons, S. (2005). Laugh and learn: Using humor to reach and teach teens. *Houston Teachers Institute* (pp. 120–137). Retrieved August 1, 2008, from http://www.hti.math.uh.edu/curriculum/guides/2005/05/05.05.08.php

Maples, M. F., Dupey, P., Torres-Rivera, E., Phan, L. T., Vereen, L., & Garrett, M. T. (2001). Ethnic diversity and the use of humor in counseling: Appropriate or inappropriate. *Journal of Counseling & Development, 79,* 53–60.

McGhee, P. (Ed.). (1989). *Humor and children's development: A guide to practical applications.* New York: Routledge.

Merriam-Webster's Student Dictionary. (2007). Retrieved July 10, 2008, from http://www.wordcentral.com/cgi-bin/student

Merriam-Webster's Online Dictionary. Retrieved July 10, 2008, from http://www.mw4.m-w.com

Parker, D. (2007). *Gifted Children and Humor.* Retrieved July 23, 2008, from http://gifteducation.suite101.com

Richman, J. (2006). The role of psychotherapy and humor for death anxiety, death wishes, and aging. *Omega, Journal of Death and Dying, 54*(1), 41–51.

Sanford, S., & Eder, D. (1984). Adolescent humor during peer interaction. *Social Psychology Quarterly, 47*(3), 235–243.

Schwartz, A. N. (2007). *Humor is a laughing matter.* MentalHelp.net. Retrieved July 30, 2008, from http://www.mentalhelp.net/poc/view_index.php?idx=119&d=1&w=5&e=151

Sultanoff, S. M. (1997). Survival of the witty-est: Creating resilience through humor. *Therapeutic Humor, 11*(5), 1–2.

Texas A&M University. (2005, February 11). Humor can increase hope, research shows. *ScienceDaily.* Retrieved August 2, 2008, from http://www.sciencedaily.com/releases/2005/02/050211095658.htm

Vereen, L., Butler, S., Williams, F, Darg, J., & Downing, T. (2006). The use of humor when counseling African American students. *Journal of Counseling & Development, 84,* 10–15.

Washington University in St. Louis (2007, August 2). Older folks don't get the joke, researchers find. *ScienceDaily.* Retrieved August 1, 2008, from http://www.sciencedaily.com/releases/2007/07/0707/3114/5027.htm

9 Adolescents, Technology, and the Internet: Coping With Loss in the Digital World

CARLA J. SOFKA

Technology is pervasive within teen culture (Pascoe, 2007), with the Pew Internet and American Life Project reporting that 93% of teens use the Internet (Lenhart, Madden, Macgill, & Smith, 2007). The current generation of adolescents—referred to by Bunn (2000) as the "young Turks of technology"—has also been has been described as "growing up online" (PBS, 2008); "coming of age online" (Harris, 2005); Generation MySpace (Kelsey, 2007); and webheads, keyboard kids, cyberchildren, and the Digital Generation (Montgomery, 2007). Blais, Craig, Pepler, and Connolly (2008) note that the Internet is a "significant aspect of the educational, social, and recreational experiences of adolescents" (p. 535). In light of the fact that individuals under the age of 30 have never known a world where the Internet did not exist in some form (Whitaker, 2002), parents whose children have experienced loss, as well as professionals providing services to bereaved adolescents, would be wise to recognize the roles that the Internet and other forms of technology may have in their process of coping with loss. In what ways are adolescents using this *thanatechnology* (Sofka, 1997)—the Internet and other resources in the digital world that are available to help them deal with death and grief? This chapter describes the appeal of digital technology among teenagers; summarizes the technology that is available for use by adolescents and how it may be used to cope with thanatology-related issues; identifies the potential benefits and risks of these resources; and discusses implications for parents, clinicians, death educators, and researchers.

THE APPEAL OF TECHNOLOGY AND THE INTERNET AMONG TEENAGERS

Why have teenagers been captivated by resources in the digital world? What's not to like about technologies that combine access to digital information with technologies for communicating with others—also referred to as information and communication technologies, or ICTs (Harris, 2005)? A growing body of literature is available to describe the study of *cyberculture,* an area of research concerned with "questions about who we are and the world we live in as affected by digital technologies" (Whitaker, 2002, p. 131). A multitude of reasons have been identified to explain the widespread use of technology among adolescents. First, more than ever before, teens are treating the Internet as a venue for social interaction (Lenhart et al., 2007). According to Pascoe (2007), social-networking sites (SNSs) are extremely popular because teen culture at this time in our country is a social culture. The digital world is a perfect example of a *participatory culture,* defined by Jenkins, Clinton, Purushotma, Robison, and Weigel (2006) as a culture with relatively low barriers to civic engagement and artistic expression, strong support for creating and sharing one's creations with others, and a process whereby the most experienced members share what is known through some type of informal mentorship. Members of participatory cultures also believe that their contributions matter, even if they don't actively contribute—"but all must believe they are free to contribute when ready and that what they contribute will be appropriately valued" (Jenkins et al., 2006, p. 7). Members also feel some degree of social connection with one another.

Second, the Internet provides adolescents with a great deal of independence, a "private space even while they're still at home" (Pascoe, 2007, p. 3). Teenagers are also attracted to the immediacy of the process of posting and receiving responses (Keller, as quoted in Natekar, 2007; Brett, as quoted in Siad, 2007), as well as having a sense of control over what little discretionary time they have available (Harris, 2005).

Third, adolescence is a time of exploration regarding one's own values and identity, and many young adults are using resources online to express and explore their forming identities (Schmitt, Dayanim, & Matthias, 2008).

While adolescents struggle with issues that may not be easy to discuss with parents or peers, Hellenga (2002) notes that Internet communication can provide a relatively safe and anonymous way to gain information and support. According to Whitaker (2002), a great deal of thought on how the Internet is impacting our identity revolves around whether access to and use of technology influences our perceptions of ourselves and how we are perceived by others. Dretzin (2008) ponders the interplay between online identity and actual identity, wondering how this interaction plays out during adolescence, a time when identity is profoundly in flux.

Fourth, adolescents who experience marginalization in their everyday life can find a sense of community online (Pascoe, 2007). Since traditionally oppressed or voiceless groups are speaking out online, Internet-savvy teenagers can be connected with others, gaining a sense of empowerment that may not otherwise be achievable (Hellenga, 2002).

Servaty and Hayslip (2001) note that loss among adolescents may alter their perception of interpersonal relationships, resulting in social isolation and a lack of social support at a time when these relationships are a crucial part of identity development and well-being. Bereaved teens can experience a heightened sense of vulnerability and a sense of difference or stigma (McCarthy, 2007). It seems logical that identifying oneself as a bereaved adolescent in an online environment where being a grieving teenager is the norm has the potential to create a sense of sameness.

Finally, technology is dramatically changing the speed at which teenagers gain tragic news, as well as the way that they mourn (Burrell, 2007). Therefore, thanatologists would be wise to learn as much as possible about the topic referred to by Natekar (2007) as *egrieving.*

ONLINE COMMUNITIES OF BEREAVEMENT

Following the events at Columbine High School, Linenthal (as quoted in Niebuhr & Wilgoren, 1999) noted that the creation of shrines following tragic deaths might indicate the desire to overcome feelings of powerlessness, to experience a sense of unity as a community of bereavement. Because of the fact that this generation has been reared on technology, Atfield, Chalmers, and Lion (2006) note that it seems only logical that teenagers turn to cyberspace during times of grief, sometimes immediately following the news of a tragedy (e.g., Siad, 2007). A variety of online communities of bereavement exist.

The first type of online bereavement community revolves around Web sites that are designed in memory of someone who has died. There are numerous ways that teenagers can use computer skills to memorialize a loved one, friend, or a pet using text, photos, and AV files. Teenagers can add a memorial to an existing online memorial site (e.g., http://www.teensremembered.org/ for teens that lost their lives in vehicle crashes) or a virtual cemetery (e.g., http://www.cemetery.org, http://www.worldgardens.com/). According to Roberts (2006), online memorials are popular because our culture is more accepting of ongoing bonds with the dead.

There are also sites that allow posting information without creating a formal memorial Web page (e.g., http://www.mycemetery.com/my/memorials.html). In addition to memorial information, some Web sites allow the creation of online guest books (e.g., http://www.legacy.com), providing an opportunity for visitors to express condolences or share memories. It is wise to investigate whether the site is free of charge or if a maintenance fee is required to preserve the site and/or the guest books beyond a free trial period. Roberts (2006) noted that 91% of individuals (largely an adult sample) who had participated in some aspect of Web memorialization found it beneficial during their bereavement. It is assumed that teenagers may also find this online participation helpful.

While grief-specific memorial sites are available, teenagers are much more likely to utilize the second type of resource, one that is already a common part of their digital existence—SNSs such as MySpace or Facebook. An SNS is a Web site that uses specialized software to enable people to connect or collaborate to form online communities and communicate with them online (Goodstein, 2007). Some SNSs have message boards that are focused on a particular experience or interest (a.k.a. groups or forums such as the bereavement group on MySpace). Magid and Collier (2007) describe message boards as resources for holding discussions and for asking questions or seeking help or advice. While the conversations are generally more in-depth, real-time personal interactions do not occur since the postings are asynchronous (they are not necessarily posted one immediately after the other—significant time can pass in between the posting and a response). Since message boards may not be monitored and postings may not be screened, users are also reminded of the need to "be careful that you don't say anything inappropriate and have a thick skin in case someone else forgets to mind their manners" (Magid & Collier, 2007, p. 98). Message boards have been used in very creative ways during times of tragedy, such as posting updates about a person's condition following an accident (e.g., St. George, 1999) or being used first as a missing persons site that changed to a condolence site and then being used to monitor the resulting court case and solicit donations to a foundation established in the victim's name (http://www.findingjackiehartman.blogspot.com).

Some SNSs have chat rooms, or online spaces often "organized by categories and topics where people have a conversation by typing and sending short messages to people on the same page in real time" (Magid & Collier, 2007, p. 95). Therefore, what a user types is instantly visible to everyone. These authors note that in-depth conversations are rare and may not be moderated, so a user should be prepared to "leave the room" if a concern arises. Mechanisms are often available to report a user who is being inappropriate or causing a disturbance.

Some SNSs provide users with the opportunity to create a Web log, commonly known as a *blog*—a public diary that is posted online and that the author or *blogger* updates on a more or less regular basis (Levine, Baroudi, & Levine Young, 2007). Posts are typically listed in reverse chronological order, and the creator of the blog usually has the option to allow readers to post responses. Boyd (as quoted in Goodstein, 2007) describes blogging as an extension of normal adolescent communication: "Teens go through a period where they express themselves loudly in order to attract others like them. It's a flocking ritual" (p. 33). Keeping a personal blog was reported by bereaved teens to be useful for "getting emotions out" and "sharing thoughts," and reading someone else's blog was helpful because the teens could "see what they have gone through" and to "know others are going through what I am" (Sofka, 2008).

Goodstein (2007) notes that the most popular blogging applications among teens are LiveJournal, Xanga, and Blogger, with many teens also using a blog as a feature on their MySpace or Facebook accounts. Huffaker and Calvert (2005) describe the possibility that teens experience a sense of empowerment in revealing thoughts and feelings without hiding behind a public mask. However, it is crucial that teens understand the impact of their decision about whether the blog will be public (readable by anyone) or private (the owner of the blog must grant access to other users).

In addition to using their SNS for documenting their experiences, thoughts, and feelings, members of an SNS also have the option of using their personal page to commemorate someone who has died. If the personal page of the deceased is maintained after death, it is also possible to add material if the page is public (open to anyone to post) or if they have been given access to private material on a site (sometimes referred to as being *friended*). Some time ago, Niebuhr and Wilgoren (1999) reported that exposure to violent deaths has grown among teenagers. Perhaps this increased exposure is one reason why adolescents are using these SNSs in fascinating and creative ways following the loss of a friend. Within hours (sometimes minutes) of a tragedy, messages expressing reactions to the tragedy are posted, often including condolence messages to the family. SNSs are being used by grieving teenagers all over the world, including England (e.g., West, 2007), Ireland (e.g., O'Brien, 2008), and Australia (e.g., Blaxland, 2007). For example, following the shooting of a 9th grader, Jordan Manners of Toronto, Canada, a candlelight vigil was quickly organized using Facebook technology, and 26 groups with more than 1,500 members were formed in a single day in memory of the victim (Siad, 2007). Even after an SNS user's death, the deceased's site "beams with life" (Belenkaya, 2006, p. 28). A friend may ask the deceased to watch over them (Natekar, 2007). Anytime, day or night, if a teenager feels alone, he or she can log in and not feel isolated (Horsley, as quoted in Belenkaya, 2006). Goodstein (2007) notes that "profiles that were once filled with light-hearted comments from friends just stopping by to say hello become filled with comments from friends who are grieving. For this generation, the printed obituary written by a newspaper with limited input from the family or a paid death notice is being replaced by online shrines where friends, family, and strangers can all remember the deceased together" (pp. 60–61).

While the use of these sites to create a community of support has the potential to be of great benefit to grieving teenagers, some situations raise concerns about the safety of or appropriateness of the use of some SNSs by this population. One controversial site that may be popular among some teens is MyDeathSpace.com. According to the home page (http://www.mydeathspace.com), "MyDeathSpace.com is an archival site, containing news articles, online obituaries, and other publicly available information. We have given you the opportunity to pay your respects and tributes to the recently deceased MySpace.com members via our comment system. Please be respectful." The entry for this Web site on Wikipedia reports that the sites receive between 15,000 and 20,000 unique visitors each day, with the creator of the site receiving 75% hate mail and 25% fan mail. In addition to the absence of consent by remaining family members or friends to post information on this site and reactions to the logo (a skull), other concerns are documented on "Action Against MyDeathSpace.com" (http://h1.ripway.com/_aamds/_index.html).

Goodstein (2007) notes that while the content posted by teens can be as simple as recording the events of the day or venting feelings out of frustration or anger, some content may appropriately be interpreted as a red flag or a cry for help. Consider postings that involve suicidal ideation or suicide that was linked to being a victim of cyberbullying. Since postings on SNSs have been linked with incidences of suicide (e.g., Megan Meier as discussed in Pokin, 2007; Joshua Ballard as discussed in Gagnon, 2005), there is intense debate about the monitoring of SNS postings versus banning the use of these sites by teenagers.

Does the Internet contribute to suicide among teens? Lee (2008) states: "Some say it's all due to the Internet, to the social-networking sites so beloved of teenagers which are quickly filled with glowing tributes to the dead, providing them with a brief, if dark, moment of fame. I don't buy that. If this were 30 years ago, we'd be blaming the telephone. The net may be a conduit for grief, but not its primary cause" (p. 8).

Malone (as quoted in O'Brien, 2008, p. 16) notes that adolescents may have a notion of "virtual life after death," divorced from the reality and finality of death and its consequences. O'Brien (2008) observes that communities and schools attempting to cope with the aftermath of suicides do so with trepidation. They have to maintain a balance between expressing respect and compassion for the deceased, and sensitivity to the grief and sadness of the bereaved, but without glorifying the action of suicide itself.

While these debates continue, it is reassuring to know that Internet resources exist to provide support to teens dealing with issues related to suicide. One site designed to commemorate those who have taken their own lives also provides links to suicide prevention information (e.g., the Wall of Angels Suicide Memorial at http://www.suicide.org/wall-of-angels-suicide-memorials.html). The parents of a teenager who committed suicide after being bullied on an SNS created a foundation in her memory that has advocated for stronger legislation related to cyberbullying, with Megan Meiers's story and the outcome of these efforts documented online (http://www.megan meierfoundation.org/story/). Draper and Le (as quoted in Magid & Collier, 2007) of the National Suicide Prevention Lifeline report that kids are, at times, using their online profiles to convey suicidal intent. They also note the strong potential for saving lives when there are postings online because "the first people to hear about kids at risk are other kids" (p. 174). Suicide prevention profiles have been set up on MySpace, Xanga, and Facebook to provide easy access to this information to anyone who should need it, and links to this information are highly visible on other relevant pages (e.g., on the MySpace link to the Good Charlotte song "Hold On"). Because of easily available links, these SNSs are a large source of referrals to the suicide prevention hotline. Draper and Le "don't know how many lives can be saved as a result of referrals through social networks, but it's certainly something that should be thought about by policy makers seeking to restrict teens' access to these sites. This is just one powerful example of how monitoring teen social networking can be much more beneficial to teens than banning it" (pp. 174–175).

SUPERCOMMUNICATION: E-MAIL, TEXT MESSAGING, AND INSTANT MESSAGING

Lenhart and colleagues (2007) describe a subset of teens—about 28% of the entire teen population—who are *supercommunicators*: teens with multiple technology options to contact friends, family, and other people with roles in their busy lives. In addition to the SNSs previously described, teens potentially have access to traditional landline phones, cell phones for verbal communication and text messaging (TM), and computers that can be used for instant messaging (IM) and e-mail.

Although e-mail is reported by some adolescents to be too formal to use with friends, they do report using e-mail with teachers and employers (Pascoe, 2007). It is extremely important to note that the published research about the use of digital technology among adolescents that informed the writing of this chapter did not specifically inquire about the use of various forms of technology to cope with loss. Data gathered by this author from a convenience sample of teenagers seeking assistance from a bereavement support organization revealed that some teenagers do use e-mail to seek support from friends while coping with loss (Sofka, 2008). It should also be noted that a professionally moderated support group sponsored by Griefnet.org, which utilizes e-mail as the sole method of communication between group members (k-2-k-teens at http://kidsaid.com/k2k_support.html), has been active and successfully supporting teens aged 13–18 for over a decade (C. Lynn, personal communication, June 19, 2008). E-mail can also be utilized to provide *e-therapy* or online counseling (see Oravec, 2000, as an excellent resource). The use of e-mail as a resource for coping with loss among bereaved teens merits further investigation. While adults often prefer e-mail when using technology to communicate with others, research conducted through the Digital Youth Project has documented that some teenagers may prefer to use TM to communicate with one another (Pascoe, 2007), with e-mail "losing its luster" (Lenhart et al., 2007, p. iv).

Although texting messages to a cell phone or other handheld device may be perceived as lacking intimacy, Pascoe (2007) notes that teens are not rendered vulnerable the same way they are in other person-to-person interactions. Initially contacting someone via TM to begin a conversation may lead to increased intimacy in subsequent communications. No research is currently available to explore the use of these various modes of communication by teens who are seeking support during times of impending loss or grief.

IM may be used by teens who do not have access to a cell phone with TM privileges. This type of computer-mediated communication occurs in real time and therefore is always interactive as opposed to TM, which potentially involves a delayed response if the recipient of the message is not able to respond immediately. IM also has the advantage of enabling communication with more than one person at a time. Research by Blais and colleagues (2008) found that using IM to communicate with best friends had a positive effect on the quality of these friendships. Pascoe (2007) also notes that some teens use IM to have important conversations that cannot be done via a traditional phone or cell phone without the risk of being overheard.

THE GOOGLE STAGE OF GRIEF

While posting to a blog on March 20, 2005, Laura at 11D noted that "maniacal googling is a new stage of grief. After denial and before resignation comes the google stage" (McKenna, 2005). Following the diagnosis of a life-threatening illness or during the grieving process, informational support or factual information about topics involving illness, death, or grief may be useful during the process of coping with these events (Sofka, 1997).

How frequently do adolescents utilize the Internet to gain information about thanatology-related topics? In a survey of 10th graders that explored adolescent cybersurfing for health information, Borzekowski and Rickert (2001) noted that 49% of the sample had used the Internet as a resource to get information about health-related issues including mental health issues, cancer, and other diseases. Following the death of a loved one due to illness, teenagers may need information to alleviate fears that the illness was contagious (Fitzgerald, 2000). While research documenting the use of thantology-specific sites among this age cohort is not currently available, it is important to be familiar with content related to death and grief that is targeted specifically for teens should they seek it out.

Some Web sites are designed for teens (http://teenadvice.about.com/od/deathgrieving/Death_Loss_Grieving.htm) or for teens and adults who have a need for information about this age group (e.g., parents, teachers, helping professionals). For example, Teen Health and Wellness (http://www.teenhealthandwellness.com) has detailed information on death and grief that can be easily located using a keyword search. Beliefnet has an advice column specifically for grieving teens that is written by Helen Fitzgerald (http://www.beliefnet.com/index/index_608.html). To identify additional resources, simply google keywords such as *teen grief* or other combinations, or *teen/adolescent* and the topic of interest, and this search engine will provide links to sites that contain written and AV resources for teens (e.g., http://www.griefworksbc.com/Teens.asp) and resources to help adults provide support to grieving teens (e.g., http://www.hospicenet.org/ html/teenager.html or http://www.dougy.org/default.asp?pid=1276972). Be aware that keyword searches will also locate content unrelated to coping with loss. Because misinformation can easily be posted online, it is important to review content before referring individuals to material posted online.

In addition to sites for informational support, the World Wide Web also contains narrative sites that provide opportunities for grieving teens to read personal stories of others or post their own story (http://www.teencentral.net—type *grief* into the Search-O-Matic—or http://www.webhealing.com/ honor.html) and expressive sites that contain artwork (e.g., http:// kidsaid.com/ storiesnart.html) or poetry (e.g., http://www.newhope-grief.org/teengrief/poetry.html). Adolescents may find it reassuring to discover that the thoughts and reactions of other teens are very similar to their own.

POTENTIAL RISKS AND CHALLENGES IN CYBERSPACE

Teenagers really are using digital technology in their everyday lives. In addition to providing a comfortable environment in which teenagers prefer to interact, there are no barriers regarding transportation and no conflicts between parents' schedules and the timing of an adolescent's desire to interact with friends. While these advantages and other benefits are important, it is crucial to recognize the potential risks and challenges that teenagers may face while using this technology.

The literature documents a wide range of double-edged swords. Hellenga (2002) acknowledges that online communication can provide adolescents who are typically shy or uncomfortable with peers with an alternative socialization ground. Stanfield (as quoted in Natekar, 2007) notes that being online may provide an excuse to avoid face-to-face interactions, which isn't always healthy. Is it possible that adolescents who spend most of their time online would never develop the skills to be successful in face-to-face social interactions (e.g., reading nonverbal social cues, confidently using verbal skills)? Is the quality of social support received online as effective as that provided in person?

While adolescents may find other like-minded teens online who are not easy to find in person, Pascoe (2007) notes that there are also subcultures online that are a little bit more dangerous: "Kids who are marginalized can find community online. . .but for kids who are engaging in pathological behaviors. . .[the Internet] can be incredibly dangerous, because they can find other people who support that kind of behavior" (p. 8). While considering the impact of Internet use on mental health, Hellenga (2002) notes the importance of investigating whether individuals who spend a great deal of time in online activities may be doing so specifically because they are lonely, maladjusted, or unhappy and may require professional help.

Safety online can be defined in a variety of ways. As previously noted, it is important for adolescents to be educated about the differences between *public* and *private* in online environments, together with the potential risks of posting personal information in a public forum. An adolescent's physical safety can be comprised by sharing one's address or making arrangements to meet a so-called virtual stranger face-to-face, since it is not uncommon for children to pretend to be older and for some adults to pretend to be younger.

Trust is a key component of safety in online environments, and one must be aware of potential ways that trust can be violated. Joinson and Dietz-Uhler (2002) note that the anonymity inherent in some Internet-based communities provides ample opportunity for participants to engage in deception. If the deception were to involve the creation and subsequent demise of a member of an online community of bereaved participants already dealing with loss, reactions to the loss of a community member could create additional challenges for people who may already be in a vulnerable emotional state. Administrators of grief-specific sites and moderators of support groups should be familiar with strategies to detect fabricated crisis or fictitious illness (Feldman, 2000).

One's emotional safety can also be impacted by cyberbullying, which can include flaming (i.e., angry or hostile comments in response to a posting), harassment, denigration, impersonation, outing and trickery, and exclusion (Kelsey, 2007). Knobel (2003) notes that a rant (simply venting) can be easily misinterpreted as a flame, and it can often be difficult to provide a fair account or interpretation of the exchanges that have occurred. A response to a question about the absence of message boards on GriefNet notes that this site does not use them since sometimes people post nasty or hurtful things and administrators or moderators do not find them before they cause some damage. While data regarding the incidence of cyberbullying within thanatology-related groups is not readily available, the reality of these inappropriate behaviors is widely documented as a risk of participating in all types of resources in the digital world (Goodstein, 2007). Raw emotions may also be shared in postings, and while they may not be intended to be offensive, it is possible that they may have a negative impact on some participants. User agreements should clearly describe the policies that exist regarding the screening or withholding of potentially objectionable postings, and moderators have a responsibility to all members to communicate in a timely manner with the author of any posting that is deemed questionable or inappropriate. Adolescents should be reminded to inform a trusted adult if they perceive or experience a threat to their safety as a result of online activities.

Those responsible for the oversight of these online resources must also consider the impact of no response from the group to a posting by the person seeking support or guidance. When members are joining a group, they should be prepared for the possibility that there are times when traffic on the site is slow, meaning that they may not get an immediate response to their posting (or perhaps no posting at all). Should members also be reminded that others are depending upon them for support, even when they themselves may not actively need, and be asked to check the site at least once during a prescribed period of time? When someone has decided to stop participating in an online community of bereavement, should they be asked to inform the group and say goodbye? These questions merit consideration.

IMPLICATIONS FOR CLINICIANS, DEATH EDUCATORS, AND PARENTS

In the past, the so-called digital divide referred to differences in one's access to technology due to the lack of physical access to a computer or the inability to afford online services. According to Dretzin (2008), "the digital divide is less about having access than it is about using the access that's available" (p. 9), with parents being in particular need of learning about the technology that is available to and being used by their teenagers. Many grief counselors and death educators may find themselves in the good but uninformed company of these parents. Prensky (2001) has described members of the D-gen (for digital generation) as digital natives, meaning that adolescents are "native speakers of the digital language of computers, video games and the Internet" (p. 1). Those of us who were not born into the digital world but have, at some later point in our lives, begun to utilize some or most aspects of technology will always be digital immigrants. One important distinction between digital natives and digital immigrants is that all immigrants, regardless of how well they adapt to their new environment, retain their "accent," or tendency to do things in the way that they were initially socialized (e.g., calling to ask if someone received your e-mail). While Prensky's comments are written in relation to students and educators in a school setting, it is not difficult to translate the implications of this distinction to the context of bereaved adolescents working with grief counselors or death educators who are unfamiliar with digital technology. Prensky states: "the single biggest problem facing education today is that our Digital Immigrant instructors, who speak an outdated language (that of the pre-digital age), are struggling to teach a population that speaks an entirely new language. This is obvious to the Digital Natives—school often feels pretty much as if we've brought in a population of heavily accented, unintelligible foreigners to lecture them. They often can't understand what the Immigrants are saying. What does 'dial' a number mean, anyway?" (p. 2).

Bridging the digital divide involves a need for digital literacy for not only the digital immigrants but also for the digital natives. Parents, grief counselors, death educators, and researchers must spend time learning about digital technology with the goal of developing a common language that can be spoken with the adolescents with whom they interact. In order to reassure parents and thanatologists that adolescents will not be harmed by use of these digital resources, adolescents also have a need for digital literacy, described by Pascoe (2007) as including the need to know how to keep themselves safe online (e.g., http://www.blogsafety or http://wiredsafety.org/), to think about the information they are putting out there, and to be able to have discussions with their parents about that information. In addition to being digitally literate, parents and thanatologists must consider the best way to have open discussions with adolescents about these resources (see Goodstein, 2007; Kelsey, 2007; Magid & Collier, 2007). As Pascoe (2007) notes, forbidding the use of technology just shuts down communication, and the teenagers will definitely find a way. Goodstein (2007) provides similar advice for parents about monitoring blogs: "Beginning a dialogue sounds a lot better than breaking and entering, online or off" (p. 50). Inviting adolescents to share tales of their adventures in the digital world, whether the genre of the tale turns out to be a drama, a comedy, or a horror story, is a useful way to help them process these experiences and to alleviate one's own worries or fears about the impact of digital technology on their social and emotional well-being.

IMPLICATIONS FOR RESEARCH

Montgomery (2007) notes the need for a conversation, informed by research, on how digital technologies can best meet the needs of children and youths. It would be wise for thanatologists to have a role in this dialogue, as well as facilitating the collection of data from bereaved youths, thereby ensuring that their voices are heard. In order to understand the potential risks and benefits of the use of digital technology in the lives of bereaved adolescents, empirical studies must be conducted that document access to and usage of thanatology-related informational resources, as well as the usage and impact (effectiveness as well as any potential risks or harm) of computer-mediated communications to specifically cope with loss-related events. It is important to understand how so-called virtual grief is similar to and different from grief that is expressed without the use of technology. However, the process of conducting research with bereaved adolescents about their use of the Internet in combination with conducting research online involves a challenging set of ethical issues (see chapter 3 in this book).

Since thanatology research is inherently interdisciplinary, ethical pluralism—having more than one ethical decision-making framework that can be used to analyze and resolve ethical issues (Ess & the AoIR ethics working committee, 2002)—may present an added challenge.

When researching issues involving death and loss, there may be ethically significant risks related to psychological or emotional harm, regardless of whether the research is conducted online.

Knobel (2003) notes that the debates involving ethics wrestle mainly with three issues: (a) the distinction between public and private space, (b) obtaining informed consent, and (c) the assurance of anonymity in research publications. The importance of protecting subjects' rights is heightened if they are minors between the ages of 12 and 18. If one's research involves the exploration of SNSs and other public spaces online, Ess and colleagues (2002) describe one broad consideration: The greater the acknowledged public nature of the venue, the less obligation there may be to protect individual privacy, confidentiality, and the right to informed consent. Knobel (2003) notes that a researcher should carefully consider participating in the online community prior to the start of research about that community since it is the responsibility of the researcher to make informed judgments about the public versus private nature of the space. Password-protected spaces are assumed to be private spaces, and archivable discussions are generally presumed to be public spaces. Although participants may be aware that the space is public, anonymity in publications cannot be promised as a result of the archived and searchable nature of cyberspace (Knobel, 2003), and participants do not expect researchers to be part of the audience (Moreno, Fost, & Christakis, 2008). Guidance is available regarding research ethics that involve issues of perceived intrusion, lurking, and disclosure of one's presence as an observer (e.g., Knobel, 2003; Leander & McKim, 2003; Moreno et al., 2008).

While it is beyond the scope of this chapter to discuss the intricate details of the decision-making process that must occur before conducting research on these topics, there are detailed and helpful resources that researchers should consult for guidance. Ess and colleagues (2002) have published a document that includes a useful list of questions for use in ethical decision-making regarding Internet research, sample consent forms, case studies, and a bibliography of additional resources. Moreno, Fost, and Christakis (2008) provide valuable information about the three levels of consent relevant to social-networking sites. Knobel (2003) provides three maxims that should guide all online research: (a) Be informed, (b) be honest and open, and (c) be prepared to invest in online communities. Failure to honor these maxims can result in "smash and grab" research that has the potential to alienate participants and make them wary of participation in subsequent studies (Knobel, 2003, p. 208).

CONCLUSION

Noting the need to understand that adolescents live in a new, massive, and complex virtual universe, Greenfield and Yan (2006) encourage us to see the Internet as a "new cultural tool kit" that provides us with an infinite series of applications (p. 392). Hellenga (2002) reminds us that the rapid growth of computer-mediated communication in all forms makes it difficult to imagine all future uses of this technology. Oltjenbruns and James (2006) encourage thanatologists to become familiar with online resources since such awareness may create opportunities for positive dialogue with teens on how to use the Internet in a safe and positive manner. Understanding adolescents' use of online resources to cope with loss will require efforts to gather data informally from the adolescents whom we serve and to formally conduct empirical research in a manner that honors and respects the challenges of data collection in cyberspace. Perhaps, with the assistance of a few bereaved adolescents who are savvy with the technical aspects of Web design and computer programming, thanatologists will be able to develop new resources that merge the latest in technology with content specific to the experiences of bereaved teenagers (e.g., how to respond to friends when they are not being helpful during times of grief, etc.). When working with current and future members of the digital generation, implementing that tried-and-true counselor's directive to "meet the clients where they are at" will require gaining a level of comfort being in cyberspace, a place where today's teenagers appear to be very comfortable. However, when learning about and using ICTs and spending time in an SNS to assist grieving adolescents, it will be important to remember to use some good old fashioned TLC.

REFERENCES

Atfield, C., Chalmers, E., & Lion, P. (2006, November 21). Safety net for grief—Anguished teens reach out across cyberspace. *The Courier Mail,* News, p. 9.

Belenkaya, V. (2006, August 20). Lost pals stay alive on web. *Daily News,* News, p. 28.

Blais, J. J., Craig, W. M., Pepler, D., & Connolly, J. (2008). Adolescents online: The importance of internet activity choices to salient relationships. *Journal of Youth and Adolescence, 37*(5), 522–536.

Blaxland, M. (2007, April 29). Grieving 4 u Amy: Teenagers share memories of friend on the net. *Sun Herald,* Hunter Extra, p. 1.

Borzekowski, D. L. G., & Rickert, V. I. (2001). Adolescent cybersurfing for health information: A new resource that crosses barriers. *Archives of Pediatric Adolescent Medicine, 155,* 813–817.

Bunn, A. (2000, August). The rise of the teen guru, *Brill's Content* (pp. 64–69). Retrieved June 18, 2008, from http://www.austinbunn.com/articles.php?target=teenguru.html

Burrell, J. (2007, January 18). Electronic age changes face of grief: IMs, Facebook allow youths to connect without having to be face to face. *Contra Costa Times,* p. A1.

Dretzin, R. (2008). *What we learned.* Retrieved June 12, 2008, from www.pbs.org/sgbh/pages/frontline/kidsonline/etc/notebook.html

Ess, C., & the AoIR ethics working committee. (2002). *Ethical decision-making and Internet research: Recommendations from the AoIR ethics working committee.* Retrieved June 10, 2008, from http://www.aoir.org/reports/ethics.pdf

Feldman, M. D. (2000). Munchausen by Internet: Detecting factitious illness and crisis on the Internet. *Southern Medical Journal, 93,* 669–672.

Fitzgerald, H. (2000). *The grieving teen: A guide for teenagers and their friends.* New York: Fireside.

Gagnon, M. (2005, December 1). Teenager posts suicide note on MySpace.com. Retrieved June 5, 2008, from http://news.newamericamedia.org/news/view_article.html?article_id=6d8134fbbe964d76f864b3b9682dcb19

Goodstein, A. (2007). *Totally wired: What teens and tweens are really doing online.* New York: St. Martin's Press.

Greenfield, P., & Yan, Z. (2006). Children, adolescents, and the Internet: A new field of inquiry in developmental psychology. *Developmental Psychology, 42*(3), 391–394.

Harris, F. J. (2005). *I found it on the Internet: Coming of age online.* Chicago: American Library Association.

Hellenga, K. (2002). Social space, the final frontier: Adolescents on the Internet. In J. T. Mortimer, & R. W. Larson (Eds.), *The changing adolescent experience: Societal trends and the transition to adulthood* (pp. 208–249). Cambridge, UK: Cambridge University Press.

Huffaker, D. A., & Calvert, S. L. (2005). Gender, identity, and language use in teenage blogs. *Journal of Computer-Mediated Communication, 10*(2). Retrieved June 18, 2008, from http://jcmc.indiana.edu/vol10/issue2/huffaker.html

Jenkins, H., Clinton, K., Purushotma, R., Robison, A. J., & Weigel, M. (2006, October 16). *Confronting the challenges of participatory culture: Media education for the 21st century* (White paper). Chicago: MacArthur Foundation. Retrieved May 21, 2008, from http://www.digitallearning.macfound.org/atf/cf/%7B7E45C7E0–A3E0–4B89–AC9C–E807E1B0AE4E%7D/JENKINS_WHITE_PAPER.PDF

Joinson, A. N., & Dietz-Uhler, B. (2002). Explanations for the perpetration of and reactions to deception in a virtual community. *Social Science Computer Review, 20*(3), 275–289.

Kelsey, C. M. (2007). *Generation MySpace: Helping your teen survive online adolescence.* New York: Marlowe & Company.

Knobel, M. (2003). Rants, ratings, and representations: Issues of validity, reliability and ethics in researching online social practices. *Education, Communication, & Information, 3*(2), 187–210.

Leander, K. M., & McKim, K. K. (2003). Tracing the everyday "sitings" of adolescents on the Internet: A strategic adaptation of ethnography across online and offline spaces. *Education, Communication, & Information, 3*(2), 211–240.

Lee, S. (2008, February 22). Lack of hope for kids that leads to despair. *Liverpool Daily Echo,* Features, p. 8.

Lenhart, A., Madden, M., Macgill, A. R., & Smith, A. (2007). *Teens and social media.* Retrieved April 14, 2008, from http://www.pewinternet.org/pdfs/PIP_Teens_Social_Media_Final.pdf

Levine, J. R., Baroudi, C., & Levine Young, M. (2007). *The Internet for dummies.* Hoboken, NJ: Wiley Publishing Company.

Magid, L., & Collier, A. (2007). *MySpace unraveled: A parent's guide to teen social networking.* Berkeley, CA: Peachpit Press.

McCarthy, J. R. (2007). "They all look as if they're coping, but I'm not": The relational power/lessness of "youth" in responding to experiences of bereavement. *Journal of Youth Studies, 10*(3), 285–303.

McKenna, L. (2005, March 17). "The Google Stage." 11D. Retrieved June 11, 2008, from http://11d.typepad.com/blog/2005/03/the_google_stag.html

Montgomery, K. C. (2007). *Generation digital: Politics, commerce, and childhood in the age of the Internet.* Cambridge, MA: MIT Press.

Moreno, M. A., Fost, N. C., & Christakis, D. A. (2008). Research ethics in the MySpace era. *Pediatrics, 121*(1), 157–161.

Natekar, A. (2007, November 12). Egrieving: Teens turning to their Web pages to mourn friends, family. Retrieved March 19, 2008, from http://www.redorbit.com/news/technology/1140749/egrieving_teens_turning_to_their_web_pages_to_mourn_friends/index.html

Niebuhr, G., & Wilgoren, J. (1999, April 28). Terror in Littleton. *New York Times.* Retrieved May 22, 2008 from http://www.nytimes.com

O'Brien, B. (2008, March 1). Suicide and what it means to the Bebo generation. *Irish Times,* Opinion, p. 16.

Oltjenbruns, K. A., & James, L. (2006). Adolescents' use of the Internet as a modality of grief support. *The Forum, 32*(4), 5–6.

Oravec, J. (2000). Online counseling and the Internet: Perspectives for mental health care supervision and education. *Journal of Mental Health,* 9(2), 121–135.

Pascoe, C. J. (2007). Interview conducted on July 17. Retrieved June 11, 2008 from http://www.pbs.org/wgbh/pages/frontline/kidsonline/interviews/pascoe.html

PBS. (2008). *Growing up online* (Documentary originally aired on January 22). Retrieved March 12, 2008, from http://www.pbs.org/wgbh/pages/frontline/kidsonline/

Pokin, S. (2007, November 10). A real person, a real death. *St. Charles Journal.* Retrieved June 10, 2008, from http://www.meganmeierfoundation.org/story/

Prensky, M. (2001). Digital natives, digital immigrants. *On the Horizon,* 9(5), 1–6. Retrieved June 19, 2008, from http://www.marcprensky.com/writing/Prensky%20–%20Digital%20Natives,%20Digital%20Immigrants%20-%20Part1.pdf

Roberts, P. (2006). From MySpace to our space: The functions of web memorials in bereavement. *The Forum, 32*(4), 1, 3–4.

Schmitt, K. L., Dayanim, S., & Matthias, S. (2008). Personal homepage construction as an expression of social development. *Developmental Psychology, 44*(2), 496–506.

Servaty, H. L., & Hayslip, B. (2001). Adjustment to loss among adolescents. *Omega, Journal of Death and Dying, 43*(4), 311–330.

Siad, S. (2007, May 25). Teens cope with grief online. *The Toronto Star,* News, p. A01.

Sofka, C. J. (1997). Social support "internetworks," caskets for sale, and more: Thanatology and the information superhighway. *Death Studies, 21*(6), 553–574.

Sofka, C. J. (2008). Unpublished data.

St. George, D. (1999, November 26). On the Web, a world of hope is spun for teen. *The Washington Post*, p. A, 1:3.

West, E. (2007, May 8). How the web is helping us deal with death. *Daily Telegraph*, p. 21.

Whitaker, J. (2002). *The Internet: The basics*. New York: Routledge.

Bereavement

PART III

As we have seen in part II, there are all too many ways in which contemporary adolescents encounter death and loss. In part III, five chapters focus on some of the most frequent and most prominent types of bereavements in the lives of adolescents that follow upon death-related losses: what life is like for an adolescent when a parent has died (chapter 10), the impact of the death of a brother or sister (chapter 11), the importance of the death of an adolescent's friend (chapter 12), implications of the death of a special celebrity (chapter 13), and distinctive problems for adolescents arising from traumatic deaths (chapter 14).

Each of these bereavement experiences is unique, with its own characteristics and qualities, but all are linked insofar as they involve losses that can have a significant impact on the life of an adolescent. Some of these bereavement situations are generally well recognized (e.g., the death of a parent or sibling), while others are not so well appreciated and may even be disenfranchised (e.g., the death of a friend or a special celebrity). Each chapter in this part explores the reactions that adolescents are likely to have to these specific types of losses, coping strategies typically used by adolescents to manage these bereavements, factors that can help or hinder such coping, the role of family and other potential helping resources, and the impact of bereavement and grief on an adolescent's emerging self-concept.

All of these bereavements can be daunting, not only when they involve some type of violent, stigmatized, or traumatic death, but also even when the relationship is one-sided, known to an adolescent only in an illusion of intimacy through his or her involvement with media personalities in a digital universe. We need better research and better appreciation of the nature and significance of these losses for developing adolescents, both for their own sakes and in order to be able to develop more effective intervention strategies. In the end, it will be the capacity of individual adolescents to construct a coherent and confident meaning to their narratives of living with these losses that will enable them to build resilient futures.

10

Life as an Adolescent When a Parent Has Died

JULIE STOKES, CATRIONA REID, AND VANESSA COOK

The death of a parent will inevitably become a key thread in an adolescent's life story (Sjoqvist, 2007). How young persons tell their story both to themselves and others will be mediated by many factors (Dowdney, 2000). Their capacity to construct a coherent and confident meaning to this narrative is a key factor in building a resilient future (Balk, 1996; Lin, Sandler, Ayers, Wolchik, & Laucken, 2004; Stokes, 2007).

At Winston's Wish (http://www.winstonswish.org.uk) many adolescents have talked openly and honestly about their individual experiences of bereavement: feelings of pain, guilt, anger, the embarrassed reactions or silence of others, and the struggle to rebuild their lives. They also share happy memories of their parents and describe the importance of remembering. It is our goal (or wish) that every bereaved child will receive timely and age appropriate support (Nugus & Stokes, 2007). However, the challenge to engage successfully with young people requires skillful assessment of need, combined with a flexible range of services. This chapter presents ideas about how adults can best understand and support adolescents coping with a parental death.

THE IMPACT OF LOSING A PARENT FOR AN ADOLESCENT

Of all the losses suffered by young people, parental death is thought to be the most traumatic and painful (Carr, 1999). Developmental tensions over dependency versus autonomy during adolescence may exacerbate this devastating and distressing experience (Balk & Corr, 2001). The effects of parental bereavement in adolescence are severe and far-reaching; it is associated with increased levels of psychiatric symptoms, such as anxiety, depression, guilt, and anger (Dowdney, 2000; Harrison & Harrington, 2001). It has also been linked to chronic illness, low self-esteem, significant disturbances in job and school performance, and difficulties in interpersonal relationships (Jacobs, 1999; Silverman, 2000; Worden, 1996). In addition to the emotional and psychological consequences, young people can experience secondary losses in previous areas of stability and control, through changes to finances, daily routines, and future plans (Stroebe, Hansson, Stroebe, & Schut, 2001).

Theories of adolescence propose that this is an age at which young people are negotiating the developmental tasks of defining their identity, individuating from the family, and establishing a place within their peer groups (Muuss, 1996). All these processes may influence, and be influenced by, adolescents' experiences of coping with the death of a parent, which may in turn have longer-term implications for adolescent development and future lives.

Important people within adolescents' lives, especially parents, influence the process of identity formation. It is not unusual for adolescents to become increasingly interested in their parents' lives and experiences at this stage, and it is thought this increased interest is part of their integrating or rejecting elements of their parents into their own identities. Losing a parent and his or her potential influence on their developing identity may make it difficult for young people to understand fully who they are or who they want to be.

Adolescents are also beginning to negotiate the task of separation and individuation from their parents. During this time they often become rebellious and defiant as one way by which they separate themselves from their parents and become more independent. A parent's death removes from the adolescent the ability to go through the natural process of separation from this parent. The relationship with the surviving parent may have implications for how their sense of self and independence develops, as well as how they later relate in any new relationships with friends, potential stepparents, or partners.

We meet many adolescents whose parents have died when they were younger but who seem to reexperience their grief as they reach this stage of their life. They are acutely aware of the absence of their parent and of the significant points in their future lives when their parent will not be present. These adolescents often benefit from learning more about their dead parent in order to come to know them in more sophisticated, adult ways. In this way the dead parent can continue to play an important and influential part in the young person's life through developing the existing continuing bond (Field, Gao, & Paderna, 2005). This process seems to reflect the developmental processes of identity development and individuation.

The following case study demonstrates how a bereaved child can develop into a very troubled adolescent if timely and appropriate support is not made available.

Case Study—Liam (16)

Liam is serving an 18-month sentence in a secure unit for theft, violent behavior, and possession of Class A drugs. Last year he was homeless and trying to survive a heroin habit, which started when he was 12. Liam's attendance at secondary school was sporadic; when he ran away from home at 14 his education ceased altogether.

The first 5 years of Liam's life had been relatively secure. However, when he was 7 family life began to change dramatically. His mother was diagnosed with a brain tumor and her prognosis was poor. Liam's parents found the stress overwhelming, and their relationship became destructive and verbally violent. While his mother deteriorated physically and cognitively, Liam's father formed a new relationship with a close family friend. During this time none of the professionals involved spoke to Liam or his younger sister, and the parents were too distracted and unavailable to talk about what was happening. Liam's mother died when he was 8. Her death was a complete shock to him, and he was not given the choice to attend the funeral. Dad's new partner moved in within 2 months, and the mother's family were so outraged that they no longer had any contact with their grandchildren. No one spoke of Liam's mother, and all photos were taken down. It was not brought up at school, and after 2 years Liam's school report described him as "a violent and angry pupil who may not cope with the transition to secondary school." No mention was made of his mother's death as a possible contributory factor to his behavior. Liam felt marginalized in his new family; he could not form an attachment with his stepmother, whom he "hated," and felt uncontrolled envy toward his sister and stepbrothers. His father was increasingly exasperated with his challenging behavior and was relieved when Liam finally left home at 14.

Boswell (1995) reported that 10% of Section 53 offenders (children convicted of the gravest crimes) had experienced the death of a parent. The cost to the state to support and rehabilitate young people like Liam is significant, especially when compared to the resources that could support community-based child bereavement services (Draper, 2008). This case study highlights not only the need for accessible community child bereavement services, but also the significant therapeutic challenge that emerges when a young person has experienced cumulative loss and insecure attachment (Brisch, 2002; Hughes, 1997).

ADOLESCENTS AND SERVICE ENGAGEMENT

The challenge for those of us working with adolescents who have been bereaved of a parent is how proactively to engage adolescents like Liam and their families. Adolescents are often considered by professionals and services to be difficult to engage. Research has found that up to 30% of young people requiring support never come into contact with mental health or counseling services (Buston, 2002; Logan & King, 2001; Meltzer, Gatward, Goodman, & Ford, 2000; Stiffman, Chen, Elze, Dore, & Cheng, 1997), and of those who do reach services, between 30% and 60% disengage prematurely (Garland & Besinger, 1996; Garland, Aarons, Saltzman, & Kruse, 2000; Young Minds Policy, 2002). Therefore, an added complication for adolescents who have lost a parent is that they may find it difficult to seek, or accept, help from services that are available to them. It may be that seeking or receiving help from an adult-led service at this time is experienced as contrary to the developmental goal of reducing dependence on adults (Wisdom, Clarke, & Green, 2006). An alternative explanation for this low engagement may be that the design and delivery of services is not appropriate or acceptable for adolescents. In keeping with this developmental stage of increasing independence and autonomy, adolescents express a desire for more flexible, collaborative counseling services, which are age appropriate and provide them with information and choice (Buston, 2002; Gibson & Possamai, 2002; Street, Stapelkamp, Taylor, Malek, & Kurtz et al., 2005). Recent research suggests that such services help adolescents to feel involved and empowered and have a positive impact on their lives, self-esteem, and sense of self (Reid, Stedmon, & Libby, 2007).

As adolescents' reactions to grief are often emotionally complex and behaviorally risky (i.e., self-harm, substance abuse, aggression), it seems particularly important that services are able to meet their needs. It is essential that the architects of child bereavement services understand how best to engage and offer support to all age groups—and not satisfy themselves with relatively easy-to-reach 8- to 10-year-olds (Stokes, 2004). To successfully engage an adolescent requires service flexibility combined with a willingness to give control over key decisions and emotional expression.

The next case study illustrates how adults can be quick to judge a young person's behavior as frustrating and inappropriate, rather than recognizing the individual's underlying distress and vulnerability.

Case Study—Becky (15)

Becky's early years were extremely chaotic, and she witnessed frequent violent outbursts between her mother and different partners. When she was 10 and living in a residential care setting, she was told that her mother had been murdered by her boyfriend. Two years later Becky was eventually placed in a permanent foster home with a view to adoption, but, not surprisingly, she found it difficult to form a secure attachment with her foster mother, Jane.

During a therapy session, Jane and Becky had been talking together warmly and respectfully. Becky became tearful when she thought about her birth mother and a day they enjoyed together on the beach, which later had been ruined by a violent, drunken argument at night. Suddenly her relaxed, reflective demeanor changed and she started laughing in an uncomfortable way. This seemingly rude/immature behavior was something Jane had witnessed before and she looked disapprovingly at Becky.

Therapist: Becky why do you think you are laughing?

Becky: (No response, but repeats the same laugh.)

Therapist: It's OK to be laughing . . . I just wondered if you had any idea what it might mean?

Jane: She tends to do that when things get tough. (There was a tone of disappointment in the foster mother's voice—who was full of hope that these sessions might enable her to reach Becky in a closer, more emotionally mature way.) Whenever things get too hard she just laughs. She's been doing it ever since she came to us.

Therapist: Oh Becky, I am really sorry. . . . I should have realized that things were getting tough for you. . . . I guess Jane knows you much better than me? … I should have given you a break.

Becky: (Starts crying, but this time with a deeper emotional connection and readily accepts a hug from Jane.)

Therapist to Jane: I think you and I will never know quite how hard her life has been.

This short, seemingly insignificant interchange shows how important it is to seek alternative meanings in adolescent behaviors that could easily be characterized as immature or rebellious. The therapist needs the confidence to be curious and nonjudgmental when discussing an adolescent's grief reactions. Research shows that adolescents value professionals who are empathic, understanding, and nonjudgmental (Buston, 2002; Gibson & Possamai, 2002). Had the therapist joined the foster mother's disapproval at that point in the process, it is very possible that Becky would have walked out and refused any further therapy.

ASSESSING THE SYSTEMS THAT IMPACT ON PARENTALLY BEREAVED ADOLESCENTS

In order to develop services that may be potentially useful to bereaved adolescents, it is vital to consider the factors that are likely to contribute to their experiences. Recent reviews of the literature (Ribbens McCarthy, 2006; Ribbens McCarthy & Jessop, 2005) have highlighted the complex social systems and psychological variables that need to be understood in order to assess and support bereaved adolescents. Essential to any assessment with bereaved adolescents is an understanding of the relationships they had with the deceased, their story of how the person died, and an account of life before and since the death. Table 10.1 presents a list of factors that can influence an adolescent's grief experience and, when present, are likely to promote resilience. All young people experience a better outcome following adverse life conditions when they have a positive relationship with an adult, engage with other people, and have a valued area of competence (Masten, Best, Garmezy, 1990). The assessment process needs to identify not only the presence or absence of such factors, but also the meaning they hold for the adolescent (Neimeyer,

Table 10.1

FACTORS THAT IMPACT POSITIVELY ON THE RESILIENCE OF AN ADOLESCENT WHO HAS EXPERIENCED THE DEATH OF A PARENT
I. ADOLESCENT
Social and adaptable temperament in infancy
Characteristics valued by others and self (talented, attractive, sense of humor, etc.)
Makes and maintains peer friendships
Has strategies to regulate emotions and behavior
Good problem-solving skills
Sets goals that are achievable
Has a feeling of control over his/her life
Positive view of self (self confidence, high self esteem, self-efficacy)
Shows a balanced acceptance and understanding of self, acknowledging both limitations and strengths
Maintains a positive internal relationship with the parent who has died
Feels able to accept the reality or idea of a surviving parent's new partner/step-parent
Hopeful outlook on life and has faith in the future
II. FAMILY
Stable and supportive home environment
Authoritative parenting style (high on warmth, boundaries, and monitoring)
Parent involved in young person's education and career development
Higher education of the parents
Socio-economic advantages
Faith and religious affiliation
Supportive connections with family and friends
Parent or main carer confident to accept support for the adolescent and themselves
Parent or carer had a positive relationship with the parent who has died
Extended family able to offer practical/emotional support valued by the parent

(*Continued*)

Table 10.1

FACTORS THAT IMPACT POSITIVELY ON THE RESILIENCE OF AN ADOLESCENT WHO HAS EXPERIENCED THE DEATH OF A PARENT (*Continued*)

III. COMMUNITY
Lives in a quality neighborhood (safe, non violent, affordable housing, recreation centers, clean air and water)
Effective schools academically and in terms of their capacity to respond to bereavement
Employment opportunities for parents and young people
Quality health and emergency care services
Availability of accessible specialist child bereavement services where they can meet other children who have been bereaved
IV. CULTURAL/SOCIETAL
Society has a low acceptance of physical violence, drug misuse, and social inequality
The government sets proactive and preventative child policies
Policies are backed by long-term funding contracts for both voluntary and state sectors
The death of a parent is accepted as a primary risk factor for all children
Government and society value and direct resources to develop community child bereavement services

Based on factors identified in "Ordinary Magic: Resilient Processes in Development," by A. S. Masten, 2001, *American Psychologist, 56,* pp. 227–238.

2005; Neimeyer, Baldwin, & Gillies, 2006; Stubbs, Alilovic, Stokes, & Howells, 2006). For example, the arrival of a new stepparent following a parental death could hold a variety of meanings for an adolescent, from extreme anger ("I hate him! He's an idiot—nothing like my dad!") to a sense of security and relief ("He looks after mum really well, and now I feel OK about going to college and leaving her.").

While it is important to understand an adolescent's personal, subjective experience of grief, it is also necessary to understand how the individual's reactions and understanding are influenced by the systems around them, including family, peer group, school, community, and society. All these levels of surrounding systems shape an adolescent's journey through the grieving process.

An adolescent's family and their patterns of interaction and communication have a profound impact on their experience and expression of their grief. The ways in which they have previously seen those around them communicate and express emotions will influence how they themselves are able to express their loss and distress following a parent's death. A study by Greef and Human (2004) indicated that intrafamilial emotional and practical support, and family hardiness contribute to resilience and enable families and adolescents to adjust and adapt successfully after the loss of a parent. The relationship that an adolescent had with the dead parent influences his or her ability to maintain a continuing bond with the remaining parent. The attachment to the remaining parent will also impact on how supported and secure the adolescent feels. A longitudinal, controlled study demonstrated that parental warmth is a significant factor in how adolescents cope with a parental death (Wolchik, Tein, Sandler, & Ayers, 2006).

The adolescent processes of individuation and separation from parents may mean they find it difficult to talk with and gain support from their remaining parent or immediate family. Therefore, other wider systems may be particularly important in providing a source of support to adolescents when a parent has died. Allowing this support can be very difficult for the remaining parent to accept as he or she will want to comfort the child and often cannot understand why the youths won't confide in them.

The peer group becomes increasingly important during adolescence. Peer relationships, acceptance, and belonging can act as a secure base for finding supportive relationships that facilitate the development of a more autonomous sense of self (Muuss, 1996; Newman & Newman, 1976). As a result, adolescents may find it easier to talk with their friends about what has happened. Friendships and meeting others of their own age with similar experiences can be significant sources of support for adolescents when a parent has died (Wood, 2003). Young people report that meeting others who understand and have similar feelings and experiences is one of the most valuable aspects of Winston's Wish residential therapeutic weekends. However, peer group acceptance and conformity are also very influential at this age, and young people are loath to be seen to be different. They often tell us that losing a parent does make them feel different and abnormal somehow. Therefore, adolescents may find it difficult to use the support of their nonbereaved peer group for fear of being rejected or stigmatized.

For most young people, school plays a major role in their everyday life. To a bereaved adolescent it may represent the only place where he or she can begin to process the loss without fear of upsetting a family member. The school environment can seem like a haven in times of family stress, and peers and adults in the school environment can be an important source of support and understanding. Losing a parent and coping with this grief can impact on young people's school performance and education (Rowling, 2003). The way in which a school responds to and supports an adolescent following the death of a parent can have a significant impact on how the youngster is able to cope with his or her grief. Table 10.2 describes the factors that young people felt were relevant on their return to school (Cook & Stedmon, 2004).

Table 10.2

ADVICE FOR TEACHERS ON SUPPORTING A PARENTALLY BEREAVED STUDENT ON HIS OR HER RETURN TO SCHOOL

- Treat young people normally, neither too gently nor too strictly.
- Provide the student with choice, especially about how to inform classmates. Seek their opinion on receiving support and the sharing of information.
- Acknowledge the loss in a thoughtful and sensitive way, perhaps through a shared card from teacher and class.
- Be wary of others overacknowledging the bereavement.
- Where there is a good relationship between student and teacher, offer the opportunity to talk, when required, and have time out in a quiet place.
- Provide a place where the student can talk, privately and confidentially. This may mean teachers offering themselves as a source of support or instead directing young people to a school counselor or a member of the staff team experienced in dealing with loss.
- Avoid putting pressure on pupils to talk about their loss.
- Ensure that all staff who need to know about the death are informed, thus avoiding any possibly embarrassing situations.
- Talk with the young person to identify a list of dates that may have particular significance (birthdays, anniversaries, etc.) and if possible make a note of these in your diary so they can be sensitively acknowledged.
- In time, discuss community support groups that may be available—especially those that provide opportunities to meet others of a similar age who have also been bereaved.

Societal values and expectations also have a huge impact on how adolescents grieve. There are certain socially accepted ways of grieving and even times for grieving. Socially determined gender roles also mean that there are certain expectations for how girls and boys will grieve. Particular difficulties may arise for adolescent boys who are not expected or allowed to cry or show their feelings. Consequently, boys often express their feelings through more socially acceptable male behaviors such as aggression or drinking. Alternatively, the prohibition of anger for girls (Jordan, 2005; Miller, 1985) is often a great obstacle to being able to fully express their grief and develop resilience.

Young males can show what Pollack (2005) calls *pseudoresilience* because of the pressure society places on boys to act tough and hide their emotions at all costs. On the outside, a boy may seem cheerful, playful, and resilient, but on the inside he may actually feel lonely, afraid, and desperate. Adults and other adolescents may be fooled into believing the stoical mask is real, rather than risk an interface with a boy's deeper hidden pain. Often there is a short window when grief will be acknowledged; afterward, a boy's disruptive behavior is the most likely thing to be noticed. The more we can sustain a healthy vulnerability in adolescent boys, the more resilient they will become and remain.

The following case study highlights how these systems influence an adolescent boy's grief following his father's death by suicide. (For more information on the impact of suicide, see chapter 5 and studies by Alilovic, 2004; Brown, Sandler, Tein, Liu, & Haine, 2007; Love, 2006; Wood, 2007.)

Case Study—Scott (15)

Scott's dad, Richard, took his own life by hanging himself. For as long as Scott could remember, his father had been violent toward his mother. In the final months, violent and unusual parental behavior had escalated, and Richard had become aggressive toward Scott. Reluctantly, Scott's mother decided to leave, for both her own and Scott's safety.

Richard's side of the family did not believe his mother's accounts of Richard's behavior and blamed her for the suicide. As a result, they no longer had contact. Scott missed the support of his uncles and male cousins, with whom he used to go and watch football. Scott also felt unable to tell his friends the full story, or to seek support from them, as he worried about what they would think of his Dad and him.

Scott lived in a small town; everyone knew what had happened, and the local paper had published it as a front-page story. Everywhere Scott went it felt like people were whispering and talking about what had happened. Some of their neighbors and friends really felt for them but were unsure what to say or do to help, so they didn't phone or visit. Scott felt isolated in a community of onlookers.

Without anyone to talk to about what had happened Scott was unable to share or express the emotions building up inside of him. He felt increasingly angry with his dad for choosing to leave him, with his mom for leaving his dad, and at himself for not stopping his dad's suicide. With no outlet for these feelings, they would build up and boil over at school or at home with his mother. Scott feared that his anger and aggression meant he was like his dad and that he might also take his own life.

With all these conflicting and strong emotions, Scott found it difficult to concentrate at school. He was easily irritated with both teachers and his friends. However, as the school was aware of what had happened to Scott's father, they made an effort to understand why his behavior may have changed. A sports teacher Scott liked offered to spend time with him talking about what had happened. As a result of these meetings, Scott had an experience of witnessing a respected male teacher talking openly about emotions, which enabled him to feel more able to share his own feelings. His teacher then referred him to a local counseling service where he was helped to find safe ways of expressing his anger, sadness, and grief and to meet others who had also been bereaved by suicide.

This case study highlights routes into engaging an adolescent, such as working at their own pace, and demonstrates how systems around them (e.g., school, community, gender and social expectations) can influence their bereavement experience.

HELPFUL APPROACHES WHEN WORKING WITH BEREAVED ADOLESCENTS

Delivering successful services for adolescents requires a collaborative approach, one that enables young people to feel empowered and independent. Adolescents need to be offered a flexible range of services that enable them to express their feelings and memories in ways that feel most acceptable to them. These services may include individual therapy, group work, telephone support, and using technologies like texting and the Internet, which are familiar and popular with young people.

Developing Positive Ongoing Conversations

Encouraging an adolescent to have imaginary, comforting, and positive conversations with a dead parent is like taking vitamins. Taking vitamins helps fight off illnesses. Likewise, simply thinking about close relationships helps a young person fight off life's adversities, such as being confronted by failure or criticism. The capacity to create adaptive internal dialogues is a feature of resilience in bereaved adolescents.

> At first I was really gutted when I didn't get picked for the school team, but I know dad would have said "keep going to training, show the coach what you're made of"—I will also try harder with my ball skills, they were my weak point during the trials.

These ongoing conversations can enable adolescents to maintain and develop their relationships with the dead parent, facilitating the adolescent processes of identity development and individuation. They also provide comfort and a sense of connection at significant milestones in an adolescent's future life. This process is a means of creating a continuing bond with the parent, one that helps young people cope with their losses (Klass, Silverman, & Nickman, 1996). Narrative methods can be used to introduce and develop these ongoing, internal conversations (White, 1988).

However, for some, an ambivalent relationship with the dead parent, or perhaps the circumstances surrounding the death, may lead to a highly complex grief journey that requires therapy before such positive internal dialogues are generated spontaneously. The following case study reflects how the circumstances of a death can complicate an adolescent's beliefs and the meaning he or she constructs following a family death.

Case Study—Natalie (14)

Natalie was going to school. At breakfast she asked her mother to iron her skirt. Her mother was annoyed at this late request and even more frustrated when Natalie decided the skirt was not short enough and now wanted her trousers ironed instead! A fairly normal encounter between an indecisive, self-absorbed adolescent and a busy working mother. However, the meaning of this encounter later led to extreme episodes of self-harm and a severe depression because Natalie's mother died in a road traffic accident on her way to work that same day.

This final encounter with her mother before her death led to intense feelings of shame and guilt. Natalie hardly talked at all; instead she expressed her self-loathing by cutting her forearm. It was 5 months before she was able to voice her destructive self-belief, "I killed my mother," and a further 8 months and several sessions of cognitive-behavioral therapy (CBT) before she was able to modify this to: "I really regret having that row with mum over breakfast because that was the last time we spoke. I never meant for her to die; I loved her and I know she loved me; I miss her so much it hurts." Through supportive therapy Natalie was able to move from a destructive conversation based on one negative encounter to a conversation that was more representative of the close relationship she and her mother had normally shared. (See Table 10.3 for an example of Natalie's thought processes.)

Using Memories to Maintain a Continuing Bond

As well as doing work to create a resilient narrative, many adolescents can benefit from using physical prompts to facilitate a helpful ongoing

Table 10.3

NATALIE'S THOUGHT PROCESSES

The thoughts below reflect the processes that Natalie engaged in to move to a set of beliefs (outlined below) that in turn released a less complicated grief reaction.

1. I can continue to have a close relationship with my mum for the rest of my life.
2. It's OK to cry, it's OK to laugh, and it's not OK to feel shame or self-hate.
3. I am not responsible for my mother's death; even though we argued and I nagged her to do the ironing for me, I never intended that she should die.
4. I can see that my attitude to things, even really bad things, makes a big difference to how I feel.
5. Now I can share stories and memories of mum with people who can listen without my becoming very upset or very angry.
6. I have met others who feel and think the same as me, so I know that this painful stuff is natural when someone you care about dies.
7. If my dad meets someone, I do not have to choose. I can relate to both my mum and a new stepmother, if that happens.
8. I now believe that life is for living. Mum would have wanted me to sort out the things I want to do, so I have made a list of my top 10 goals, and now I am going to go for them.

relationship with a dead parent. In recent years, resources such as memory boxes (Stokes, 2004, 2007) have been used to reinforce identity and, where appropriate, consciously focus on positive memories of unconditional love and respect from the deceased parent. Maintaining secure attachments and having positive stories to share is a key characteristic of bereaved adolescents who are perceived as resilient. While the bereavement literature confirms the importance of continuing bonds, it rarely links to the memory processes required to build adaptive links to a dead parent (Lohnes, 1994). When does a young person want to avoid reminiscing? How do different deaths affect an adolescent's capacity to remember? What do they do to retain secure memories? Which memories feel safe to rehearse with which people? Which are intrinsic to helping the adolescent define his or her own identity?

The following case study demonstrates the importance of providing props for an adolescent to refer back to when he or she is feeling unconfident.

Case Study—Leanne (14)

When Leanne was 10, her mother was given a diagnosis of secondary breast cancer; 2 years later she died. During that time Leanne's mother traveled a parallel path of maintaining hope that she would live but also wanted to prepare a memory box for her daughter just in case the doctors were right. The memory box contained a variety of objects, each one reflecting a story that would give Leanne a sense of being special and loved, and remind her of early childhood memories that may be lost if not rehearsed. The box also contained a bottle of her mother's perfume that was sprayed on a soft scarf, which became a nighttime comforter all through the teenage years. Some of the items in the box (e.g., letters) were prepared for later after she died.

Leanne took great pride in her memory box, which she chose to keep in her bedroom, underneath her bed. In the early months after her mother died she needed to look through it almost every night with her dad. As time moved on she used it more sparingly and only showed it to those she really trusted. As she entered her teenage years Leanne was surprised to find herself full of renewed grief for her mother; finding out more about her mother as a person and adding this information to her memory box helped her to develop the relationship she had with her mother. She realized she could continue to develop and add to her memory box throughout her life as a means of continuing to value and develop the relationship she had with her mother. She knew it would continue to remind her of her mother in a way that was both painful and comforting. Leanne was slowly developing her own mechanism for holding on while letting go. These memories reaffirmed her sense of self, allowing her to build a resilient mind-set as she encountered future changes, such as a new school, dad's new partner, and stepsiblings. Her mother's guidance was there for her to help her develop a positive mind-set, to make effective personal relationships and good friends, and to feel confident in her own capacity to be a mother should that time come. (For further information on supporting a child when a parent is ill, see Christ [2000], Stokes & Stubbs [2007], and *The Mummy Diaries* [n.d.].)

For Leanne it was relatively easy to access positive memories of her mother, but it is important to consider how we work with young people who have difficulty finding positive memories of their parent, either due to ambivalent relationships prior to their death or as a result of the way they died (e.g., suicide). Some of the young people we work with are trying so hard to repress these difficult memories that it prevents them from being able to recall any positive memories of their parent. For these young people it is important to allow them to acknowledge and voice these difficult memories and hold them alongside positive memories, in order to help them create a full and coherent narrative. Releasing these frozen feelings or memories can help adolescents with complicated grief to move forward (Goldman, 2001). For young adolescents whose parent had a traumatic death, this release is an important process in helping them to separate the *person* who died and their relationship with them, from the *way* in which they died. Releasing difficult feelings or memories can also be important in helping to decrease intrusive thoughts relating to the negative memories they have been trying to repress. Adolescents bereaved through suicide have reported finding it helpful to be able to remember both good and bad memories, as that helped them establish a narrative and to dilute feelings of anger, blame, rejection, and guilt (Wood, 2007).

> When I realized, cause I didn't know that he was depressed or an alcoholic at the time, cause I was too young apparently, so after knowing that, about 3 months after he died it was like "wow, so I wasn't the only cause," but I thought I was the only cause . . . if I forgot the depressive, alcoholic bit then I'd really believe it was my fault.

Wood found this form of cognitive process enabled young people bereaved by suicide to construct a more robust and adaptive continuing bond with their dead parents.

Finding Alternatives to Talking

Many adolescents find it difficult to express their feelings verbally; therefore, it is important for professionals to offer them alternative ways to explore their memories and emotions following a bereavement. Internet sites provide young people with a means of expressing and normalizing their emotions through online therapeutic activities and securely monitored interactive forums where they can meet other bereaved young people (e.g., http://www.rd4u.org.uk or http://www.winstonswish.org.uk). These forums can provide a nonthreatening neutral space in which young people can talk anonymously without needing to worry about other's immediate reactions.

Research is also needed to understand more fully the role that vehicles like music or physical activity can have for a parentally bereaved adolescent. Preliminary findings from an ethnographic study (Brewer & Sparkes, 2008) suggest that involvement in sport and physical activity provides a useful means of coping with bereavement for some adolescents, through expressing emotions, enhancing resilience, providing social support, and establishing a continuing bond. Success in sport can be an important and concrete way for the young person to succeed and feel a sense of pride, which can be inwardly shared with their dead parent. Similarly, the role of physical activity has been useful in team building on peer group interventions and in therapeutic activities. An example of this therapeutic activity is the "Anger Wall" where adolescents spend time thinking about and writing down some of the more difficult feelings they may find hard to express. What they have written is then pinned to an outdoor wall, and they are given the chance to physically express some of these feelings by running at the wall and throwing wet clay bombs at the written emotions. Although research into the role of physical activity in grief resolution in is its infancy, there is a wealth of research evidence for the beneficial effects of exercise for alleviating and preventing mental health problems (e.g., Biddle, Fox, & Boutcher, 2000), which suggests that physical activity may prove equally helpful in work with bereaved adolescents.

At Winston's Wish we recognized that the success for engaging older adolescent boys within the families referred was limited. We have therefore recently developed an "Outward Bound" therapeutic program specifically for adolescents aged 14–17 based on a range of physically challenging activities situated in a remote location. Throughout this program adolescents are encouraged to step outside their safety zone both physically, through these activities, and emotionally, through their expression of their grief, in order to build confidence and self-esteem. This form of activity-based therapeutic intervention is in keeping with previous research findings, which show that adolescent males value approaches that are more action than talk focused (Smith, 2004).

CONCLUSION

Few experiences are as devastating for a young person as the loss of a parent. If invited to write their autobiography, the death of a parent would inevitably be in the first chapter—and for most in the first paragraph. It is a life-changing experience. However, if young people are actively supported in their grief, bereavement can also be a conduit to emotional growth and learning. It is our responsibility to successfully engage young persons in ways that feel right for them; demonstrate perceptive, thorough assessment skills; and then offer flexible, accessible, age-appropriate interventions.

A resilient mind-set paves the way forward so the adolescent can develop into adulthood, empowered with choices, opportunities, and the personal resources to maximize his or her full potential. We know from the resilience literature that it is the attitude of adolescents to their losses that will ultimately define how they tell their survival story. Crucially, the systems that surround them—their family, friends, school, the media, online social-networking sites, and so forth—will also have a huge influence. As educators we can use an impressive range of culturally diverse resource material (e.g., http://63.134.200.198/documents/TeenageGriefProfessionalDevelopmentMaterials.pdf) to help those best placed to support a young person. At Winston's Wish we frequently hear that meeting other bereaved young people has been a critical factor in building a confident self-identity. Perhaps one of the main challenges is to create opportunities that enable bereaved adolescents to come together. In doing so, we will witness young people who show great empathy and have a greater appreciation of life and relationships than many of their nonbereaved peers—a privilege to witness and be part of.

REFERENCES

Alilovic, K. (2004). Beyond the Rough Rock: Offering a specialised group for families bereaved by suicide. In J. A. Stokes (Ed.), *Then, now & always . . . supporting children as they journey through grief,* (pp. 154–178). Cheltenham, UK: Winston's Wish.

Balk, D. E. (1996). Models for understanding adolescents coping with bereavement. *Death Studies, 20,* 367–387.

Balk, D. E., & Corr, C.A. (2001). Bereavement during adolescence: A review of research. In M. S. Stroebe, R. O. Hansson, W. Stroebe, & H. Schut (Eds.), *Handbook of bereavement research: Consequences, coping and care* (pp. 199–218). Washington, DC: American Psychological Association.

Biddle, S., Fox, K. R., & Boutcher, H. (2000). *Physical activity and psychological well-being.* London & New York: Routledge.

Boswell, G. (1995). *Violent victims: the prevalence of abuse and loss in the lives of section 53 offenders.* UK: Princes Trust.

Brewer, J., & Sparkes, A. C. (2008, July). *The meanings of sport and physical activity in the lives of bereaved children: Insights from an ethnographic study.* Presented at the International Conference on Grief and Bereavement in Contemporary Society, Melbourne, Australia.

Brisch, K. H. (2002). *Treating attachment disorders: From theory to therapy.* New York: Guilford.

Brown, A. C., Sandler, I. N., Tein, J.-Y., Liu, X., & Haine, R. A. (2007). Implications of parental suicide and violent death for promotion of resilience of parentally bereaved children. *Death Studies, 31,* 301–335.

Buston, K. (2002). Adolescents with mental health problems: What do they say about health services? *Journal of Adolescence, 25,* 231–242

Carr, A. (1999). *The handbook of child and adolescent psychology.* London: Routledge.

Christ, G. H. (2000). *Healing children's grief: Surviving a parent's death of cancer.* New York: Oxford University Press.

Cook, V., & Stedmon, J. (2004). *Adolescents' experience of returning to school following the death of a parent.* Unpublished doctoral dissertation, University of Bristol, UK.

Dowdney, L. (2000). Childhood bereavement following parental death. *Journal of Child Psychology & Psychiatry and Allied Disciplines, 41,* 819–830.

Draper, A. (2008). *Constructions of childhood parental bereavement.* Unpublished doctoral thesis, Doctoral in Systemic Psychotherapy, Tavistock Clinic (London) & University of London.

Field, N., Gao, B., & Paderna, L. (2005). Continuing bonds in bereavement: An attachment theory perspective. *Death Studies, 29,* 277–299.

Garland, A., Aarons, G., Saltzman, M., & Kruse, M. (2000). Correlates of adolescents' satisfaction with mental health services. *Mental Health Services Research, 2,* 127–139.

Garland, A., & Besinger, B. (1996). Adolescent's perceptions of outpatient mental health services. *Journal of Child and Family Studies, 5,* 355–375.

Gibson, R., & Possamai, A. (2002). What young people think about CAMHS. *Clinical Psychology, 18,* 20–24.

Goldman, L. (2001). *Breaking the silence: A guide for helping children with complicated grief—Suicide, homicide, AIDS, violence and abuse* (2nd ed.). New York: Brunner-Routledge.

Greef, A. P., & Human, B. (2004). Resilience in families in which a parent has died. *The American Journal of Family Therapy, 32,* 27–42.

Harrison, L., & Harrington, R. (2001). Adolescents' bereavement experiences: Prevalence, association with depressive symptoms and use of services. *Journal of Adolescence, 24,* 159–169.

Hughes, D. (1997). *Facilitating developmental attachment: The road to emotional recovery and behavioural change in foster and adopted children.* New York: Rowman & Littlefield.

Jacobs, S. (1999). *Traumatic grief: Diagnosis, treatment and prevention.* Philadelphia: Brunner/Mazel.

Jordan, J. V. (2005). Relational resilience in girls. In S. Goldstein & R. B. Brooks (Eds.), *Handbook of resilience in children* (pp. 79–91). New York: Kluwer Academic/Plenum Publishers.

Klass, D., Silverman, P. R., & Nickman, S. (Eds.) (1996). *Continuing bonds: New understandings of grief.* Washington, DC: Taylor & Francis.

Lin, K., Sandler, I., Ayers, T., Wolchik, S., & Laucken, L. (2004). Resilience in parentally bereaved children and adolescents seeking preventive services. *Journal of Clinical Child and Adolescent Psychology, 33,* 673–683.

Logan, D. E., & King, C. A. (2001). Parental facilitation of adolescent mental health utilization: A conceptual and empirical review. *Clinical Psychology: Science & Practice, 8,* 319–333.

Lohnes, K. (1994). *Maintaining attachment to a dead parent in childhood: A developmental perspective.* Unpublished doctoral thesis, University of Michigan, Ann Arbor.

Love, H. (2006). *Suicide bereaved children and young people's experience of a specialist group intervention: An Interpretative phenomenological analysis.* Unpublished doctoral dissertation, University of Exeter, UK.

Masten, A. S. (2001). Ordinary magic: Resilient processes in development. *American Psychologist, 56,* 227–238.

Masten, A. S., Best, K. M., & Garmezy, N. (1990). Resilience and development: contributions from the study of children who overcome adversity. *Development and Psychopathology, 2,* 425–444.

Meltzer, H., Gatward, R., Goodman, R., & Ford, T. (2000). *The mental health of children and adolescents in Great Britain.* London: Social Survey Division of the Office for National Statistics. Retrieved May 13, 2008, from http://www.statistics.gov.uk/downloads/theme_health/KidsMentalHealth.pdf

Miller, J. B. (1985). *The construction of anger in women and men: Work in progress no 4.* Wellesley, MA: Stone Centre Working Paper Series.

The Mummy Diaries (n.d.). Channel 4. Retrieved June 13, 2008, from http://www.channel4.com/health/microsites/M/mummy_diaries/

Muuss, R. E. (1996). *Theories of adolescence.* New York: McGraw-Hill.

Neimeyer, R. (2005). Grief, loss and the quest for meaning. *Bereavement Care, 24*(2), 27–30.

Neimeyer, R., Baldwin, S., & Gillies, J. (2006). Continuing bonds and reconstructing meaning: Mitigating complications in bereavement. *Death Studies, 30,* 715–738.

Newman, P. R., & Newman, B. M. (1976). Early adolescence and its conflict: Group identity versus alienation. *Adolescence, 11,* 261–274.

Nugus, D., &. Stokes, J. A., (2007). Bridging the gap: 15 years of service development and delivery: A model for community–based child bereavement services in the UK. *Grief Matters, 10*(2), 36–41.

Pollack, W. S. (2005). Creating genuine resilience in boys and young males. In S. Goldstein & R. B. Brooks (Eds.), *Handbook of resilience in children* (pp. 65–77). New York: Kluwer Academic/Plenum Publishers.

Reid, C. B. R., Stedmon, J., & Libby, S. (2007). *The meaning of using mental health services during adolescence.* Unpublished doctoral dissertation, University of Plymouth, UK.

Ribbens McCarthy, J. (2006). Resilience and bereaved children: Developing complex approaches. *Grief Matters, 9*(3), 58–61.

Ribbens McCarthy, J., & Jessop, J. (2005). *The impact of bereavement and loss on young people.* York, UK: The Joseph Rowntree Foundation.

Rowling, L. (2003). *Grief in school communities: Effective support strategies.* Bucks, UK: Open University Press.

Silverman, P. R. (2000). *Never too young to know: Death in children's lives.* New York: Oxford University Press.

Sjoqvist, S. (2007). *Still here with me: Teenagers and children on losing a parent.* London & Philadelphia: Jessica Kingsley.

Smith, J. M. (2004). Adolescent males' view on the use of mental health counseling services. *Adolescence, 39,* 76–82.

Stiffman, A. R., Chen, Y., Elze, D., Dore, P., & Cheng, L. (1997). Adolescents' and providers' perspectives on the need for and use of mental health services. *Journal of Adolescent Health, 21,* 335–342.

Stokes, J. A. (2004). *Then, now & always . . . Supporting children as they journey through grief.* Cheltenham: Winston's Wish.

Stokes, J. A. (2007). Resilience and bereaved children: Helping a child to develop a resilient mind-set following the death of a parent. In B. Munroe & D. Oliviere (Eds.), *Resilience in palliative care: Achieving in adversity* (pp. 39–65). Oxford, UK: Oxford University Press.

Stokes, J. A., & Stubbs, D. (2007). *As big as it gets: Supporting a child when a parent is seriously ill.* Cheltenham: Winston's Wish.

Street, C., Stapelkamp, C., Taylor, E., Malek, M., & Kurtz, Z. (2005). *Minority voices: Research into the access and acceptability of services for the mental health of young people from Black and ethnic minority groups.* London: Young Minds Publications.

Stroebe, M., Hansson, R., Stroebe, W., & Schut, H. (2001). *Handbook of bereavement research: Consequences, coping, and care.* Washington, DC: American Psychological Association.

Stubbs, D., Alilovic, K., Stokes, J., & Howells, K. (2006). *Family assessment: Guidelines for child bereavement practitioners.* Cheltenham: Winston's Wish.

White, M. (1988, Spring). Saying Hullo again: The incorporation of the lost relationship in the resolution of grief. *Dulwich Centre Newsletter,* 29–36.

Wisdom, J., Clarke, G. N., & Green, C. A. (2006). What teens want: Barriers to seeking care for depression. *Administration and Policy in Mental Health and Mental Health Services Research, 33*(2), 133–145.

Wolchik, S. A., Tein, J. Y., Sandler, I. N., & Ayers, T. S. (2006). Stressors, quality of the child–caregivers relationships, and children's mental health problems after parental death: The mediating role of self-system beliefs. *Journal of Abnormal Child Psychology, 34*(2), 221–238.

Wood, L. (2003). *Adolescents' experiences of a residential weekend for bereaved families: An interpretative phenomenological analysis.* Unpublished master's thesis, University of Bath, UK.

Wood, L. (2007). Continuing bonds after suicide: Bereavement in childhood. Unpublished doctoral dissertation, London.

Worden, J. W. (1996). *Children and grief: When a parent dies.* New York: Guildford.

Young Minds Policy. (2002). *Young minds policy for mental health services for adolescents and young adults.* London: Young Minds Publications. Retrieved June 1, 2008, from http://www.youngminds.org.uk/adolescentpolicy/YM_Adol_Policy.pdf

11

Sibling Bereavement During Adolescence

DAVID E. BALK

E. O. Poznanski, a professor of psychiatry at the University of Michigan, stimulated the spate of research into adolescent sibling bereavement with this quote: "The reaction of children to the death of a sibling would appear to provide the opportunity to study bereavement issues more clearly than in the case of the death of a parent" (Poznanski, 1979, p. 57). Dissertations and peer-reviewed journal articles on adolescent sibling bereavement appeared in the decade following this quote and continued thereafter. The researchers seemed unfazed by the cautions Poznanski mentioned about embedded problems, such as a preceding state of parental withdrawal if the sibling had been chronically ill, sibling rivalry, and parental grief.

Researchers into adolescent sibling bereavement have examined a fairly limited, associated number of topics. American researchers, influenced by psychology's predominant focus on the individual, have examined self-concept, peer relations, emotional reactions, grief reactions, religion and spirituality, surviving a suicide, sibling death from terminal illness, things that help and hinder bereavement recovery, and effects on schoolwork; some research attention has also focused on continuing bonds and on family influence upon the bereaved adolescent (see particularly Balk, 1983; Balmer, 1992; Davies, 1991, 2003; Hogan, 1987). British researchers, influenced by sociology and social policy analysis and a predominant focus on society and culture, have examined sibling bereavement within the overall context of the family, the school, and the culture and have championed continuing bonds and meaning making (see particularly Ribbens McCarthy, 2006; Riches & Dawson, 2000). This chapter reviews these topics: self-concept, emotional reactions, the family, continuing bonds, sibling death from terminal illness, things that help and hinder bereavement recovery, religion and spirituality, peer relationships, sibling suicide survivors, and effects on schoolwork.

SELF-CONCEPT

A teenager whose brother died said about her maturity, when viewed on a scale from 1–10, "Before Andrew's death, I was about a 7. Now, it depends. In general, I'd say 9. I started questioning everything after his death, and I learned a lot from it; feeling all these emotions and dealing with them made me feel more mature" (Balk, 1981, p. 135).

Crisis theory highlights that poorly managing a threatening situation produces both short- and long-term deleterious effects on self-efficacy (Moos & Schaefer, 1986). In league with crisis theory's understanding of the injurious outcome of a crisis to self-concept, viewpoints stressing the volatile, mercurial nature of adolescence suggested that poorly resolved life crises undermine achieving a mature, stable personal identity (Freud, 1971; Hall, 1904; Kaufman, 1979). Little if any attention was given to the notion that crises stimulate positive growth and development, and little credence was given research findings that noted (a) resiliency is the norm in adolescent responses to anticipated and unexpected life crises, and (b) only a small percentage of adolescents around the world experience overt or covert disturbance (Bandura, 1964/1980; Offer, 1969; Offer, Ostrov, & Howard, 1977).

Balk (1983) examined whether adolescents bereaved over a sibling's death showed self-concept problems when compared to national samples of healthy and clinically disturbed adolescents. He administered the Offer Self Image Questionnaire for Adolescents (OSIQ; Offer et al., 1977), a self-report inventory developed for use with and normed on adolescents. The OSIQ has 11 subscales measuring such areas as moral values, vocational aspirations, family relationships, peer relationships, and psychopathology. On 10 of the 11 subscales, bereaved adolescents had scores no different than the scores of same-age, same-sex healthy adolescents. However, on moral values, the bereaved adolescents' scores were 1 standard deviation higher than the scores of their healthy, nonbereaved peers. These scores on moral values provide one indication that coping with bereavement can propel adolescents into maturity beyond that of their unaffected peers.

The bereaved adolescents grouped according to high, average, and low self-concept scores: (a) 25%–30% whose self-concepts were considered more mature than those of most adolescents, (b) the majority (more than 50%) whose self-concepts were considered like those of most adolescents, and (c) a small minority (15%–20%) whose self-concepts were lower than the self-concepts of most adolescents. These findings oppose assertions that life crises necessarily damage adolescent integration of a stable identity, and they support Offer's (1969) longitudinal findings that adolescents typically respond well when faced with family tragedies. Hogan and Greenfield (1991) found that adolescents with low self-concept were particularly vulnerable to long-term negative outcomes following a sibling's death. Likely in this research we have a glimpse of contributing factors to prolonged grief disorder.

EMOTIONAL REACTIONS

A 14-year-old teenager whose older brother had died said, "I felt like my life was just shattered. It was like this big jolt in my life, and I felt really little compared to the whole world. . . . I had this feeling like so empty inside. . . . I hurt so bad, going numb was the only way to deal with it" (Balk, 1981, p. 286).

While numerous emotions have been reported for sibling-bereaved adolescents, two emotional reactions typically studied have been depression and anxiety. Anxiety and depression found in adolescents following a sibling's suicide provide one example (Dyregov & Dyregov, 2005). Balmer (1992) reported sibling-bereaved adolescents' scores on standardized instruments were more indicative of depression than were the scores of nonbereaved matched controls.

Emotions that adolescents said described them in the months following their siblings' deaths were shock, guilt, confusion, depression, fear, loneliness, and anger. Over time fewer adolescents indicated that these emotions described their ongoing reactions to their siblings' deaths, but a notable minority (28%–45%) still reported guilt, confusion, depression, anger, and loneliness. Over half said they were convinced in the first few months after their sibling died that their feelings would not subside. Nearly two thirds said their feelings had become less intense over time; however, one third said the intensity of their feelings had increased (Balk, 1983).

THE FAMILY FOLLOWING ADOLESCENT SIBLING BEREAVEMENT

A teenager whose brother had died said, "All kinds of changes occurred in my family. My parents almost had a divorce. Tension rose, a lot of hostility; they got in a lot of fights. They are all right again now" (Balk, 1981, p. 305).

Hogan and Balk (1990) demonstrated that bereaved mothers and fathers held distinctly different assessments of their adolescents' self-concepts and bereavement reactions to a sibling's death. The mothers' assessments diverged significantly from what the adolescents reported about themselves. Specifically, the mother, father, and one adolescent from 14 families in which a child had died completed Hogan's Inventory of Sibling Bereavement (HSIB: Hogan, 1990). The adolescents answered for themselves, and the parents answered as they expected the adolescents would respond to the HSIB. Mothers assessed the adolescents' self-concepts to be more mature and their grief to be more distressing that what either the fathers or the adolescents indicated. Further, the fathers' and adolescents' scores were in substantial agreement.

These findings called into serious question commonly held views that mothers have more reliable understandings of adolescents than do fathers. In private, bereaved mothers at meetings of the Compassionate Friends and in university courses expressed relief over such data: They felt reprieved from always having to be the accurate, sensitive touchstone for the family.

In conversations with bereaved siblings, Hogan (1988) uncovered a significant issue within bereaved families following the death of a child. Bereaved adolescents camouflaged their grief as a means to rescue their families from dissolution. The intense pain and distress of bereavement threatened their parents' well-being and the survival of their families. Expressing grief only seemed to elicit more distress in the family. Frequently parents misconstrued camouflaged feelings in one of two ways: either (a) "My adolescent is strong, doing well, and not suffering from grief's distress" or (b) "My adolescent is insensitive, does not care, and has not been touched by my child's death."

In consort with Hogan's findings about camouflaged feelings, Balmer (1992) learned that her bereaved adolescent subjects seldom spoke with their parents about grief following a sibling's death. Parents concluded that the adolescent did not and would not speak to anyone about these matters and were surprised to find how eager their adolescents were to talk with a researcher when offered the opportunity. The adolescents had, in actuality, been concerned about their parents' health following the death and were "merely attempting to protect them from further pain by refusing to initiate conversations about their own worries, fears, and concerns" (Balmer, 1992, p. 173).

Balmer (1992) noted that "the family plays an important and powerful mediating role for adolescents who are faced with life crises" (pp. 169–170). She determined that family climate, particularly interrelationships reflecting cohesion and healthy expressions of conflict, served to buffer sibling-bereaved adolescents from adjustment problems following a sibling's death.

Balk (1983) devised a family coherency scale in which bereaved adolescents indicated how close they felt to each family member prior to the sibling's death and how often they engaged in important, personal conversations with each family member prior to the sibling's death. The scores were aggregated as a measure of family coherency, with two thirds of the adolescents grouped into greater family coherency and one third into less family coherency.

Discriminant function analysis was used to see whether family coherency influenced sibling-bereaved adolescents' responses in the few months after the death and at a later point in time. This multivariate statistical technique provides information that can be used to sketch a psychologically meaningful profile of the adolescents in each group (Tatsuoka, 1970).

After the death, four reactions characterized adolescents in families with greater coherency: shock, fear, loneliness, and the attribution that these feelings would never subside. After the death, two reactions characterized adolescents in families with less coherency: guilt and not discussing the death. When some time had passed, only depression distinguished the adolescents from a family with greater coherency. Several emotional responses characterized sibling-bereaved teenagers in families with less coherency: numbness, relief, confusion, fear, loneliness, and anger. What psychologically meaningful profiles can we deduce from these statistical results?

Profile of a Teenager From a Family With Greater Coherency

Sixty-three percent of the sibling-bereaved adolescents fit this profile. When their sibling died, they were faced with a shattered family environment, an environment that previously had been a source of security. They were shocked, lonely, and afraid. The teenagers believed the intense feelings would never go away. In time these teenagers report they began to share their feelings and thoughts with their families, especially with their mothers. Now they feel depressed about their sibling's death. Confusion is nonexistent for them, probably because questions about the death have been both welcomed and answered. They have no guilt.

How does the family with greater coherency influence bereavement resolution for these teenagers? It seems that a tradition of greater family coherency helps sibling-bereaved adolescents work through problems by using the family as a resource. At the same time, these adolescents develop an enduring sadness regarding the death. Perhaps this enduring sadness is the natural price paid for close personal sibling bonds severed by death.

Profile of a Teenager From a Family With Less Coherency

Thirty-seven percent of the adolescents fit this profile. Personal conversations within the family were practically nonexistent. Feelings of closeness were minimal. Adolescents did not see family ties as a source of strength, support, or security. These young persons talked to no one in the family about the death. Threats to the family's survival posed by the sibling's death were not distressing to the adolescents. They felt guilty when the death occurred. Over time, a sense of confusion developed, also feelings of numbness, fear, and loneliness. A feeling of relief emerged over time: relief that they had survived the problems the death brought to their lives.

How does the family with less coherency influence bereavement resolution for these teenagers? Lack of close emotional ties and of personal conversations insulated the teenagers initially from many emotions. The family is not a resource, and its dissolution is not a concern. Over time, these teenagers tend especially to feel confused as questions about the death and about reactions to it simply are not discussed. Perhaps an enduring confusion about the death is a natural price paid when a family with distant relationships experiences the death of a child.

Greater family coherency promotes understanding and acceptance of differences, and fosters a sense of togetherness, whereas less family coherency inhibits expression of differences or indicates, at another extreme, that each person is on their own. It is not that much of an insight to see connections between family issues following sibling death and the growing research support for the singular importance of positive, consistent parenting in the lives of bereaved children and adolescents (Sandler et al., 2003; Worden, 1996).

Riches and Dawson (2000) invoked family systems theory to examine effects of adolescent sibling bereavement. Family systems theory talks about emotional balance, roles, rules, and interaction processes; family systems theory emphasizes that the death of a family member unsettles a family's emotional balance and leads often to adjustments in terms of defining roles, enforcing rules, and governing communication (see Nadeau, 1997; Shapiro, 1994). For example, a rule in a family could be that expressing emotions signifies weakness, and therefore expressions of grief will be stifled; by contrast, another family's rule could be that open communication of feelings signifies trust and health, and therefore expressing feelings of grief will be accepted.

The empty space left by the dead sibling can prove problematic for individuals and for family adjustment. The empty space can highlight the bereaved sibling's confusion over his or her own place in the family. Different interpretations of the empty space may not be tolerated; discrepancies in coping with bereavement can become matters of secondary distress in the family as can different trajectories in the resolution of grief (Riches and Dawson, 2000). To see an eloquent depiction of the trauma to a family following a child's death and the impact on the surviving adolescent, view the remarkable film *Ordinary People,* Robert Redford's exquisite rendering of Judith Guest's (1976) novel.

CONTINUING BONDS

A teenager whose sibling had died from cancer said, "You can never forget somebody you are that close to all your life" (Balk, 1981, p. 288).

Attachment theory provides a powerful framework for understanding and examining child-parent relations and bereavement following the death of a parent or child. An important explanatory mechanism within attachment theory is Bowlby's (1980) notion of an attachment schema an infant forms in early interactions with a caregiver: The quality of the attachment bonds with the caregiver influences interpersonal attachments over the life span.

Sibling relations provide a fruitful area for deploying attachment theory. The notion of an attachment schema formed in infancy and remolded thereafter in response to interpersonal circumstances can help explain the impact of sibling relationships on development and the reason sibling relationships sundered by death become matters for bereavement. What I have not found examined are the influences that types of attachment bonds between siblings have on responses to sibling death. Thus, an area of importance for research with practical significance for grief counselors is what the trajectories are of adolescent bereavement when sibling relationships sundered by death are marked by (a) secure attachments, (b) anxious-avoidant attachments, and (c) anxious-ambivalent attachments (see Mallinckrodt, Gantt, & Coble, 1995).

Hogan and DeSantis (1992) and Davies (1991) were the first scholars to mention that continuing bonds marked adolescent sibling bereavement. Hogan and DeSantis (1992, p. 164) talked of "an ongoing attachment" characterized by an "emotional and social relationship or bond between the deceased and bereaved sibling" that has at least six facets: (a) regrets, such as missing a confidant; (b) endeavors to understand, such as learning more about the circumstances of the sibling's death; (c) catching up, that is, a need to inform the dead sibling of events since the death, such as, reassuring the dead sibling that the family was well; (d) reaffirming the emotional bond between the dead sibling and the bereaved adolescent, such as, expressing love for the sibling who died; (e) continued influence of the sibling, such as, the deceased sibling was an ongoing, positive role model; and (f) reuniting with the sibling in the afterlife.

Packman, Horsley, Davies, and Kramer (2006) address the remarkable shift in bereavement thinking that has occurred since the notion of continuing bonds captured the imagination of thanatologists. These authors examine how the concept of continuing bonds (a) applies to sibling relationships and sibling bereavement and (b) suggests clinical interventions with bereaved families. With an appreciative nod to family systems theory, Packman and colleagues talk about the impact of sibling death on a family and how family communication and family cohesion influence the family's adjustment and recovery.

The clinical implications for sibling bereavement above all include positive, consistent parenting (see Sandler et al., 2003; Worden, 1996). For this reason, parents are encouraged to model continuing bonds by keeping linking objects (for instance, by carrying photos in their wallets), by admitting to having internal conversations with the dead child, and by listening attentively to what the bereaved adolescent has to say (Packman et al., 2006). Parents can also encourage bereaved siblings to participate in bereavement groups. It is crucial for parents to remain patient with sibling-bereaved adolescents who keep their thoughts and feelings in check, and whose form of connection to the dead sibling is discrepant from what a parent expects (for instance, in music the parent neither appreciates nor understands).

PEER RELATIONSHIPS

A teenager whose sibling died said, "With my good friends, they were with me through the whole thing. They were with me the whole time, and we got closer. But other kids didn't know what to say to me. They would either look at me with real sad eyes or pity just pouring out or come up real happy. I was something to talk about and look at when I walked down the hall. I hated it. They didn't know how to deal with it" (Balk, 1981, p. 105).

An observation from Silver and Wortman (1980) that outsiders typically underestimate the intensity and the duration of distress caused by life crises applies to bereavement: unaffected persons seldom appreciate the ongoing demands and anguish that the bereaved experience. The issue is further complicated by the anxiety and discomfort many persons feel when around someone who is grieving. Few persons, if they have not been bereaved themselves, have the poise and courage to remain attentive to someone who is bereaved.

This observation about outsiders' ignorance concerning the effects of bereavement and discomfort when in the presence of a griever uncannily depicts a contextual problem that bereaved adolescents face. Many persons figuratively or literally leave the room when grief enters. Bereaved adolescents say they learned who their real friends were in the aftermath of a sibling's death, and in many cases, new friendships had to be made as old friends, weary of the intensity and duration of the grief, drifted away.

Conversations with peers about one's grief, supposedly a means to cash in on social support, can backfire: nonbereaved acquaintances find such conversations unappealing and indicate such conversations possess a short shelf life. To prevent the loss of friends, some bereaved adolescents stop sharing their thoughts and feelings about the death. Bereaved adolescents appreciated most the friends who allowed them (a) to respond as the occasion demanded and (b) to escape at times from their distress. One can see in these accommodating and responsive peers' intuitive enactments what we now call the dual process model of coping with loss (Stroebe & Schut, 1999).

SIBLING DEATH FROM TERMINAL ILLNESS

A teenager whose brother died of leukemia said, "Sam went through lots of times when he seemed to be getting better and then would get worse. Tension rose then, with everybody. There was a lot of hostility. Everybody understood what was going on, but . . . I couldn't stand to see Sam suffer. I told a counselor I thought it would be better if Sam died. He was shocked I could talk about it as easily as I could" (Balk, 1981, p. 305).

An assumption among some in thanatology is that anticipated deaths are less difficult on the griever than are sudden deaths. Anticipatory grieving or anticipatory mourning is thought to enable persons to prepare themselves for the impending loss (see Rando, 2000). Empirical research does not give unequivocal support to this notion that anticipated grievers fare better than sudden grievers (Gilliland & Fleming, 1998), and strong objections have been raised as to the reality of anticipatory mourning (Fulton, 2003). There is also recognition that a drawn-out death filled with pain and physical disfigurement—as well as financial strain and interpersonal conflict—interferes with cognitive functioning and can exacerbate bereavement (Mackenzie, Smith, Hasher, Leach, & Behl, 2007).

Parents with children grieving a sibling's death from cancer commonly express concern for them, and note with regret that equal parenting had been neglected due to greater priority given to meet their terminally ill child's needs (deCinque, Monterosso, Dadd, Macpherson, & Aoun, 2006). These parents recognized their own bereavement created obstacles in providing support to their living children. The parents even seemed aware that their children adjusted so that they did not add to the distress of the parents. Feeling unable to meet the needs of their bereaved children, the parents said sources outside the family need to provide support for bereaved siblings.

Birenbaum (2000) reported secondary data analysis of adolescents' responses across time following the death of a sibling from cancer. The author had been the principal investigator of a longitudinal study into home care when a child has a terminal illness. The influence of Lindemann (1944) can be seen in terms of the physical and psychosocial responses that Birenbaum and his associates examined.

The researchers gathered data from 12- to 19-year-old adolescents on four separate occasions: before the sibling died, 2 weeks after the death, 4 months after, and 12 months after. Because of loss of research participants over time (12 of the 22 dropped out by the 12-month follow-up), the researchers acknowledged they could not present longitudinal findings but rather "a cross sectional analysis at four points in time" (Birenbaum, 2000, p. 386).

The psychosocial symptoms most seen before the death were arguing, irritability, disobedience, impulsivity, hyperactivity, secretiveness, moodiness, worrying, sadness, and feeling unloved. At 12 months following the death, nearly all of these psychosocial symptoms were still in evidence, with a few new ones added and some less prominent: The bereaved adolescents were even more likely to argue and be sad, irritable, and hyperactive; they also had a greater propensity to daydream, have problems concentrating, show off, and demand attention. At the same time, they were much less disobedient at home than they had been in the few weeks prior to the death. Impulsivity, hyperactivity, demanding attention, sadness, daydreaming, and feeling unloved were all at higher levels in the bereaved adolescents than levels reported in nonbereaved peers.

The physical symptoms most seen before the death were stomach aches, asthma, headaches, nausea, and general aches and pains. At 12 months after the sibling's death, three physical symptoms were more prominent than others: headaches, nausea, and stomach aches. All of these physical symptoms were considerably higher than what are found in nonbereaved children and adolescents.

WHAT HELPS AND WHAT HINDERS BEREAVEMENT RECOVERY

A sibling-bereaved adolescent asked if she had advice for bereaved adolescents said, "I think it's important for them to talk with someone else with a problem like theirs. 'Cause I think it will help them deal with it better and get through it. The first year I think is the hardest" (Balk, 1981, p. 299).

Lehman, Ellard, and Wortman (1986) provided a classification of bereaved persons' perspectives of social support actions that help and others that hinder bereavement recovery. Among actions deemed helpful were being present, expressing concern, allowing opportunity to express feelings, and being in contact with someone who had been in similar circumstances. Among actions deemed unhelpful were giving advice, encouraging the person to get on with life, and saying "I know how you feel."

Hogan and DeSantis (1994) surveyed bereaved adolescents on what helped and hindered them to cope with their sibling's death. Some things that helped were in the individual's self-control, such as, doing things to reduce stress or relying on personal beliefs. Other helps came (a) from family members who offered solace or helped the adolescents to understand their reactions were normal and (b) from friends who were available with caring and love. Some help came from professionals such as ministers or psychologists, and some found peer support groups helpful.

Some things that hindered adolescents in their sibling bereavement were outside the individual's self-control; particular examples include being imploded with intrusive thoughts and images, experiencing intense loneliness and guilt, and realizing the permanence of the sibling's death. Arguments with family members were very unhelpful in coping with grief. Insensitivity of outsiders—particularly persons who said they know how the adolescent felt or who advised the person on how to grieve—hindered coping. For some sibling-bereaved adolescents a problem arose out of seeing the injustice and unfairness that their sibling's death had revealed characterizes the world.

RELIGION AND SPIRITUALITY

A sibling-bereaved adolescent said, "I think in part the anger that I felt towards God just didn't help at all. Religion doesn't too terribly much help me now. I still feel the anger, but our minister has helped a great deal. I think the peace I find in it helps, knowing that Randy is in heaven with God. Even though I am angry at God and the fact that Randy is with Him and not with us. It's a comfort in a way just knowing that if there wasn't any religion in my life at all, the confusion of why would be even greater. At this point I know that God must have some reason. I don't know what it is, and if I did I probably wouldn't understand it anyway. But there is a reason, and it better have been a good one" (Balk, 1981, p. 298).

The dangerous opportunities of growth and dissolution that life crises present can manifest in existential issues about the meaning and/or absurdity of life. Religious beliefs in a just and caring God can be tested severely. It is possible that a transformation in development coming out of a life crisis can be a faith consciousness beyond what the person held prior to grappling with the crisis (see Batten & Oltjenbruns, 1999; Fowler, 1981; Moos & Schaefer, 1986; Tedeschi & Calhoun, 2006).

Religion affords some persons a means to determine the personal significance of a sibling's death (see Moos & Schaefer, 1986) and thus affords a help in coping with bereavement (Balk, 1996). Nearly three fourths of 144 bereaved siblings told Hogan and DeSantis (1992) they believe they will be reunited with their sibling in heaven. Sibling-bereaved adolescents were more inclined to tell Balk (1991) that religion helped them cope than that it was not of any help.

Batten and Oltjenbruns (1999) present sibling bereavement as a catalyst for spiritual development in adolescents. They argue that the criteria for transformative powers in a life crisis are present in sibling bereavement: time for reflection, a permanent and serious impact on the person's life, and struggle to find emotional balance severely jeopardized by a life event.

Applying these ideas about crises as potentially transforming experiences to adolescents whose siblings had died 3 to 19 months ago, Batten and Oltjenbruns conducted interviews and analyzed them for themes. Major themes uncovered were all seen as part of new perspectives on self, others, a higher power, life, the sibling relationship, and death (see Attig, 1996). The adolescents' grappling with bereavement had led to "changing understanding of life's meaning" and "it is these changed perspectives about life's meaning that constitutes spiritual growth" (Batten & Oltjenbruns, 1999, p. 542).

SIBLING SUICIDE SURVIVORS

When asked about thoughts of suicide, a bereaved adolescent whose sibling had died said, "I don't know what I hoped to accomplish. I didn't want to feel hurt any more, but I knew if I did do it I would be hurting others more because I knew how hurt they were from Phil being gone" (Balk, 1981, p. 293).

Centers for Disease Control mortality findings indicate that the great majority of adolescents and young adults who complete suicide leave behind sibling survivors to cope with the traumatic aftermath (Gallo & Pfeffer, 2003). One aspect of the trauma from these deaths is the heightened risk for prolonged grief disorder in suicide survivors who have close attachments to the siblings who took their lives (Mitchell, Kim, Prigerson, & Mortimer-Stephens, 2004): More intense symptoms of complicated grief are reported significantly more often in suicide survivors with close attachments to the deceased than in survivors with distant attachments. One surprise in a study by Mitchell and colleagues (2004) is that siblings' prolonged grief disorder over suicide was less intense than symptoms in parents and spouses over suicides and was more like the grief of in-laws and coworkers to suicides.

Sibling suicide survivors feel ashamed, guilty, and abandoned, but their loss is often overlooked, and their grief not validated. According to Dyregrov and Dyregrov (2005, p.714), sibling suicide survivors are "forgotten grievers." These Norwegian bereavement researchers found age differentiated the impact of sibling suicides: Younger siblings were more at risk than older siblings for prolonged grief disorder and for such clinical symptoms as depression and anxiety. In league with the social interpretation frameworks that some thanatologists place on bereavement (Goss & Klass, 2005; Ribbens McCarthy, 2006; Walter, 1999), the Dyregrovs emphasize that difficulties in sibling suicide bereavement for young persons are largely relational and social; examples would be being shunned by peers and masking one's feelings of dismay lest friends, uncomfortable with the realities surrounding grief over a suicide, abandon them.

EFFECTS ON SCHOOLWORK

A sibling-bereaved adolescent said, "School wasn't the most important thing. I had to get myself back together. I was more with people, and I don't believe that you get everything out of a book 'cause you have a lot more to learn out of life itself. I'm starting to study more again. I don't study as much as I used to. But I want to get into college" (Balk, 1981, p. 295).

Disrupted work productivity, problems staying on task, and difficulties concentrating are three symptoms in Lindemann's (1944) acute grief syndrome. School performance for many bereaved adolescents provides the major measure of work-related grief, and grades offer a summative indicator of school performance.

The great majority of sibling-bereaved adolescents in Balk's (1983) research indicated their study habits and grades were negatively affected following the death; for many, however, as time passed they said their grades and study habits improved. The reasons given for improved study habits and grades had to do with stopping feeling guilty and wanting to make something of their lives. While bereaved adolescents in Balmer's (1992) research reported problems concentrating, there were no differences in their grades and the grades of matched nonbereaved controls. Because these bereaved adolescents were experiencing anxiety and depression as well as other adjustment problems, Balmer doubted securing grades was a useful measure of adjustment following sibling death. She noted as well that there are numerous problems in obtaining reliable data.

SUMMARY COMMENTS

This chapter looked at various strands in the research tapestry woven since the early 1980s about adolescent sibling bereavement. Topics examined were self-concept, emotional reactions, the family, continuing bonds, sibling death from terminal illness, things that help and hinder bereavement recovery, religion and spirituality, peer relationships, sibling suicide survivors, and effects on schoolwork. On the whole, since the start of the 21st century there seems to be less research attention paid to adolescent sibling bereavement than was the case in the 1980s and 1990s.

Researchers have yet to conduct longitudinal studies using control groups to examine the trajectory of adolescent sibling bereavement. Some areas for investigation seem clear: (a) types of attachment and the sequelae of adolescent sibling bereavement; (b) family issues during a child's terminal illness and after the death; (c) adolescent sibling bereavement in cultures and with nationalities other than Euro-American; (d) adolescent sibling bereavement in diverse racial and ethnic groups; (e) adolescent sibling bereavement in varied constellations other than the two-parent nuclear family; and (f) interventions aimed to promote positive, consistent parenting of sibling-bereaved adolescents.

REFERENCES

Attig, T. (1996). *How we grieve: Relearning the world.* New York: Oxford University Press.

Balk, D. E. (1981). *Sibling death during adolescence: Self-concept and bereavement reactions.* Unpublished doctoral dissertation, University of Illinois at Urbana-Champaign.

Balk, D. E. (1983). Adolescents' grief reactions and self-concept perceptions following sibling death: A case study of 33 teenagers. *Journal of Youth and Adolescence, 12,* 137–163.

Balk, D. E. (1991). Sibling death, adolescent bereavement, and religion. *Death Studies, 15,* 1–20

Balk, D. E. (1996). Models for understanding adolescent coping with bereavement. *Death Studies, 20,* 367–387.

Balmer, L. E. (1992). *Adolescent sibling bereavement: Mediating effects of family environment and personality.* Unpublished doctoral dissertation, York University, Toronto.

Bandura, A. (1980). The stormy decade: Fact or fiction? In R. E. Muuss (Ed.), *Adolescent behavior and society: A book of readings* (pp. 22–31). New York: Random House. (Reprinted from *Psychology in the Schools,* 1964, *1,* 589–595)

Batten, M. & Oltjenbruns, K. A. (1999). Adolescent sibling bereavement as a catalyst for spiritual development: A model for understanding. *Death Studies, 23,* 529–546.

Birenbaum, L. K. (2000). Assessing children's and teenagers' bereavement when a sibling dies from cancer: A secondary analysis. *Child Care, Health and Development, 26,* 381–400.

Bowlby, J. (1980). *Attachment and loss. Volume III. Loss: Sadness and depression.* New York: Basic Books.

Davies, B. (1991). Long term outcomes of adolescent sibling bereavement. *Journal of Adolescent Research, 6,* 83–96.

Davies, B. (2003). The study of sibling bereavement: A historical perspective. In I. Corless, B. B. Germino, & M. A. Pittman (Eds.), *Dying, death, and bereavement: A challenge for living* (2nd ed., pp. 287–302). New York: Springer Publishing.

deCinque, N., Monterosso, L., Dadd, G., Macpherson, R., & Aoun, S. (2006). Bereavement support for families following the death of a child from cancer: Experience of bereaved parents. *Journal of Psychosocial Oncology, 24,* 65–83.

Dyregrov, K. & Dyregrov, A. (2005). Siblings after suicide: "The forgotten bereaved." *Suicide and Life Threatening Behavior, 35,* 714–724.

Fowler, J. W. (1981). *Stages of faith: The psychology of human development and the quest for meaning.* San Francisco: Harper & Row.

Freud, A. (1971). Adolescence as a developmental disturbance. In *The writings of Anna Freud* (Vol. VII, pp. 39–47). New York: International Universities Press.

Fulton, R. (2003). Anticipatory mourning: A critique of the concept. *Mortality, 8,* 342–351.

Gallo, C. L & Pfeffer, C. R. (2003). Children and adolescents bereaved by a suicidal death: Implications for psychosocial outcomes and interventions. In R. A. King & A. Apter (Eds.), *Suicide in children and adolescents* (pp. 294–312). New York: Cambridge University Press.

Gilliland, G. & Fleming, S. (1998). A comparison of spousal anticipatory grief and conventional grief. *Death Studies, 22,* 541–569.

Goss, R. E. & Klass, D. (2005). *Dead but not lost: Grief narratives in religious traditions.* Walnut Creek, CA: AltaMira Press.

Guest, J. (1976). *Ordinary people.* New York: Viking Press.

Hall, G. S. (1904). *Adolescence: Its psychology and its relations to physiology, anthropology, sociology, sex, crime, religion, and education* (Vol. 1). New York: D. Appleton.

Hogan, N. S. (1987). *An investigation of the adolescent sibling bereavement process and adaptation.* Unpublished doctoral dissertation, Loyola University, Chicago.

Hogan, N. S. (1988). The effects of time on the adolescent sibling bereavement process. *Pediatric Nursing, 14,* 333–335.

Hogan, N. S. (1990). Hogan Sibling Inventory of Bereavement. In J. Touliatos, B. Perlmutter, & M. Straus (Eds.), *Handbook of family measurement techniques* (p. 524). Newbury Park, CA: Sage.

Hogan, N. S., & Balk, D. E. (1990). Adolescent reactions to sibling death: Perceptions of mothers, fathers, and teenagers. *Nursing Research, 39,* 39–36.

Hogan, N. S., & DeSantis, L. (1992). Adolescent sibling bereavement: An ongoing attachment. *Qualitative Health Research, 2,* 159–177.

Hogan, N. S., & DeSantis, L. (1994). Things that help and hinder adolescent sibling bereavement. *Western Journal of Nursing Research, 16,* 132–153.

Hogan, N. S., & Greenfield, D. B. (1991). Adolescent sibling bereavement: Symptomatology in a large community sample. *Journal of Adolescent Research, 6,* 97–112.

Kaufman, B. (1979). Object removal and adolescent depression. In A. French & I. Berlin (Eds.), *Depression in children and adolescents* (pp. 109–128). New York: Human Sciences Press.

Lehman, D. R., Ellard, J. H., & Wortman, C. B. (1986). Social support for the bereaved: Recipients' and providers' perspectives on what is helpful. *Journal of Counseling and Clinical Psychology, 54,* 438–446.

Lindemann, E. (1944). Symptomatology and management of acute grief. *American Journal of Psychiatry, 101,* 141–149.

Mackenzie, C. S., Smith, M. C., Hasher, L., Leach, L., & Behl, P. (2007). Cognitive functioning under stress: Evidence from informal caregivers of palliative patients. *Journal of Palliative Medicine, 10,* 749–758.

Mallinckrodt, B., Gantt, D. L., & Coble, H. M. (1995). Attachment patterns in the psychotherapy relationship: Development of the client Attachment to Therapist scale. *Journal of Counseling Psychology, 42,* 307–317.

Mitchell, A. M., Kim, Y., Prigerson, H. G., & Mortimer-Stephens, M. (2004). Complicated grief in survivors of suicide. *Crisis: The Journal of Crisis Intervention and Suicide, 25,* 12–18.

Moos, R. H., & Schaefer, J. A. (1986). Life transitions and crises: A conceptual overview. In R. H. Moos (Ed.), *Coping with life crises: An integrated approach* (pp. 3–28). New York: Plenum.

Nadeau, J. (1997). *Families making sense of death.* Thousand Oaks, CA: Sage.

Offer, D. (1969). *The psychological world of the teenager.* New York: Basic Books.

Offer, D., Ostrov, E., & Howard, K. I. (1977). The self-image of adolescents: A study of four cultures. *Journal of Youth and Adolescence, 6,* 265–280.

Packman, W., Horsley, H., Davies, B., & Kramer, R. (2006). Sibling bereavement and continuing bonds. *Death Studies, 30,* 817–841.

Poznanski, E. O. (1979). Childhood depression: A psychodynamic approach to the etiology and treatment of depression in children. In A. French & I. Berlin (Eds.), *Depression in children and adolescents* (pp. 46–68). New York: Human Sciences Press.

Rando, T. A. (Ed.). (2000). *Clinical dimensions of anticipatory mourning: Theory and practice in working with the dying, their loved ones, and their caregivers.* Champaign, IL: Research Press.

Ribbens McCarthy, J. (2006). *Young people's experiences of loss and bereavement: Towards an interdisciplinary approach.* New York: Open University Press.

Riches, G., & Dawson, P. (2000). *An intimate loneliness: Supporting bereaved parents and siblings.* Philadelphia: Open University Press.

Sandler, I. N., Ayers, T. S., Wolchik, S. A., Tein, J-Y., Kwok, O-M., Haine, R. A., et al. (2003). The Family Bereavement Program: Efficacy evaluation of a theory-based prevention program for parentally-bereaved children and adolescents. *Journal of Consulting and Clinical Psychology, 71,* 587–600.

Shapiro, E. (1994). *Grief as a family process: A developmental approach to clinical practice.* New York: Guilford.

Silver, R. L., & Wortman, C. B. (1980). Coping with undesirable life events. In J. Garber & M. E. P. Seligman (Eds.), *Human helplessness: Theory and applications* (pp. 279–340). New York: Academic Press.

Stroebe, M. S., & Schut, H. (1999).The Dual Process Model of coping with bereavement: Rationale and description. *Death Studies, 23,* 197–224.

Tatsuoka, M. (1970). *Discriminant analysis: The study of group differences.* Champaign, IL: Institute for Personality and Ability Testing.

Tedeschi, R. G., & Calhoun, L. G. (2006). Time of change? The spiritual challenges of bereavement and loss. *Omega, Journal of Death and Dying, 53,* 105–116.

Walter, T. (1999). *On bereavement: The culture of grief.* Philadelphia: Open University Press.

Worden, J. W. (1996). *Children and grief: When a parent dies.* New York: Guilford.

12

Death of a Friend During Adolescence

HEATHER L. SERVATY-SEIB

This chapter examines adolescent experiences involving the death of a friend or peer. After noting that losses associated with adolescent friend death are often disenfranchised, both in society and in the empirical research, the chapter highlights factors that contribute to the importance of friend death during adolescence and argues on behalf of the need for increased empirical attention in this area. The chapter then explores existing empirical research on adolescents' reactions to friend death, factors that appear to affect those reactions, coping strategies used by friend-bereaved adolescents, and the role that others can play in supporting these adolescents. The chapter concludes with recommendations for future research.

THE DISENFRANCHISED NATURE OF ADOLESCENT FRIEND DEATHS

Adolescents who experience the death of a friend or peer have been referred to as a hidden population (Sklar & Hartley, 1990) and their grief is commonly considered disenfranchised (Doka, 2002). When an adolescent dies, he or she leaves behind a family devastated by the off-time and often sudden loss of a member of its youngest generation. In contrast to the apt recognition afforded the parents of deceased young people, the grief of the friends of deceased adolescents generally goes unnoticed, is minimized, or is misunderstood (Hooyman & Kramer, 2006; Oltjenbruns, 1996; Podell, 1989, Sklar & Hartley, 1990). Survivor-friends, as they have been referred to by Sklar and Hartley, have few rights as mourners (Sklar, 1991) and do not have established social roles or expectations to guide them through the process of their grief (Deck & Folta, 1989). Even the level of friend involvement in formal death rituals (e.g., funerals, burial ceremonies) is left to the family to decide (Smith, 1996). In addition, informal conversations about death losses are generally more oriented toward adults than they are adolescents (McNeil, Silliman, & Swihart, 1991). As a result, grieving friends may begin to internally question how appropriate it is for them to openly express their reactions as they do not want to be disrespectful to the experiences of the family (Werner-Lin & Moro, 2004). Sklar and Hartley (1990) concluded that grieving friends may even be a hidden population to themselves in that the bereaved friends (mostly college-aged students) they studied were surprised to learn that best friend was even a *category* of individuals who could mourn.

The disenfranchisement of the survivor-friend experience of adolescents also exists in the thanatological literature. Although research on friend death has increased over the past decade, McCarthy (2006) highlights the fact that studies of peer bereavement "are still largely undeveloped and tend to rely quite haphazardly on opportunistic or volunteer samples, often of American college students" (p. 104).

IMPORTANCE OF ADOLESCENT FRIEND DEATHS

The lack of empirical attention given to the area of friend death is both surprising and troubling (Balk, 1991). Friendships are central to the daily life and development of adolescents. In addition, a large number of individuals will experience the death of a friend or peer during adolescence, and the studies that do exist suggest that the grief following the death of a friend can be as intense as that following the death of an immediate family member.

Although friendships are vital relationships regardless of age as they involve "choice, sharing, valuing, loyalty, and pleasure" (Deck & Folta, 1989, p. 78), they are arguably most essential during adolescence when young people are working to separate from their families and seeking like-minded peers who can support their emerging identities. Research suggests that friends provide cognitive and social resources that facilitate young people's negotiation of normative developmental transitions and the stress that often accompanies such transitions (Hartup, 1996). It is important to note, however, that scholars call for a more nuanced view of adolescent friendships, moving beyond the basic fact of having or not having friends to a focus on the qualitative and identity-related nature of such relationships (Bukowski, Newcomb, & Hartup, 1996; Newcomb & Bagwell, 1996).

Determining the prevalence of friend death during adolescence is a challenging task, but existing research suggests that the death of a friend during this life phase is unfortunately not an uncommon occurrence. Discussing findings in order based on the chronological age of their samples allows for interesting comparisons across the developmental phase of adolescence. Dise-Lewis (1988) studied early adolescents (aged 11 to 14 years) and found that 12% reported the death of a friend during the past year. Rheingold and colleagues (2004) used data from the National Survey of Adolescents with a representative sample of over 4,000 U.S. adolescents aged 12 to 17 and found that 20.3% had experienced the death of a friend during the previous year. Schachter (1991) found that 87% of the 13- to 19-year-olds she surveyed had experienced the death of a friend at some point in their lives. Using a similar high-school-aged sample, Ewalt and Perkins (1979) found that 40% had experienced the death of a close friend. Their data is in line with Ringler and Hayden (2000) who found that 43.5% of their college student sample reported experiencing the death of a peer while in high school. Balk (1997) studied the death experiences of 994 college students and found that 60% had at some point experienced the death of a friend. Twenty-seven percent of these deaths had occurred within the past year, while 38% had occurred during the previous 2-year period. These numbers suggest that a conservative estimate would be that 10%–20% of adolescents are likely to be bereaved following the death of a friend within the previous year, while from 40% to 60% are likely to experience the death of a friend by the time they reach age 18.

The likelihood of experiencing the death of a friend during adolescence may be affected by certain demographic factors. More specifically, research has suggested that "females, older adolescents, adolescents with lower household incomes, and those of minority race/ethnicity (with the exception of Asian/Pacific Islanders) are at increased risk of death of a friend within the past year" (Rheingold et al., 2004, p. 1). The differential death rates based on sex and race/ethnicity add further information to consider (Kung, Hoyert, Xu, & Murphy, 2008). The death rate for male adolescents aged 15–19 is nearly twice as high as that for female peers, whereas the death rate for adolescent males ages 20–24 is three times as high as for females in the same age group. With regard to race/ethnicity, African American males in the 15–19 year age range have a death rate almost 50% higher than their White male peers, and this gap rises to 60% higher for those in the 20–24 year age range. Overall, adolescents are more likely to grieve the death of a male peer and perhaps most likely a minority male; adolescent females, and perhaps most likely minority females, are more likely to identify themselves as bereaved following the death of a peer.

Scholars have frequently identified the sudden, violent, preventable, and overall human-induced causes of death during adolescence as a critical factor in why the effects of peer deaths need to be closely monitored (Gordon, 1986). In fact, a recent report by the Centers for Disease Control and Prevention (CDC) indicates that the most common causes of death for adolescents ages 15–24 continue to be accidents, homicides, and suicides, in that order (Heron, 2007). In addition, African American males in the 20–24 year range are four times more likely to die of homicide than their White male peers, while White males in this same age group are twice as likely to die from suicide than are African American males. Although suddenness itself has not consistently been shown to affect grief intensity, research with adults does suggest that perceived preventability (Guarnaccia, Hayslip, & Landry, 1999) and/or the shocking nature of a death (Gamino, Sewell, & Easterling, 2000) are positively associated with strong manifestations of grief. Deaths due to accidents, homicide, and suicide give rise to concerns about the interaction between trauma and grief, a critical factor to consider when working with young people grieving the death of a peer (Webb, 2002).

Both scholars and young people consider the death of friend during adolescence to be a significant life event that may result in reactions similar to those experienced after the death of an immediate family member. Researchers examining the experiences of middle (e.g., Chapman, 2003; Rynearson, Favell, Belluomini, Gold, & Prigerson, 2002) and late adolescents (e.g., Oltjenbruns, 1998; Schnider, Elhai, & Gray, 2007) have frequently grouped participants together regardless of whether they experienced the death of an immediate family member or a friend. Such merging reflects Archer's (1999) premise that kinship (with its coinciding shared genetic material) is not the sole or even perhaps best predictor of grief intensity. Dise-Lewis (1988), in her work to create a life events and coping inventory for young people, asked early adolescents (aged 11–14 years) to generate and then rank stressful life events. Participants in this study not only identified friend death as one of the life events they considered to be stressful, they ranked it as 10th on a list of 125 life events. Items ranked higher included immediate family-related events such as the death of a parent or other close family member, parents divorcing, and parent going to jail.

With regard to differential grief intensity, findings suggest that the grief responses of adolescent survivor-friends may be comparable to those of adolescents grieving the deaths of immediate family members. For example, some scholars (e.g., Dyregrov, Gjestad, Wikander, & Vigerust, 1999; Sklar & Hartley, 1990) found the data they gathered from bereaved friends to be similar to the data from investigations done by others who studied adolescents grieving familial death losses. By contrast, Lurie (1993) collected data from adolescents' grieving friends or family members; her findings were generally similar between the groups, although she did find that survivor-friends scored higher than adolescents grieving family death losses on anger/hostility. Cohen (2005) examined longitudinal data from late adolescents (aged 18–19 years at the start of the investigation) grieving either the death of a close friend or family member. Overall, she found that mother, father, and sibling death losses resulted in differential negative effects over time with regard to depression, mastery, engagement with life, and work/school functioning, but that the death of a friend was not associated with detrimental changes in these variables.

REACTIONS TO THE DEATH OF A FRIEND DURING ADOLESCENCE

Although adolescent grief responses following the death of a friend or peer are primarily marked by a significant degree of variability (Bragdon, 2006; Johnson, 2006; Saffer, 1986), there are some prominent reactions noted in the empirical literature (e.g., Brooks-Harris, 2001; Henschen & Heil, 1992; Swihart, Silliman, & McNeil, 1992; Vernacchia, Reardon, & Templin, 1997). The two most commonly cited responses include a sense of shock or disbelief and a feeling of anger. Other frequently observed manifestations of grief include sadness and crying, concerns about personal mortality, negative effects on concentration and academic functioning, anniversary or other triggering events, and greater appreciation of life or friends.

Single life events do not necessarily cause psychiatric symptoms or disorders; however, research does suggest that the death of a friend can be a risk factor in the development of certain mental health conditions. Meyer and colleagues (1993) studied the relationship between undesirable life events and depression in adolescents aged 11–16 and found that depressed adolescents had experienced more events than their nondepressed peers. One of these undesirable life events that depressed adolescents had experienced significantly more often than the nondepressed adolescents was the death of a peer. Brent and colleagues (1993b) found that those who had witnessed the suicidal death of a peer had higher rates of anxiety disorders than a matched control group. In their work with the National Survey of Adolescents data (representative sample of over 4,000 U.S. adolescents aged 12–17), Rheingold and colleagues (2004) found that the death of a friend within the previous year was associated with substance abuse/dependence. The authors noted that this result may indicate that bereaved adolescents drink to cope with a friend's death, but that it could also point to the idea that adolescents who abuse substances may be more likely to have friends who engage in high-risk behavior and are, therefore, more likely to die. Also related to substance issues, Kitamura and colleagues (1999) studied a small sample of Japanese women aged 19–25 and found that the early death of a close friend was a significant predictor of current levels of problem drinking.

With regard to the risk for suicide-related symptoms, research does suggest that adolescents who have experienced the suicidal death of a family member or friend have a stronger attraction to death and a weaker attraction to life (Gutierrez, King, & Ghaziuddin, 1996) and are more likely to have considered suicide, made a plan for suicide, or attempted suicide (Ephraim, 1998). In addition, Conrad (1992) surveyed high school students and found that self-hurters were much more likely than other adolescents to know a person who had committed suicide.

FACTORS AFFECTING REACTIONS TO FRIEND DEATH

Research suggests that individual and death-related factors must be considered when examining adolescents' grief reactions to a friend's death. More specifically, the nature of the personal relationship with the deceased has been found to associate with the intensity of grief responses. Related to relationship quality, there appear to be contexts (e.g., sports teams, hospital wards) within which adolescents form particularly strong bonds with one another, bonds that may affect their grief following the death of a peer. A less clear picture emerges in terms of how factors such as cause of death; time since death; and sex, race, and age of the mourner may affect grief reactions.

Adolescents play various roles in each others' lives, and in general the research suggests that those who were closer to the deceased exhibit higher levels of both negative and positive grief responses. Servaty-Seib and Pistole (2006) found that closeness to a deceased high school peer predicted grief intensity, while other individual and death-related factors did not. McNeil and colleagues (1991) found that those closest to a high school classmate who died from leukemia were more likely to report having trouble talking about the death and paying attention in class than less close peers. The closer peers were also more likely to express a belief that this death changed them in some way, including heightening their awareness of their own mortality and increasing both their thoughts about life after death and their concern about the people they loved.

Brent and colleagues (1993a) found that high school students who were closer to a peer who committed suicide were more likely than nonclose peers to develop a new-onset depression following the death. Closeness was also associated with severity of PTSD symptomatology (Brent et al., 1993b). Although not related to symptoms per se, Woodford (2007, p. ii) found that those college students who reported higher levels of closeness to their deceased friend were more likely to equally endorse both a "continuing bonds" and "broken ties" description of their grief experience, while those less close were more likely to pick only one or neither description as fitting their experience.

It is important to note the possibility that the cause of death, specifically a suicidal death loss, overrides closeness as a predictor of grief. Thus, O'Brien, Goodenow, and Espin (1991) found that the duration and intensity of grief following a peer's suicidal death were not associated with the closeness of the relationship with the deceased. Podell (1989) also highlighted the need to look beyond basic closeness to examine how important the deceased peer was in maintaining the bereaved person's self-esteem and sense of personal identity.

Adolescent friend death losses can be particularly intense when they are experienced in contexts that foster increased cohesion and greater perceived similarity, such as exists on athletic teams, in times of war, and within medical units. Henschen and Heil (1992) interviewed 10 former college football players who experienced the death of a teammate

4 years prior. They argued that the responses of the participants were similar to others grieving significant death losses, but that the athletic setting with its focus on invincibility may have contributed to an even more intense response, including a high level of shock and disbelief. Participants reported vivid memories of the death; four described feeling a little "weird" due to the power of the memories. Vernacchia, Reardon, and Templin (1997) also described the grief responses of a college basketball team immediately following the death of a teammate. The authors emphasized the public nature of such deaths and the fact that the grief in reaction to their teammate's absence appeared to unfold over time as the team engaged in their routine activities (e.g., practices). They also highlighted issues of glorification and memorialization that seem common in athletic-related death losses (e.g., wearing the deceased's number, dedicating the play of games to the deceased). McNeil and colleagues (1991) also described the way in which high school football players used similar processes to honor a deceased teammate following his death. It is worth noting that all participants discussed in the above studies were male and as such may have been more instrumental (Martin & Doka, 1999) in their grief and, therefore, more attracted to active and physical ways in which to express their grief.

The experience of the death of a so-called buddy during a time of war is the most commonly cited traumatic loss indicated by soldiers (Garb, Bleich, & Lerer, 1987). For example, van der Kolk (1985) interviewed Vietnam veterans who had and had not developed PTSD. He found that those who had developed the disorder were more likely than those who had not to have been adolescents during their time in combat. The author argued that these younger soldiers had used their buddies as the intermediary stage between dependency on their family and emotional maturity. These younger soldiers had then experienced the death of their buddies as more extreme than those who were beyond adolescence at the time of combat—as narcissistic injury rather than object loss.

Gemma (1996) described her grief group work with adolescents on an acute-care unit of a large urban pediatric hospital where there was a fairly consistent group of young people who were admitted and readmitted and whose relationships evolved over time. She explained that the group she facilitated following the death of one of the teens, allowed the members to express a whole range of feelings including their sadness in missing her; their anger for her leaving them; "their heightened sense of vulnerability, the reworking of their defensive maneuvering, and their renewed determination to be careful and compliant with their treatment" (pp. 223–224). Gemma noted that they grieved for their deceased friend and also for themselves.

Although it makes intuitive sense that violent and human-induced causes of death would be associated with higher grief intensity as compared to illness-related causes, such a conclusion cannot be clearly drawn from the empirical literature available on the adolescent experience of friend death. Most of the literature on the experience of friend death does focus on this age group's most common causes of death, traumatic accidents, suicides, and homicides. Not only are peer deaths as a result of illness rarely a focus, there are currently no solid comparisons of grief intensity based on the cause of the peer's death. Servaty-Seib and Pistole (2006) did not find suddenness of death to be a predictor of grief following the death of a friend. However, their assessment of suddenness was researcher- rather than participant-determined, and their sample of survivor-friends was a subset of their overall sample. Research has examined predictors of symptoms within specific cause-of-death groups. More specifically, Brent and colleagues (1993a) found that adolescent peers who were most likely to experience a new-onset depression following the suicidal death of a peer "were more likely to have viewed the scene of death or witnessed the suicide, discovered the victim at the scene of the death, to have known the suicidal plans of the victim, to believe they could have prevented the suicide, and to have spoken with the victim the day of the suicide" (p. 1193). In a similar vein, Melhem and colleagues (2004) examined the relationships among complicated grief, PTSD, depression, and history of physical or mental illnesses in a group of friends and acquaintances of adolescents who had committed suicide.

The length of time since the death of a peer does not appear to predict the grief intensity of survivor-friends. Dyregrov and colleagues (1999) found no significant changes in scores on the Hogan Grief Reactions Checklist between 1 month and 9 months following a peer death loss. Servaty-Seib and Pistole (2006) did not find an association between time since death and the grief intensity of high school students who experienced the death of a peer. In addition, McNeil and colleagues (1991) found that those high school students who were most distressed immediately after the death of their peer were those who tended to have the most intense long-term reactions. Researchers have also found pronounced reactions associated with the death of a friend 3 (Bragdon, 2006), 4 (Henschen & Heil, 1992), and even 5 years (Sklar & Hartley, 1990) following the death loss.

Demographic variables such as sex, age, and race/ethnicity have received little empirical attention as factors potentially related to reactions of adolescents grieving the death of a peer. High school females may be more likely than males to perceive themselves to have been close to the deceased peer, acknowledge personal growth following the death, think it would take them longer to overcome the loss, and indicate a belief that they will never get over the death (Dyregrov et al., 1999). Melhem and colleagues (2004) found that those who exhibited complicated grief following the suicidal death of a peer were more likely to be female. In contrast, Servaty-Seib and Pistole (2006) did not find sex to be a predictor of grief intensity following the death of a high school peer, and Woodford (2007) found no sex differences in college students' endorsement of a specific mode of bereavement (e.g., continuing bonds or broken ties). With regard to age, Woodford found that older college students (grieving the death of a friend) were less likely to endorse either mode of bereavement description offered to them than were their younger counterparts; they preferred to offer their own description of their grief experience.

A significant majority of investigations focused on the experience of adolescents grieving the death of a friend have used primarily White participants in their samples or have not clearly identified the race/ethnicity of participants. However, recent dissertation research done by Bragdon (2006) and Johnson (2006) may represent a move toward the use of more diverse samples. Bragdon interviewed 12 college-aged males grieving the death of male friends, and while 8 were White, 2 were African American, and 2 were Hispanic; no differences based on race/ethnicity were reported. Johnson (2006) interviewed a sample of 21 African American females aged 16–19 years and reported on their diverse experiences with the death of a friend.

ADOLESCENT APPROACHES TO COPING WITH FRIEND DEATH

Adolescents grieving the death of a friend appear to use what Martin and Doka (1999) called expressive or instrumental approaches, as well as intrapersonal approaches to coping (Balk, 1997; Bragdon, 2006; Dyregrov, Kristoffersen, Mattiesen, & Mitchell, 1994; Johnson, 2006; Ringler & Hayden, 2000). With regard to the empirical literature, talking about the experience, a clearly more expressive action, was the most commonly indicated helpful response. A primary theme in the research was adolescents' preference for talking about the death with friends rather than with parents or other adults. More specifically, Balk studied college students grieving the deaths of friends or family members and found that those who had experienced the death of a friend preferred talking with friends, while those grieving a familial death preferred to speak with their mothers. Dyregrov and colleagues asked high-school-aged survivor-friends whom they preferred to talk to; 80% indicated a same sex friend, 7% indicated a friend of the opposite sex, and 13% indicated their mother.

It is important to note that Balk (1997) found that although his participants desired to speak with friends about their grief experience, they also reported that their peers appeared uninterested or uncomfortable with the prospect of engaging in such conversations. In a similar vein, Johnson (2006) noted that although environmental supports such as friends and family appeared useful to survivor-friends, there were also challenges in these areas. Cohen (2005) actually studied the longitudinal effect of having support from peers and found that support did not moderate the relationship between loss and the outcome variables (e.g., depression, mastery, school and work functioning), but peer support did have an independent and adaptive effect on these variables.

More instrumental actions were also frequently noted in the research, including attending the funeral, engaging in personalized mourning behaviors, and being physically active. Although adolescents do report attending the funerals of their deceased friends, they indicated not knowing how to act, what to say, or even what to wear (Bragdon, 2006; Dyregrov et al., 1999; Schachter, 1991). They may also not attend out of fear of losing control of their emotions (Johnson, 2006). Even more than attending the funeral, adolescent survivor-friends appear comforted by personalized memorials and rituals. They engaged in activities such as visiting the grave, lighting candles and writing poems, and cherishing objects such as clothing and yearbooks. These personal actions also extended over time as Dyregrov and colleagues found that 83% of adolescents wanted to mark a deceased peer's birthday in class, and 52% thought it was "right" to remember him in class on the anniversary of his death date. Physical release through activities such as exercise, working out, and engaging in sports was also noted in the research. Bragdon (2006) found other more negative risking-taking actions in her male sample (18- to 22-year-olds) of survivor-friends including fighting, using drugs, and skipping school.

Research also suggests that adolescents may use intrapersonal strategies to cope with the death of a friend. Two studies (Johnson, 2006; Swihart et al., 1992) found that adolescents in their investigations appreciated the opportunity to think alone about their loss. In addition, male and female adolescents reported religion, spirituality, and prayer as important in their coping. Johnson (2006) found a close connection between metaphysical ideas and meaning making, with metaphysical ideas helping bereaved adolescents to "'stay connected' to their deceased friends, gain control over their lives, heal, and 'move on'" (p. i). However, the relationship between religion and the functioning of survivor-friends appears to be quite complex. Park and Cohen (1993) found a positive relationship between intrinsic religious beliefs and distress following the death of a friend. They argued that those who are highly religious may have to engage in a great deal of cognitive restructuring in order to integrate the experience of a friend's death with the core assumptions of their faith.

THE ROLE OF FRIENDS, PARENTS, AND EDUCATIONAL INSTITUTIONS IN SUPPORTING ADOLESCENTS GRIEVING THE DEATH OF A FRIEND

The role that others can play in supporting friend-bereaved adolescents is an area in particular need of further empirical attention. Friends, parents, and educational institutions are all critical elements in adolescents' lives, and all have the potential to influence survivor-friends' experience of grief.

Although more research is needed with regard to how adolescent peers understand grief and how they interact with survivor-friends, the investigations that are available suggest that adolescents of all ages could benefit from learning more about grief and about how best to interact with bereaved peers. Dyregrov and colleagues (1999) found that high-school-aged survivor-friends struggled with hurtful comments made by peers, and Saffer (1986) found that those in his grief support group "felt they were outcasts from the rest of the student body" (pp. 743–744), whom they perceived as aloof. In a similar vein, Balk (1997) found that "college students not touched by bereavement demonstrate both ignorance and fear when in the presence of a grieving peer" (p. 216). Both Balk and Dyregrov and colleagues argue the need for psychoeducational training programs to foster the social support skills of nonbereaved peers. Such programs would need to incorporate relevant research. For example, research on the perspectives of nonbereaved college-aged peers offers insights into important elements to be included in curricula. Kubitz, Thornton, and Robertson (1989) found that nonbereaved college students' ratings of the interpersonal attractiveness and functioning of another student grieving the death of a friend varied based on sex, type of death, and the intensity of symptoms. More specifically, men were rated lower on functioning if they displayed high intensity grief, whereas the perceived functioning of women did not vary based on the displayed level of grief. Men were also viewed as more interpersonally attractive if they exhibited low intensity grief, whereas women were viewed as more attractive if their grief matched the type of death loss (i.e., low for expected and high for sudden). These findings suggest the need for educating peers on the idiosyncratic nature of grief regardless of sex and type of death. In terms of support, Ringler and Hayden (2000) found that friend-bereaved adolescents highly rated supportive actions such as listening, understanding of feelings, and physical expressions of support (e.g., hugging). In addition, bereaved high-school-aged and college-aged students (subsets of each sample were survivor-friends) have positive perceptions of support-intended messages focused on offering one's presence ("being there"), expressing the willingness to listen, and expressing care and concern, but negative perceptions of messages focused on giving advice and minimizing other's feelings (Servaty-Seib & Burleson, 2007; Rack, Burleson, Bodie, Holmstrom, & Servaty-Seib, 2008). Rack and colleagues also found that the perception of messages varied based on sex and cause of death.

It is important to note that even if adolescents gain an accurate sense of grief and what the bereaved perceive as supportive, they may still choose not to interact and support bereaved peers. Woodford (2003) attempted to study nonbereaved college students' intentions to interact with a peer grieving a friend's death through the use of the Theory of Planned Behavior (TPB; Ajzen, 2006). Although intention to interact was not predicted by the three primary elements of TPB (i.e., attitude, subjective norms, perceived control), Woodford found that the strongest predictor of intention was the perceived positive effect that such an interaction would have on the bereaved peer. Although the majority of students indicated that interacting with a bereaved peer would be anxiety provoking and uncomfortable, these negative self-concerns did not predict intention. These findings have powerful implications for the content of programs designed to increase nonbereaved college student interaction with bereaved peers.

Little is known about the role that parents can and should play in supporting their adolescent children who have experienced the death of a same-age peer. High-school-aged students who experienced the death of a peer to leukemia perceived minimal support from their parents and viewed their parents as uncomfortable and even uninterested (Swihart et. al., 1992). In contrast, Ringler and Hayden (2000) found that college students thinking back on peer death losses in high school overwhelmingly reported support from at least one parent. A parental focus on listening rather than offering advice or disregarding feelings was viewed positively by the adolescents (McNeil et al., 1991). Dyregrov and colleagues (1994) highlighted the importance of parental involvement when a peer dies and found that those high-school-aged adolescents who were told about a peer's death by their parents and talked with their parents about the death exhibited fewer intrusive images and less depression than those who were told by their siblings or friends and then subsequently interacted primarily with their friends.

The impact of adolescent deaths on educational institutions cannot be ignored. Swihart and colleagues (1992) recommend that when responding to an adolescent death it is important to treat the whole school as a system. Although offering a complete summary is beyond the scope of the present chapter, there are multiple resources available that describe postvention responses and recommendations following the death of high-school-aged (e.g., McCarthy, 2006; Thompson, 1990) and college-aged adolescents (e.g., Levine, 2008; Rickgarn, 1996; Streufert, 2004), often following suicidal deaths. There is a real need, however, for more research that evaluates the effectiveness of such postvention work, particularly from the perspective of the students. McNeil and colleagues (1991) found that the bereaved high school students they studied appreciated the spontaneous classroom-based opportunities for discussion and the sharing of thoughts and feelings that occurred after a peer's death. Although the activities sponsored by the school, such as an information meeting, a student assembly, and a class audiovisual presentation, were well attended, the students only rated the audiovisual presentation as helpful to them in their coping. However, the students did perceive the school staff as having acted appropriately and appeared to value adult presence more than any specific actions that were taken.

Somewhat in contrast, Dyregov, Wikander, and Vigerust (1999) found that students were overwhelmingly positive (96% rated as very good or good) with regard to the efforts the school had put in place to support them following the sudden death of their classmate. The students particularly appreciated the support of their teacher and the ritual activities in which they could participate. A critical point from this study is the need for a grief hierarchy to be determined following the death of a young person. The authors recommend a process of asking classmates of the deceased and his or her family about who his or her closest friends were. They found that those who were most close to the adolescent viewed the efforts of the school as not enough, while those who were less close to the young man perceived that the school was focusing too much on the death. The use of a grief hierarchy would allow for more nuanced attention for those who are differentially affected. One consistent point in these studies is the need expressed by school staff for more education and preparation to help them be better able to assist students in negotiating the process of coping with a peer's death.

DIRECTIONS FOR FUTURE RESEARCH

Recommended areas for future research can be grouped into improvements in focus and method/design. With regard to focus, more research is needed in the area of factors that may affect adolescents' reactions to the death of a peer. Although some risk factors appear clear (e.g., close relationship with the deceased), more research regarding potential differential effects based on cause of death, sex, age, and race/ethnicity would be valuable. In addition, although closeness has been examined, a more nuanced examination of the relationships between bereaved adolescents and their deceased friend (e.g., roles the deceased played, shared identity aspects) would add to the literature. More research is also needed on the coping efforts of adolescent survivor-friends and the roles that peers, parents, and educational institutions can play in facilitating the adaptive coping of these bereaved young people. With regard to design, more racially and ethnically diverse and non-U.S. samples are needed, and longitudinal investigations are required to determine which coping and support efforts contribute to the healthy processing of adolescent grief following the death of a friend.

REFERENCES

Ajzen, I. (2006). *Constructing a TpB questionnaire: Conceptual and methodological considerations.* Retrieved April 8, 2008, from http://people.umass.edu/aizen/tpb.html

Archer, J. (1999). *The nature of grief: The evolution and psychology of reactions to loss.* London: Routledge.

Balk, D. E. (1991). Death and adolescent bereavement: Current research and future directions. *Journal of Adolescent Research, 6,* 7–27.

Balk, D. E. (1997). Death, bereavement and college students: A descriptive analysis. *Mortality, 7,* 207–220.

Bragdon, P. K. (2006). *Young male adult's experience of the death of a peer: Grief and bereavement.* Retrieved May 12, 2008, from ProQuest Digital Dissertations (AAT 3206663).

Brent, D. A., Perper, J. A., Moritz, G., Allman, C., Liotus, B. S., Schweers, J., et al. (1993a). Bereavement or depression? The impact of the loss of a friend to suicide. *Journal of the American Academy of Child & Adolescent Psychiatry, 32,* 1189–1197.

Brent, D. A., Perper, J. A., Moritz, G., Friend, A., Schweers, J., Allman, C., et al. (1993b). Adolescent witness to a peer suicide. *Journal of the American Academy of Child & Adolescent Psychiatry, 32,* 1184–1188.

Brooks-Harris, J. E. (2001). Saying goodbye ten years later: Resolving delayed bereavement. *Journal of College Student Psychotherapy, 16,* 119–134.

Bukowski, W. M., Newcomb, A. F., & Hartup, W. W. (1996). Friendship and its significance in childhood and adolescence: Introduction and comment. In W. M. Bukowski, A. F. Newcomb, & W. W. Hartup (Eds.), *The company they keep: Friendship in childhood and adolescence* (pp. 1–15). New York: Cambridge University.

Chapman, M. V. (2003). Social support and loss during adolescence: How different are teen girls from boys? *Journal of Human Behavior in the Social Environment, 7,* 5–21.

Cohen, E. (2005). *Bereavement during the adolescent to young adult transition: A developmental resilience model.* Retrieved May 12, 2008, from ProQuest Digital Dissertations (AAT 3172770).

Conrad, N. (1992). Stress and knowledge of suicidal others as factors in suicidal behavior of high school adolescents. *Issues in Mental Health Nursing, 13,* 95–104.

Deck, E. S., & Folta, J. R. (1989). The friend-griever. In K. Doka (Ed.), *Disenfranchised grief: Recognizing hidden sorrow* (pp. 77–89). Lexington, MA: Lexington Books.

Dise-Lewis, J. E. (1988). The life events and coping inventory: An assessment of stress in children. *Psychosomatics Medicine, 50,* 484–499.

Doka, K. (Ed.). (2002). *Disenfranchised grief: New directions, challenges, and strategies for practice.* Champaign, IL: Research Press.

Dyregrov, A., Wikander, A. M., & Vigerust, S. (1999). Sudden death of a classmate and friend: Adolescents' perception of support from their school. *School Psychology International, 20,* 191–208.

Dyregrov, A., Gjestad, R., Wikander, A. M., & Vigerust, S. (1999). Reactions following the sudden death of a classmate. *Scandinavian Journal of Psychology, 40,* 167–176.

Dyregrov, A., Kristoffersen, J. I., Mattiesen, S. B., & Mitchell, J. T. (1994). Gender differences in adolescents' reactions to the murder of their teacher. *Journal of Adolescent Research, 9,* 363–383.

Ephraim, T. A. (1998). *Adolescent coping strategies after a suicide or other loss by death: A retrospective study.* Retrieved May 14, 2008, from ProQuest Digital Dissertations (AAT 9812017).

Ewalt, P. L., & Perkins, L. (1979). The real experience of death among adolescents: An empirical study. *Social Casework, 60,* 547–551.

Gamino, L. A., Sewell, K. W., & Easterling, L. W. (2000). Scott and White grief study—phase 2: Toward an adaptive model of grief. *Death Studies, 24,* 633–660.

Garb, R., Bleich, A., & Lerer, B. (1987). Bereavement in combat. *Psychiatric Clinics of North America, 10,* 421–436.

Gemma, P. B. (1996). Helping adolescents deal with death on an inpatient pediatric unit. In P. Kymissis & D. A. Halperin (Eds.), *Group therapy with children and adolescents* (pp. 217–224). Washington, DC: American Psychiatric Association.

Gordon, A. K. (1986). The tattered cloak of immortality. In C. A. Corr & J. N. McNeil (Eds.), *Adolescence and death* (pp. 16–31). New York: Springer Publishing.

Guarnaccia, C. A., Hayslip, B., & Landry, L. P. (1999). Influence of perceived preventability of the death and emotional closeness to the deceased: A test of Bugen's model. *Omega, Journal of Death and Dying, 39,* 261–276.

Gutierrez, P., King, C. A., & Ghaziuddin, N. (1996). Adolescent attitudes about death in relation to suicidality. *Suicide and Life-Threatening Behavior, 26,* 8–18.

Hartup, W. W. (1996). The company they keep: Friendships and their developmental significance. *Child Development, 67,* 1–13.

Henschen, K. R., & Heil, J. (1992). A retrospective study of the effect of an athlete's sudden death on teammates. *Omega, Journal of Death and Dying, 25,* 217–223.

Heron, M. P. (2007). Deaths: Leading causes for 2004. *National Vital Statistics Reports, 56*(5). Hyattsville, MD: National Center for Health Statistics.

Hooyman, N. R., & Kramer, B. J. (2006). *Living through loss: Interventions across the life span.* New York: Columbia University Press.

Johnson, C. M. (2006). *When friends are murdered: A qualitative study of the experience, meaning and implications for identity development of older adolescent African American females.* Retrieved May 11, 2008, from ProQuest Digital Dissertations (AAT 3211714).

Kitamura, T., Kijima, N., Sakamoto, S., Tomoda, A., Suzuki, N., & Kazama, Y. (1999). Correlates of problem drinking among young Japanese women: Personality and early experiences. *Comprehensive Psychiatry, 40,* 108–114.

Kubitz, N., Thornton, G., & Robertson, D. U. (1989). Expectations about grief and evaluation of the griever. *Death Studies, 13,* 39–47.

Kung, H. C., Hoyert, D. L., Xu, J. Q., & Murphy, S. L. (2008). Deaths: Final data for 2005. *National Vital Statistics Reports, 56*(10). Hyattsville MD: National Center for Health Statistics.

Levine, H. (2008). Suicide and its impact on campus. In H. L. Servaty-Seib & D. J. Taub (Eds.), *Assisting bereaved college students* (pp. 63–76). San Francisco: Jossey-Bass.

Lurie, C. (1993). The death of friends vs. family member in late adolescence: The role of perceived social support and self-worth. Unpublished master's thesis, Colorado State University, Fort Collins.

Martin, T., & Doka, K. (1999). *Men don't cry . . . women do: Transcending gender stereotypes of grief.* Philadelphia: Routledge.

McCarthy, J. R. (2006). *Young people's experiences of loss and bereavement.* New York: Open University Press.

McNeil, J. N., Silliman, B., & Swihart, J. J. (1991). Helping adolescents cope with the death of a peer: A high school case study. *Journal of Adolescent Research, 6,* 132–143.

Melhem, N. M., Day, N., Shear, M. K., Day, R., Reynolds, C. F., & Brent, D. (2004). Predictors of complicated grief among adolescents exposed to a peer's suicide. *Journal of Loss & Trauma, 9,* 21–34.

Meyer, P. A., Garrison, C. Z., Jackson, K. L., Addy, C. L., McKeown, R. E., & Waller, J. L. (1993). Undesirable life-events and depression in young adolescents. *Journal of Child and Family Studies, 2,* 47–60.

Newcomb, A. F., & Bagwell, C. L. (1996). The developmental significance of children's friendship relations. In W. M. Bukowski, A. F. Newcomb, & W. W. Hartup (Eds.), *The company they keep: Friendship in childhood and adolescence* (pp. 289–321). New York: Cambridge University Press.

O'Brien, J. M., Goodenow, C., & Espin, O. (1991). Adolescents' reactions to the death of a peer. *Adolescence, 26,* 431–440.

Oltjenbruns, K. A. (1996). Death of a friend during adolescence: Issues and impacts. In C. A. Corr & D. E. Balk (Eds.), *Handbook of adolescent death and bereavement* (pp. 196–215). New York: Springer Publishing.

Oltjenbruns, K. A. (1998). Ethnicity and the grief response: Mexican American versus Anglo American college students. *Death Studies, 22,* 141–155.

Park, C. L., & Cohen, L. H. (1993). Religious and nonreligious coping with the death of a friend. *Cognitive Therapy and Research, 17,* 561–577.

Podell, C. (1989). Adolescent mourning: The sudden death of a peer. *Clinical Social Work Journal, 17,* 64–78.

Rack, J. J., Burleson, B. R., Bodie, G. D., Holmstrom, A. J., & Servaty-Seib, H. L. (2008). Bereaved adults' evaluations of grief management messages: Effects of message person centeredness, recipient individual differences, and contextual factors. *Death Studies, 32,* 399–427.

Rickgarn, R. L. V. (1996). The need for postvention on college campuses: A rationale and case study findings. In C. A. Corr & D. E. Balk (Eds.), *Handbook of adolescent death and bereavement* (pp. 273–292). New York: Springer Publishing.

Rheingold, A. A., Smith, D. W., Ruggiero, K. J., Saunders, B. E., Kilpatrick, D. G., & Resnick, H. S. (2004). Loss, trauma exposure, and mental health in a representative sample of 12–17-year-old youth: Data from the national survey of adolescents. *Journal of Loss & Trauma, 9,* 1–19.

Ringler, L. L., & Hayden, D. C. (2000). Adolescent bereavement and social support: Peer loss compared to other losses. *Journal of Adolescent Research, 15,* 209–230.

Rynearson, E. K., Favell, J. L., Belluomini, V., Gold, R., & Prigerson, H. (2002). Bereavement intervention with incarcerated youths. *Journal of the American Academy of Child & Adolescent Psychiatry, 41,* 893–894.

Saffer, J. B. (1986). Group therapy with friends of an adolescent suicide. *Adolescence, 21,* 743–745.

Schachter, S. (1991). Adolescent experiences with the death of a peer. *Omega, Journal of Death and Dying, 24,* 1–11.

Schnider, K. R., Elhai, J. D., & Gray, M. J. (2007). Coping style use predicts posttraumatic stress and complicated grief symptom severity among college students reporting a traumatic loss. *Journal of Counseling Psychology, 54,* 344–350.

Servaty-Seib, H. L., & Burleson, B. R. (2007). Bereaved adolescents' evaluations of the helpfulness of support-intended statements: Associations with person centeredness and demographic, personality, and contextual factors. *Journal of Social and Personal Relationships, 24,* 207–223.

Servaty-Seib, H. L., & Pistole, M. C. (2006). Adolescent grief: Relationship category and emotional closeness. *Omega, Journal of Death and Dying, 54,* 147–167.

Sklar, F. (1991). Grief as a family affair: Property rights, grief rights, and the exclusion of close friends as survivors. *Omega, Journal of Death and Dying, 24,* 109–121.

Sklar, F., & Hartley, S. F. (1990). Close friends as survivors: Bereavement patterns in a "hidden" population. *Omega, Journal of Death and Dying, 21,* 103–112.

Smith, H. I. (1996). *Grieving the death of a friend.* Minneapolis, MN: Augsburg Fortress.

Streufert, B. J. (2004). Death on campuses: Common postvention strategies in higher education. *Death Studies, 28,* 151–172.

Swihart, J., Silliman, B., & McNeil, J. (1992). Death of a student: Implications for secondary school counselors. *School Counselor, 40,* 55–60.

Thompson, R. A. (1990). Strategies for crisis management in the schools. *NASSP Bulletin, 74,* 54–58.

van der Kolk, B. A. (1985). Adolescent vulnerability to posttraumatic stress disorder. *Psychiatry, 48,* 365–370.

Vernacchia, R. A., Reardon, J. P., & Templin, D. P. (1997). Sudden death in sport: Managing the aftermath. *The Sport Psychologist, 11,* 223–235.

Webb, N. B. (2002). Traumatic death of a friend/peer: Case of Susan, age 9. In N. B. Webb (Ed.), *Helping bereaved children: A handbook for practitioners* (2nd ed., pp. 167–193). New York: Guilford.

Werner-Lin, A., & Moro, T. (2004). Unacknowledged and stigmatized losses. In F. Walsh & M. McGoldrick (Eds.), *Living beyond loss: Death in the family* (2nd ed., pp. 247–271). New York: W. W. Norton & Co.

Woodford, J. A. (2007). *An exploratory examination of traditional-age college students' bereavement after the death of a peer.* Retrieved May 12, 2008, from ProQuest Digital Dissertations (AAT 3255543).

Woodford, L. M. (2003). *Sharing the pain with friends: Grief and support among late adolescent women.* Retrieved May 12, 2008, from ProQuest Digital Dissertations (AAT NQ73332).

13

Adolescent Bereavement Over the Deaths of Celebrities

CHRISTOPHER W. HALL AND ROBYN A. REID

Adolescence is viewed as a normative period of change and transition in physical, cognitive, psychosocial, and spiritual domains. Establishing a sense of identity is a central task in the psychosocial development of adolescence (Erikson, 1968, 1980). The engagement and exploration with questions such as who am I, how do I see myself, how do others view me, and how we connect or ally with others are all aspects of this process of identification. Erikson (1980) described identity as a process of defining oneself relative to shared characteristics with others. Identity is a process of connecting internal self-perceptions with the perception of self as part of a social environment (Josselson, 1987). The developmental tasks of adolescence include decreased identification with and separation from parents, developing interest in sexuality and relationships, and attaining a sense of self and identity and stable character formation (Blos, 1941, 1979).

Identity formation is the dynamic process of forming an identity through assimilation and accommodation. As new crises and challenges are confronted, belief systems are reexamined to cope with the new information. Assimilation occurs when new information is interpreted in a manner that fits with the individual's current knowledge and beliefs, with accommodation taking place when the individual makes changes in the self to account for new experiences (Whitbourne, 1986).

To date the influence of celebrity figures upon adolescent development has been largely neglected in the research literature (Giles & Maltby, 2004). The impact upon the adolescent following the death of public figures is even more neglected as an area of intellectual inquiry.

Over the last century the appearance of the mass media has increased the sphere of influence over adolescent socialization from peers, family, neighbors, teachers, and faith communities to include television, radio, print media, popular culture, and the Internet. This mass media pervasiveness has profoundly changed the social and cultural milieu for today's adolescent. The role of the mass media in relationship to theoretical models of development, however, has received scant attention (Giles & Maltby, 2004).

Adolescents of today have not just changed incrementally from those of the past as has happened between previous generations. A significant discontinuity has taken place. This discontinuity is the arrival and rapid dissemination of digital technology over the last few decades of the 20th century. Adolescents today represent the first generations to grow up with this new technology. The ubiquitous presence of e-mail, cable television, the Internet, blogs, texting, and mobile telephones has become integral to the lives of adolescents. Adolescents' use of digital media has become so widespread that the term *digital natives* (Prensky, 2001) now refers to the generations growing up immersed in technology who are native speakers of the digital language of computers and the Internet.

A 2005 study (Roberts, Foehr, & Rideout, 2005) found that children ages 8 to 18 typically spend a third of their day, approximately 8.5 hours, using media, including screen media, music, computers, gaming, and print. The most frequently used media format is screen media followed closely by music. A second study published in the same year (Lenhart, Madden, & Hitlin, 2005) found that 87% of adolescents aged 12–17 use the Internet, half of this group using the Internet on a daily basis. Of adolescents online, 75% regularly used instant messaging, nearly double the 42% rate of adults. Some authors have explained this increased use of media during adolescence by the fact that more time is spent alone, often in a private bedroom, during this period (Steele & Brown, 1995).

The types of communication and the access to information about others' lives and their communities make it easier to find arenas of self-expression and identification with subcultures allowing young people a diverse sense of belonging, while in some ways maintaining an individual and anonymous participation. The emergence of mass media has also created a vehicle for the targeting and marketing to young people as sources of revenue and profit.

One impact of this increased usage of media is the increased importance that media figures exert upon the lives of adolescents. A study by Bonn and Lomore (2001) found that 75% of young adults reported a strong attachment to more than one celebrity idol at some point in their lives. These celebrities were primarily actors, musical artists, and athletes, but also included a variety of other figures. One of the phenomena that occurs when a celebrity dies is the rapid diffusion of news. People seek out more information about the celebrity, and the event and the media feed this demand.

The nomenclature for describing the relationship with a media figure or celebrity is diverse, with terms such as *reference idol* (McEvoy & Erickson, 1981), *hero* (Bromnick & Swallow, 1999), *celebrity* (Giles & Maltby, 2004), and *human brands* (Thomson, 2006) often used interchangeably. There is general agreement that, as Larson (1995) suggests, media figures play an important role in adolescent development as they offer a variety of possible identities that a young person might wish to experiment with and provide examples "of how to think and feel in different circumstances" (p. 538). Romantic attachments to a musician or movie star may enable a young person to act out an imaginary relationship at a safe distance and to fantasize "about possible selves or situations" (Steele & Brown, 1995, p. 565).

Attachment to media figures in general is referred to as a *parasocial* relationship, a one-sided friendship one has with a mass communication persona or character (Horton & Wohl, 1956). Although all the interaction is one-way, the person feels as if they know the figure as they would a friend. While such relationships are imaginary, they are nevertheless experienced as real, with parasocial relationships sharing many similarities with actual social relationships (Perse & Rubin, 1989). These relationships may occur through such activities as watching TV or attending a concert, which lead to a feeling of intimacy or friendship. However, such relationships do not require changes to a person's attitudes, beliefs, or behaviors (Babb & Brown, 1994; Horton & Wohl, 1956). The other occurrence may be a process of identification with the celebrity via self-defining relationships that promote a sense of desired connection to a person and group and do involve changes to attitudes, beliefs, and behaviors. Research shows that the greater the identification, the more likely the imitative behaviors will happen—even the destructive ones such as suicide. Stack (2000), in a review of 293 suicide studies, found that the death by suicide of an entertainment or political figure was 14.3 times more likely to produce a copycat effect when compared to noncelebrities.

There has been a growth of celebrity shows such as *Big Brother* where ordinary individuals can be catapulted to instant celebrity and their lives chronicled in minute detail, providing a vehicle for others to experience a sense of intimacy and identification. The paparazzi and intrusions into the private lives of celebrities allow the adolescent access to unprecedented levels of personal information about celebrities and their daily lives. In addition, parents are frequently unfamiliar with technology and may be alienated from the full extent of their adolescents' usage and engagement with it.

The adolescent search for a stable sense of personal identity is marked in part by a process of emotional separation from their parents and gravitation toward the peer group. As part of this process, adolescents often form secondary attachments to figures they encounter in the popular media. From sporting figures, political leaders, actors, musical performers, and entertainers, adolescents can feel that they personally know these famous personalities and often develop in this relationship an "illusion of intimacy" (Schickel, 1985, p. 29) with them. It is believed that these parasocial attachments foster the transition to adulthood in much the same way that relationships with peers do, serving as important arena in which the development of a mature adult identity takes place (Adams-Price & Greene, 1990; Greene & Adams-Price, 1990).

THE NATURE OF CELEBRITY

The Australian wildlife expert and television personality Steve Irwin, "the Crocodile Hunter," reached an audience of 500 million people through media exposure after his death, with his Web site inundated by visitors and donations increasing dramatically as a result of publicity after his sudden death (Brown & Fraser, 2007). Irwin embodied the Australian working-class man and created the assumption that the private and public person were the same. Therefore, people felt they knew him and identified with his values around his love of family, his country, and wildlife and conservation. The media and worldwide communication brought into being the ritual sharing of emotion by large populations (Gibson, 2007).

Celebrities like Angelina Jolie and Bono may also bring world attention to issues such as poverty, AIDS-related diseases, and African orphans. The capacity for actors and celebrities to influence social attitudes and behaviors is significant. Christopher Reeve contributed to neurological research in an attempt to reverse or improve the outcomes for those like him with spinal injury. Since his diagnosis of Parkinson's disease, Michael J. Fox has become a spokesperson for that disease (Brown & Fraser, 2007).

Adolescents of all backgrounds form complex identifications with celebrities (Ali, 2002). This phenomenon has implications for adolescents who may be especially vulnerable to both identification and parasocial relationships as they undergo the process of identity formation with respect to both gender and personality. The increasing interactivity and sophistication of the World Wide Web means that celebrity and fame increase in cultural relevance, significance, and influence. Identification means that ritualized practices of fans can create communal identification, which promotes a sense of group belonging. Fans can offer their opinions and create a sense of belonging through a sense of exclusivity (Soukup, 2006).

Virtual communities become bound together by values, identity, and association, linked by the object of their adoration. They may function as a public service to other fans through the sharing of information, recruitment of others to the group and the celebrity, and as a mediating influence and advocate for the celebrity. Adolescents can become the so-called authority about the celebrity and gain peer esteem. They can create their own interpretations and adaptations of celebrity work, through creation of Web sites and the production and dissemination of images and texts. Young people can voice opinions and values by aligning themselves with celebrities to whom they feel connected, or even experiment with clothing or behaviors, which are made more legitimate because of the celebrity and their fan base. There may be a perceived mutual interaction between the fan and celebrity, particularly where the celebrity visits the Web site (Soukup, 2006).

While some aspect of popular culture may be produced by the celebrity's promotional team, once released into circulation, control is delivered into the hands of the adolescent fan who can influence the success or failure of the celebrity. Young people may gain increased status and overcome alienation and invisibility via the formation of strong bonds within cybercommunities (Soukup, 2006).

Evidence suggests that young people learn from the values, beliefs, and behaviors of the characters that they watch (Signorielli & Kahlenberg, 2001). There are, however, distortions in television, as many occupations or situations from real life are not considered entertaining enough, so that many sexual stereotypes persist with women and ethnic minorities in less glamorous roles and an underrepresentation of some roles, coupled with preference for medical and legal shows (Hoffner et al. 2006). Young adults are influenced by portrayals of success and wealth (Hoffner & Cantor, 1991).

Media activities are important determinants of adolescent cognitions and behaviors and may even regulate mood. They enable teenagers to explore romantic relationships vicariously and may influence self-esteem through a sense of belonging and identification with subcultures. Adoration and consuming behaviors, however, have been found to have a detrimental effect upon both mental and physical health (Chiou, Huang, & Chuang, 2005).

A study conducted in Hong Kong by Fu and Yip (2007) found that people impacted by a celebrity's suicide were 5.93 times more likely to have a severe level of suicidal ideation than people not affected, and that both short- and long-term risk for suicide was greater following celebrity suicide. Evidence showed an association between celebrity suicides or death and a subsequent increase in the suicide rate. The research explored whether celebrity suicide was an independent risk factor, as opposed to other vulnerability for suicide. The study found that celebrity suicide could trigger suicidal ideation in anyone regardless of whether they were vulnerable for suicide. This finding has implications for the management of celebrity deaths in the media. How the event is managed and reported may increase the risk of suicide for those who may not have been deemed vulnerable prior to the event. The study emphasized the important role that media play in the responsible reporting of these deaths (Fu & Yip, 2007).

Adolescents are potentially more vulnerable than older persons because of their cognitive immaturity, emotional immaturity, disenfranchised grief, limited experience, and risk factors such as substance abuse/use, as well as lack of prior experience with grief. Those working with young people would be prudent to be alert to the impact of a celebrity death, especially on those adolescents who are already seen to be at risk, and to remain vigilant in case those not considered vulnerable may become so.

ATTACHMENT STYLES AND CELEBRITY

Wayment's (2006) study of attachment style and its relationship to empathy and helping following collective loss revealed that the more secure the attachment style, the greater the empathy and helping behaviors. Attachment styles are "internal working models" (Wayment, 2006, p. 2) of the self and others that are formed in early childhood and that continue to impact upon relationships in adult life. Secure attachment is characterized by individuals who have a strong sense of their self-worth, along with positive views of self and others. These positive attributions enable them to believe they are worthy of love and support, and to enjoy closeness and dependence on others. They generally experience success in their social relationships and have a sense of well-being (Bartholomew, 1990; Bowlby, 1973; Collins & Read, 1990). Those with anxious-ambivalent attachment feel negative about themselves but positive about others. Those with an avoidant attachment style are often emotionally distant and not as trusting of others, thus avoiding intimacy. Those who are disorganized/disoriented have negative views of self and others. Mikulincer, Florian, and Weller (1993) found that when individuals are threatened attachment patterns are more likely to be triggered to assist with coping.

Adolescents with avoidant or disorganized attachment styles may be less resilient in the face of loss. It may be hypothesized that those with less comfort around trust and intimacy may fare more badly because of a lack of help-seeking behavior or comfort with self-disclosure (Parkes, 2006).

Attachment style can predict the likelihood of positive qualities in relationships with others, with secure attachments more likely to facilitate the development of autonomy and independence in adolescents. In the course of their development, adolescents must negotiate the tension between the desire for independence and maintaining a sense of closeness and intimacy (Baltes & Silverberg, 1994). Psychological well-being is positively related to attachment to parents and peers, and a stronger predictor of a school/work identity, whereas attachment to peers is a stronger predictor of relational identity and a positive predictor of problem behavior (Armsden & Greenberg, 1987). Positive relationships of support create the optimal environment for the development of autonomy in adolescents and the effective development of psychosocial skills. The combination of developing independence within supportive relationships fosters the greatest likelihood of positive developmental outcomes (Noom, Dekovic, & Meeus, 1999). Regardless of age, admirers often speak of celebrities as though there were some sort of relationship between them (e.g., Adams-Price & Greene, 1990; Cohen, 1997).

According to Caughey (1984, 1994) who conducted research on celebrity influence from a relational perspective, celebrity idols frequently serve as idealized self-images for their admirers because they possess qualities or traits admirers would like to develop, or refine, in themselves. In his research Caughey reports how research participants engaged in a range of behaviors intended to bring about changes in behavior, physical appearance, values, and attitudes so as to bring these aspects of themselves more in line with their image of their idol. As mentor and role model, celebrity idols may inspire efforts at self-transformation that affect, in profound and meaningful ways, many different areas of their admirers' lives.

Caughey's work also examined and emphasized the importance of considering what individuals put into their relationships with their idols, and their perceptions concerning the extent to which they and their idols share a special connection or bond. Many of his participants engaged in a range of behaviors that serve, in his words, as symbolic substitutes for genuine interaction. These behaviors include collecting mementos, collecting newspaper and magazine clippings, joining fan clubs, writing letters, or making other efforts to contact or meet the idol. Caughey also discussed how significant events in the idol's life often come to assume a critical importance in the life of the admirer, affecting the admirer's well-being as though they were events in his or her own life, or perhaps in a close friend or family member's life. In sum, individuals appear to invest in their relationships with their favorite media personalities in much the same way as they invest in relationships with partners in real relationships.

Given that most adolescents have access to their idols only in media time, research by Bonn and Lomore (2001) found that neither the passage of time nor the real-life death of the idol necessarily served as impediments to the establishment of celebrity attachments. It is therefore important not to assume that media personalities from the past cannot serve as meaningful and influential figures in the lives of today's adolescents. Bonn and Lomore (2001) also found that few of the celebrities identified by young adults in their study were individuals whose media personas were decidedly negative and likely to give rise to concern from parents or others because of their behavior or the values they espouse.

THE DISENFRANCHISED NATURE OF CELEBRITY GRIEF

In many respects, Western societies take a dim view of these parasocial or fantasy relationships and of the individuals who experience them. Caughey (1984, p. 65) states "those who have been through intense media relationships often recall them with embarrassment, and those outside them often respond with derision." Intense relationships with media figures are often viewed as abnormal, even pathological, and the fan as disturbed and mentally ill (Caughey, 1984).

These losses remain largely disenfranchised, that is, they involve a "grief that persons experience when they incur a loss that is not or cannot be openly acknowledged, publicly mourned, or socially supported" (Doka, 1989, p. 4). The grieving norms of the adolescent are fundamentally shaped by the "feeling rules" (Hochschild, 1979, p. 551) of parents, other adults, peers, and the media itself. Many of the problems encountered by adolescents grieving the death of a celebrity represent the failure of one part of this social system to understand the meaning, significance, and experience of the loss. Points of empathic failure can occur at the level of self, family, larger community, and transcendent reality (Neimeyer & Jordan, 2002).

At the level of the self, adolescents can disenfranchise themselves through denial or disapproval of some aspect of their own grief experience (Kauffman, 1989). Lack of social sanction, fear of social disapproval, or peer rejection can inhibit the expression of grief following the death of a loved celebrity. The grief experienced through the loss of parasocial relationships can also be disenfranchised within the family when a parent, or another family member, may attempt to condemn or control the grief reactions of the adolescent, or simply fail to allow and accept differing bereavement responses. The larger community can disenfranchise the grief of adolescents following the death of a celebrity when the loss is unrecognized in a variety of social contexts. This failure may take the form of peer relationships, teachers, and faith communities who may not fully appreciate the nature and intensity of the loss experience. The death of a celebrity as a result of drug overdose or suicide can be met with negative social judgment and derision. The death of a public figure can also provoke a sense of disconnection from one's spiritual system of belief. In the case of celebrity death as a result of drug overdose or suicide, the bereavement can prompt larger questions of meaning, such as the adverse religious judgment of the deceased, or the death may challenge previously held religious or spiritual beliefs.

SOCIAL FUNCTIONS

For some adolescents the mourning of celebrities provides an important bridge to dealing with grief in their own lives. Expressing this sense of loss on the Internet and with peers provides a sense of connection and community. The power of these affiliations and attachments can bind grievers together and create a sense of intimacy and connection. Mourning the death of a celebrity can reawaken previous losses and provide a new opportunity to express feelings of loss. In connection with the celebrity, the adolescent can recognize qualities and values, which may be shared. The confrontation of the mortality of the public figure can also activate the adolescents' own death anxiety.

TYPES OF LOSS

Loss of a Perceived Relationship: The Unique Image or Persona With Which to Identify

Adolescents who form strong attachments to celebrities and who feel that the relationship has intimacy, friendship, and reciprocity will mourn the loss of that individual as they would a real friendship. Celebrities may have unique ways of dressing or using particular styles of makeup. For example, the rock group KISS spawned a generation of look-a-like fans. Those young people who identify with subcultures in order to experiment with their looks, image, and presentation to others may find the celebrity's absence disruptive to the formation of their identity and may have difficulty negotiating social situations and communication that no longer contains material or content with the celebrity as the focus. There is also evidence that celebrity suicide may even be imitated given high levels of identification and distress for vulnerable individuals (Stack, 2000).

Loss of Mood Regulation and Comfort

Adolescent experiences, which are commonly depicted in soap operas and popular music, enable adolescents to live vicariously through their favorite celebrity and in music via their identification and social activities. The regular contact and predictability of favorite activities and celebrities may provide a buffer against lack of control or constant change, hence creating a source of comfort. In the case of music there may be the capacity for the mood to be regulated or enhanced and even for increased expression of emotional states via the performance of lyrics and music.

Loss of Mediator With Peers: Source of Focus for Communication/Socialization

Activities on Internet-based fan Web sites allow adolescents to become authorities about their celebrities, which may provide them with status and prestige with their peers. Discussing celebrity lives, fashions, and products provides a relatively safe jumping-off point for conversations with other teens. Experimenting with images, looks, values, and behaviors when part of a fan club provides legitimacy to adolescents' activities, particularly if their chosen celebrity is colorful or outrageous. There is less likelihood of criticism and a greater feeling of solidarity as there is safety in numbers and a sense of belonging and even elitism.

Loss of Particular Celebrity Product

The media manipulate the celebrity and their product. In fact, much of the celebrity machine is geared toward making profits through the sales of products such as movies and clothing. When the celebrity dies, these products become collectable, and frequently valuable, as they no longer are readily available. Access to information, products, and contact may be lost and cause distress.

Loss of Sense of Self/Identity

The sense of identification with celebrities involves a change in values, beliefs, and behaviors, which over time can be inculcated into the personality. When a celebrity dies—especially one who is representative of an era—a generation can mourn that individual's passing and feel in some sense as if a part of them has also gone, never to be the same again. The assassinations of John F. Kennedy and John Lennon caused a rending of the social fabric and a public outpouring of grief. This public impact may have been due to their capacity for inspiring people toward peace in their music and speeches. Ironically, these men of peace were murdered, and their deaths seemed emblematic of the social problems of the day. People can often recall with great clarity where they were and what they were doing at exactly that moment of assassination. Such was the power of the grief and shock for many. Music is often an integral part of growing up since songs are often chosen to represent important moments in life or they are heard at particular times, which embeds them in memory. When we hear them played we can be transported to another time and place and relive aspects of our childhood and growing up. Music therapy has grown around the importance of music and lyrics to the individual, and much of music has generational aspects, which are unique to the era in which they are prominent, such as rock and roll and other forms of popular music.

The cybercommunities and their members may participate in a number of ways. They may provide the comfort of anonymity and unrestricted expression of thoughts and feelings. Some individuals may experience a measure of social success via the Internet, not available to them in real life. There may be avenues of expression or participation not otherwise available because of factors such as age, culture, political, or financial constraints. When a celebrity dies, the cybercommunity may provide a powerful rallying point for mutual grieving and solace. Likewise, the removal of celebrity contact or product may be very distressing for some individuals; for those who are vulnerable, it may even lead to self-destructive behaviors.

IMPLICATIONS FOR PRACTICE

Gender, social context, developmental tasks, socialization, styles of grieving, and the social environment will influence interventions intended to help bereaved adolescents. Given the disenfranchised nature of parasocial relationship loss, it is clear that many of the strategies one might use to address disenfranchised losses can equally be applied in this context (Doka, 2002). These strategies include the use of public and private ritual, and engagement in the spontaneous memorializing of public figures, which overcomes the sense of powerlessness and generates further social support and solidarity in the face of loss.

The use of technology itself can be helpful. For example, following the death of Princess Diana, mourners could download the order of service and effectively become private participants in a public ritual. The use of the extended communities of care on the Internet, including social-networking Web sites such as Facebook and Web fan sites, also provides an avenue of communication and elaboration for grieving adolescents. The use of linking objects, such as memorabilia and music, provides a continuing connection, as do the representations of the deceased through photography and video. The empowerment of family, schools, and the wider community in recognizing and validating the sense of loss, as well as the further strengthening of social support, can also work toward an amelioration of this loss experience. These experiences of loss provide teachable moments for the adolescents where important lessons about loss can be learned.

IMPLICATIONS FOR FUTURE RESEARCH

Only a handful of studies have examined the power of living celebrity influences upon adolescents in general, with even less consideration given to the bereavement experience of adolescents following celebrity death. We know little about how the degree of attachment to celebrities impacts the process by which a sense of identity is formed in adolescence. We need further data on what leads some adolescents to adopt aspects of celebrity identities as their own and to identify adolescents whose identifications with media personalities may lead them to emulate the self-destructive aspects of their celebrity idols through drug misuse, alcoholism, and suicide. The disenfranchised quality of these losses is also reflected in the lack of research activity in this area. The dim view of fantasy relationships and the ensuing pressure not to appear different may lead adolescents to downplay the idol's actual degree of influence. There is a need to supplement the self-reports of adolescents with data from other sources, such as peers and parents, and to consider behavioral measures of celebrity influence. Little is known about the process of parasocial relationships and bereavement across cultures, and how these relationships change across time.

CONCLUSION

Adolescents are exposed to an increasingly diverse range of media and technology, which facilitates the development of parasocial relationships and identification with celebrity figures. These relationships are both common and influential in the lives of adolescents. The loss of these relationships through the death of public figures is frequently experienced as an authentic and significant loss. Although largely disenfranchised by society, the death of a celebrity presents a challenge to our conventional understanding of relationships and calls out for a more complete scientific analysis of these phenomena.

REFERENCES

Adams-Price, C., & Greene, A. L. (1990). Secondary attachments and adolescent self concept. *Sex Roles, 22,* 187–198.

Ali, S. (2002). Friendship and fandom: Ethnicity, power, and gendering readings of the popular. *Discourse: Studies in the Cultural Politics of Education, 23,*153–165.

Armsden, G. C., & Greenberg, M. T. (1987). The inventory of parent and peer attachment: Individual differences and their relationship to psychological well-being in adolescence. *Journal of Youth and Adolescence, 18,* 39–53.

Babb, V., & Brown, W. J. (1994, July). *Adolescents' development of parasocial relationships through popular television situation comedies.* Paper presented to the annual conference of the International Communication Association, Sydney, Australia.

Baltes, M. M., & Silverberg, S. (1994). The dynamics between dependency and autonomy: Illustrations across the life span. In D. L. Featherman, R. M. Lerner, & M. Perlmutter (Eds.), *Life-Span Development and Behavior* (Vol. 12, pp. 41–90). Hillsdale, NJ: Lawrence Erlbaum.

Bartholomew, K. (1990). Avoidance of intimacy: An attachment perspective. *Journal of Social and Personal Relationships, 7,* 147–178.

Blos, P. (1941). *The adolescent personality: A study of individual behavior.* New York: Appleton-Century.

Blos, P. (1979). *The adolescent passage: Developmental issues.* New York: International Universities Press.

Bonn, S. D., & Lomore, C. D. (2001). Admirer-celebrity relationships among young adults: Explaining perceptions of celebrity influence on identity. *Human Communication Research, 27*(3), 432–465.

Bowlby, J. (1973). *Attachment and loss. Separation: Anxiety and anger* (Vol. 2). New York: Basic Books.

Bromnick, R. D., & Swallow, B. L. (1999). I like being who I am: A study of young people's ideals. *Educational Studies, 25,* 117–128.

Brown, W. J., & Fraser, B. P. (2007, May). *Mediated involvement with a celebrity hero: Responses to the tragic death of Steve Irwin.* Paper presented at the annual meeting of the International Communication Association, San Francisco, CA. Retrieved June 3, 2008, from http://www.allacademic.com/meta/p170914_index.html

Caughey, J. L. (1984). *Imaginary social worlds.* Lincoln: University of Nebraska Press.

Caughey, J. L. (1994). Gina as Steven: The social and cultural dimensions of a media relationship. *Visual Anthropology, 10,* 126–135.

Chiou, J. S., Huang, C., & Chuang, M. C. (2005). Antecedents of Taiwanese adolescents' purchase intention toward the merchandise of a celebrity: The moderating effect of celebrity adoration. *The Journal of Social Psychology, 145*(3), 317–332.

Cohen, J. (1997). Parasocial relations and romantic attraction: Gender and dating status differences. *Journal of Broadcasting and Electronic Media, 41,* 516–529.

Collins, N. L., & Read, S. J. (1990). Adult attachment, working models, and relationship quality in dating couples. *Journal of Personality and Social Psychology, 58,* 644–663.

Doka, K. J. (Ed.) (1989). *Disenfranchised grief: Recognizing hidden sorrow.* Lexington, MA: Lexington Books.

Doka, K. J. (Ed.) (2002). *Disenfranchised grief: New directions, challenges, and strategies for practice.* Champaign, IL: Research Press.

Erikson, E. H. (1968). *Identity, youth, and crisis.* New York: Norton.

Erikson, E. H. (1980). *Identity and the life cycle.* New York: Norton.

Fu, W-W., & Yip, S. F. (2007). Long-term impact of celebrity suicide on suicidal ideation: Results from a population-based study. *Journal of Epidemiology and Community Health, 61*(6), 540–546.

Gibson, M. (2007). Some thoughts on celebrity death: Steve Irwin and the issue of public mourning. *Mortality, 12*(1), 1–3.

Giles, D. C., & Maltby, J. (2004). The role of media figures in adolescent development: Relations between autonomy, attachment, and interests in celebrities. *Personality and Individual Differences, 36,* 813–822.

Greene, A. L., & Adams-Price, C. (1990). Adolescents' secondary attachments to celebrity figures. *Sex Roles, 23,* 335–347.

Hochschild, A. R. (1979). Emotion work, feeling rules, and social structure. *American Journal of Sociology, 85,* 551–575.

Hoffner, C., & Cantor, J. (1991). Perceiving and responding to mass media characters. In J. Bryant & D. Zillmann (Eds.), *Perceiving and responding to the screen: Reception and reaction processes* (pp. 63–101). Hillsdale, NJ: Lawrence Erlbaum.

Hoffner, C. A., Levine, K. J., Sullivan, Q. E., Crowell, D., Pedrick, L., & Berndt, P. (2006). TV characters at work: Television's role in the occupational aspirations of economically disadvantaged youths. *Journal of Career Development, 33*(1), 3–18.

Horton, D., & Wohl, R. R. (1956). Mass communication and parasocial interaction: Observations on intimacy at a distance. *Psychiatry, 19,* 215–229.

Josselson, R. (1987). *Finding herself: Pathways to identity development in women.* San Francisco: Jossey-Bass.

Kauffman, J. (1989). Intrapsychic dimensions of disenfranchised grief. In K. J. Doka (Ed.), *Disenfranchised grief: Recognizing hidden sorrow* (pp. 25–29). Lexington, MA: Lexington.

Larson, R. W. (1995). Secrets in the bedroom: Adolescents' private use of media. *Journal of Youth and Adolescence, 24,* 535–550.

Lenhart, A., Madden, M., & Hitlin, P. (2005). *Teens and technology: Youth are leading the transition to a fully wired and mobile nation.* Retrieved June 1, 2008, from http://www.pewInternet.org/pdfs/PIP_Teens_Tech_July2005web.pdf

McEvoy, A., & Erickson, E. L. (1981). Heroes and villains: A conceptual strategy for assessing their influence. *Sociological Focus, 14,* 111–122.

Mikulincer, M., Florian, V., & Weller, A. (1993). Attachment styles, coping strategies, and posttraumatic psychological distress: The impact of the gulf war in Israel. *Journal of Personality and Social Psychology, 64,* 817–826.

Neimeyer, R. A., & Jordan, J. R. (2002). Disenfranchisement as empathic failure: Grief therapy and the co-construction of meaning. In K. J. Doka (Ed.), *Disenfranchised grief: New directions, challenges, and strategies for practice* (pp. 95–117). Champaign, IL: Research Press.

Noom, M. J., Dekovic, M., & Meeus, W. H. J. (1999). Autonomy, attachment and psychosocial adjustment during adolescence: A double-edged sword? *Journal of Adolescence, 22,* 771–783.

Parkes, C. M. (2006). *Love and loss: The roots of grief and its complications.* London: Routledge.

Perse, E. M., & Rubin, R. B. (1989). Attribution in social and parasocial relationships. *Communication Research, 16,* 59–77.

Prensky, M. (2001). *Digital natives, digital immigrants.* Retrieved June 1, 2008, from http://www.marcprensky.com/writing

Roberts, D. F., Foehr, U. G., & Rideout, V. (2005). *Generation M: Media in the lives of 8–18 year-olds.* Retrieved June 1, 2008, from http://www.kff.org/entmedia/upload/Generation-M-Media-in-the-Lives-of-8–18-Year-olds-Report.pdf

Schickel, R. (1985). *Intimate strangers: The culture of celebrity.* Garden City, NY: Doubleday.

Signorielli, N., & Kahlenberg, S. (2001). Television's world of work in the nineties. *Journal of Broadcasting & Electronic Media, 45,* 4–22.

Soukup, C. (2006). Hitching a ride on a star: Celebrity, fandom, and identification on the World Wide Web. *Southern Communication Journal, 71*(4), 319–337.

Stack, S. (2000). Media impacts on suicide: A quantitative review of 293 findings. *Social Science Quarterly, 81,* 957–971.

Steele, J. R., & Brown, J. D. (1995). Adolescent room culture: Studying media in the context of everyday life. *Journal of Youth and Adolescence, 24,* 551–576.

Thompson, M. (2006). Human brands: Investigating antecedents to consumers' strong attachments to celebrities. *Journal of Marketing, 70,* 104–119.

Wayment, H. A. (2006). Attachment style, empathy, and helping following a collective loss: Evidence from the September 11 terrorist attacks. *Attachment & Human Development, 8*(1), 1–9.

Whitbourne, S. K. (1986). *The me I know: A study of adult identity.* New York: Springer-Verlag.

14

Adolescent Bereavement and Traumatic Deaths

ANDREA C. WALKER

Adolescent traumatic bereavement is characterized by the interaction of traumatic loss with developmental tasks involving both differentiating from family and developing increased social support outside of the family. During the loss of a parent, for instance, these dynamics can create a unique experience of desiring independence from parents while simultaneously mourning the loss of a parent. The violent nature of a death can further complicate the bereavement experience. The purpose of this chapter is to review issues related to adolescent bereavement and traumatic death, with special attention to the risks of complicated grief. The chapter will discuss (a) the challenges specific to traumatic death, (b) traumatic death within the developmental stages of adolescence, (c) grief challenges nested within specific relationships to decedents and types of traumatic losses, and (d) review of available literature on successful therapeutic approaches to treatment of adolescent traumatic grief. Throughout the chapter, the terms *complicated grief* and *prolonged grief disorder* are used interchangeably.

TRAUMATIC DEATH

Adolescents who experience a traumatic death may be significantly challenged in finding resolution to the confusion and devastation that often times accompanies such a loss. Both intense, chronic stress and trauma can impair brain systems in such a way that impedes normal cognitive efforts to make sense of the loss (Neimeyer, Herrero, & Botella, 2006). In response to the experience, adolescents may perceive death itself as traumatic and thus be inhibited in addressing the normative tasks of bereavement. Adolescents may also be strained in the normal oscillation between restoration and loss-oriented thoughts (Stroebe & Schut, 1999) due to the discomfort involved in remembering the circumstances around the death, causing the adolescent to avoid those thoughts altogether (Brown & Goodman, 2005). Essentially, the adolescent may be experiencing both bereavement and posttraumatic stress disorder (PTSD) symptoms (Pfefferbaum et al., 2000).

Traumatic grief may result from deaths involving a combination of (a) the degree of physical or emotional proximity to the deceased, as with a family member or peer; (b) stigma associated with the death, such as in loss of a family member to suicide or HIV/AIDS; and (c) the presence of violent death, as in community disasters, murders, or accidents. Degree of closeness is associated significantly with traumatic death outcomes: Persons losing a family member or close friend experience the highest degree of PTSD symptoms (Pfefferbaum et al., 1999). Stigma-related deaths, as in suicide, also increase the amount of trauma experienced. Cerel, Fristad, Weller, and Weller (1999) found higher rates of anxiety and a greater association of long-term problems with suicidal versus nonsuicidal deaths. Traumatic distress may occur in survivors of violent deaths (Currier, Holland, Coleman, & Neimeyer, 2008) and may lead to a trajectory of prolonged grief disorder (Prigerson et al., 1999; Prigerson & Jacobs, 2001; Zhang, El-Jawahri, & Prigerson, 2006). In summary, central to understanding the adolescent's grief involving a traumatic death is an examination of the interplay of developmental stage and associated tasks with the increased complexity of bereavement in response to interacting issues related to (a) the closeness of the person who died, (b) violence, and/or (c) stigma of the loved one's death.

ADOLESCENT DEVELOPMENT AND TRAUMATIC GRIEVING

Adolescent development is characterized by physical, cognitive, social, spiritual, and emotional change and transition (Noppe & Noppe, 2004). Solipsistic thinking characterizes this stage, in that adolescents tend to perceive themselves as being at the center of others' worlds and that their situations are unique (Elkind, 1967). Balk (2008) identified specific developmental tasks of adolescence, including differentiating from family and forming autonomous identity, formulating career goals, and developing intimate relationships, which underscore the need to further scrutinize separate tasks within the trajectory of adolescence.

Early adolescence tends to characterize conflicts of separation versus safety; middle adolescence, independence versus dependence; and later adolescence, closeness versus distance (Fleming & Adolph, 1986). In addition, as cognitive sophistication increases throughout adolescence from concrete-operational to more formal operational (Piaget, 1972), those who experience death will be confronted with increasingly less clear-cut ways of explaining and understanding death. Although there is considerable overlap among issues and conflicts affecting early, middle, and later adolescents, a general consideration of these conflicts and tasks may provide a critical lens through which a better understanding of adolescents' experiences with traumatic death may be reached.

Early and Middle Adolescence

Development of family narratives in the form of reminiscing, discussing, and explaining emotional expression is particularly important for early adolescents (Bohanek, Marin, & Fivush, 2008) to interpret their experiences with traumatic death. Lenhardt and McCourt (2000) suggested that calm, self-possessed adolescents may not be processing their grief and may be vulnerable to complication, resulting in a greater likelihood of developing prolonged grief disorder, resulting in compromise of major developmental task completion (see Balk, 2008).

As adolescents struggle to establish their identity, a process heightened in early and middle adolescence, the thought of actually "not being" may present seemingly insurmountable perplexity. Fear of their own deaths and those of loved ones may lead to increased risk-taking behaviors as adolescents challenge their very mortality (Noppe & Noppe, 2004). Homicides, suicides, and accidents, which may be exacerbated by risk-taking behaviors, are responsible for most adolescent deaths across the globe (Fingerhut, 2004; Fingerhut & Warner, 2006).

In response to being reminded of the stark reality of their mortality, as well as physiological changes involved in puberty, early and middle adolescents may feel emotional fluctuations. Instead of expressing them, however, they may attempt to hide or control emotions because of fear of not being alike or accepted by their peers (Fleming & Balmer, 1996).

As a result, adolescents may have brief eruptions of emotions (Noppe & Noppe, 2004; Waisanen, 2004). The process of developing a sense of fairness and justice (see Fleming & Adolph, 1986) may be further assaulted in the case of traumatic death, as adolescents are not yet fully capable of negotiating the demands emerging from social context (Noppe & Noppe, 2004).

Later Adolescence

As adolescents age, they may perceive the world through increasing shades of gray and less in terms of black and white. The increased cognitive development afforded to later adolescents may also increase the difficulty in making sense of traumatic deaths. Much of the literature on this age group, as well as on complicated grief risk factors and the meaning-making theoretical perspective intended to be generalized to some adults, has been conducted on college students. I will draw from this literature to provide a platform of traumatic death from the perspective of the later adolescent.

Researchers have found that 30% of all college students are within 12 months of having experienced the death of a family member or a friend (Balk & Walker, 2008), and many of these deaths are traumatic. At a time when social support is needed the most, college students may be proximally distant from usual support systems (Schnider, Elhai, & Gray, 2007), exacerbating the development of prolonged grief disorder and stress-related problems. Insomnia, for instance, is much higher among traumatically bereaved, as opposed to normally bereaved, college students (Hardison, Neimeyer, & Lichstein, 2005). This study also found that impaired daytime functioning and increased use of substances to fall asleep were also associated with complicated grief, indicating the risk of substance abuse and failure to reach educational goals. Sophomore college women grieving death by homicide, suicide, or accident are much more likely to have acute stress disorder than those not experiencing traumatic death (Green et al., 2001). Also, perhaps not surprisingly, separation distress occurs at a much higher rate in African Americans than in Whites (Neimeyer, Baldwin, & Gillies, 2006).

Grieving in later adolescents can take on a much more complex trajectory than in younger and middle adolescents. Avoidant emotional coping, as opposed to engagement-ruminative, was significantly related to greater complicated grief in college students (Schnider et al., 2007). The process of recovery has been found to be associated with both continuing bonds and meaning reconstruction, in that more meaning making relates to less complicated grief and, at least within the first year following the loss, more continuing bonds relate to more complicated grief (Neimeyer, Baldwin, & Gillies, 2006). Perhaps because the deaths are unnatural and nonsensible, it may be much more difficult to make sense of violent death, making complicated grief outcomes much more likely in response to such deaths (Currier, Holland, & Neimeyer, 2006).

Beyond Adolescence

As the cognitive processing of traumatic deaths increases in later adolescents, renegotiating the events may also continue even further into the adolescent's life, facilitating continual sense making of the loss. Revisiting the grief, as one develops cognitively, incorporates additional depth to what was previously understood, constructs more meaning regarding the loss, and facilitates ongoing adjustment (Oltjenbruns, 2007). Traumatized adolescents consequently may reconcile ongoing grieving tasks throughout their lives, extending beyond their current experience of the death. Thus, the adolescent's challenge in grieving may be more complex than that of an adult.

RELATIONSHIPS TO DECEDENTS

Parental Loss

Traumatic losses can result in complicated grief for adolescents, particularly when those deaths involve parents. Adolescents may experience a sense of abandonment from a parent's death. Using an attachment theory perspective, Freudenberger and Gallagher (1995) suggested that children and adolescents may experience denigrated self-image and turn to substance abuse to compensate for the lost object (or parent). Simultaneous to feelings of abandonment from parental deaths, adolescents have a strong need for acceptance from a peer group, which can exacerbate cognitive dissonance during this event. For instance, adolescent response to the death of a parent may be characterized by denial or suppression of emotional expression because of fear that one might be exposed as being different from peers whose parents are both alive (Harris, 1991), as well as to prevent perception of one's regressing to an earlier developmental stage (Garber, 1995). Development of a sense of identity may be particularly inhibited with parental death.

Maternal Versus Paternal Loss

Maternal death, as opposed to paternal, may be accompanied by increased likelihood of complicated grief (Lenhardt & McCourt, 2000). Females, in particular, who are proceeding through a separation-individuation process are likely to identify more strongly with their mothers than males and may thus experience higher risk for complicated grief than males (LaSorsa & Fodor, 1990). Unless surviving fathers encourage grief expression in their children, unresolved grief in females may be more likely (Lenhardt & McCourt, 2000). Death of a father may also instigate trauma for surviving adolescent children. In an emotional description of an undergraduate student's personal experience with loss, Waisanen (2004) reveals the horror involved in watching her father die a slow and debilitating death from cancer. The traumatic death of this father fostered complicated grief responses.

Suicide

Parental deaths by suicide are likely to have a devastating impact on surviving adolescents. In fact, the associated trauma can be so intense that the ability of a survivor to reestablish his or her life narrative, or to make meaning of the loss, is significantly impaired (Neimeyer, Herrero, & Botella, 2006). In a study of Indian children ages 6–16 (mean age 12.2), child survivors of suicide were found to have higher rates of depressive disorders, PTSD, and panic disorder than children who had not experienced a suicide (Sethi & Bhargava, 2003). Three participants discovered the body of a person who died, and all were diagnosed with PTSD. The suicide survivors also experienced increased difficulties with peers, siblings, school, and leisure activities.

Murder

Intimate partner femicide (IPF), the murder of a woman by an intimate partner, involves the mothers of approximately 3,300 children annually (Lewandowski, McFarlane, Campbell, Gary, & Barenski, 2004). In a qualitative study of 10 families, seven caregivers reported that grieving children presented a myriad of troubles: (a) mental health issues of depression, anxiety, prolonged grief, and posttraumatic stress symptoms; (b) physical health problems, including asthma, weight and appetite changes, and somatic complaints; (c) behavioral changes of general rebellion, destructive and impulsive behaviors, peer-related problems, and illegal activity; and (d) drop in academic performance (Hardesty, Campbell, McFarlane, & Lewandowski, 2008). Those who indicated proximity to the event, in terms of discovering the body or hearing or seeing the murder, all reported adverse health effects; those who were not exposed to the murder reported no physical health problems. Instances of both suicide and homicide may increase the risk of the surviving adolescents' becoming suicidal (Brent et al., 1992; Hardesty et al., 2008).

HIV/AIDS

Rotheram-Borus, Weiss, Alber, and Lester (2005) studied the impact of parental death due to HIV/AIDS on the emotional distress and high-risk behaviors of adolescents. The stigma associated with HIV/AIDS may further exacerbate the grief of parental loss. Results of the study indicated that parental death was not associated with a drastic change in emotional and behavioral functioning of the surviving adolescents. Both emotional distress and contact with juvenile justice system peaked during the year prior to parental death and declined steadily during the year following the death. Only depressive symptoms increased after the death, returning to normal within a year. These results provide insight into the traumatic nature of witnessing first-hand the dying process of a parent and the social stigma of living with a parent with HIV/AIDS, whose death may bring a degree of solace as an adolescent faces the finality of the loss.

Community Disaster

Since community disasters often involve massive catastrophe and multiple deaths, they may involve greater instances of PTSD along with complicated grief than other types of traumatic death. Children who lost parents on September 11 needed help both with PTSD and with bereavement (Cohen, Goodman, Brown, & Mannarino, 2004). A study investigating the Oklahoma City bombing found that youths who lost an immediate family member experienced greater PTSD than did anyone else (Pfefferbaum et al., 1999, 2000). In measuring a sample of children and adolescents whose fathers were New York City servicemen who lost their lives on September 11, Brown and Goodman (2005) found that those experiencing the traumatic death were impaired in fulfillment of normative bereavement tasks. Potentially comforting reminders of their dead fathers instead became intrusive triggers of anxiety-provoking memories.

As might be expected, adolescents living in war zones are at greater risk for both complicated grief and PTSD (Layne et al., 2001). Missing friends and family breakdown could have as significant an effect on well-being of Bosnian adolescents as exposure to war-related events (Lynne & Konstantinos, 2005). In cases of extreme exposure to trauma, such as in the Rwandan genocide, in which multiple family members were killed or disfigured with children watching nearby, survivors must deal not only with traumatic grief but also with survivor guilt and survivor burden (Gupta, 2008). In one case in particular, a girl and her brother hid in a tree while watching the murder of nearly 20 of her family members, including her parents. Then, tragically, the girl's brother fell out of the tree, soon facing his own murder; the girl's resulting survival guilt was seemingly insurmountable. In numerous other examples, surviving adolescents are left to care for younger siblings while trying to recover from the multiple, violent deaths of parents and other family members (Gupta, 2008). For most of us, recovery from the grief associated with multiple losses involving such brutality is incomprehensible and challenges the very heart of human spirit.

Sibling Loss

The violent death of a sibling can cause trauma as adolescents grieve the losses directly as well as adjust to family disruption resulting from grief of other family members. In a study by Lohan and Murphy (2002), parents reported that the grief responses of siblings of children who had died violently did not change much up to 2 years after the child's death. Results indicated that adolescents mostly talk to their mothers about their grief. Early adolescent boys (ages 10 to 14 years) were perceived by both mothers and fathers as having the lowest degree of difficulty in this group as compared to all ages of adolescents; inversely, younger adolescent daughters were reported as having greater difficulties with family relationship issues. Mothers of middle adolescent boys (ages 15–19) reported increased physical and self-destructive behaviors in this group, whereas fathers did not. Mothers described middle adolescent daughters (ages 15–19) with the greatest degree of detail, indicating a struggle with reestablishing their identities in the wake of sibling loss

(Lohan & Murphy, 2002). From a psychodynamic perspective, Ainslie and Solyom (1986) describe how an adolescent sibling who was encouraged to nearly ignore the death of her infant brother struggled to resolve her grief after the birth of her own daughter later in adulthood. If not properly addressed at the time of death, sibling death can result in later complications.

Peer Loss

The nature of the death of a peer, in terms of its unexpectedness and likelihood of involving violence, can influence the degree of trauma enveloped in the associated grieving of an adolescent. In comparison to the loss of a grandparent, loss of a friend in general has been shown to be associated with higher levels of grief, highlighting the importance of perceived closeness of the decedent in grief (Servaty-Seib & Pistole, 2006). In comparison to those who lost an acquaintance, adolescents who lost a friend in the Oklahoma City bombing displayed significantly more severe PTSD (Pfefferbaum et al., 1999, 2000). Dyregrov, Gjestad, Wikander, and Vigerust (1999) studied the grief reactions of a sample of 26 adolescents in Norway experiencing the sudden death of a classmate from accident, finding that grief level was similar to that of adolescents who had lost siblings. The criteria for classification of prolonged grief disorder include duration of symptoms beyond 6 months: Many of these adolescents reported persistent distress at 9 months.

Death of a peer due to suicide may further exacerbate traumatic grief. For example, in adolescents exposed to a peer's suicide, researchers (Melhem et al., 2003) found complicated grief significantly associated with (a) females, (b) feelings of personal responsibility, (c) interpersonal conflict, (d) previous history of depression, and (e) a family history of anxiety disorders. One must also consider the likelihood that adolescents who have a preexisting vulnerability to complicated grief may be more likely to be friends with adolescents who also are emotionally vulnerable and, as in this study, commit suicide. Further research examining traumatic peer death is needed.

THERAPEUTIC INTERVENTIONS

The tumult of both the developmental stage of adolescence and the violent nature of the death loss requires that therapeutic interventions reflect sensitivity to anxiety-provoking triggers and compassion for additional challenges afforded to these victims regarding traumatic grief. Whitaker (1985) suggested that developmental complications can result from failure of an adolescent or young adult to appropriately grieve a parental death as a result of avoidance or emotional distancing. In cases of such denial, more demonstrative, instrumental interventions, beyond "conventional talking psychotherapy" (p. 241), may be needed, such as visiting the grave in the presence of the psychotherapist. By contrast, adolescents have been found to prefer discussing losses with their peers (Dyregrov et al., 1999; McNeil, Silliman, & Swihart, 1991) and usually identify peers as being the most able to provide unconditional support (Hogan & DeSantis, 1994); these studies have investigated same-age losses, including peers and siblings. Waisanen (2007) indicated that many of her peers did not seem to know how to respond to her requests for support in discussing the stress related to the slow death of her father to cancer. Different types of losses may thus call for different types of therapeutic approaches.

Parental Suicide

Parental suicide challenges the very core of a person's prior life narrative and nullifies the emotional meaning and structure of one's life (Neimeyer, Herrero, & Botella, 2006). Adolescent survivors, many of whom still dominantly operate under concrete-operational thinking, are left to make sense of the reasons for their parent's suicide and cope with the added strain from the stigma assigned to suicidal death (Cerel et al., 1999). Since long-term psychological and social outcomes are at greater risk, some researchers (Mitchell et al., 2006) emphasize the importance of early interventions.

These interventions should incorporate careful communication with children and adolescents regarding the parental suicide. Mitchell and colleagues (2006) recommended that therapists communicate clearly, not substituting any words for *suicide,* and be aware of children's cognitive development. These researchers recommend therapeutic support groups specifically designed for adolescents bereaved of parental suicide; adolescents can fulfill their need for peer acceptance through interactions with peers who have had similar death experiences. In turn, adolescents may begin to feel reduction in social anxiety, leading to reestablishing identity and self-esteem. Mitchell and colleagues (2007) describe an 8-week program, the Children's Survivors of Suicide (SOS) Bereavement Support Group, structured to provide education and therapy guiding alteration of negative thoughts, feelings, and behaviors of surviving children by encouraging verbal, written, and drawing skills. Although the group targets ages 7–13, it may be altered to provide more appropriate activities for later adolescents.

Whether working with groups or individuals, therapists of suicide survivors should demonstrate empathic listening and compassionate concern for the adolescents. Therapists should focus on reestablishing coherence of the client's life narrative or self-identity (Neimeyer et al., 2006). In doing so, the therapist should help clients (a) integrate the suicide event into personal narratives, (b) reconstruct the image of their dead parent, and (c) explore those aspects of the loss that cause ongoing distress and promote growth. Neimeyer and colleagues described an adult woman, who as an early adolescent discovered her mother's dead body to suicide; the recovery process involved reestablishing meaning in her life such that she could forgive her mother, releasing her shame regarding the event, and renewing her capacity to love. Working with an adolescent should involve these same tasks, but therapists should facilitate meaning making in consideration of the adolescent's current life narrative, involving school, peer group, surviving family, and so forth. Therapists should also acknowledge the need for adolescents to revisit the grief to establish additional or altered meaning (Oltjenbruns, 2007) as their cognitive ability continues to develop, a process which may possibly last throughout their life spans.

Community Disaster

In the wake of the September 11 disaster, clinicians in New York City began to come together to develop interventions for children suffering from community disaster. Children needed not only intervention for PTSD symptoms, but also help with grieving the loss of their parent, a resulting state known as childhood traumatic grief (CTG) (Cohen et al., 2004). Cohen and colleagues compared the effectiveness of two types of therapies, trauma-focused cognitive-behavioral therapy adapted for CTG (TF-CBT) and client-centered therapy (CCT), finding TF-CBT to be more successful at incorporating the needs of both trauma and bereavement into a single therapeutic approach. For families generally operating successfully before the traumatic event, the strength-based approach of CCT may be more appropriate in addressing nontrauma related issues. An Internet-based CBT treatment program has been developed for those suffering from complicated grief, with promising results (see Wagner, Knaevelsrud, & Maercker, 2005). Considering the extensive use of technologically advanced modes of communication by most adolescents today, such a program may be appropriate for this group.

Traumatic disasters such as described above have occurred around the globe. Using examples from children in Rwanda after the 1994 genocide; in Sierra Leone after the 1999 rebel invasion; and in Kabul, Afghanistan, during the Mujahideen period, Gupta (2008) highlighted the importance of art therapy in working with severely traumatized children from numerous backgrounds. Many of the children in her examples experienced extreme violence and resulting trauma because of sudden and graphic deaths of family members, oftentimes while children watched nearby. Art therapy provided children and adolescents with a way to express confusing, painful feelings that might otherwise go unarticulated.

A UNICEF sponsored School-Based Psychosocial Program for War-Exposed Adolescents was implemented using a sample of 87 students from schools in Bosnia and Hercegovina. This program involved a 20-session trauma/grief-focused group with four modules designed to (a) reduce acute stress, (b) process traumatic experiences therapeutically, (c) facilitate adaptive grieving in response to loss, and (d) promote progressive developmental adaptation by engaging in current and planning future life tasks (Layne et al., 2001). Results indicated success in that participants experienced significant reductions in posttraumatic stress, depression, and grief symptoms after undergoing the treatment group.

Environmentally At-Risk Adolescents

One population particularly vulnerable to traumatic grief involves inner-city adolescents, who may experience repeated, sometimes violent, losses. These losses may be disenfranchised due to lack of recognition by others or fragmented social and familial resource support systems (Crenshaw & Garbarino, 2007). Adolescents in this population are often preoccupied with death circumstances and are inhibited from recalling any pleasant memories of the person. Authors modified a previous treatment model (Cohen & Mannarino, 2004) to specifically target adolescents who experience repeated violent death. Crenshaw and Garbarino recommend that therapists first target triggers related to anxiety-provoking images and then assist adolescents in developing a more positive context for their memories. Therapists should also provide families of children with education about the traumatic grief symptoms adolescents may exhibit. Finally, therapeutic efforts should emphasize and target the core need to construct meaning of the event, which may be done by helping the adolescent to reconcile aspects of his or her current life circumstances and develop future goals to make sense of the loss.

CONCLUSION

In summary, I would like to make a few closing comments intended to provide more comprehensive insight on the overall position of adolescent bereavement and traumatic death as it pertains to research and practice. Although literature affords us ample information regarding the developmental context of adolescents, empirical studies measuring cognitive processes that early and middle adolescents undergo while adjusting to death, particularly traumatic death, are rare. Nevertheless, several empirical studies provide rich, relevant data on grieving in college students, even pertaining to traumatic death, but caution must be used in generalizing results to other later adolescents who are not in college. Also, we must remember that although the mean age of these study participants was within 18–22 years, the range included a few nontraditional students of adult age.

Further, research has provided some information on types of traumatic losses and relationships to the decedent, the most at-risk of which appears to be suicide. Studies comparing occurrence of complicated grief by type of death are scarce, however, and most merely compare violent losses with nonviolent losses. Studies comparing grief by relationship to decedent are more common, with parental loss suggested to be the most significant for adolescents. Those experiencing compounded stressors of multiple losses involving intense brutality, as experienced in war-exposed countries, may be experiencing the most devastating grief, but these populations are sorely understudied.

Despite these limitations, certain themes pervade the literature, and useful suggestions can be made for practitioners. In the first place, adolescents need to make sense of the death, and emotional and cognitive development may mediate this process. It seems that, although emotional reaction may be more volatile, cognitive acceptance of the loss at younger ages dominated by more concrete thinking is easier to reach. Later adolescents, who are developing more abstract modes of thinking, and who may be grappling with the existential questions about reality and self, may be the most unable to make sense of such senseless acts as traumatic deaths.

Second, the concept of a life narrative, or one's perceived position in relation to the rest of the world, may be most compromised in the case of adolescents dealing with traumatic death. Not only must they make sense of the death itself, but adolescents must integrate the loss into their self-concept. In the best of circumstances, adolescents need self-concept development, but the loss of a significant relationship that helps to define self, and the added confusion when that loss is traumatic or violent, may considerably retard the process. The risk of future challenges resulting from problems in developing a consistent life narrative is immense.

Finally, adolescents need to understand and prepare for the ongoing interface with grief and with the decedent throughout their lives. This final step involves a teleological unfolding, focusing both on restoration and future goals in life without the decedent, as well as the continued review of changes over time in the adolescent's relationship with the person who died. Adolescents should be assured that continually reconciling the lost relationship as it is imagined to have developed may characterize normative bereavement and that not doing so may also characterize normative bereavement.

Therapeutic interventions should specifically address the issues and be constructed to facilitate the flow through these steps. I suggest a combination of support group with individual and/or family therapy, as well as flexibility to work with adolescents targeting goals simultaneously. The initial issue of sense making may be the most challenging in cases of traumatic death, so care should be taken in giving adolescent survivors ample time to reflect on the significance of the death. Interactions should encourage exploration of a life narrative in terms of school, peer group, part-time job, and surviving family, as these issues generally pertain to adolescents. To address the third issue, adolescents may be asked to describe the relationship with the decedent as it might have developed 5, 10, and even 20 years from now. This activity may further help the adolescent make sense of the loss.

As with any population of people, there may be greater within-group than between-group variance. Therapeutic interventions must thus consider the individual needs of the adolescent who may be experiencing any of a number of possible combinations of losses, type(s) of losses, and available resources. Central to facilitating such an adolescent's recovery is an understanding of what we already know about adolescents, as presented in this chapter, coupled with openness to those things that we do not yet know.

REFERENCES

Ainslie, R. C., & Solyom, A. E. (1986). The replacement of the fantasized Oedipal child: A disruptive effect of sibling loss on the mother-infant relationship. *Psychoanalytic Psychology, 3*(3), 257–268.

Balk, D. E. (2008). The adolescent's encounter with death. In K. J. Doka & A. S. Tucci (Eds.), *Living with grief: Children and adolescents* (pp. 25–42). Washington, DC: Hospice Foundation of America.

Balk, D. E., & Walker, A. C. (2008). Prevalence and severity of college student bereavement. In D. Balk (Chair), *New understandings of college student bereavement.* Symposium conducted at the annual conference of the Association for Death Education and Counseling, Montreal, Quebec, Canada.

Bohanek, J. G., Marin, K. A., & Fivush, R. (2008). Family narratives, self, and gender in early adolescence. *Journal of Early Adolescence, 28,* 153–176.

Brent, D. A., Perper, J. A., Moritz, G., Allman, C., Friend, A., Schweers, J., et al. (1992). Psychiatric effects of exposure to suicide among the friends and acquaintances of adolescent suicide victims. *Journal of American Academy of Child and Adolescent Psychiatry, 31,* 629–640.

Brown, E. J., & Goodman, R. F. (2005). Childhood traumatic grief: An exploration of the construct in children bereaved on September 11. *Journal of Clinical Child and Adolescent Psychology, 34,* 248–259.

Cerel, J., Fristad, M., Weller, E., & Weller, R. (1999). Suicide-bereaved children and adolescents: A controlled longitudinal examination. *Journal of the American Academy of Child & Adolescent Psychiatry, 38*(6), 672–679.

Cohen, J., Goodman, R. F., Brown, E. J., & Mannarino, A. (2004). Treatment of childhood traumatic grief: Contributing to a newly emerging condition in the wake of community trauma. *Harvard Review Psychiatry, 12,* 213–216.

Cohen, J. A., & Mannarino, A. P. (2004). Treatment of childhood traumatic grief. *Journal of Clinical Child and Adolescent Psychology, 33,* 819–831.

Crenshaw, D. A., & Garbarino, J. (2007). Hidden dimensions: Profound sorry and buried potential in violent youth. *Journal of Humanistic Psychology, 47,* 160–174.

Currier, J. M., Holland, J. M., Coleman, R. A., & Neimeyer, R. A. (2008). Bereavement following violent death: An assault on life and meaning. In R. G. Stephenson & G. R. Cox (Eds.), *Perspectives on violence and violent death* (pp. 177–202). Amityville, NY: Baywood.

Currier, J. M., Holland, J. M., & Neimeyer, R. A. (2006). Sense-making, grief, and the experience of violent loss: Toward a mediational model. *Death Studies, 30,* 403–428.

Dyregrov, A., Gjestad, R., Wikander, A. M. B., & Vigerust, S. (1999). Reactions following the sudden death of a classmate. *Scandinavian Journal of Psychology, 40,* 167–176.

Elkind, D. (1967). Egocentrism in adolescence. *Child Development, 38,* 1025–1034.

Fingerhut, L. A. (2004). International collaborative effort on injury statistics: 10-year review. *Injury Control and Safety Prevention, 11,* 297–301.

Fingerhut, L. A. & Warner, M. (2006). The ICD-10 injury mortality diagnosis matrix. *Injury Prevention: Journal of the International Society for Child and Adolescent Injury Prevention, 12,* 24–29.

Fleming, S. J., & Adolph, R. (1986). Helping bereaved adolescents: Needs and responses. In C. A. Corr & J. N. McNeil (Eds.), *Adolescence and death* (pp. 97–118). New York: Springer Publishing.

Fleming, S., & Balmer, L. (1996). Bereavement in adolescence. In C. A. Corr & D. E. Balk (Eds.), *Handbook of adolescent death and bereavement* (pp. 139–154). New York: Springer Publishing.

Freudenberger, H. J., & Gallagher, K. M. (1995). Emotional consequences of loss for our adolescents. *Psychotherapy, 32,* 150–153.

Garber, B. (1995). Mourning in adolescence: Normal and pathological. *Adolescent Psychiatry, 12,* 371–387.

Green, B. L., Krupnick, J. L., Stockton, P., Goodman, L., Corcoran, C., & Petty, R. (2001). Psychological outcomes associated with traumatic loss in a sample of young women. *American Behavioral Scientist, 44,* 817–837.

Gupta, L. M. (2008). Addressing traumatic losses among war-affected children in the developing world: Lessons learned for future post-conflict interventions. Paper presented at the annual conference of the Association for Death Education and Counseling, Montreal, Quebec, Canada.

Hardesty, J. L., Campbell, J. C., McFarlane, J. M., & Lewandowski, L. A. (2008). How children and their caregivers adjust after intimate partner femicide. *Journal of Family Issues, 29,* 100–124.

Hardison, H. G., Neimeyer, R. A., & Lichstein, K. L. (2005). Insomnia and complicated grief symptoms in bereaved college students. *Behavioral Sleep Medicine, 3,* 99–111.

Harris, E. S. (1991). Adolescent bereavement following the death of a parent: An exploratory study. *Child Psychiatry and Human Development, 21,* 267–281.

Hogan, N. S., & DeSantis, L. (1994). Things that help and hinder adolescent sibling bereavement. *Western Journal of Nursing Research, 16,* 132–153.

LaSorsa, V., & Fodor, I. (1990). Adolescent daughter/midlife mother dyad: A new look at separation and self-definition. *Psychology of Women Quarterly, 14,* 593–606.

Layne, C. M., Pynoos, R. S., Saltzman, W. R., Arslanagic, B., Black, M., Savjak, N., et al. (2001). Trauma/grief-focused group psychotherapy: School-based postwar intervention with traumatized Bosnian adolescents. *Group Dynamics: Theory, Research, and Practice, 5,* 277–290.

Lenhardt, A. M. C., & McCourt, B. (2000). Adolescent unresolved grief in response to the death of a mother. *Professional School Counseling, 3,* 189–196.

Lewandowski, L. A., McFarlane, J., Campbell, J. C., Gary, F., & Barenski, C. (2004). "He killed my mommy!" Murder or attempted murder of a child's mother. *Journal of Family Violence, 19,* 211–220.

Lohan, J. A., & Murphy, S. A. (2002). Parents' perceptions of adolescent sibling grief responses after an adolescent or young adult child's sudden, violent death. *Omega, Journal of Death and Dying, 44,* 77–95.

Lynne, J., & Konstantinos, K. (2005). Exposure to political violence and psychological well-being in Bosnian adolescents: A mixed methods approach. *Clinical Child Psychology and Psychiatry, 10*(2), 157–176.

McNeil, J. N., Silliman, B., & Swihart, J. J. (1991). Helping adolescents cope with the death of a peer: A high school case study. *Journal of Adolescent Research, 6,* 132–145.

Melhem, N. M., Day, N., Shear, M. K., Day, R., Reynolds, C. F., & Brent, D. (2003). Predictors of complicated grief among adolescents exposed to a peer's suicide. *Journal of Loss and Trauma, 9,* 21–34.

Mitchell, A. M., Wesner, S., Brownson, L., Dysart-Gale, D., Garand, L., & Havill, A. (2006). Effective communication with bereaved child survivors of suicide. *Journal of Child and Adolescent Psychiatric Nursing, 19,* 130–136.

Mitchell, A. M., Wesner, S., Garand, L., Gale, D. D., Havill, A., & Brownson, L. (2007). A support group intervention for children bereaved by parental suicide. *Journal of Child and Adolescent Psychiatric Nursing, 20,* 3–13.

Neimeyer, R. A., Baldwin, S. A., & Gillies, J. (2006). Continuing bonds and reconstructing meaning: Mitigating complications in bereavement. *Death Studies, 30,* 715–738.

Neimeyer, R. A., Herrero, O., & Botella, L. (2006). Chaos to coherence: Psychotherapeutic integration of traumatic loss. *Journal of Constructivist Psychology, 19,* 127–145.

Noppe, I. C., & Noppe, L. D. (2004). Adolescent experiences with death: Letting go of immortality. *Journal of Mental Health Counseling, 26,* 146–167.

Oltjenbruns, K. A. (2007). The importance of a developmental context: Childhood and adolescence as an example. In D. Balk, C. Wogrin, G. Thornton, & D. Meagher (Eds.), *Handbook of thanatology: The essential body of knowledge for the study of death, dying, and bereavement* (pp. 143–149). Northbrook, IL: Association for Death Education and Counseling.

Pfefferbaum, B., Gurwitch, R. H., McDonald, N. B., Leftwich, M. J., Sconzo, G. M., Messenbaugh, A. K., et al. (2000). Posttraumatic stress among young children after the death of a friend or acquaintance in a terrorist bombing. *Psychiatric Services, 51,* 386–388.

Pfefferbaum, B., Nixon, S. J., Cucher, P. M., Tivis, R. D., Moore, V. L., Gurwitch, R. H., et al. (1999). Posttraumatic stress responses in bereaved children after the Oklahoma City bombing. *American Academy of Child & Adolescent Psychiatry, 38,* 1372–1379.

Piaget, J. (1972). Intellectual evolution from adolescence to adulthood. *Human Development, 15,* 1–12.

Prigerson, H. G., & Jacobs, S. C. (2001). Traumatic grief as a distinct disorder: A rationale, consensus criteria, and a preliminary empirical test. In M. S. Stroebe, W. Stroebe, & R. O. Hansson (Eds.), *Handbook of bereavement research* (pp. 613–645). Washington, DC: American Psychological Association.

Prigerson, H. G., Shear, M. K., Jacobs, S. C., Reynolds, C. F., Maciejewski, P. D., Davidson, J. R. T., et al. (1999). Consensus criteria for traumatic grief. *British Journal of Psychiatry, 174,* 67–73.

Rotheram-Borus, M. J., Weiss, R., Alber, S., & Lester, P. (2005). Adolescent adjustment before and after HIV-related parental death. *Journal of Consulting and Clinical Psychology, 73,* 221–228.

Schnider, K. R., Elhai, J. D., & Gray, M. J. (2007). Coping style use predicts posttraumatic stress and complicated grief symptom severity among college students reporting a traumatic loss. *Journal of Counseling Psychology, 54,* 344–350.

Servaty-Seib, H. L., & Pistole, M. C. (2006). Adolescent grief: Relationship category and emotional closeness. *Omega, Journal of Death and Dying, 54,* 147–167.

Sethi, S., & Bhargava, S. C. (2003). Child and adolescent survivors of suicide. *Crisis, 24,* 4–6.

Stroebe, M., & Schut, H. (1999). The dual process model of coping with bereavement: rationale and description. *Death Studies, 23,* 197–224.

Wagner, B., Knaevelsrud, C., & Maercker, A. (2005). Internet-based treatment for complicated grief: Concepts and case study. *Journal of Loss and Trauma, 10,* 409–432.

Waisanen, E. M. (2004). Daddy. *Journal of Loss and Trauma, 9*, 291–298.

Whitaker, L. C. (1985). Visiting the parental grave in psychotherapy. *Psychotherapy, 22*(2), 241–247.

Zhang, B., El-Jawahri, A., & Prigerson, H. G. (2006). Update on bereavement research: Evidence-based guidelines for the diagnosis and treatment of complicated bereavement. *Journal of Palliative Medicine, 9*, 1188–1203.

PART IV

Interventions

As part of their assigned topics, many of the earlier chapters in this book have suggested various ways to help adolescents who are experiencing a life-threatening illness, a significant death or other loss, or bereavement and grief resulting from such a death or loss. The six chapters in part IV take up constructive interventions in more robust and direct ways. These discussions cover a broad range of topics: teaching adolescents about death, bereavement, and coping (chapter 15); camps and support groups for adolescents (chapter 16); counseling for adolescents with life-threatening illness (chapter 17) or for bereaved adolescents (chapter 18); and therapy for adolescents experiencing prolonged grief disorder (chapter 19). Chapter 20 adds advice on how to help caregivers who are experiencing compassion fatigue or burnout as a result of their work with the adolescents and their family members described in earlier chapters.

There is much that can be done to prepare adolescents in advance to cope in constructive ways with death and bereavement experiences, to offer support when such experiences are encountered, and to intervene when difficulties arise. It is a privilege to be admitted into the life of an adolescent who is trying to cope with death-related experiences and to be able to provide assistance to such adolescents in ways described in the chapters in this part.

15

Educating Adolescents About Death, Bereavement, and Coping

ROBERT G. STEVENSON

Adults sometimes ask why adolescents should be burdened with dark thoughts of death and loss. These adults feel that adolescents do not need to learn about the reality of death because, unlike younger children, they have internalized an understanding that death is universal and irreversible, and that the body no longer functions after death. What more need an adolescent learn? Why would any adolescents want to focus on such topics or to learn in any formal way about death and grief, at a time in life when they are so full of vitality? Why learn about death when one is still learning to live? The questions seem logical, but are based on an illusion that can disappear in an instant. The questions are complicated by the very different ages at which adolescence is said to end in different cultures or countries. A young person considered an adolescent in one country may be a productive citizen and parent in another.

AN EXAMPLE: A COMMUNITY IN BERGEN COUNTY, NEW JERSEY

A decade ago in Bergen County, New Jersey, there was a community that could easily be seen as an example of small-town America. Because the topic of death seemed so remote, local schools offered nothing related to death education. In just a few months, that illusion was shattered by a series of tragic deaths.

A high school freshman was accidentally shot and killed by a classmate as they examined his father's off-duty revolver. The community was shocked, but they expressed their grief and tried to move on.

Less than 2 months later, the young son of a high school coach died after a battle with leukemia. Many people had raised money for a bone marrow transplant for this young man. His death came as an emotional blow that touched countless people beyond his immediate family and friends. Losses such as this, where so many are affected, can result in what is called community grief. This type of grief raises issues that go beyond an individual's grief experience. Students were among those most affected.

Since the young man's death was not entirely unexpected, school officials believed that the adolescents in their care were handling it well. School leaders chose to believe these bereaved youngsters needed no special support. Requests by school staff to involve others in developing a plan of support were turned down. Staff members even reached out to educators in other districts, and several teachers and staff members went to a workshop in a nearby regional high school. In that district there was a teacher who had designed a death education course for students and developed support programs for all staff.

That summer, a teenage girl who appeared to be responding well to treatment for a chronic illness, lapsed into a coma while on vacation at the shore. After several days on life support, she died. A number of individuals stepped forward to help the young people of the town. A local clergyman held a prayer service while the girl was in the hospital and encouraged her friends and classmates to write letters of support. At the girl's funeral, young people played key roles in the ceremony (with an adult beside them to offer support if it was needed). The public high school (located near the church) announced it would be open after the service with cool drinks, and the school's guidance personnel were made available to speak with any young people who wished to do so. After these events the community was more sensitive to the needs of adolescents. Over the next 10 years, three high school students were struck by trains in two separate incidents. In each case, the school and community responded more effectively than had been the case earlier.

Each of the deaths experienced by this community affected the town's young people. To plan for the aftermath of one death is important, but that alone may not be enough. There may be several losses that affect an entire community, or a community loss may combine with personal losses of individuals in that community. Planning for the grief that follows a single loss may not be effective when grief associated with multiple losses is the issue. This community learned through experience how to help young people who are faced with community grief.

This story is typical of the way in which many American communities deal with death and grief. They deny them until a crisis forces them to confront their sad reality. When people finally take action, mistakes may be made—even with the best of intentions—and the lessons learned from a crisis may be forgotten when life returns to normal and people have the chance to return to their previous "cocoon" of denial.

To avoid such a return to isolation, with its associated lack of support, some communities have developed specific programs to help adolescents and their families cope with dying, death, grief, and loss. Families, schools, and religious institutions all play important roles. Because many programs are based in the schools, this area of study has come to be known as death education. Death education is "that formal instruction which deals with dying, death, grief, loss, and their impact on the individual and humankind" (Stevenson, 1984, p. 141). Such formal instruction may occur at home with family members, in religious institutions, or in schools.

Other countries have examined programs offered to adolescents in America and have started developing responses tailored to the needs of young people in their own cultures. Japan, Greece, and Korea are all developing and implementing death education programs in their countries based on their cultures, traditions, and religious beliefs. In Japan, Alfons Deeken has been a prime mover in their death education movement, the first in Asia. Deeken is a German-educated Jesuit priest who teaches at Sophia University in Tokyo. Although not focused on young people as much as on adults, one element of his work has been to bring death education to Japanese junior and senior high school students (Deeken, 1999).

In Greece, Merimna was founded in 1995 by Danai Papadatou and a group of scientists to support children who face life-threatening illnesses or who are mourning the loss of a beloved person (Stavros S. Niarchos Foundation, 2006). Merimna offers education programs for educators in Greek schools, together with counseling for children and adolescents.

Korea is just starting to develop programs for adolescents. A team of Korean students visited a number of authors and colleges in 2007 to learn about American death education. The program in Korea is funded by private industry, not the government, but its aims seem to parallel those of programs developed earlier in Japan.

DEATH EDUCATION

Death education begins in the home. Parents are the first and most important teachers of their children. They model coping behaviors as they themselves try to cope with the losses they encounter in life. In an ideal situation, young people can turn to family members for information and support in time of crisis, building on a foundation established early in life. However, emotional ties and concern about saying the wrong thing can hinder open family discussion of sensitive issues, such as the taboo topics of sex and death. If parental concern over possible misstatements, or the influence of cultural taboos, is strong enough, such discussions may not take place at all. Parents may wish to protect young persons from unpleasant reality, or they may want to preserve their vision of the innocence of childhood for as long as possible.

It is also true that, for a variety of reasons, some families do not fulfill their potential as a safe, nurturing place for each of their members. Although the concept is overused and often misapplied, dysfunctional families do exist. The dysfunction may be in the area of communication, or it may come as a result of family secrets (emotional baggage from the past). In such situations, family members may need help from some outside source to function more effectively in times of grief or other death-related crises. Often, families turn to religious institutions that also provide death education, although diversity of religious belief in pluralistic societies and across cultures, or even lack of such belief, makes it difficult to generalize about the impact of religion in the education of adolescents about death.

Christians may view death as punishment for sin. Some Christians attribute their feelings of guilt to a traditional religious portrayal of death. Nevertheless, their faith can also offer comfort in times of grief. Jesus said, "Blessed are those who mourn for they shall be comforted" (Matthew 5:4). The comfort is said to come through the belief that Jesus is the resurrection and the life, and that one who believes in him "will live, even when he dies" (John 11:25).

Eastern religions speak of death as transition as the life force moves on to a new plane of existence or another life in this world. Eastern faiths, such as Hinduism, Buddhism, or Taoism, do not speak of personal salvation. There is common ground, however, in religious teachings about death. In general, religious belief offers explanation for events that may otherwise seem incomprehensible (Why did he have to die?). These beliefs can calm fears regarding the fate of the deceased (heaven, reunion with Brahma, movement to a new life through reincarnation) and through ritual (wakes, shiva, cremation, graveside services) can be a source of communal strength. Also, when one feels hopeless, religion can be a source of hope. It can be hoped that the deceased is now beyond this so-called vale of tears and that those who mourn may one day be reunited with their loved one, or it can be comfort to believe that a loved one has now escaped the ever-turning wheel of reincarnation (birth, decay, death, and rebirth). Religion generally offers the belief that life continues in some form after the event of physical death and may help the bereaved to move on with their lives.

Because death education is at its best when it is not done in isolation, teachers must try to be conscious of the many influences in the lives of their students. Familial, cultural, regional, and religious differences must all be acknowledged if death education is to be truly responsive to the needs of students.

THE ROLE OF THE SCHOOL

Death education in the United States and Canada has developed primarily in colleges and high schools. In other countries it is centered on agencies outside of the formal school setting, although staff from agencies may be called on to present programs in schools. Death education programs have developed in three primary areas (Stevenson, 2001):

- Prevention—courses that present facts about the physical aspects of death, the psychosocial effects of death on the survivors, and methods of coping with dying, death, and grief
- Intervention—school support in the midst of crisis
- Postvention—continued support by the school community after a death

Death education does *not* include every course or curriculum that mentions death. Hamlet's soliloquy or *Romeo and Juliet* may well be used in a death education context, but their inclusion in a curriculum does not, by itself, transform an English literature course into a death education curriculum. In a school setting, death education includes those courses, curricula, counseling programs, and support services that offer a structured approach to issues dealing with dying, death, grief, loss, and their impact on the students, staff, their families, their friends, and society.

After over 3 decades of death education in American schools, the need for such courses and programs is clearer than ever. Although some would like to cling to the illusion that death does not touch the lives of adolescents, the reality is quite different. In the United States, 1 in every 750 young people of high school age dies each year. Each of those deaths affects not just the students at one school, but at schools throughout the area. One in 20 young people will lose a parent to death by their senior year in high school (Critelli, 1979). Sibling deaths, celebrity deaths (of adolescents' heroes or cult figures), and staff deaths also affect high-school-age adolescents. Potentially, there are students trying to cope with their grief in every class in every school. Thus, the difference among adolescents is not about whether they have been affected by grief. They differ in their degree of success in coping with that grief. In other countries where death is not nearly as remote (attributable to such factors as poverty, disease, and war), there is more need to help adolescents understand what they are going though when they experience grief. There is also a need to do so in a manner that takes into account, and respects, local culture and traditions.

The link between death education and schools is natural because grief can have a dramatic impact on the learning process and can affect a student in a number of ways (Stevenson, 1986):

- Academic—a shorter attention span, difficulty in remembering facts, lower grades, and/or a lowered level of self-confidence regarding school assignments
- Behavioral—disruptive classroom behavior; poor attendance; more frequent visits to the school nurse; increased absence due to "illness" or injury; greater frequency of accidents; withdrawal from school sports or other school activities; and/or acting-out, punishment-seeking, or even violent behaviors
- Emotional—greater need for teacher attention and support; apathy; a general loss of interest in school; altered relationships with staff and peers; greater feelings of anger or guilt; and sadness or an inability to enjoy life, including school

A school or classroom can be turned upside down by the physical and emotional demands of the grief process and the disruption that even a few of the possible reactions listed above can cause. The larger the number of affected students, the greater is the potential disruption of the educational process.

Further, there are some students who are "at risk" in special ways. Some bereaved students try to numb their emotional pain by self-medicating with alcohol or drugs. This attempt to cope with the pain of grief can be seen as the cause of problems when it may, in fact, be a symptom of unresolved grief. Some students are coping with greater burdens imposed by more than one loss. Multiple losses are so common that they should be seen as the rule and not an exception. Multiple losses can involve personal losses of each individual, or they may be of the type that affects an entire community.

COMMUNITY GRIEF

Some deaths impact an entire community. These present a special type of grief situation because an entire school, town, or region can be involved. In 1986 the National Association of Secondary School Principals distributed a set of guidelines for developing a protocol for a school's response to community grief (Stevenson & Powers, 1986). It was based on questions to be answered when a school must address community grief. These questions include the following: Who should inform the students of the event (loss)? Where and how should this communication be done? How might students react? What may complicate a student's response? And what personnel are available both within and outside the school community to assist with this task? (Stevenson & Stevenson, 1996). The process of developing a structured death education program within a school system can help prepare both students and staff to answer these questions and to respond more effectively in times of crisis.

In interviews with death education students, the two benefits most frequently identified were a lessening of fear and anxiety regarding death, and improved communication by students. Young people said that before taking a death education course, they believed they could not discuss the topic of death. This silence increased their fear of death and hindered communication with family members and others who might have offered support. After taking a death education course, students spoke of bringing class materials home and of discussing death and grief with family members, often for the first time. As students spoke more openly about the topic, they felt their fear and anxiety lessened. As one student said, "Before I took a death education course I thought about death all the time, but I couldn't talk about it. Since taking this course I talk about death with a lot of people . . . so I don't have to think about it any more" (Stevenson, 1984, p. 54). The object here is *not* to eliminate a fear of death, but to bring it to a level which is less threatening to a student. It is often said that knowledge is power; in this case, the knowledge provided is about dying, death, and grief.

Improvement also took place in home–school communication. Parents who were interviewed said that they were more likely to notify the school after a family death. These same parents expressed appreciation for the assistance they felt their children had received in preparing to face the inevitable losses of life. When a death had already occurred, the school was seen as providing support that was less encumbered with personal and family grief as the student recovered from the loss.

In addition to student grief, death education has come to play an important role in four areas of prevention: depression and suicide, HIV and AIDS, adolescent violence, and future parenting skills.

Depression and Suicide

Death education curricula have been used as a means to inform students about symptoms of depression and warning signs of suicide. Studies of the impact of adolescent suicide show that the suicide of a peer encourages "suicidal thinking, suicide attempts and higher depression" (Feigelman & Gorman, 2008, p. 191). Based on this study, the authors recommend that "in the months immediately following such events, youth offering reports of the loss of a friend to suicide should be offered suicide risk screening as a matter of course" (p. 192).

Brent and his colleagues (1992) reported that depressed adolescents with suicidal ideation have rates of major depressive disorder, anxiety disorder, substance abuse, conduct disorder, and attention deficit hyperactivity disorder much higher than a demographically matched community-based comparison group. They also showed increased rates of new-onset major depression and PTSD at baseline and follow-up assessments in relation to the comparison group. Depression and PTSD co-occurred with traumatic grief, an expected finding since bereavement is a common risk factor for all three conditions.

HIV/AIDS

The incidence of HIV infection and AIDS has increased dramatically among adolescents in North America. For this reason, almost all health education curricula address the means of HIV transmission and symptoms of AIDS. Death education curricula discuss related issues. Death education students have at times assumed a proactive stance in helping schools develop policies related to HIV and AIDS. Such program content would be difficult in countries that do not allow such discussions in a school setting. In these cases, information would be best supplied to family adults so that they could convey it to their adolescents.

Violence and War

The growing number of violent adolescent deaths has pushed this topic to the forefront of death education. High-school-age adolescents serving time for violent crimes in Bergen County, New Jersey, were five times more likely to have lost a parent through death or abandonment before age 5. It was felt that unresolved childhood grief was a major source of their violence. As part of their rehabilitation, a death educator was called in to consult with correctional personnel in developing ways to facilitate resolution of their grief. Death education curricula address the causes, risks, and consequences of violent behavior; social and psychological factors behind the increase in adolescent violence; and nonviolent alternatives to violence, such as peer mediation. However, there is a growing belief among adolescents that there can be so-called good violence to redress wrongs and restore balance in a society or a life (Stevenson & Cox, 2008). There is a parallel between this good violence and the ethical/religious doctrine of just war that makes an examination of violence and war important topics in death education.

In the United States, war is traditionally seen as something that happens "over there" in other places. Studies of grief among Bosnian youths indicate that, "students and leaders involved in receiving or delivering a group-based intervention for psychosocial difficulties related to the Bosnian conflict identified the impacts of the program to be both broad in scope and primarily positive" (Cox et al., 2007, p. 319). It was also found that most of the negative evaluations were influenced by difficulties associated with changing negative stereotypes of school personnel, students, and parents relating to providing or receiving mental health services in schools. A factor that may be important in understanding adolescent grief in war-torn countries was identified by Carlton-Ford (2008) in Baghdad, where he observed "a broad social context involving the presence of foreign forces . . . combined with general violence," and also observed "a heightened sense of self, at least to the extent that one's self is tied to one's nation" (p. 53).

Another factor not often addressed by traditional death education is the situation of adolescents in countries coping with trauma related to war who may also have their grief complicated by mental health difficulties, including PTSD, depression, and anxiety (Ehntholt & Yule, 2006).

Parenting Skills

The degree of difficulty that a child experiences when coping with grief has been linked to how well the child's parents cope with their grief (Sandler et al., 2003; Worden, 1996). Also, young children relate to death differently than do adolescents and adults. Death education curricula seek to prepare adolescents to help future children understand and cope in effective ways with this difficult topic.

QUALIFICATIONS OF DEATH EDUCATORS

When death intrudes in a school routine, guidance counselors, child study team members, a school nurse, or outside support personnel from nearby agencies are typically the people expected to "handle" the situation. In some cases, they do not have the preparation or background experience for this task. Even when they have specific training, their time is limited.

Parents are the first death educators. Outside the home, death educators are most frequently classroom teachers and school counselors. Currently, this topic does not require special certification, as might be the case in health education or psychology in some states. Part of the difficulty in requiring special certification comes from the wide variety of sponsoring disciplines in American schools. Death education curricula have been developed in health, family living, English, social studies, and science departments. Death education teachers in public schools are certified as educators and have some background in child or developmental psychology, but they often have no formal training in death education. It may be difficult to find such training since teacher preparation programs have yet to recognize the need to prepare teachers to cope with the impact of death in the classroom. In private and parochial schools the preparation base is even more varied, since in most states less formal preparation is required of staff members than in public schools. In addition, there may be staff members who would be uncomfortable teaching death education curriculum because of unresolved grief in their own lives.

Staff development programs and workshops have provided an ongoing means of staff preparation for death education. Assisting students to cope with death is *not* a job for one or two staff members. The entire staff should be involved at *some* level since there often are situations where they may be needed. Also, since bereaved students can be found in every class, all staff members should be aware of ways in which they can help. If not able to help actively, they should at least be aware of how to avoid inadvertently adding to a student's problems.

Staff development programs have been offered to teaching staff, school nurses, guidance counselors, aides, and administrators. The involvement of administrators is important because they develop school response protocols related to death and other crises. They will also evaluate the performance of the staff members implementing death education curricula.

In response to a lack of standardized staff preparation or teacher certification requirements, the Association for Death Education and Counseling (ADEC) developed a program for certification of professional death educators (now offering the credential of Certified in Thanatology [CT]). ADEC is an international organization of professionals involved in the areas of death education and grief counseling. To obtain certification as a professional death educator, a candidate must demonstrate appropriate educational preparation and work experience, show evidence of good character, and pass a comprehensive examination on essential core knowledge related to death and grief. Since this program was started in 1981, hundreds of candidates have received professional certification. Having an accepted standard for preparation of educators has been an aid to administrators and a comfort to the parents of students in death education courses.

HIGH SCHOOL DEATH EDUCATION CURRICULA

Setting standards for staff selection and preparation has been difficult, but such standards now exist. Establishing standards for high school death education curricula has been an equally difficult task. A curriculum is a statement of priorities. It is important that these curricula be written by professional educators, but priorities must reflect those of parents and of the community as a whole. Such curricula should also reflect current research, since knowledge in the field has been growing and evolving at a rapid rate. The curriculum development process should allow input by parents and concerned community members. Any final death education curriculum must be accepted by the governing board of the school or school district. The open nature of such a curriculum development process helps to establish lines of communication between home and school and allows educators to address possible community concerns regarding death education. Cognitively, adolescents are no longer children, but they are not yet adults. Although they may be able to handle the *intellectual* requirements of college death education classes, the *emotional* component of death education makes it important to remember that school curricula must be age appropriate in both content and methodology.

There are other decisions that must be made regarding adolescent death education. They can again be stated in the form of questions:

- What will be the offering discipline(s) for the death education course or units? The subject area in which death education takes place will shape what is taught and how it is presented. It must be determined whether death education will be placed in a single curriculum area or will be multidisciplinary, involving several academic departments. These decisions will also determine who the evaluators will be and the standards by which the curriculum and teacher will be evaluated.
- What will be the format for the death education curriculum? Some schools offer death education as a separate course, while others have infused the death education curriculum into existing courses.
- Will this course be required? The content of death education curricula may well be important for all people at some time. This does not mean that every student will benefit from a course offered at a set point in their academic experience. This possible problem can be avoided by making death education courses, or units, elective in nature. If their background makes it difficult for them to participate in a standard death education class, alternatives can be offered to such students.
- Are there risks in death education? Even the strongest supporters would agree there are risks in any course whose content holds strong potential for emotional involvement. It is important to de-

> termine to what extent these risks can be addressed in advance and how to avoid possible negative effects. It is also important to differentiate between real areas of concern and myths about death education propagated by Phyllis Schlafly and her lobbying group, the Eagle Forum.

Schafly (1988, p. 22) has written that death education is "one of the nasty little secrets of public school education." She presents educators and parents as adversaries. In fact, death education as it exists bears no relationship to Schlafly's presentation. The model used by death educators seeks to reinforce the family as a positive support for students. Open home–school communication encourages parent–teacher cooperation to benefit the young adults, about whom both groups care. The counseling dimension of grief support involves certified school personnel. Knowing when to make appropriate referral of students who need additional support is part of the responsibility of every teacher.

Constructive criticism of death education comes from English researcher Sonja Hunt (personal communication, July 14, 1983). She pointed out that there are events and processes in life that leave a distinct mark on an individual. Death is such an event, and grief is such a process. She cautioned that educators need to be aware of the possible consequences of their work before attempting instruction that could affect the grief process. She also asked educators to show clearly why schools would be an appropriate place for such interventions.

Basically, Hunt cautioned educators to examine death education lessons and their possible effects *before* implementing such lessons in the classroom. She also encouraged ongoing programs of evaluation of death education curricula and professional development programs. The last 2 decades have shown the wisdom in her critique. Professional journals (such as *Death Studies; Illness, Crisis and Loss;* and *Omega, Journal of Death and Dying*) regularly publish research results evaluating the effects of death education. Professional organizations regularly offer workshops, symposia, and extension courses to develop and enhance the skills needed by death educators.

MODELS OF HIGH SCHOOL DEATH EDUCATION CURRICULA

In its earliest form, education about death was simply a part of life. Death was all around in the natural order of things. People died at home, and their family and friends were a part of that process. This arrangement is still the case in much of the world. A person dies at home, and the whole village joins with the family in the rituals that express grief over the loss. In America, however, the second half of the 19th century and the first half of the 20th century saw death increasingly separated from life. It was this artificial division that was, perhaps, the major reason why death education was felt to be increasingly needed.

Death education was introduced into high schools beginning in the late 1960s. The first curriculum materials available to educators were divided into two categories: prepared units (with supplementary materials), which were fully developed, ready-to-use lesson plans (e.g., Berg & Daugherty, 1972), and unstructured learning opportunities and objectives to be used by educators in developing their own lessons (e.g., Mills, Reisler, Robinson, & Vermilye, 1976). Both types saw death education as a series of discrete topics aimed at answering student questions about death and its effects. Both relied on outside experts (funeral directors, doctors, nurses, clergy) coming into the classroom to supplement the work of the teacher.

As more information became available about dying, death, grief, and loss, curricula became model centered. A lesson would typically start with a psychological model, such as the Five Stages of Death and Dying developed by Elisabeth Kübler-Ross (1969). Her model provided a way for students to look at an experience that was new to them. The structure of a given model made the topic seem less confusing and gave a basis for comparing loss experiences. Additional models of grief soon appeared from a variety of writers; newer thinking on bereavement, grief, and mourning is also available (e.g., Corr, Nabe, & Corr, 2009). The drawback of some of the early models was that as they were used more frequently, they often came to have a life of their own. In extreme cases, the integrity of the model actually became more important than the individual experience it was intended to describe. This problem was of special importance in applying the model to other countries. If the model was given priority, it could keep caregivers and educators from seeing the real needs of individuals from a different culture.

There are common themes among curricula. Some themes appear in almost every death education course, while others are used selectively, depending on subject area and instructor. Three widely used resources (O'Toole, 1989; Stevenson, 1990; Zalaznik, 1992) are representative of death education curricula. These three curricula contain themes such as Aging; Change and Loss (as a part of life); a Child's Understanding of Death; Illness; Communication and Language; Cultural and Historical Perspectives on Grief; Definitions of Death; Economic and Legal Aspects of Death; Ethics, Euthanasia, and the "Right to Die"; Family as Support; Feelings; the Grief Process; HIV and AIDS; the Experience of Loss (permanent vs. temporary); Quality of Life; Religious and Philosophical Views of Death; Right to Life/Right to Choose; Rituals of Death and Mourning (Funerals); Suicide and Suicide Prevention; Views of Life after Death; and Violence.

The amount of time spent on an individual theme will vary based on the needs of the students and on significant current events. The latest approach to death education involves reintegration of life and death as part of a natural cycle, using a style similar to narrative counseling. Stories, rather than psychological or behavioral models, are used to provide a new focal point for lessons in death education. Stories have long been used in elementary classrooms; their use is now being introduced on the high school level. These stories allow educators to bring a multicultural perspective to death education. Lessons can blend modern models and traditional symbols that have brought comfort to bereaved individuals literally for centuries (see, e.g., Gignoux, 1998). The rituals of storytelling allow an educator to move easily into an explanation of the rites of passage that have helped previous generations to cope with the same issues these students now face. Repeating the stories heard in class to parents and others continues the process of communication; it also brings other people and their unique points of view into the educational process. As students become more comfortable telling the stories they have learned, they are more likely to begin to piece together the stories of their own lives and to share those stories with others. This narrative construction and sharing allows high school students to build a view of life and death upon a foundation that incorporates their personal stories. Shaping and telling their personal stories has become a new method for dealing with personal grief.

CONCLUSION

Students of any age cannot be shielded from the reality of death in their lives. Education can play a positive role in preparing adolescents to cope with the reality of dying, death, and grief. Schools wishing to implement such a program should consider the following points:

- The process of implementing a death-related curriculum should be open, and input should be sought from students, parents, and community members.
- Educators must be qualified, both academically and emotionally, for this challenging topic.
- Curricula must be age-appropriate and sensitive to the varied backgrounds, cultures, and experiences of individual students.
- Death education instructors can be valuable resources in facing crises other than death.
- Death education courses can impart knowledge; assist students in coping more effectively with dying, death, and grief; and develop communication and parenting skills.

Physical illness can strike an individual at any time. For that reason, society recommends, and may even require, immunization to lessen the pain and suffering caused by such illness. Treatment after the fact is often more difficult. Death and grief can also strike at any time. Death education can be viewed as a form of immunization. Experience has shown that it can help adolescents to face the pain and suffering such events can cause.

REFERENCES

Berg, D. W., & Daugherty, G. G. (1972). *Perspectives on death.* Baltimore, MD: Waverly Press.

Brent, D. A., Perper, J. A., Moritz, G., Allman, C., Friend, A., Schweers, J., et al. (1992). Psychiatric effects of exposure to suicide among the friends and acquaintances of adolescent suicide victims. *Journal of American Academy of Child and Adolescent Psychiatry, 31,* 629–640.

Carlton-Ford, S. (2008, March 3). Rare examination reveals adolescent reaction to Iraq War. *Health & Medicine Week,* pp. 53–75.

Corr, C. A., Nabe, C. M., & Corr, D. M. (2009). *Death and dying, life and living* (6th ed.). Belmont, CA: Cengage Wadsworth.

Cox, J., Davies, D. R., Burlingame, G. M., Campbell, J. E., Layne, C. M., & Katzenbach, R. J. (2007). Effectiveness of a trauma/grief-focused group Intervention: A qualitative study with war-exposed Bosnian adolescents. *International Journal of Group Psychotherapy, 57,* 319–346.

Critelli, C. (1979, January 26). Parent death in childhood. Paper presented at the Columbia-Presbyterian Medical Center Symposium, *The Child and Death,* New York.

Deeken, A. (1999). Evolving Japanese perspectives on death and dying. *Budhi: A Journal of Ideas and Culture, 3*(2/3), 215–232.

Ehntholt, K. A., & Yule, W. (2006). Practitioner review: Assessment and treatment of refugee children and adolescents who have experienced war-related trauma. *Journal of Child Psychology and Psychiatry, 47,* 1197–1210.

Feigelman, W., & Gorman, B. S. (2008). Assessing the effects of peer suicide on youth suicide. *Suicide & Life-Threatening Behavior, 38,* 181–194.

Gignoux, J. H. (1998). *Some folk say: Stories of life, death, and beyond.* New York: FoulkeTale Publishing.

Kübler-Ross, E. (1969). *On death and dying.* New York: Macmillan.

Mills, G. C., Reisler, R., Robinson, A. E., & Vermilye, G. (1976). *Discussing death.* Palm Springs, CA: ETC Publishing.

O'Toole, D. (1989). *Growing through grief.* Burnsville, NC: Mountain Rainbow Publications.

Sandler, I. N., Ayers, T. S., Wolchik, S. A., Tein, J-Y., Kwok, O-M., Haine, R. A., et al. (2003). The Family Bereavement Program: Efficacy evaluation of a theory-based prevention program for parentally-bereaved children and adolescents. *Journal of Consulting and Clinical Psychology, 71,* 587–600.

Schlafly, P. (1988, April 13). Death education comes into open. *The Brooklyn Spectator,* p. 21.

Stavros S. Niarchos Foundation. (2006). *The Friends of Merimna.* Retrieved June 10, 2008, from http://www.stavrosniarchosfoundation.org

Stevenson, R. G. (1984). *A death education course for secondary schools: "Curing" death ignorance.* Unpublished doctoral dissertation, Fairleigh Dickinson University, Teaneck, NJ.

Stevenson, R. G. (1986). Measuring the effects of death education in the classroom. In G. H. Paterson (Ed.), *Children and death* (pp. 201–207). London, Ontario: King's College.

Stevenson, R. G. (1990). Contemporary issues of life and death. In J. D. Morgan (Ed.), *Death Education in Canada* (pp. 140–161). London, Ontario: King's College.

Stevenson, R. G. (2001). *What will we do? Preparing a school community to cope with crises* (2nd ed.). Amityville, NY: Baywood.

Stevenson, R. G., & Cox, G. (Eds.). (2008). *Perspectives on violence and violent death.* Amityville, NY: Baywood.

Stevenson, R. G., & Powers, H. L. (1986). How to handle death in the school. *Tips for Principals.* Reston, VA: National Association of Secondary School Principals.

Stevenson, R. G., & Stevenson, E. P. (Eds.). (1996). *Teaching students about death: A comprehensive resource for educators and parents.* Philadelphia: The Charles Press.

Worden, J. W. (1996). *Children and grief: When a parent dies.* New York: Guilford.

Zalaznik, P. H. (1992). *Dimensions of loss & death education* (3rd ed.). Minneapolis, MN: Edu-Pac Publishing Company, Inc.

16

Camps and Support Groups for Adolescents

STACY F. ORLOFF, DONNA ARMSTRONG, AND STACY S. REMKE

Many hospice programs and children's grief centers, alone or in collaboration with other organizations, offer specialized camps, retreats, support groups, and programs for bereaved adolescents or adolescents with a life-threatening or life-limiting illness. Some programs also take into account the needs of family members of these adolescents. Much of what is known about these programs comes from descriptions in various publications (e.g., Creed, Ruffin, & Ward, 2001; Klontz, Bivens, Leinart, & Klontz, 2007; LoCicero, Burkhart, & Gray, 1998; Martinuik, 2003; Nabors et al., 2004; Schachter, 2007; Schachter & Georgopoulos, 2008; Summers, 1993), conversations between care providers, and comments from participants or other anecdotal information. Much less is known about the long-term therapeutic value or demonstrated efficacy of such services (e.g., Currier, Holland, & Neimeyer, 2007; Forte, Hill, Pazder, & Feudtner, 2004). This fact often makes it difficult for providers to determine best practices when designing and implementing their own specialized services for ill and bereaved adolescents.

This chapter describes some of the principles that have emerged to guide several of the specialized retreats, camps, and support groups currently available for adolescents. The chapter also offers extended examples from three providers to illustrate both challenges and responses that have emerged in their experiences. Unless specifically identified, these programs are available to all adolescents regardless of the illness or type of death they are encountering.

NEEDS AND RESPONSES

The Harvard Child Bereavement Study provided longitudinal data about children and adolescents who had experienced the death of a parent. On that basis, Worden (1996) identified four tasks of mourning that can help clinicians identify interventions to assist bereaved adolescents. The four tasks are (a) "to accept the reality of the loss" (p. 13); (b) "to experience the pain or emotional aspects of the loss" (p. 14); (c) "to adjust to an environment in which the deceased is missing" (p. 15); (d) "to relocate the deceased person within one's life and find ways to memorialize that person" (p. 15). These tasks can help to ground the development and implementation of each of the programs outlined in this chapter.

In addition, national events have highlighted the need for programs to serve adolescents affected by traumatic loss such as school shootings and natural disasters. Additional needs include clinical services for teens whose loved ones died as a result of violence, including murder, suicide, and domestic violence. In fact, many hospices and children's grief centers are treating more and more adolescents whose loved ones died from unnatural causes. Responses have gone beyond individual and family counseling to include the types of programs described in this chapter.

The number of bereavement groups, specialized retreats, support groups, and other programs provided by hospices and grief centers has grown over the last several years. With this growth have also come some lessons learned by these providers. Above all, it is critically important for providers to consider the unique developmental needs of the adolescent and to understand the role of an adolescent's peer group in determining social mores and acceptable behavior. Social support is vitally important, and many bereaved teens fear losing their peer group if they unmask and share their depth of despair and sadness (Christ, Siegal, & Christ, 2002).

It is also important to appreciate that the extracurricular life of the typical teenager is very full. Besides school activities, many teenagers also maintain part-time jobs or have other commitments outside of school that may limit their availability to take part in programs like those described in this chapter.

Finally, providers typically find themselves wondering what type of program will best serve the needs of the adolescents in their communities. Clearly, there is no unique path to success in sponsoring these specialized services. And it is difficult to continue to offer these services when turnout is low. There are, however, some important factors to consider that will increase the potential success of these camps, retreats, support groups, or other specialized services.

CAMPS AND RETREATS FOR ADOLESCENTS

In England, the Winston's Wish program (http://www.winstonswish.org.uk) has developed a successful program of weekend residential camps for bereaved children and adolescents, with a separate, accompanying program for parents and/or guardians of those young people (Stokes, 2004). Many of the principles and activities that are central to that program can also be seen in three examples of American programs.

The Hospice of the Florida Suncoast, Clearwater, Florida, Camp Triple L/Camp Erin

In 1983 the Hospice of the Florida Suncoast in Clearwater, Florida (http://www.thehospice.org), established a program that specialized in services for children. Only 3 years later, in 1986, the Child and Family Support Program held its first children's bereavement camp, Camp Triple L (Love, Laughter, Leisure). Begun as a day retreat, Camp Triple L has evolved to a weekend bereavement camp for children ages 8 to mid-adolescence. Recently, the Hospice of the Florida Suncoast has received long-term funding from the Moyers Foundation, bringing it into a close affiliation with Camp Erin, a national effort by the Moyers Foundation to ensure children across the country have access to quality bereavement camps.

Camp Erin/Camp Triple L take place each spring, with as many as 90 campers attending in many years. Eventually, it was decided to limit camp attendance to bereaved children between the ages of 8 and 16 and to institute staffing ratios of 1:2 for campers. Currently, the camp will not accept more than 64 campers, which allows full utilization of eight cabins with 8 bereaved campers in each. Four cabins are for male campers, and four for female campers. Cabins are also divided by age, leaving one full cabin for male teens, and one for female teens. All potential campers are evaluated for camp appropriateness prior to releasing a camp application to their parent or guardian. Returned applications are carefully reviewed prior to accepting the child or teen to camp. This screening is necessary to ensure that the weekend experience is a positive one for all bereaved campers.

The Hospice uses a retreat center that can easily accommodate the needs of this camp. The retreat center is located on a river, so water sports such as canoeing are available. There are two swimming pools, a full kitchen, and staff who do all the cooking. Food is served in a buffet line, and campers may serve themselves. Cabins are carpeted; air conditioned with ceiling fans (a must in Florida); and have bunk beds, bathrooms, and showers. Campers bring their own bedding. There are many private meeting rooms, so each group has its own private space for bereavement groups. There is also a large room that accommodates the entire camp (campers and volunteers) for full camp meetings and a memorial service.

The Hospice provides transportation to the camp from one of its community service centers. All campers and their families arrive at the community center and are greeted by volunteers and hospice employees responsible for the final check-in process; calming the nerves of parents/family members; receiving luggage and medication; and distributing camp name badges, which are immediately placed on the camper for the duration of the weekend. Dinner is provided to campers when they arrive at the site.

The primary goal of this weekend bereavement camp is to provide bereaved children and teenagers a safe and therapeutic environment in which they can share their feelings, give and receive support, and learn some new effective coping strategies. Through carefully planned social and therapeutic activities, bereaved teenagers are able to share their stories. They frequently express shock and surprise upon acknowledging that there are many other teenagers who are experiencing similar thoughts, feelings, and experiences (see Morin & Welsh, 1996). Each year the Child and Family Support Program staff creatively develops a camp theme such as "putting the pieces together" or "follow your yellow brick road." This theme is reflected through the specially crafted therapeutic activities in each bereavement group, the camp-wide memorial service, and the large camp art project completed by the end of the weekend.

As an example, for the camp theme "putting the pieces together," each camper and staff created a puzzle piece that depicted their deceased loved one. The large camp activity consisted of each camper putting his or her piece on a large predrawn master board where the metaphor of putting the pieces of your life back together could be visibly seen. Another year, campers decorated yellow foam blocks, using different kinds of art supplies to memorialize their loved ones. The foam blocks were then hot glued on a large piece of fabric (the size of a large quilt) that had a predrawn yellow brick road leading to an emerald city where everyone has the skills necessary to work toward their goals.

A camp reunion is held approximately 3 weeks after Camp Erin/Camp Triple L. Campers' families are invited to one of the Hospice's service centers for a pizza dinner and a planned night of sharing. Each cabin shares special memories and camp highlights. Many camp pictures are shown through a special PowerPoint presentation. Family members can speak to the camp staff and volunteers to learn more about how their individual child(ren) did. Follow-up counseling can be requested. All campers and parents or guardians receive an evaluation in the mail to complete and return.

Over the last several years, fewer bereaved teenagers have attended camp. One year, the camp date was changed from spring to fall to see if that would positively impact camp attendance. In actuality, fewer bereaved teens attended camp that year due to the high impact of attendance at high school football games. The Child and Family Support Program counselors informally discussed this diminished attendance with bereaved teens being seen individually or through support groups held at high schools. Many teens expressed discomfort committing to attending a weekend retreat with other teenagers they didn't know, the difficulty of getting a weekend off work, or their reluctance to spend the weekend with younger children. After taking all of these points under consideration, the staff proposed offering a 1-day bereavement retreat for teens.

CUBE

CUBE (Caring, Understanding, Believing, and Empowerment) is a 1-day retreat for bereaved adolescents held at one of the Hospice of the Florida Suncoast's community service centers. This retreat was developed in 2006 after careful and deliberate planning, including time spent with bereaved teens asking them their preferences. CUBE usually attracts approximately 12 teens and can accommodate up to 20. As with all other weekend retreats, prospective bereaved adolescents are nominated and screened by the Child and Family Support Program staff prior to being invited to the CUBE day.

Taking the needs of adolescents into consideration, this retreat begins midmorning on either a weekend or day off from school and ends at 4 in the afternoon. During these 6 hours, the teens, together in one group, participate in many different activities that revolve around the six themes, or sides of a cube: physical, emotional, cognitive, spiritual, social, and historical. Throughout the day and during the many different activities, the bereaved teens and group facilitators engage in different conversations related to loss.

At the conclusion of the day, the teens participate in a celebration in which they honor the memory of their deceased family member. They often choose to share contact information with each other and make plans to stay in touch. An informal evaluation is completed prior to leaving the retreat, and a more formal evaluation is mailed to the adolescent's home after the event.

Camp Hope

Begun in 1997, this retreat was originally developed for bereaved spouses and their minor-aged children. Families with children as young as 3 were able to attend. Over the years, as the needs of families seen by the Hospice of the Florida Suncoast have changed, this retreat's focus changed to a weekend retreat for bereaved families and children. The commonality for all families is that they are bereaved. The relationship to the deceased and the nature of the death may vary. Camp Hope is limited to no more than 8 to 10 families. It is held at the same retreat center as Camp Erin/Camp Triple L.

Structured similarly to Camp Erin/Camp Triple L, families attending Camp Hope stay in cabins with a common dayroom dividing the cabin in the middle. Females stay on one side of the cabin, and males on the other. The decision to divide families in this way was not made easily. After much thought, the Child and Family Support Program staff decided this arrangement would provide for greater sharing among all the different families and provide bereaved children and teens the opportunity to bond and seek support from other retreat attendees. This arrangement has served this retreat well, and the parents and children all seem to easily accommodate to these sleeping arrangements.

Camp Hope is also similar to Camp Triple Erin/Camp Triple L in that all retreat activities are centered around a theme that changes annually. Children and adolescents are divided by age into different bereavement groups that meet throughout the weekend. Adult family members are also divided into different groups based on number of attendees. One year, the retreat theme was "finding your way through grief." Retreat staff discussed how lighthouses were used to guide boats into a safe harbor and that their light was a beacon for safety and security. Activities in bereavement groups as well as the family memorial service all used the lighthouse metaphor to support this theme.

Attendance is sometimes an issue for bereaved teens for the same reasons listed above. There is, however, often a greater influence for bereaved teens to attend this retreat since all other family members are attending. Special emphasis is placed on accommodating the needs of adolescents through nighttime planned activities.

Hospice of the Bluegrass, Lexington, Kentucky, Great Escape: A Family Bereavement Camp

Great Escape: A Family Camp (http://www.hospicebg.com) is a weekend camp for parents or guardians, children, and adolescents who have experienced a death in the family. Families are referred from hospice staff and from the community. They represent the myriad types of illnesses and deaths served by the hospice and encountered in the community. Retreat activities include recreational activities, grief education, expression of feelings, and memorialization of the loved one. All aspects of this retreat, including sleeping accommodations, meals, and recreational activities, focus on the family being together.

The camp is held at an Easter Seal facility that is accessible to individuals with disabilities. The camp is arranged in villages, each with three to four cabins. Each village may house one to two families, depending on the size of the family. Each family is assigned one or two (more if needed) family "buddies" or counselors. The buddies assist families in getting small children ready in the mornings and before activities, help out at meal times, and eat with families. There are also trained camp staff available to assist with campfires and lead recreation activities, including the low ropes and obstacle course.

During the weekend, the children's groups are divided by age. Parents and guardians are in a group together. The primary focus of the bereavement groups is to provide opportunities to share psychoeducational information about grief, express feelings, and memorialize the deceased loved one. Activities are tailored to group age and developmental needs. The methods used include sharing circle, scrapbooking, journaling, guided imagery, nature walks, and yoga. The obstacle course is also integrated into the theme of the weekend.

The goals of the teen group are to tell the story of the death, increase expression of feelings through music, and memorialize the deceased through scrapbooking. Teens also participate in a low ropes course where they learn to trust and work with others to accomplish a goal. After this particular activity, teens participate in a sharing circle where they often identify that they need "help in getting to the other side" during their grief process (see Ens & Bond, 2005). Families are also given opportunities to express grief as a family. There is a sacred space where families are encouraged to place photos or remembrances of the deceased.

Families also participate in an opening ceremony, which utilizes a flag ritual to recognize the deceased loved one. The closing ceremony ends the camp and recognizes the accomplishment all campers have achieved by sharing their grief journey.

Teen Retreat

Hospice of the Bluegrass also sponsors an overnight teen grief retreat titled Crisis Is Danger and Opportunity, or CIDAO. The primary focus of this retreat is to bring bereaved teens together so that they can share their stories of loss and participate in art activities, journaling, photography, and memorialization. Many professional articles (e.g., Nabors et al., 2004) note the value of being with others who have gone through similar experiences. During this retreat, staff from a regional wilderness camp assist in leading teens in therapeutic recreational exercises. After each activity, teens divide into small groups and process their experiences in sharing circles. This retreat is staffed by hospice staff and trained bereavement volunteers.

Securing teens' commitment to attend a weekend retreat can be difficult. Over the years, the number of participants varied from 6 to 22. As registration decreased, staff tried to determine why teens were not attending the grief retreat. Teen availability is always an issue because of their involvement in academics, sports, and other extracurricular activities. Many teens are employed and do not want to or cannot afford to give up a paycheck for the weekend. And, of course, there are competing social activities that attract the interest of many adolescents. Staff from Hospice of the Bluegrass also noted that they were offering fewer high school bereavement groups, which impacted the number of teens referred to the teen retreat. Due to lack of response, this teen retreat has been temporarily suspended and is planned to be held again as a 1-day retreat.

Rapids of Life

Rapids of Life is a 1-day rafting retreat for adolescents ages 9–16 who have experienced the loss of a loved one or are coping with anticipatory grief issues related to the illness of a loved one. As with other special programs, the nature of the illnesses and deaths may vary. Participants are referred by both hospice staff and the community. All adolescents, staff members, and volunteers complete a guided rafting trip on the Little Pigeon River in Tennessee. The rafting trip lasts approximately an hour and a half.

This river trip serves as a metaphor for the adolescent's experiences in coping with a family member's illness or death. After the rafting experience, the teens meet as a group to process their experience. This program structure gives them a chance to be with and bond with other teens who may be experiencing similar feelings. Finally, the teens complete an art activity allowing them to decorate an oar with the name of the deceased and art or symbols representing the deceased and feelings of grief.

Healing Hooves

Healing Hooves is a 1-day bereavement retreat utilizing equine therapy. It is a collaborative effort between Hospice of the Bluegrass and Central Kentucky Riding for Hope. Central Kentucky Riding for Hope is a nonprofit NARHA (North American Riding for the Handicapped Association) certified organization that provides horseback riding for therapeutic, social, and recreational purposes for children and adults with all types of disabilities. It is held at the Central Kentucky Riding for Hope facility located within the Kentucky Horse Park in Lexington, Kentucky.

The 1-day retreat is for children and teens ages 7–17 who have experienced the loss of a loved one. Unmounted activities with a horse provide a unique way for children to express their grief. Care of the horse is also taught to illustrate the value of nurturing and self-care. Two participants (closely related in age) are paired with both a bereavement counselor and an equine specialist. Participants share their stories and create adornments for their horses, which symbolize feelings of grief. Other activities include completing an obstacle course with the horse, grooming the horse, and painting the horse with symbols of remembrance.

Participants are also given the opportunity to journal about their experiences throughout the day. At the end of the day, participants present the horses to their families and discuss the symbolic adornments and painting on their horses.

Children's Hospitals and Clinics, Minneapolis, Minnesota, Camp Connect

In 1998, a community coalition of pediatric providers and grief and loss specialists in Minnesota created a camp for bereaved youngsters ages 8–18 (http://www.childrensmn.org). In the early stages of the camp's development, professionals experienced in working with bereaved children and teens met to develop a flexible curriculum. Structured around a series of reflective and active activities, the children and teens have opportunities for formal and informal processing of their grief in a supportive setting of mentors and peers. The camp meets for 1.5 days, usually Saturday morning to Sunday noon, on a spring weekend. In earlier years, the camp focused on children and teens who have lost a sibling. More recently, the camp expanded to include a variety of loss experiences.

Camp staff includes social workers, chaplains, child life specialists, nurses, bereavement counselors, and others. Campers are organized into cabins by age group. Staff are assigned to each group for the duration of camp, allowing supportive relationships and trust to develop.

The teen group includes campers ages 13 to 18. Typically about five to eight bereaved teens attend Camp Connect. They are welcome to attend camp three times. Older teens are also able to return as junior counselors, moving into a peer mentorship role and enabling them to support other bereaved teens by sharing and modeling their own growth through grief.

Activities vary year to year, shaped by input from previous participants and the observations of camp staff. Nature walks, outdoor activities, and games, as well as campfire gatherings and food fights tend to be staples of the curriculum. The sharing of a storybook on a theme related to grief is also a regular feature. While geared to appeal to the wide range of ages, the teens often have commented this activity is "young" for them. Yet staff have observed that even in dissecting the activity, lots of good sharing and discussion between the teens seems to emerge. This process also allows teens an opportunity to observe their own skills and awareness that are distinct from the younger campers.

Each camper receives a curriculum booklet that includes the camp schedule and activities. This loose-leaf journal, organized by tabs and topics, includes topics such as the impact of loss, reflections about life before and after the death event (recalling), identifying strategies for self-care, writing a letter to their deceased loved one (readjusting), and finally, reengaging in life.

Camp Connect activities include expressive arts, campfires, and sharing circles. An annual ritual includes a campfire and sharing circle. Campers write a letter to their deceased loved one. If they want, they may share the letter with the circle and then "send" it to their loved one by placing the letter into the fire. This ritual is often a very emotional and powerful experience for campers and staff alike as they witness the profundity of the grief present in the circle and feel supported by their peers and supporters. One year, a music therapist participated in Camp. During the Fire Circle he walked in the woods around the campfire area, beating drums, musically affirming and amplifying the words and actions happening within the circle. Those present later commented that the drums added an important and powerfully evocative element to the ritual.

Feedback from teens who have attended Camp Connect has been overwhelmingly positive. The greatest complaint has been the limitation of camp attendance to 3 years. The policy limiting attendance to three times was made in order to balance the numbers of teens who want to attend camp with the number of newly bereaved teens. Other factors considered in making this difficult decision included staffing needs, space at the camp facilities, and cost.

Teens who choose to become junior counselors are included in the planning stages of the annual Camp experience. They provide input regarding potential activities and receive training on their roles. They also become acquainted with the Camp staff who will be supervising them and who will be available for support and assistance throughout Camp. On several occasions, teen campers have developed romantic feelings for other campers. Staff have monitored and intervened as needed to ensure appropriate support for the normal developmental processes behind these impulses, while also looking out for the interests of all the campers. Such normal teen exploits should be anticipated and dealt with gently and respectfully, understanding that these impulses are normal and even reflect efforts to reinvest in life in the midst of grief.

RETREATS FOR TEENS WITH SERIOUS ILLNESSES

Although this chapter has focused primarily on specialized services for bereaved adolescents, there also are some regional summer camps that provide services for seriously ill teens, particularly teens with cancer and other life-limiting illnesses or conditions. What follows is a brief summary of one such camp in Kentucky. Readers may wish to locate similar camps in their regions.

Indian Summer Camp is a camp for any child ages 6–18 who has been diagnosed with cancer. Although it is not sponsored by Hospice of the Bluegrass, the staff from the hospice may refer ill teens to this camp. It does not matter if they are currently in treatment, posttreatment, or remission. Indian Summer camp is a 6-night, 7-day camp. Most campers stay for the full week, although some campers attend for fewer days depending on their health status. Indian Summer Camp is a private, nonprofit, all-volunteer organization directed by an independent advisory board. It is similar to other camps for children such as the Hole in the Wall camps, Muscular Dystrophy Camps, and ROCK (Reach out to Cancer Kids) Camp sponsored by the American Cancer Society.

Typically, 75–80 kids attend Indian Summer Camp. There are 40 nonmedical volunteers and 10–15 medical volunteers at all times, including at least 1 full-time doctor. Medical staff may administer chemotherapy and other types of treatment at the facility as needed. Children and their medical team plan as carefully as they can for this once-a-year experience, and treatment is scheduled around the camp as much as possible. Children can attend Indian Summer Camp more than once; many campers attend for up to 10 years. After the age of 18, campers graduate to become counselors-in-training. After 1 year, they become counselors and may continue to come back year after year.

The focus of Indian Summer Camp is having fun, being a kid, and "reclaiming that moment of innocence" according to Amy Oliver-Steinkuhl, Indian Summer Camp Director. Camp activities include boating, tubing, swimming, scuba diving, arts and crafts, archery, basketball, soccer, fishing, campfires, and dances. Children and teens stay in cabins by age group and often have the same cabin mates year after year.

Strong bonds are created during the week and throughout the years. Some campers keep in touch through the year via phone and e-mail. When a camper dies, a letter is mailed to the parents of all the kids who were in the deceased camper's cabin. Deaths of campers are critical life events for all camp participants, particularly ill children and adolescents, and it is incumbent upon camps to develop plans for acknowledging the bereavement such deaths produce. As Rich (2002) noted, some camp directors and other adults prefer to avoid any references to death, dying, or bereavement.

According to Camp Director Amy Olvier-Steinkuhl, "For teens, camp is probably the best social support." It is the one place where they are "not different." In many cases, it may be the first real positive peer interaction they have had. Teens receive so much positive reinforcement being around other teens who "are walking the same path." The positive impact of a camping experience is echoed in the literature. For example, Wellisch, Crater, Belin, and Weinstein (2006) report that oncology campers have positive memories regarding camp experiences and showed positive improvements over time. Indian Summer Camp also holds a teen retreat in the fall for any teen between ages 13–18 who has been diagnosed with cancer.

SPECIALIZED GRIEF SUPPORT GROUPS

Bereavement groups for teens can offer a good opportunity to check in with teens about how they are functioning in their grief, to enable them to share similar experiences and learn from one another, and to assist them in accessing the support they may need to address their concerns.

The Dougy Center in Portland, Oregon

The Dougy Center (http://www.GrievingChild.org), founded in 1982 by Beverly Chappell (2008), is a well-known organization that has become a model for many grief support programs for children, adolescents, and their families across the United States and abroad. The Dougy Center currently provides "24 age-specific groups for children ages 3–5, 6–12, 10–14, teens, young adults, and concurrent groups for their adult family members. Some of the groups are loss-specific, including for those impacted by parent death, sibling death, murder, suicide, sudden death, and death following a long-term illness" (Schuurman, 2008, p. 256). According to Schuurman, support in a group setting may provide assistance to children and adolescents who often give voice to the following statements: (a) "Hey, maybe I'm not crazy"; (b) "I'm not alone"; (c) "Someone else cares what I'm going through"; (d) "My feelings matter and

I get to express them"; and (e) "I get to express—or not express—what I feel in ways that help me" (pp. 259–261). Practical advice is provided by the Dougy Center in a booklet entitled *Helping Teens Cope with Death* (1999).

Children's Hospitals and Clinics, Minneapolis, Minnesota

Two examples of specialized bereavement groups for adolescents are offered by the Children's Hospitals and Clinics in Minneapolis.

The Healing Quilt

The Healing Quilt is an 8- to-10-week bereavement group. Group members are selected according to ages, with a minimum of five teens in each group. Concurrent parent/guardian and school-aged groups are offered at the same time. Families can come together and meet in groups designed to address their divergent needs.

The Healing Quilt groups have usually emphasized talking and the sharing of feelings and concerns. Some ritual for expectations of the group setting can be very useful, even when simple in design. For example, one group started each session by checking in to see how the week had been and passing around a talisman to signify who held the floor to speak. Another group began by repeating a set of affirmations encouraging self-respect, personal empowerment, and self-care during their own grief journey. It can be a powerful exercise to help the group develop its own norms and expectations for how it will run after being given some basic guidelines by those facilitating the group.

The Healing Quilt groups focus on grief normalization, education about the grieving process, and opportunities for reflecting upon one's experiences and feelings. It is important to help teens differentiate between thoughts, feelings, impulses, and fears versus actions because developmentally teens struggle between feeling invincible and concerned for their own mortality. Also, building an awareness of supportive structures, as well as providing information about confidential resources for one-to-one counseling and assistance, can be very helpful to those teens struggling with overwhelming feelings and concerns. Their needs may be outside the frame of reference provided by their peers or their own experiences so far. Facilitators would do well to note the tension between the common dramatic expressions of many teens and the need to take seriously impulses or thoughts toward self-destruction, joining the dead person, and other signals of distress that need attention (Melhem, Moritz, Walker, Shear, & Brent, 2007; Walker & Shaffer, 2007).

In one teen group meeting, a 14-year-old girl, Alice, made a number of self-critical comments in the group. She described herself as a bad student, unable to keep up with class work in high school, which she had started that fall. She said that she used to be a good student but didn't seem to be able to manage the change to the new school. She hung her head and looked down as she spoke. Her teachers had been sending letters home to her parents identifying her poor performance. When she was encouraged to share more details of her experiences in school, she told how she was often preoccupied in class and had trouble paying attention. It came to light that she was thinking about her brother. She was unable to stop remembering how he had looked in the last few days before he had died the previous spring. At that time, Alice was attending middle school, surrounded by teachers, peers, and friends who had known her and her brother for many years. They were well aware of her family situation and the stresses upon her family that the current high school was not.

During the group session, Alice received positive feedback and empathy from her peers. They shared similar experiences of being preoccupied by disturbing images for a time, having troubles with school performance, and so forth. They also offered reassurances that these things would get better. The group facilitator followed up with Alice's family after the group session, encouraging them to meet with staff at the high school to explain her situation and plan for a more supportive approach to solving her school problems. For Alice and her parents, this interpretation offered an "aha" moment, allowing them to reframe the issue. Alice wasn't a poor student at all, though her school performance was very much affected by a common expression of grief: preoccupation with intrusive and disturbing memories. Anticipatory guidance was also offered, framing these phenomena as a phase that was likely to resolve over time and also identifying resources for counseling should that become necessary or desired. Perhaps most importantly, Alice heard from teenagers like her that she was okay and that they understood what she was going through. Several weeks later, she appeared to be in much better spirits; she reported she was getting help from her teachers and doing better at school.

Reinterpretation of or reframing issues in light of normative grief and accessing emotional support as well as practical assistance helped this young teen resolve the problems that were disturbing her. It is important to note the role of knowledgeable facilitators who understand how grief can manifest in teens over time so that issues can be identified and addressed in productive ways.

Family Support Activities

The Family Support Program is a closed 8-week bereavement group that meets during the evening. The evening begins with all families sharing a dinner meal together. After dinner, the children move into groups divided by age. The adults divide into groups based on their relationships to the deceased. Groups focus on telling the story, life changes, sharing memories, and self-care. The teen group has used music, journaling, guided visualization, and art activities to address grief.

At the end of each 8-week session, families have a memory feast. The memory feast is a potluck meal where families bring a food that the deceased loved one enjoyed. Additionally, each family member has the opportunity to share a story about the significance of the food. Past graduates of the family support program are also invited to attend this closing session. Program participants also participate in a balloon release. Individual groups are facilitated by staff members and trained bereavement volunteers.

Annie's Hope, St. Louis, Missouri

In addition to its programs for children, adolescents, and families who have already experienced a death, Annie's Hope (http://www.annieshope.org) offers its Horizons program. This is an anticipatory grief support program offering assistance to families facing an impending death and providing assurance that ongoing support will be available to youngsters after the death occurs.

SUMMARY

Rich (2002) described an oncology camp in Hawaii in which the adult leadership was heavily focused on providing a fun and safe experience for participants. Sadly, these adult leaders appear to have been unmindful of the bereavement needs of participants who were aware of the deaths of some former campers, so much so that these adults attempted to inhibit or marginalize expressions of grief. Some campers themselves, helped by sympathetic counselors, organized ad hoc, impromptu rituals to allow expressions of grief. Camp administrators chastised the counselors who participated in these rituals when they arrived late for a staff meeting.

Unlike this example, programs of the type described in this chapter focus on active listening to identify with adolescent participants their specific needs in coping with death-related encounters. Such programs are sensitive to the unique needs and experiences of each individual, as well as the resources available in a given community. They strive to normalize the grief process, build in supports and opportunities for adolescents to process their experiences, and offer anticipatory guidance for teens and their parents or guardians. Successful programs for adolescents—whether they take the form of camps, day or weekend retreats, support groups, or other specialized services—base their services on well-researched and documented bereavement theory (Balk & Corr, 2001). Such programs also draw on a growing body of experience and practice of the type described in this chapter.

REFERENCES

Balk, D. E., & Corr, C. A. (2001). Bereavement during adolescence: A review of research. In Stroebe, M. S., Hansson, R. O., Stroebe, W., & Schut, H. (Eds.), *Handbook of bereavement research: Consequences, coping, and care* (pp. 199–218). Washington, DC: American Psychological Association.

Chappell, B. J. (2008). *Children helping children with grief: My path to founding The Dougy Center for Grieving Children and Their Families.* Troutdale, OR: NewSage Press.

Christ, G. H., Siegal, K., & Christ, A. E. (2002). Adolescent grief: It never really hit me . . . until it actually happened. *Journal of the American Medical Association, 288,* 1269–1279.

Creed, J., Ruffin, J., & Ward, M. (2001). A weekend camp for bereaved siblings. *Cancer Practice, 9*(4), 176–182.

Currier, J. M., Holland, J. M., & Neimeyer, R. A. (2007). The effectiveness of bereavement interventions with children: A meta-analytic review of controlled outcome research. *Journal of Clinical Child & Adolescent Psychology, 36,* 253–259.

The Dougy Center. (1999). *Helping teens cope with death.* Portland, OR: Author.

Ens, C., & Bond, J. B. (2005). Death anxiety and personal growth in adolescents after the death of a grandparent. *Death Studies, 29,* 171–178.

Forte, A. L., Hill, M., Pazder, R., & Feudtner, C. (2004, July 26). Bereavement care interventions: A systematic review. *BMC Palliative Care, 3,* 3. Retrieved June 19, 2008, from http://www.biomedcentral.com

Klontz, B. T., Bivens, A., Leinart, D., & Klontz, T. (2007). The effectiveness of equine-assisted experiential therapy: Results of an open clinical trial. *Society and Animals, 15,* 257–267.

LoCicero, J. P., Burkhart, J., & Gray, S. (1998). Camp Carousel: A weekend grief retreat. *American Journal of Hospice and Palliative Care, 15*(1), 25–27.

Martiniuk, A. (2003). Camping programs for children with cancer and their families. *Support Care Cancer, 11*(2), 749–757.

Melhem, N. M., Moritz, G., Walker, M., Shear, M. K., & Brent, D. (2007). Phenomenology and correlates of complicated grief in children and adolescents. *Journal of the American Academy of Child and Adolescent Psychiatry, 46*(4), 493–499.

Morin, S., & Welsh, L. (1996). Adolescents' perceptions and experiences of death and grieving. *Adolescence, 31,* 585–595.

Nabors, L., Ohms, M., Buchanan, N., Kirsch, K. L., Nash, T., Passik, S., et al. (2004). A pilot study of the impact of a grief group for children. *Palliative and Supportive Care, 2,* 403–408.

Rich, M. D. (2002). Memory circles: The implications of (not) grieving at cancer camps. *Journal of Contemporary Ethnography, 31,* 548–581.

Schachter, S. R. (2007). Bereavement summer camp for children and teens: A reflection of nine years. *Palliative and Supportive Care, 5,* 315–323.

Schachter, S. R., & Georgopoulos, M. (2008). Camps for grieving children: Lessons from the field. In K. J. Doka & A. S. Tucci (Eds.), *Living with grief: Children and adolescents* (pp. 233–251). Washington, DC: Hospice Foundation of America.

Schuurman, D. (2008). Grief groups for grieving children and adolescents. In K. J. Doka & A. S. Tucci (Eds.), *Living with grief: Children and adolescents* (pp. 255–268). Washington, DC: Hospice Foundation of America.

Stokes, J. A. (2004). *Then, now & always . . . Supporting children as they journey through grief: A guide for practitioners.* Cheltenham, England: Winston's Wish.

Summers, K. H. (1993). Camp Sunrise: Supporting bereaved children. *American Journal of Hospice and Palliative Care, 10*(3), 24–27.

Walker, P., & Shaffer, M. (2007). Reducing depression among adolescents dealing with grief and loss: A program evaluation report. *Health & Social Work, 32*(1), 67–69.

Wellisch, D. K., Crater, B., Belin, T. R., & Weinstein, K. (2006). Psychosocial impacts of a camping experience for children with cancer and their siblings. *Psychology, 15*(1), 56–65.

Worden, J. W. (1996). *Children and grief: When a parent dies.* New York: Guilford.

17

Psychotherapeutic Approaches for Adolescents With Life-Threatening Illnesses

MICHELLE R. BROWN AND BARBARA SOURKES

So much of adolescence is an ill-defined dying,
An intolerable waiting,
A longing for another place and time,
Another condition.

—Theodore Roethke (1908–1963)

Roethke (1957) captures the essence of adolescence: the quest, the restlessness, and the inner turbulence that accompany the opening of new horizons toward the future. The presence of life-threatening illness, whether newly diagnosed in adolescence, or as a preexisting condition, adds layers of complexity to a life stage already characterized by flux. In the words of 19-year-old Katharine, who had been diagnosed with osteogenic sarcoma at the age of 16:

> Younger children are not developed in themselves yet, in their own persons, in their own individualism. They can still be with their mother. Older people are away from their mother; they're detached, more adult. When you're in the middle, parents don't want to let you go. You want to be set free a little bit, but you want to be able to come back. I just felt that I was denied any sort of chance. I wish I could look back and see: "Would Katharine have been popular? Would Katharine have had lots of boyfriends? Would Katharine have starred on the varsity?" I look now, and would that have been what I wanted? I don't know. I never had the chance to find out.

> Instead it was decided for me: "You are going to mature very fast right now. You have to make life-and-death decisions. You have to accept things that children who are young adults between the ages of thirteen and nineteen don't normally have to face." It's like: "Grow up right now and become what you have to become to deal with this." I never had the chance to be sweet sixteen. . . . I had to automatically be an adult, and it was very hard. (Sourkes, 1982, pp. 101–102)

This chapter provides an overview of the role of psychotherapy for the adolescent living with a life-threatening illness. Salient psychological issues including those of identity, autonomy/dependence, and future orientation are examined. Attention is also paid to variations, which may exist as a function of socioeconomic status, cultural, and ethnic background.

THE ROLE OF PSYCHOTHERAPY

Adolescents with a life-threatening illness typically enter psychotherapy because of the stress engendered by the illness, rather than being referred for treatment of intrapsychic or interpersonal concerns. Psychological treatment is not always indicated, as sadness and anxiety are universal reactions to prolonged illness and treatment. However, under sustained stress, such responses may progress to major clinical disorders that may ultimately necessitate psychotherapy and/or psychotropic medication. Both parents and clinicians often underestimate the degree of emotional distress experienced by pediatric populations with chronic illness. Differential diagnosis may be difficult for nonmental health providers since normal emotions of sadness and grief overlap with symptoms of clinical depression (e.g., crying, decreased appetite, difficulty sleeping, and decreased attention and concentration; Kersun & Shemesh, 2007; Shemesh et al., 2005). The therapist, by assessing the severity of symptoms, particularly in terms of intensity and duration relative to the child's current reality, can determine if psychotherapy is necessary, or whether existing supportive services (e.g., child life, ongoing relationships with physicians and nurses) would suffice. Some adolescents turn to chaplains rather than mental health professionals.

Psychotherapy is the treatment modality unique to the mental health professional (Sourkes, 2000). Within its framework, the adolescent seeks to integrate the facets of his or her life through various modes of verbal and nonverbal expression (e.g., art). For some, self-help techniques such as relaxation, guided imagery, and hypnosis may be integrated into the psychotherapy to reduce symptoms of nausea, fatigue, insomnia, and pain (Kazak, 2005; Kazak et al., 1996; Kersun & Shemesh, 2007; Steif & Heiligenstein, 1989). These techniques are not restricted to psychotherapeutic intervention and may be employed by other disciplines trained in their methodology.

Psychotherapy can facilitate psychological adjustment with adolescents by promoting developmentally appropriate discussions around their illness and prognosis (Brown & Sourkes, 2006). Abstract reasoning enables adolescents to anticipate the future in a way that many younger children cannot (Aldrich, 1974; Brown & Sourkes, 2006). Responding to adolescents' questions about death (e.g., "What's happening to me? What will happen if . . . ? Am I dying?") requires careful exploration of what is already known by the teen, what is really being asked (the question behind the question), and why the question is being asked at this particular time and in this setting (Brown & Sourkes, 2006; Sourkes, 1992). Parents, in their own struggle with grief, sometimes discourage such questioning or provide optimistic responses in an attempt to avoid the pain associated with threatened loss. As a result, it is not uncommon to hear adolescents' frustration or resignation emerge in comments such as: "My parents won't face the fact that I'm dying."

Psychotherapy can provide adolescents with a space of their own where thoughts and feelings are protected and confidential. In this setting, emotions can be expressed openly without fear of others' reactions, such as the adolescent who feels that his or her feelings are too painful for the family to bear.

> You are the only person I can talk to about my illness. My mother always starts to cry when I bring it up with her. My dad tells me not to worry, that everything will work out fine. My friends, they just don't get it. You get it. And you don't try to make me feel better. You let me be me. (Fifteen-year-old girl prior to heart transplant.)[1]

Through psychotherapy, adolescents can experience a sense of stability and continuity during a time that may otherwise feel chaotic and unanchored. The therapeutic relationship in and of itself may be a profound intervention, even when issues of death and loss are not explicitly addressed. Oftentimes, mental health providers working with adolescents facing a life-threatening illness feel pressured to elicit the teens' emotions around their prognosis and assist them in finding some meaning in their illness or impending death. However, such therapist-driven goals are typically not therapeutically indicated. Rather, the therapist should follow and respect adolescents' cues to ensure that issues important to them are addressed.

> Over the course of her two years in therapy, Elle, a 17-year-old with acute myelogenous leukemia, rarely spoke of her illness. In her final weeks of life, her therapist asked Elle to describe her understanding of her current medical state and prognosis, concerned that Elle did not appreciate the gravity of her illness. Elle responded somewhat dismissively stating, "I know I'm going to die. I just don't see much point in talking about it. It's not how I want to spend my last days."[1]

Individual psychotherapy can also play a critical role by helping adolescents formulate a hierarchy of their chosen goals (e.g., graduation from high school, foreign travel, admission to college). For this reason, adolescents have the right to know their diagnosis and prognosis. The information can provide a time context within which to organize and reorganize priorities, thereby instilling an increased sense of control over the time remaining.

Family therapy is often provided in combination with individual psychotherapy to open the lines of communication between adolescents and their families about topics that parents are uncertain about how to approach. The father of an adolescent with cystic fibrosis stated:

> If I could change anything, I would have spoken to Rachel a lot sooner about how she was doing. There was a lot of time spent with an elephant under the rug, that sort of thing that nobody wanted to talk about. So, I'm glad we finally got around to it. . . She never brought it up trying to protect us and we never brought it up trying to protect her. . . . So I went to see a counselor who suggested, "Well, why don't you talk to her about it?" and I said, "Oh no, she's got enough on her plate already. I don't want to burden her with this," and he said, "No, no. You know she's grown up with this. She knows it better than anybody what her life expectancy is and what the prognosis is." And he was right. When I did mention it to Rachel, that's just what she said. She said, "You know, I know what my situation is like and I never wanted to bring it up because I didn't want to make it harder for you." So being able to talk to her about it was the first best thing that happened. (Kuttner, 2003)

As echoed in these words, parents often avoid discussions with their teens about the possibility of death. Yet, as with Rachel, most adolescents who have lived with the cumulative toll of illness and treatment have acquired an accurate understanding of their life-threatened status or impending death long before others discuss it with them. Parents are often unsure of how to initiate such conversations and are fearful of unleashing overwhelming emotion. Furthermore, they may avoid the topic in an attempt to shield their children from the family's grief, or for fear of instilling terrifying thoughts that their teen has not yet even considered. A recent study (Kreicbergs, Valdimarsdottir, Onelov, Henter, & Steineck, 2004) found that bereaved parents who had discussed impending death with their child had no regrets about doing so. This assessment was in sharp contrast to some of the parents who had avoided such openness.

The family therapist can facilitate conversations about death between adolescents and their family. This intervention may occur through a series of discussions that take place over a period of time (with the family's verbal and nonverbal cues guiding the pace) or by providing brief consultation to the family so that they feel more capable of pursuing such discussions on their own. Of course, it is important to consider that variations in cultural background will influence the suitability of such therapeutic goals. Lee (1983), for example, recommends an approach for Asian-American families that focuses more on problem-solving and goals than on emotional expression, self-assertion, or acquisition of insight.

A focus on the well siblings must also be an aspect of the family work. Too often, the siblings stand outside the spotlight of attention, even though they have lived through the illness experience with the same intensity as the child and parents (Bluebond-Langner, 1996; Sourkes, 1980). Mariesa, a 16-year-old well sibling, comments on her experience throughout the course of her younger sister's illness:

> Everyone in my family was always calling [and asking], "How's Mikaela doing? How is the little angel?" And then with me, I was like, "What about me?" No one ever asked about me. No one cared anymore. From that moment on, it was not about me anymore. It was, "Oh, you have another daughter? We didn't notice." From that point on, everyone always cared about Mikaela and it made me feel like no one cares about me just because I'm not the one who is physically sick. (Kuttner, 2003)

Healthy siblings experience many of the same issues as the ill child: loss of control and predictability over their schedules, loss of a personal identity (e.g., being identified as the sibling of a dying child), and loss of interpersonal relationships (because of changes in routine that exclude them from their normal social opportunities; McSherry, Kehoe, Carroll, Kang, & Rourke, 2007). The healthy siblings share common questions and concerns; some they raise with parents, professionals, or another trusted adult, and others they harbor silently. Their concerns include fear of becoming ill, guilt for escaping the disease, and anxiety resulting from a lack of information or misinformation (Sourkes, 1980). Rarely mentioned but often present is the unacceptable feeling of shame at having a so-called different family, marked by an ill-sibling who is disfigured or dying. Siblings may also harbor anger around diminished attention and nurturance from their parents, especially when the ill teen is in the hospital. Siblings who themselves are feeling deprived may also resent stepping in as surrogate parents for younger brothers and sisters. Once home, siblings may resent the extra attention and privileges accorded to the ill teen, shifting their complaint from that of too little attention to preferential treatment. Parents, meanwhile, are struggling to maintain equality and normality when, in fact, a distinctly abnormal factor in the family constellation exists.

Adolescents may express their thoughts about treatment options and awareness of living with the threat of death to individuals other than their parents or primary physician. The therapist can be an important liaison at critical junctures in the illness trajectory. Parents, teens, and treatment providers may hold differing opinions regarding the goals for treatment. On the one hand, physicians may recommend an aggressive course of treatment, while the adolescent and parents are concerned about the pain and suffering associated with such an approach. On the other hand, physicians may encourage a transition to palliative care, while the family still wishes to exhaust every possible life-prolonging option. Under such circumstances, the therapist can clarify these differing perspectives and their implications and facilitate discussions toward a common treatment goal. Furthermore, the risk of miscommunications and misunderstandings (albeit unintended) that may have lasting emotional repercussions for the family is reduced.

> A 17-year-old boy with end-stage pulmonary disease was encouraged by the medical team to agree to a DNR (do not resuscitate) order given his advanced condition. However, the child and the mother refused, wanting the treatment team to pursue every available life-sustaining measure. Every day on rounds, the medical team tried to persuade them to change their minds, pointing out how much additional pain and suffering could be involved. Although their intention was caring, the team's persistence caused

the boy and his mother to feel judged and unsupported throughout the remaining days of his life. (Sourkes et al., 2005, p. 369)

Differing priorities may also lead to misunderstandings especially when curative and palliative care are perceived as mutually exclusive. For example, an adolescent's behavior might be perceived as nonadherent and oppositional when he or she misses medications or procedures that are time consuming or painful. However, the teen may be asserting that quality of life and/or comfort is more important than curative efforts. By evaluating the unique characteristics of each adolescent and family (e.g., personal and religious beliefs, hopes related to treatment), the therapist is able to advocate for the individual needs of each patient.

As a liaison between the adolescent, family, and/or treatment team, the therapist must also evaluate culturally defined characteristics of each patient. Culturally defined health beliefs and practices can significantly influence acceptance of and adherence to prescribed therapies, the degree and quality of parental involvement in patient care, and the family's relationship with health care staff. Behavior viewed in isolation of the cultural context is often misinterpreted by the treatment providers. For example, "resistances" observed among Asian Americans (hesitancy to open up, tendency to give limited information) may be mislabels. While openness may be embraced by European Americans, Asian Americans have been taught that premature disclosure of emotions to a stranger is an indication of lack of self-control, immaturity, and a cause for shame. As a cultural broker, the therapist can raise awareness of cultural influences at play, thereby facilitate understanding, communication, and the development of a treatment plan that is congruent with a family's cultural heritage (Trill & Kovalcik, 1997).

THEMES IN PSYCHOTHERAPY

Identity

The quest for identity is the foremost task of adolescence (Erikson, 1968). It is the period of life when defining and sharing oneself outside the sheltered context of the family, as well as envisioning the future, becomes paramount. A life-threatening illness invariably alters the adolescent's sense of personal identity. Whereas the illness may initially be perceived as an external intruder, over time it transforms itself into an internalized part of the adolescent's physical and emotional being. This process is often noted through subtle shifts in language (e.g., *the illness* becomes *my illness*). The risk for an adolescent is when his or her identity becomes overridingly that of "a patient" rather than that of "a teenager who is living with/has an illness/condition" (Sourkes, 1982, p. 35).

Restrictions imposed by illness and treatments interfere with experiences through which adolescents ordinarily develop their sense of competence, self-worth, and positive self-esteem (McSherry et al., 2007). School is the defining structure of normal life for all children and adolescents, and affords opportunities for achievement in both academic and extracurricular/social domains. Yet, school attendance for adolescents with a life-threatening illness is often sacrificed to hours spent at clinic visits, outpatient treatment, hospitalizations, and home. Less visible effects of the disease process and its treatment, including neurocognitive deficits and altered mental status, can significantly impair academic and social functioning. Overwhelming fatigue commonly limits adolescents' ability to remain in school full-time and thereby reduces opportunities for learning as well as socialization. Furthermore, physical limitations from specific symptoms and handicaps can also be profoundly disruptive (Evan, Kaufman, Cook, & Zeltzer, 2006; Freyer, 2004).

> When asked about the illness's impact on her life, a 19-year-old responded, "I wasn't like this before. I had interests. I went out with my friends. I used to take acting and dance classes. I had goals. Now I can hardly get out of bed." (Brown & Sourkes, 2006, p. 593)

The effects of illness and its treatment on physical appearance can also influence adolescents' developing sense of self. Physical changes of puberty bring about heightened concern with body image for all adolescents. Given that self-image and worth are often bound up with outward appearance, the visible markers of illness, whether temporary or permanent (e.g., hair loss, drastic changes in weight, stunted growth, wheelchair dependence, amputation), place ill adolescents at even greater risk for poor body image and related feelings of inferiority and low self-esteem. Compounding their own difficulty in adjusting to an altered body image is their fear of others' reactions to their appearance. Peers—usually responding out of their own discomfort and fear—may shy away from or even taunt the ill teens, only serving to reinforce their belief that they no longer belong. Such shame and embarrassment can lead to adolescents refusing to return to school and withdrawing from other activities. In turn, the maintenance of preexisting relationships and the development of new peer relationships are hindered (Easson, 1985).

> Following a long course of steroids and an extended absence from school, a 16-year-old expressed reluctance to participate in social activities with peers from school, stating that no one would recognize her since she had become so "fat." (Brown & Sourkes, 2006, p. 593)

> Katharine reflected on how she had looked and felt when her weight had dropped to seventy pounds during chemotherapy: "It's very hard. You lose all self-pride and self-respect. You lose 'self' really, because physically you lose so much weight." (Sourkes, 1982, p. 103)

For adolescents who are ill, their emerging sense of sexual identity is also complicated by the effects of disease and treatment. Sexual development may be interrupted, delayed, or permanently disrupted.

Furthermore, as social opportunities for the ill adolescent are significantly reduced, so too are the normative interactions through which sexual knowledge is typically obtained and experimentation occurs (Easson, 1985; Stevens et al., 1996). Unfortunately, adolescents with life-limiting conditions and disabilities receive less information about sex from their health care providers compared to healthy peers. Furthermore, their education typically focuses on limitations and vulnerabilities related to sexuality, rather than options for sexual expression (Berman et al., 1999; Cromer et al., 1990). Professionals often mistakenly assume that teens who are seriously ill have little concern about their sexual functioning. Although adolescents tend not to initiate the topic, most are relieved to voice their questions and concerns when a team member with whom they feel comfortable broaches the subject. The therapist's discomfort in handling sexual concerns—or the denial of their importance—can handicap the therapeutic process by closing off a crucial avenue of disclosure. Acknowledgement of sexual activity and the impact of the illness upon it is necessary if the adolescent is to communicate with candor (Sourkes, 1992).

> An 18-year-old who had had a leg amputated expressed fears about his sexual functioning, and about how his girlfriend would react. On a clinic visit shortly after his surgery, he greeted the therapist: "You'll be glad to know I still work!" Before the therapist had time to respond, the boy added, laughing: "I was glad, too." (Sourkes, 1992, p. 280)

There are also concerns more subtle than those about actual sexual performance. For example, most children undergoing chemotherapy will temporarily lose body hair, a common side effect of many drugs. There is much focus on the visible loss of hair on the head, from both a cosmetic and symbolic point of view. In contrast, adolescents rarely mention the impact of the loss of pubic hair. Yet, as a perceived threat to a newly emerging sexual identity, this loss may actually be more devastating.

Fertility issues also become more salient as adolescents begin to contemplate long-term relationships and parenthood. Options in reproductive technology are often presented to ill adolescents at the time of their diagnosis or treatment. Despite such advances, many adolescents nevertheless confront another facet of loss: "A 17-year-old girl who had been treated for uterine cancer cried, 'The biggest scar is not having my own babies.' Her grief was palpable and profound" (Sourkes, 1992, p. 281). It is reasonable to assume that discussions about sexuality with ill adolescents may engender deep feelings of sadness and disappointment for both the patient and provider. However, this emotional reaction should not dissuade discussions of what is possible for these adolescents (Cheng & Udry, 2002). Rather, it is the pursuit of such possibilities that can promote the development of personal identity even as death approaches.

Independence/Dependence

Serious illness may substantially interfere with critical life experiences necessary for achieving the typical developmental goals of adolescence. Chief among these is the development of personal independence and self-confidence acquired through gradual separation from parents (Freyer, 2004). Yet, adolescents who are ill are catapulted back into an enforced dependency. They require assistance with the most basic of tasks, such as personal hygiene or eating. They must endure a lack of privacy over their physical and emotional boundaries at exactly the time that self-control is so paramount developmentally. Milestones that represent increasing independence, such as obtaining a driver's license or employment, may be delayed or missed altogether and highlight the disruption of the normal passage from childhood toward adulthood.

The very nature of illness, treatment, and the medical environment makes adolescents acutely vulnerable to a sense of loss of control. Adolescents' efforts to maintain or regain a sense of control may manifest as rebellion or refusal to follow the prescribed treatment regimen, leading professionals to label them dismissively as difficult or noncompliant. Any approaches or techniques that increase adolescents' participation and choices in the situation, from the most concrete (e.g., scheduling of medications or appointments) to those of symptom relief (e.g., self-hypnosis) to the most profound and abstract (e.g., treatment decisions) will increase their sense of mastery and esteem.

Among healthy adolescents, parents typically attempt to adjust their supervisory practices to allow for more freedom and independent decision making. However, parents of adolescents who are ill tend to be overprotective, vigilant, and inflexible—even punitive—in their fear of the possible repercussions of nonadherence. Yet, these parenting behaviors can in turn create heightened conflict if the adolescent's desire for more autonomy is disregarded. Alternatively, adolescents who have come to rely primarily on others for extended periods of time may become overly dependent and less confident in their own abilities to cope with the challenges at hand. This sense of vulnerability may discourage the adolescent's effort toward individuation (Evan et al., 2006).

As adolescents progressively separate from parents, identification with peers becomes more important. However, the desire to fit in with peers may be at odds with restrictions imposed by their illness or treatment regimen, and efforts to seek acceptance from others may put their health at greater risk. Examples include a teen with cystic fibrosis who feels pressured to smoke when socializing with friends or a severely immunocompromised teen who refuses to wear a face mask in public. Despite their cognitive ability to reason abstractly and anticipate the future, adolescents in fact tend to be behaviorally impulsive and present focused, with limited willingness to consider the possibility of a negative outcome. This is particularly the case when no immediate consequences are evident. Adolescents' sense of omnipotence, or invulnerability to potential negative consequences, only compounds the problem. Thus, even adolescents who "know" that their health status is precarious may skip medications or other therapies with the reasoning that "nothing will happen to me." It is often not until late adolescence or early adulthood when an adequate appreciation of hypothetical future consequences of illness begins to emerge with more gravity and consistency.

The capacity for and role of decision making on the part of adolescents has recently come into sharp focus in the field of pediatric palliative care, from clinical, legal, and ethical perspectives (Institute of Medicine, 2003; NHPCO, n.d.; Sourkes et al., 2005). There is an increasing sense among health care providers that adolescent autonomy should be respected and their preferences be given substantial consideration should they wish to participate in the decision-making process. Certainly, a confluence of factors (e.g., age, developmental and cognitive maturity) will affect the degree to which an adolescent's wishes are factored into decisions. In actual practice, the medical team tends to be more comfortable supporting autonomy when the adolescent is assenting to the treatment plan rather than expressing any form of dissent. Adolescents may also defer medical decisions to family members. Yet, this reliance on family members can elicit concerns from the medical team when the parents' medical decisions go against medical advice; the assumption being that if the adolescent truly understood the implications of their parents' medical decision, the adolescent might choose differently for him- or herself.

> A 17-year-old boy with hemophilia who was also HIV-positive referred to his condition exclusively as an "immune system disorder" (i.e., he never acknowledged the terms HIV or AIDS). However, he was knowledgeable and open about all blood and safe-sex precautions. On each of his admissions, when the physicians asked him whether he had any question about the exact nature of his condition or his treatment, he would calmly shake his head "no" and say: "If you have anything to discuss, you can talk to my parents." Although the team was chagrined at times with his non-involvement in decisions, he was clearly comfortable delegating to his parents. He avidly continued his schoolwork, socialized with friends, and responsibly managed his own care and risk to others up to the time of his death.[1]

Cultural factors will also shape the degree of personal autonomy afforded to and desired by adolescents. Hispanic families, for example, traditionally place high value on respecting authority figures (Rothe, 2005). Hierarchical relationships are established, and, as such, adolescents tend to accept authority unquestioningly and comply with directions from elders. Giving assent is considered a sign of respect, even when the adolescent is in disagreement with the issue in question. This value system can be problematic for health care providers who attach greater importance to the wishes of the individual adolescent than those of the family.

Future Orientation and Goals

> I turn to the first page, which is not a part of [my] journal, but a private goal sheet not meant to ever be seen by anyone. Of course I have many more goals than are written here, but these are the two most important ones, the ones I must accomplish before dying in order for my life to have been worthwhile. . .

1. lose virginity
2. make a contribution—publication of [my] journal
(Sixteen-year-old boy with brain tumor in a novel by Schreiber, 1983, p. 22)

Adolescence is a time of great anticipation as teens ponder who they will become and what they will accomplish. Yet, such considerations can be complicated and poignant for adolescents who are living with a life-threatening condition. Academically, these adolescents may be performing months or years behind peers as a result of prolonged school absence or the cognitive effects of the illness or treatment. Well-intentioned teachers at times promote students through the system even if academic goals are not adequately met. While the ill students (and even parents) may appreciate this advancement at the time, upon graduation they are left unprepared for the real world. Conversely, attempts to treat ill teens as normal create unrealistic expectations and place stressful performance demands on them. In either extreme, these adolescents are left with diminished confidence in their ability to achieve future success. Furthermore, in circumstances of prognostic uncertainty or unexpected medical setbacks, adolescents may lose motivation, asking themselves, "What's the use of committing to this?" If their attitude of hopelessness and despair endures over an extended period of time, future-oriented behaviors may cease, leading to withdrawal and depression.

For adolescents from impoverished families, even greater despair may stem from potential future losses for their family than from the threat of personal loss. Immigrant families may have endured enormous sacrifice to provide a better life for their children, leaving behind family and support systems in their native country. Hopes for the future hang upon the adolescent's educational and/or professional success. Facing death, adolescents may fear the future of their family. First- and even second-generation Americans may have served as the sole interpreter for the family and wonder how the family will manage in their absence. They may grieve their inability to provide for their family financially and feel remorseful about the costs related to health care, which will further burden their family.

The overarching task for adolescents living with a life-threatening condition is to learn to tolerate the uncertainty of their life condition as they move forward through time. Their challenge is to create a balance between the demands of their illness and their hopes for the future, while finding meaning in their present relationships and accomplishments. Members of the family or treatment team may become confused or concerned when a teen facing death refers to future dreams. Often, these hopes and wishes are mistaken for ignorance and denial (e.g., "Doesn't he know he is going to die? Someone needs to tell him."). Adherence to future goals to the exclusion of impinging reality may signify fear and dysfunction. However, most adolescents are able to acknowledge and have meaningful discussions about the reality of their impending death, yet focus on future milestones that they may not live to see. This adaptive process is a source of coping and strength rather than a detriment (McSherry et al., 2007). Psychotherapy can play a vital role in supporting this process.

> In the days before her death, a 20-year-old with end-stage pulmonary disease asserted that she was the most able of the three siblings to attend to their ailing mother and described detailed plans for her long-term care. During the conversation, she spontaneously noted that her own death would likely precede the implementation of such plans and then returned to talk about her hopes and wishes for the future.[2]

A clinical nurse specialist reflected on her conversations with Rachel, a 17-year-old girl living with cystic fibrosis:

> Living with knowing that you are dying is a balancing act. And Rachel really showed me this through one of her stories. We were having a very intense talk about what she wanted it to look like . . . her end of life. And she said very seriously that when she is to die, she wanted to be here . . . in a hospice surrounded by friends and family, and surrounded by people that knew how to take care of her . . . and she was talking about the nurses and the doctors that can help her not feel scared. . . . and then she said, "but I have another way that I'd like to die . . . I would like to be sitting on my front porch, wrapped in an afghan with a rocking chair and my husband holding my hand." And all I did was reflect that that would be a nice way. And to me that just spoke about the hope that we always have; that we have a rich full life, we have relationships that matter, we are supported in our pain. . .with also hanging on to the fact that she knows that it might look very different for her. (Kuttner, 2003)

IMPLICATIONS FOR END-OF-LIFE CARE

> I was brought up to believe that life is a gift. God gives life as a gift with no strings attached. It should be a given, just to live. Then if you want to work

> to be different things, you work for that. But you shouldn't have to struggle just to live. (Reflections of an adolescent just prior to death; Sourkes, 2000, p. 265)

Decisions during the end-phase of life are difficult, since there can no longer be any promise of prolonged time. Concerns about quality of life often emerge as the dominant theme.

> A 16-year-old girl with cystic fibrosis intermittently refused ventilatory support during sleep due to the chest pain caused by the air pressure from the bi-pap machine. She also frequently declined at least one of the four scheduled respiratory therapy treatments each day and decided to postpone the recommended gastronomy tube to facilitate nutritional intake. The medical team perceived her "non-adherent behavior" as indifference towards a possible lung transplant. She, however, clearly lamented her quandary in stating, "Why should I try so hard and endure so much pain if, in the end, a lung is not available for transplant, or even worse, if I get a lung and the transplant fails?"[3]

Adolescents will vary in their approach to balancing curative efforts and comfort measures. Regardless of their decisions, the goals for the therapist remain the same: to foster an independent sense of self, to support their developing autonomy, and to promote a sense of agency in their pursuit of future aspirations. In this way, adolescents living with life-threatening illness can strive toward the same developmental accomplishments as their healthy peers, albeit with dramatically different issues. By supporting this process, the therapist can contribute importantly to the young person's experience of life despite the sadness of an untimely death.

In our clinical experience, we have encountered many professionals who feel that adolescents are the most painful age group to face: just as they are beginning to negotiate an independent existence, that moving forward is dramatically disrupted or irreversibly halted. Yet, in counterpoint, many teens have noted that they experienced their battle with illness not solely as an assault against their developing sense of self, but also as a source of personal growth and competence (Evan et al., 2006). While acknowledging their physical and emotional suffering, they can also attest to previously unknown courage, maturity, and life perspective that their healthy peers have yet to appreciate. It is such resilience, wisdom, and sensitivity that touches us both personally and professionally and inspires us to continue our work with these remarkable young people.

NOTE

1. Case example taken from the authors' professional experiences.
2. Case example taken from the authors' professional experiences.
3. Case example taken from the authors' professional experiences.

REFERENCES

Aldrich, C. (1974). Some dynamics of anticipatory grief. In B. Schoenberg, A. Carr, & A. Kutscher (Eds.), *Anticipatory grief* (pp. 3–9). New York: Columbia University Press.

Berman, H., Harris, D., Enright, R., Gilpin, M., Cathers, T., & Bukovy, G. (1999). Sexuality and the adolescent with a physical disability: Understandings and misunderstandings. *Issues in Comprehensive Pediatric Nursing, 22*(4), 183–196.

Bluebond-Langner, M. (1996). *In the shadow of illness: Parents and siblings of the chronically ill child.* Princeton, NJ: Princeton University Press.

Brown, M. R., & Sourkes, B. (2006). Psychotherapy in pediatric palliative care. *Child and Adolescent Psychiatric Clinics of North America, 15*(3), 585–596.

Cheng, M. M., & Udry, J. R. (2002). Sexual behaviors of physically disabled adolescents in the United States. *Journal of Adolescent Health, 31*(1), 48–58.

Cromer, B. A., Enrile, B., McCoy, K., Gerhardstein, M. J., Fitzpatrick, M., & Judis, J. (1990). Knowledge, attitudes and behavior related to sexuality in adolescents with chronic disability. *Developmental Medicine and Child Neurology, 32*(7), 602–610.

Easson, W. M. (1985). The seriously ill or dying adolescent. Special needs and challenges. *Postgraduate Medicine, 78*(1), 183–184, 187–189.

Erikson, E. (1968). *Identity: Youth and crisis.* New York: Norton.

Evan, E. E., Kaufman, M., Cook, A. B., & Zeltzer, L. K. (2006). Sexual health and self-esteem in adolescents and young adults with cancer. *Cancer, 107*(7 Suppl.), 1672–1679.

Freyer, D. R. (2004). Care of the dying adolescent: Special considerations. *Pediatrics, 113*(2), 381–388.

Institute of Medicine. (2003). *When children die: Improving palliative and end-of-life care for children and their families.* Washington, DC: National Academies Press.

Kazak, A. E. (2005). Evidence-based interventions for survivors of childhood cancer and their families. *Journal of Pediatric Psychology, 30*(1), 29–39.

Kazak, A. E., Penati, B., Boyer, B. A., Himelstein, B., Brophy, P., Waibel, M. K., et al. (1996). A randomized controlled prospective outcome study of a psychological and pharmacological intervention protocol for procedural distress in pediatric leukemia. *Journal of Pediatric Psychology, 21*(5), 615–631.

Kersun, L. S., & Shemesh, E. (2007). Depression and anxiety in children at the end of life. *Pediatric Clinics of North America, 54*(5), 691–708, xi.

Kreicbergs, U., Valdimarsdottir, U., Onelov, E., Henter, J. I., & Steineck, G. (2004). Talking about death with children who have severe malignant disease. *New England Journal of Medicine, 351*(12), 1175–1186.

Kuttner, L. (Writer) (2003). *Making every moment count* [Motion picture]. National Film Board of Canada and Still Water Pictures.

Lee, E. (1983). A social systems approach to assessment and treatment for Chinese American families. In M. McGoldrick, J. Pearce, & J. Giordano (Eds.), *Ethnicity and family therapy* (pp. 302–318). New York: Guilford.

McSherry, M., Kehoe, K., Carroll, J. M., Kang, T. I., & Rourke, M. T. (2007). Psychosocial and spiritual needs of children living with a life-limiting illness. *Pediatric Clinics of North America, 54*(5), 609–629, ix–x.

National Hospice and Palliative Care Organization (NHPCO). (n.d.). *ChIPPS 0.8169 Bibliography Summary of the Ethics and Decision-Making Subgroup.* Retrieved August 28, 2008, from http://www.nhpco.org/14a/pages/index.cfm?pageid=3409

Roethke, T. (1957). *Words for the wind.* London: Secker & Warburg.

Rothe, E. M. (2005). Hispanic adolescents and their families: Sociocultural factors and treatment considerations. *Adolescent Psychiatry, 28,* 251–278.

Schreiber, M. (1983). *Princes in exile.* New York: Beaufort Books.

Shemesh, E., Annunziato, R. A., Shneider, B. L., Newcorn, J. H., Warshaw, J. K., Dugan, C. A., et al. (2005). Parents and clinicians underestimate distress and depression in children who had a transplant. *Pediatric Transplantation, 9*(5), 673–679.

Sourkes, B. (1980). Siblings of the pediatric cancer patient. In J. Kellerman (Ed.), *Psychological aspects of childhood cancer* (pp. 47–69). Springfield, IL: Charles C Thomas.

Sourkes, B. (1992). The child with a life-threatening illness. In J. Brandell (Ed.), *Countertransference in child and adolescent psychotherapy* (pp. 267–284). New York: Jason Aronson.

Sourkes, B. (2000). Psychotherapy with the dying child. In H. Chochinov & W. Breitbart (Eds.), *Handbook of psychiatry in palliative medicine* (pp. 265–272). New York: Oxford.

Sourkes, B., Frankel, L., Brown, M., Contro, N., Benitz, W., Case, C., et al. (2005). Food, toys, and love: Pediatric palliative care. *Current Problems in Pediatric and Adolescent Health Care, 35*(9), 350–386.

Sourkes, B. M. (1982). *The deepening shade: Psychological aspects of life-threatening illness.* Pittsburgh, PA: University of Pittsburgh Press.

Steif, B. L., & Heiligenstein, E. L. (1989). Psychiatric symptoms of pediatric cancer pain. *Journal of Pain and Symptom Management, 4*(4), 191–196.

Stevens, M. E., Steele, C. A., Jutai, J. W., Kalnins, I. V., Bortolussi, J. A., & Biggar, W. D. (1996). Adolescents with disabilities: Some psychosocial aspects of health. *Journal of Adolescent Health, 19,* 157–164.

Trill, M. D., & Kovalcik, R. (1997). The child with cancer: Influence of culture on truth-telling and patient care. *Annals of the New York Academy of Sciences, 809,* 197–210.

18 Counseling Approaches for Bereaved Adolescents

PHYLLIS KOSMINSKY AND DEIRDRE LEWIN

More than any other stage of life, adolescence is about transformative change. Physical growth and development are the most apparent, but the interior changes that occur are just as dramatic and arguably more challenging for adolescents. So much change cannot help but produce a sense of disorganization, disorientation, and even despair for many adolescents as they struggle to gain a foothold in the world and a sense of their place in it. The experience of losing a loved one at this stage of life is a further stressor, one that can easily result in an overload of an adolescent's nascent coping capacities.

Assessment of the needs of adolescents who have suffered the loss of a family member or a close friend must be made within the context of their developmental stage. The defining task of adolescence is to find one's way across a great divide, leaving behind the world of childhood, with little assurance of what awaits us on the other side or if we will make it across in one piece. It is at this very point, when the world feels frighteningly unknowable and unpredictable, that an adolescent most needs people to depend on for protection and guidance. This is just the role that a parent, a sibling, or a close friend can play in the life of an adolescent, and it is this loss of reassuring connection that many adolescents describe when asked about how they have been affected by their loss (Christ, Siegel, & Christ, 2002).

RATIONALES FOR INTERVENTION

What We Have Learned About How Adolescents Adapt to Loss

The focus on research-based practice or research-informed practice is relatively new in the field of bereavement counseling, and certainly among clinicians, research is still only a small part of what informs their practice (Sandler et al., 2003). Much of what clinicians bring to their work with bereaved adolescents is based on experience, instincts, and common sense. Isolation hurts; support helps. Emotionally absent or critical parenting hurts; attentive, empathic parenting helps. Clinicians hold these beliefs to be self-evident. Research can challenge or provide support for these assumptions, but more importantly, it can suggest directions for the development of interventions that strengthen bereaved adolescents' capacities for healing from loss and mediate the negative effect of factors that get in the way of their healing.

Previously, Valentine (1996) reported on findings from studies of adolescent loss indicating that adjustment is mediated by three kinds of protective factors: family environment, support networks, and personality characteristics. Studies since that time have provided additional evidence of the value of protective factors and of potential complications when these factors are absent or compromised. While most of the research available 10 years ago related to the loss of a parent, more studies have been conducted since that time concerning the loss of siblings and friends. It is also important to note that factors are interrelated (Christ, 2000; Hogan & DeSantis, 1996a, 1996b). With respect to family environment, a consistent finding concerning the loss of a parent is the importance of the surviving parent's well-being and the quality of this parent's relationship with the child or adolescent (Horsley & Patterson, 2006). Key to this relationship is the balance the parent is able to strike between setting limits and allowing the adolescent age-appropriate autonomy. In her study of the impact of a parent's death from cancer, Christ (2000) found that "setting appropriate limits, appreciating and fostering the child's skills and abilities" (p. 187), and providing both nurture and encouragement of the adolescent's independence, were parenting factors that were associated with better outcomes in younger adolescents. By contrast, in those families where the surviving parent had difficulty tolerating young adolescents' "coexistent needs for dependence and independence" (Christ, 2000, p. 189), there was considerably more conflict and deterioration of the relationship between parent and adolescent, with negative impact on the adjustment to loss.

Summarizing research on adolescent response to the loss of a sibling, Horsley and Patterson (2006) note that family communication is crucial to the adjustment of surviving siblings, who "often feel overlooked and consequently alone in their grief" (p. 121). Open communication and support provide the adolescent with an environment in which "a normal course of adolescent development can resume" (p. 121). Conversely, these authors report, researchers have found that adolescents who do not have the opportunity to talk about a death can struggle for years to come to terms with their loss. In addition to allowing for emotional expression, families with open communication are also better equipped to address adolescents' questions about the circumstances of a death or the nature of the illness. For example, in a family where questions are allowed, an adolescent might express anxiety about his or her own risk of cancer.

Hogan and DeSantis (1996a) were among the first to investigate factors that help or hinder adolescents' ability to cope with the death of a sibling. Positive adjustment was associated with an ability to overcome feelings of helplessness, to feel hopeful rather than hopeless about the future, and to find meaning in a sibling's death. These characteristics in turn were stronger among adolescents who engaged in activities that "increased their sense of resiliency and ability to effect and to anticipate events associated with sibling death" (Hogan & DeSantis, 1996a, p. 184). Adjustment was more difficult for adolescents who felt overwhelmed by the finality and irrevocability of the death, which "increased their sense of vulnerability and exacerbated their grief" (Hogan & DeSantis, 1996a, p. 184). Finally, Hogan and DeSantis (1996b) suggest that an adolescent's capacity to harness feelings of hopefulness and mastery following a sibling's death is positively associated with his or her ability to maintain a continuing bond with a deceased brother or sister. In these authors' view, "ongoing attachment . . . is the silent variable" that allows loss to be an opportunity for personal growth and enables grieving adolescents to become resilient survivors (p. 251). Others have expanded on the importance of continuing bonds in adolescent bereavement and the implications of this finding for practice (DeVita-Raeburn, 2004; Packman, Horsley, Davies, & Kramer, 2006).

Evidence of the Impact of Bereavement Therapy

Does offering support through either individual therapy or groups help or hinder the healing process? Controversy over this question was sparked by an article by Neimeyer (2000), which included a summary of a doctoral dissertation (Fortner, 1999) indicating that bereavement counseling may in fact be harmful. Subsequent analysis demonstrated that the methods and conclusions of this dissertation were flawed (ADEC, 2007). In a continuing effort to resolve this issue, Larson and Hoyt (2007) reviewed more than 50 studies in this field and concluded that there are adequate data to affirm the value of interventions for the bereaved.

A meta-analysis conducted by Hoag and Burlingame (1997) provided support for the use of group therapy with children and adolescents. The authors looked at 56 studies conducted over 23 years and including a variety of group therapies with subjects aged 4 through 18. Results indicated that "group treatment was significantly more effective for children than wait-list and placebo control groups" (Hoag & Burlingame, 1997, p. 234). Further substantiation comes from adolescents' evaluation of their experience in groups. Over 2 years, 142 adolescents in support groups were asked to rate their experience in support groups, and 85% rated it as very to extremely positive/helpful (Author's files, the Den for Grieving Kids, 2006/2007).

While research and clinical anecdotal materials offer support for the value of individual and group interventions for bereaved teens, questions regarding who benefits and to what extent remain. Forte, Hill, Pazder, and Feudtner (2004) reviewed 74 studies and found that except for the value of antidepressant medication, there was no clear evidence for the efficacy of bereavement services for adults and children. A similar conclusion was reached by Currier, Holland, and Neimeyer (2007) who conducted a meta-analysis of 13 studies of grief interventions with children. However, the authors note that interventions provided "in a time sensitive manner and those that implemented specific selection criteria produced better outcomes than investigations that did not attend to these factors" (p. 253). We hope that continuing investigation will shed further light on these questions and give direction to the development of interventions for bereaved adolescents.

THE TREATMENT PROCESS: USING WHAT WE HAVE LEARNED

Goals of Treatment: Uncomplicated Mourning

At its most basic, bereavement counseling with normal grief begins with an understanding of the loss and the implications of the loss; proceeds with a process in which the bereaved moves toward integrating the reality of the loss and adjusting emotionally and behaviorally; and ends (to the extent that it ever ends) with an increasing involvement with and commitment to new people and new experiences, while retaining an ongoing connection to the person who has died (Balk, 2004).

For an adolescent, the trajectory of grief recovery is mediated by the maturation of emotional and intellectual capacity. The ability to think abstractly, to project into the future, and to think beyond the boundaries of self all contribute to the complexity of the individual's response to loss. With maturity comes a deeper understanding of death and with it the potential for a deeper appreciation of love and connection as precious and tenuous elements of human existence.

Of course, intellectual and emotional development do not occur in tandem. It is often the case that younger adolescents in particular understand intellectually realities that they cannot integrate emotionally. The life-threatening illness and death of a sibling, or the sudden death of a parent, are events that create a sense of unreality and a loss of balance in people of all ages and levels of experience. It is no surprise to find that at a time of life when one's emotional muscle is still in the process of developing, the weight of grief can be too much to bear. The consequences of this overtaxing of the adolescent's ability to cope emotionally may be seen in a variety of acting-out behaviors, the most common of which include risk taking, sexual activity, and substance abuse. Sadness and anger erupt unpredictably and with propulsive force, and adolescents are incapable of explaining to those around them what they are feeling, why they are feeling it, and what others can do to help.

If grieving adults typically arrive for treatment knowing that they need help and having some sense of what kind of help they need, the same cannot be said for adolescents. The first goal of treatment with adolescents must realistically be to engage the client and to develop a rapport, while recognizing that there may be deep ambivalence about participating in treatment. Trust is not automatic. It must be earned, and an important part of earning it is establishing upfront our willingness to listen, not to assume that we know what the client needs.

Emotional Expression: Accessing and Expressing Feelings About the Loss

While some bereaved adolescents enter the clinician's office with a sense of relief about being able to let their feelings out, many are reluctant to talk about their grief or to show strong emotions. ("If I talk about this I'll start to cry, and I don't want to cry.") The goal of therapy in this regard is not to push the adolescent to express feelings about the loss, but to offer a place where it is safe to do so.

The opportunity bereavement counseling offers to talk about feelings can be especially important given the developmental imperatives of adolescence—the need to detach from parents and to identify with peers. A young woman who does not want to burden her father with her grief, and who is reluctant to be "depressing" around her friends, may find that talking with a counselor relieves at least some of her feelings of unreality about the loss or isolation from those around her. In the safety of the therapist's office (individually or in a group with other bereaved adolescents), feelings can be expressed and questions can be posed that are not acceptable anywhere else in the adolescent's world.

Restoring Meaning: Making Sense of the Loss

The importance of meaning making as an element of adaptation to loss has been elaborated by Nadeau (1998) and Neimeyer (2001). Questions typically on the minds of adolescent clients include the following: Why did this happen? What is life going to be like now? What is the meaning of the loss/how do I make it meaningful? How do I keep the person in my life but make room for new relationships and experiences?

Why did this happen—to my parent, to my family, to *me?* Presented as a question, this is at the same time a statement, a declaration of disbelief, refusal, outrage. The unfairness of losing a loved one is something people of all ages feel, but the timing of some losses increases their sting. Adolescence is not supposed to be about death: It is supposed to be about life. A parent, sibling, or friend is supposed to be there, sharing the adventure and providing support in the rough times. For a bereaved adolescent, the sense of having been chosen arbitrarily to endure the death of a loved one is intensified because the occurrence of loss is so infrequent this early in life. As often happens when people can't understand why something has happened to them, adolescents may look for explanation in their own behavior, their own failure to protect, to care for, to love. One of the goals of therapy is to bring these beliefs to light and help clients consider alternative explanations that do not place the blame for the death on their shoulders.

Concerns about how their life will be impacted by the loss arise before or soon after it occurs, and these concerns persist. The clinician can encourage the adolescent client to express these concerns and can initiate discussion about what can be done on a practical level to maintain as much as possible the client's involvement with activities and friends. Other family members can be brought into this discussion as needed to help them understand the adolescent's concerns and to enlist their cooperation, to the extent they are able to provide it.

Restoring Control: From Powerlessness to Mastery

The transition from childhood to adulthood involves an increasing appreciation of one's ability to influence the direction of one's life, to anticipate an outcome and work toward its realization. Like so much else in the young person's emerging sense of self, this feeling of personal empowerment is just beginning to develop, and it can be shattered by loss. For this reason, restoring a sense of control—or restoring at the very least the individual's confidence that some degree of control is possible—is particularly important in working with adolescent clients.

Goals of Treatment: Complicated Mourning

As noted earlier, within the field of bereavement work an increasing emphasis on the demarcation of grief in an extreme or extended form has influenced the evolution of approaches to treatment. Three types of obstacles to normal grieving that arise in many cases of complicated bereavement have been identified, and caregivers need to be aware of their potential impact when working with bereaved adolescents.

Addressing Relational Conflict

Intimate human relationships are seldom without some elements of ambivalence, and this is certainly true of relationships between adolescents and their family and friends. With age and wisdom, we may come to understand that even if the people we love are not perfect, we can still love them. Conflicts that loom large when we are teenagers resolve when we become adults, and under the most fortunate of circumstances we have a chance at resolution and healing. But when a loved one dies during adolescence, this opportunity evaporates, often leaving behind regret, guilt, anger.

Addressing Relational Abuse

The intensity of these feelings will be that much greater if the relationship was not only conflictual, but abusive. A child who grows up with an abusive parent or sibling will be left, in the event of that individual's death, with a mixture of feelings that can be very difficult to acknowledge and even harder to live with. If the abuse was not generally known, there may be pressure to grieve for someone whose death is a relief, whose memory the adolescent is unwilling to honor. Like many victims of abuse, a bereaved adolescent may harbor feelings of responsibility for the abuse. These feelings can alternate with grief and rage, making it impossible for the adolescent to find an emotional balance point.

Addressing Trauma in the Mode of Death

There is also ample evidence that trauma relating to the manner of death creates special difficulties for recovery from bereavement, and this must be addressed in considering treatment goals. Trauma can refer not only to sudden, violent death, but also to death following a long debilitating illness. Where trauma compounds grief, sadness and loss are often accompanied by symptoms such as intrusive thoughts, anxiety attacks, nightmares, and other troubling reminders of the death. If an adolescent witnessed the death or feels any sense of responsibility for the events which caused it, the resulting guilt may be so intense as to lead to thoughts of suicide (Cohen, Mannarino, & Deblinger, 2006). All of these thoughts and feelings are likely to increase an adolescent's sense of being different from his or her peers, of having been damaged by the death. If not addressed, the effects of trauma may compromise an adolescent's development and adjustment to the loss.

A young person who has been a caregiver to an ill parent who dies is likely to feel many conflicting emotions: a sense of personal failure and guilt about not having been able to save the parent, a feeling of relief that must mean they are "bad", anger about the death, and resentment toward the surviving parent. An adolescent's feelings of resentment and anger are likely to be compounded if, in the wake of the death, he or she is faced with additional responsibilities within the family.

TREATMENT APPROACHES

Individual Treatment

In this section, we suggest approaches to individual treatment with bereaved adolescents that take into account the developmental needs of adolescents, treatment rationales, and treatment goals that we have summarized thus far. How do we put what we have learned from research into practice with bereaved adolescents?

Studies of adolescent coping in response to the death of a loved one and other major stressors have identified the importance of family environment, support networks, and personality characteristics (Balk & Corr, 2001; Lin, Sandler, Ayers, Wolchik, & Leucken, 2004; Valentine, 1996). Summarizing the clinical implications of these studies, Valentine suggests that professional interventions with adolescents who are coping with death focus on "building better relationships with parents, siblings and other extended family, and in building a better external support system in the community" (p. 328). Also, professionals can help their adolescent clients to develop "individual coping styles, social skills, communication and cognitive skills, self esteem, self confidence and autonomy. In so doing, the adolescent can develop a sense of control at a time when he or she might be feeling helpless and lost" (p. 328).

A major shift in our understanding of what it means to heal from grief—the identification of continuing bonds with deceased loved ones—has led to further elaboration of best practice with bereaved adolescents. Based on their findings concerning the importance of continuing bonds in adolescents coping with sibling loss, Packman and colleagues (2006) suggested that a key role for professionals is to help parents encourage activities that facilitate the maintenance of these bonds.

Many adolescent clients find that writing about their loved one and recording memories in a journal helps them maintain a sense of connection and lessens their anxiety about forgetting the person and the life they shared. Adolescents often gravitate toward music that expresses their feelings, and they may respond positively to the invitation to bring in music that has meaning for them as they come to terms with their loss (Pipher, 1996). Along with discussing the adolescent's own experience, it can be useful to bring into the discussion the experiences of others as represented in literature and film (DeVita-Raeburn, 2004).

Christ and colleagues (2002) note that younger adolescents may be reluctant to talk about a parent's illness, but at the same time, may have mistaken ideas and fears concerning the cause of their parent's death. Often simply asking, "Is there anything about your mother's death you wonder about?" allows an adolescent to express these thoughts and fears, including the fear of their own genetic predisposition to illness.

Directed questioning can also help an adolescent to identify the "cognitive legacy" left to them by the person who has died (Valentine,

1996). For example, a young person can be asked: How are you like your mother (or father or brother)? What do you like to do that your mother taught you to do? What was your father like as a parent? What do you imagine telling your own children about their grandmother or grandfather? Such questions clarify and strengthen the bereaved adolescent's sense of ongoing connection to the person who has died.

Later, questions about the meaning of the loss can be raised, though it is often the client who initiates such observations about how he or she imagines the loss will affect the course of his or her life. People young and old express sadness and longing but also reflect on how the experience of losing a loved one has deepened their understanding of life and their ability to feel compassion for others (Valentine, 1996).

Designing Interventions for Adolescents With Complicated Bereavement

In this section, we suggest additional techniques that have been useful in working individually with adolescents whose grief is complicated by relationship factors or by the circumstances of the death as described above. The overall goal of these techniques, as Rando (1993) has observed, is to uncomplicate the mourning—not to "cure" the grief but to set the individual on a course of healing that is not unduly compromised by factors secondary to the loss itself.

Cohen, Mannarino, and Deblinger (2006) use the term *childhood traumatic grief (CTG)* to refer to a condition in which "both unresolved grief and post traumatic stress disorder (PTSD) symptoms are present, often accompanied by depressive symptoms as well" (p. 17). This constellation of symptoms has been described elsewhere under the diagnostic heading of "complicated grief" or "traumatic grief" (Prigerson et al., 1999). Adolescents with CTG have become "'stuck' on the traumatic circumstances of the death and *cannot fully grieve the death of the loved one*" (emphasis added; Cohen et al., 2006, p. 19). It is important to note that according to these authors, the critical factor in diagnosing CTG is not the circumstances of the death, but how they affect the individual. For example, in a child or adolescent with CTG, memories of the horrible manner in which the person died interfere with access to positive memories of the deceased. The survivor avoids thinking about the person because even positive memories "segue into traumatic reminders of the death" (Cohen et al., 2006, p. 18).

The research-supported treatment model that Cohen and colleagues (2006) have developed for these children and adolescents is Trauma Focused Cognitive Behavioral Therapy (TF-CBT). The authors describe TF-CBT as a *skills and strength-based model* that begins with *psychoeducation* of the client and parents regarding the nature and impact of trauma and continues with instruction in *relaxation* techniques (focused breathing and meditation) and *affective expression and modulation* (encouraging the client to experience and express emotions and to manage difficult affective states). The next phase of treatment, construction of a *trauma narrative,* is meant to provide for gradual desensitization of the emotionally charged content that causes the client to continually reexperience the traumatic events. This is both the most difficult, and according to the authors, ultimately the most helpful phase of treatment for many adolescents. Much more than simple storytelling, the process of narrative construction provides an opportunity for a survivor to *reconstruct* the story of what happened, incorporating information that they did not have at the time and correcting cognitive misperceptions that can lead to inappropriate feelings of guilt, responsibility, and anxiety.

In some situations, the lack of information about the actual circumstances of a loved one's death may lead an adolescent to imagine horrible scenes of a loved one's suffering or disfigurement. This was the case with one young woman we worked with whose father committed suicide. Her mother was reluctant to discuss the manner of death, a gunshot to the stomach. The girl was under the mistaken impression that her father had shot himself in the head and imagined his head being blown apart. Identifying and correcting such inaccurate cognitions is part of what the authors describe as "processing the traumatic experience" (Cohen et al., 2006, p. 142). Once these distortions are identified, cognitive processing techniques are used to correct them and to reinforce more accurate and constructive thoughts.

The protocol developed by Cohen and colleagues incorporates a number of elements that we have found to be clinically useful in working with bereaved adolescents when grief is complicated by trauma. The following case examples illustrate the importance of psychoeducation, instruction in self-soothing and emotion regulation, and processing of a trauma narrative.

When an adolescent is present when a loved one dies, the likelihood is great that he or she will be troubled by images of the death and thoughts about the loved one's suffering and death. As discussed elsewhere (Kosminsky, 2007), it may be necessary to address the traumatic components of a person's experience of death before doing other work relating to the loss. In other words, feelings about how the person died can be so upsetting that they overwhelm the individual's grief and produce an enveloping sense of confusion. People who experience traumatic loss describe being "blown apart" or "shattered" by the combination of terror and lack of control that characterize response to trauma. Some degree of coherence in the individual's sense of self must be restored before such persons can proceed to the work of confronting and grieving their loss. One approach to consider is Eye Movement Desensitization and Reprocessing (EMDR) (Shapiro, 2001).

Developed by Francine Shapiro in the 1980s, EMDR has been used effectively to treat clients with trauma for the past 20 years, although some continue to question why it works and whether the unique components of the technique represent a significant departure from or improvement over other methods (Shapiro, 2001). EMDR combines elements of cognitive-behavioral therapy with some form of visual, tactile, or auditory bilateral stimulation, for example, an oscillating light beam that the client visually tracks while holding his head still, so that only his eyes move back and forth. We have found EMDR to be extremely useful in providing relief for some bereaved clients (children and adults) who have symptoms of posttraumatic stress. Readers are encouraged to consult the additional references provided here (Shapiro, 2001; Tufnell, 2005) regarding EMDR, the use of which requires formal training and supervised practice. Modifications of the adult protocol for use with younger adolescents and children have been developed and used in the treatment of trauma, including traumatic loss (Tufnell, 2005).

Group Treatment Approaches

The value of group therapy approaches with adolescents makes intuitive sense given their growing reliance on peers during this period of their lives. In times of stress, they tend to turn to friends for advice, reality testing, and support. A support or therapy group meets both their developmental needs and offers special benefits related to the unique issues that adolescents struggle with when they are grieving.

The bereavement support groups we describe in this section are just that: support groups, not therapy groups. As such, they are designed to encourage participants to express and explore feelings and share memories, but not to interpret the deeper psychological meaning of participants' comments or to explore the earlier roots of present reactions.

While a mental health or nursing professional typically leads a therapy group, many support groups for children and teens are led by trained volunteers, as in the widely used Dougy Center model (Dougy Center for Grieving Children, 1999). Carefully selected volunteers are educated about the manifestations of grief, normal and complicated grief, listening skills, and group management techniques. Group activities aimed at eliciting feelings and reviving memories, and projects that develop group cohesion are typical in these groups.

Support, Role Definition, and Self-Identity Issues

As important as friends are during the adolescent years, an adolescent who is grieving may find that his or her friends are not able to provide much needed comfort and support, or that he or she does not want to depend on them in this way. The sense of being "the only one" who knows what grief feels like may create a gap too wide for even the closest friends to bridge. At the same time, family members who would otherwise be a source of support for a grieving young person, such as a surviving parent, are often deeply involved in their own struggle to come to terms with the loss. Depression, financial or legal problems, and just coping with the needs of everyday life without the person who has died distract them and decrease their availability, so that adolescents feel uncertain about where to turn.

Comments typically made by members of adolescent bereavement groups suggest that these groups can be a welcome source of support and valuable advice. As one newly bereaved teen said, "I can't talk about this stuff at home. My mom cries and my sister gets mad, so I just shut up. In the group people KNOW what it's all about." Group facilitators can promote a sense of group cohesion and mutual understanding by asking questions that help group members identify common elements in their experiences.

A death in the life of an adolescent does not necessarily result in long-term maladjustment. In fact, there are situations where spiritual growth (Leighton, 2008) and a natural resilience can obviate immediate and long-term negative outcomes (Christ, 2000). We also know that support is one of the vital elements in ensuring a constructive adjustment to the changes that death brings to a young person's life; where this may be lacking or depleted in their lives, a group of peers can help fill that vacuum.

Isolation

The feeling that "I'm having to go this alone" is pervasive among bereaved teens, and not without reason. Unlike, for example, a teen whose parents have been divorced, teens experiencing bereavement are not likely to find among their friends and classmates a natural cohort of peers who have had a similar experience. Sibling bereavement is an even rarer phenomenon than the loss of a parent, and therefore particularly challenging and isolating for an adolescent (Worden, Davies, & McCown, 1999).

For this reason, groups meet a very real need in helping bereaved teens know that they are not alone in their struggles. It is impressive to observe the response of teens when they first enter a bereavement support group and see 5 to 10 peers in the room. A sense of relief at not being alone is often the first benefit that they report. In one high school group, a girl who had been referred because of her increased withdrawal and negativism following the death of her primary caregiver, her grandmother, was surprised on her first visit to the group to see that there were about 10 other students. She said, "That tells me that I am not the only one dealing with the feelings and thoughts that I have, and it's a place where I can feel comfortable."

In the safety of the group, bereaved teens find much in common. There is a wide range of feelings that are less socially acceptable than others and so often not easily expressed in everyday life: Anger; fury at being abandoned; relief that the person has died; belief that the teen him- or herself was neglectful and may have caused the death; secrets like talking to the deceased, his or her abuse of alcohol or drugs, or other illicit behaviors; or even the content of dreams may not be safely expressed outside of the circle of other bereaved teens. But within the group, these reactions are received as familiar and shared experiences.

Normalization

The normalization of grief is one of the major advantages of groups. Being with others who are dealing with the loss of loved ones, adolescents are able to recognize that their reactions to death are not strange or unhealthy. At the same time, they are able to identify aspects of their relationship and their loss that make it unique. Decreased isolation also promotes emotional healing by helping adolescents gain access to feelings that have been repressed or denied. Hearing others express openly feelings that might seem shameful or wrong can trigger access to these feelings, making it possible to express them, address the related issues, and so reduce their potency. Adolescents realize that they will not be ostracized or criticized for expressing their feelings. Group members can often stimulate a conversation that, in a safe nonjudgmental atmosphere, can enable someone to express their own shameful secrets, as a group member so explicitly explained in talking about why she comes to her group: "It helps you to feel good about your lost one instead of thinking bad, or that it's your fault."

Another area where a group's reflection of the "normal" is invaluable is related to new roles that may be assumed or placed upon an adolescent when the death of a significant family member results in shifting roles within the family. Adolescents need clarification of reasonable role expectations, especially at a time when a death may have placed upon them what seem wholly unreasonable expectations, such as "you have to be the man of the family now." Other adolescents can be remarkably perceptive when it comes to sniffing out and debunking the unrealistic roles into which others may have cast them. This process of reality testing within the group can give members the confidence to decide for themselves what roles they are or are not willing to accept. The group can play a crucial role in reflecting to an adolescent what are and are not normal and reasonable role expectations, helping to keep a balanced view of self at a time when the developing self is so vulnerable.

Finally, it is important to recognize the impact not only of who died, but also how they died. Homicide and suicide are particularly problematic. Violent death, especially when gang related, complicates group dynamics. Fear, shame, and split loyalty, particularly where there is conflict between law enforcement and the teens in the community, creates difficult issues for adolescent mourners and facilitators alike. One out of four gang members die within 4 years of joining a gang, and in some low-income housing projects, belonging to a gang is the only way to survive the street life that is the norm for many teens (Venkatesh, 2008). Homicides are the second leading cause of death for teens, and the main cause of death for African American males in the United States, with a rate almost six times higher than that of White males. The phenomenon is no longer limited to inner cities. Service providers must recognize the reality that violence is a significant part of many adolescents' lives, one that raises complex issues that can significantly complicate efforts to support grieving adolescents.

Overall, there is ample research to uphold the clinical impression that youngsters who are provided help, either through individual or group work, have better clinical outcomes than those who do not. These findings aside, clinical experience shows that adolescents who receive help can find companionship where there might have been isolation, clarity where there might have been confusion and guilt, and normality at a time when the world seems upside down. Perhaps most important of all for adolescents, for whom being like others of their age is so important, is that "we get to share our feelings with people like us."

CONCLUDING COMMENTS

Our purpose in this chapter has been to highlight what we know about how adolescents experience loss, what we know about factors that help or inhibit an adolescent's incorporation of the experience of loss into his or her identity in a way that allows for continued growth and involvement with life, and how to apply this knowledge in counseling bereaved adolescents. Research in the field of bereavement, and our own experience working with adolescents individually and in groups, provides ample support for the value of intervention, particularly with adolescents who have experienced a traumatic loss.

Certainly, much remains to be learned about how adolescents grieve and how to support their healing (Currier et al., 2007). Yet, we know enough about adolescence, about mourning, and about emotional recovery to provide meaningful support for bereaved adolescents and to prepare them for the losses they are likely to face in the future. As adults who have had our own significant losses, we can offer hope to bereaved adolescents and help them imagine a meaningful future. While each of us must find our own way out of the painful place we enter when a loved one dies, we can, along with parents, teachers, and other adults who touch the lives of bereaved adolescents, offer a guiding hand, an open heart, and the reassurance that comes from our simply being present.

REFERENCES

Association for Death Education and Counseling (ADEC). (2007). *Grief counseling helpful or harmful? A new examination of the evidence.* Retrieved June 3, 2008, from http://www.adec.org/documents/Grief_Counseling_Helpful_or_harmful.pdf

Balk, D. E. (2004). Recovery following bereavement: An examination of the concept. *Death Studies, 28,* 361–374.

Balk, D. E., & Corr, C. A. (2001). Bereavement during adolescence: A review of research. In M. S. Stroebe, R. O. Hansson, W. Stroebe, & H. Schut (Eds.), *Handbook of bereavement research* (pp. 199–218). Washington, DC: American Psychological Association.

Christ, G. (2000). *Healing children's grief.* New York: Oxford University Press.

Christ, G., Siegel, K., & Christ, A. (2002). Adolescent grief: "It never really hit me . . . until it actually happened. *Journal of the American Medical Association, 288,* 1269–1278.

Cohen, J. A., Mannarino, J. R., Deblinger, E. (2006). *Treating trauma and traumatic grief in children and adolescents.* New York: Guilford.

Currier, J. M., Holland, J. M., & Neimeyer, R. A. (2007). The effectiveness of bereavement interventions with children: A meta-analytic review of outcome research. *Journal of Clinical and Adolescent Psychology, 36*(2), 253–259.

DeVita-Raeburn, E. (2004). *The empty room: Surviving the loss of a brother or sister at any age.* New York: Scribners.

Dougy Center for Grieving Children (1999). *Helping teens cope with death.* Portland, OR: The Dougy Center.

Forte, A. L., Hill, M., Pazder, R., & Feudtner, C. (2004, July 26). Bereavement care interventions: A systematic review. *BMC Palliative Care, 3,* 3. Retrieved June 19, 2008, from http://www.biomedcentral.com

Fortner, B. V. (1999). *The effectiveness of grief counseling and therapy: A quantitative review.* Unpublished dissertation, University of Memphis, TN.

Hoag, M. J., & Burlingame, G. M. (1997). Evaluating the effectiveness of child and adolescent group treatment: A meta analysis. *Journal of Clinical Child Psychology, 26,* 234–246.

Hogan, N. S., & DeSantis, L. (1996a). Adolescent sibling bereavement: Toward a new theory. In C. A. Corr & D. E. Balk (Eds.), *Handbook of adolescent death and bereavement* (pp. 173–195). New York: Springer Publishing.

Hogan, N. S., & DeSantis, L. (1996b). Basic constructs of a theory of adolescent sibling bereavement. In D. Klass, P. R. Silverman, & S. L. Nickman (Eds.), *Continuing bonds: New understandings of grief* (pp. 235–254). Washington, DC: Taylor & Francis.

Horsley, H., & Patterson, T. (2006). The effects of a parent guidance intervention on communication among adolescents who have experienced the sudden death of a sibling. *American Journal of Family Therapy, 34*(2), 119–137.

Kosminsky, P. (2007). *Getting back to life when grief won't heal.* New York: McGraw-Hill.

Larson, D. G., & Hoyt, W. (2007). What has become of grief counseling? An evaluation of the empirical foundations of the new pessimism. *Professional Psychology: Research and Practice, 38,* 347–355.

Leighton, S. (2008). Bereavement therapy with adolescents: Facilitating a process of spiritual growth. *Journal of Child and Adolescent Psychiatric Nursing, 21*(1), 24–34.

Lin, K., Sandler, I., Ayers, T. S. Wolchik, S., & Luecken, L.(2004). Resilience in parentally bereaved children and adolescents seeking preventive services. *Journal of Clinical Child and Adolescent Psychology, 33,* 673–683.

Nadeau, J. (1998). *Families making sense of death.* Thousand Oaks, CA: Sage.

Neimeyer, R. A. (2000). Searching for the meaning of meaning: Grief therapy and the process of reconstruction. *Death Studies, 24,* 541–558.

Neimeyer, R. A. (Ed.). (2001). *Meaning reconstruction and the experience of loss.* Washington, DC: American Psychological Association.

Packman, W., Horsley, H., Davies, B., & Kramer, R. (2006). Sibling bereavement and continuing bonds. *Death Studies, 30,* 817–841.

Pipher, M. (1996). *Reviving Ophelia: Saving the selves of adolescent girls.* New York: Berkley Publishing Co.

Prigerson, H. G, Shear, M. K., & Jacobs, S., Reynolds, C.F., Maciejewski, P.K., & Davidson, J.R. (1999). Consensus criteria for traumatic grief: A preliminary empirical test. *British Journal of Psychiatry, 174,* 67–73.

Rando, T. A. (1993). *Treatment of complicated mourning.* Champaign, IL: Research Press.

Sandler, I. N., Ayers, T. S., Wolchik, S. A., Tein, J-Y., Kwok, O-M., Haine, R. A., et al. (2003). The Family Bereavement Program: Efficacy evaluation of a theory-based prevention program for parentally-bereaved children and adolescents. *Journal of Consulting and Clinical Psychology, 71,* 587–600.

Shapiro, F. (2001). *Eye Movement Desensitization and Reprocessing: Basic principles, protocols and procedures.* New York: Guilford.

Tufnell, G. (2005). Eye Movement Desensitization and Reprocessing in the treatment of pre-adolescent children with post-traumatic symptoms. *Clinical Child Psychology and Psychiatry, 10,* 587–600.

Valentine, L. (1996). Professional interventions to assist adolescents who are coping with death and bereavement. In C. A. Corr & D. E. Balk (Eds.), *Handbook of adolescent death and bereavement* (pp. 312–328). New York: Springer Publishing.

Venkatesh, S. (2008). *Gang leader for a day: A rogue sociologist takes to the streets.* New York: Penguin.

Worden, J. W., Davies, B., & McCown, D. (1999). Comparing parent loss with sibling loss. *Death Studies, 23,* 1–15.

19

Therapy for Adolescents Experiencing Prolonged Grief

DAVID A. CRENSHAW AND LINDA C. HILL

Charles Dickens's remarkable and memorable opening to *A Tale of Two Cities* aptly characterizes much of what occurs in the adolescent period of human development. Dickens stated, "It was the best of times, it was the worst of times, it was the age of wisdom, it was the age of foolishness, it was the epoch of belief, it was the epoch of incredulity, it was the season of Light, it was the season of darkness, it was the spring of hope, it was the winter of despair, we had everything before us, we had nothing before us" (Dickens, 1859/2003, p. 5). Adolescence is a time of polarities and superlatives, where everything makes sense and nothing makes sense; a time of omnipotence that when punctured quickly plummets into utter helplessness; a time of great hopes and dreams, and conversely, emotional crashes and desperate despair; and a time of rare opportunity; and a time when frightening hazards must be confronted. Adolescents cognitively grasp the realities of death better than younger children but emotionally are particularly vulnerable for that same reason. Timing also bears heavily on adolescents: If confrontation with death of someone close occurs at just the point when they are moving autonomously in the direction of claiming a life of their own, it can be devastating—like pulling the emotional floor right out from under them (Crenshaw, 2002a).

ATTRIBUTIONS AND MEANINGS FOR ADOLESCENTS

McCarthy (2007; see also chapter 2 in this book) observed that significant bereavement is reported by the majority of young people in contemporary Western societies. According to studies examining the prevalence of adolescent grief, at least 90% of teens have directly experienced a loss associated with death (Ewalt & Perkins, 1979; Harrison & Harrington, 2001). Yet, as McCarthy points out, youth bereavement has garnered little attention from mainstream services or academics. She noted that this marginality is paralleled in young people's everyday bereavement experiences. McCarthy argued that there has been an overemphasis in academic and professional circles on cognitive understandings of death and individual intrapsychic processes and responses to relevant development tasks. What has been neglected in her view is the key feature of youths' experiences of bereavement, their relative powerlessness, rather than any specific features of cognitive or affective responses. In addition, McCarthy advocated for more attention to the meanings that youths attribute to their experiences and the relation of these attributions to risk for negative outcomes associated with bereavement. McCarthy presented case studies that illustrated how young people are active agents in their family peer group contexts and that bereavement needs to be viewed in a relational context.

Consistent with the recommendations of McCarthy that the meanings and attributions of bereaved youths need to be carefully attended to, research has indicated that grief intensity is related to perceived emotional closeness to the deceased person (Servaty-Seib & Pistole, 2006). Adolescents may well experience more intense grief over the death of a friend than a grandparent, but this cannot be assumed to be the case; rather, it needs to be explored with each unique adolescent in terms of the meaning and impact for that individual.

TRAUMATIC AND/OR STIGMATIZED DEATHS

The attributions and meanings assigned to a death by an adolescent take on renewed significance if the death is either traumatic or evokes meaning that is stigmatizing. A significant factor in recovering from a traumatic loss is the ability to place the experience with the death of someone emotionally close in a meaningful context, to be able to develop a cohesive and coherent narrative related to such an otherwise emotionally devastating experience (Crenshaw, 2006, 2007; Siegel, 1999).

Studies of major natural disasters validate the importance of well-timed treatment to avoid long-term mental health problems among adolescents. Following the catastrophic earthquakes in Armenia in 1988, untreated adolescents as well as a group who received trauma-focused group and individual psychotherapy were followed over a 5-year period (Goenjian et al., 2005). Although the intervention period was relatively brief, 6 weeks of treatment given 1.5 years after the disaster, the results indicated that the brief trauma/traumatic grief–focused psychotherapy was effective in reducing PTSD symptoms and depression in relation to the untreated adolescents. The authors recommended the implementation of mental health intervention programs in schools after disasters to reduce trauma-related psychopathology. Most trauma/traumatic grief protocols place emphasis on exploring meaning and perspective while creating trauma narratives (Cohen, Mannarino, & Deblinger, 2006).

Stigma-related deaths such as parental death due to HIV or suicide can pose special problems for adolescents since peer acceptance and the wish to be perceived as no different from others are powerful drivers of adolescent behavior. In a study of the impact of parental death because of HIV on 414 adolescents studied over a 6-year period, it was found that bereaved adolescents had significantly more emotional distress, negative life events, and contact with the criminal justice system than nonbereaved teens (Rotheram-Borus, Weiss, Alber, & Lester, 2005). Depressive symptoms following the death increased in bereaved adolescents, although 1 year later the symptoms of depression were no greater than the nonbereaved group. An interesting finding in this study was that sexual risk behaviors increased following the death for bereaved adolescents. Becoming sexually active may represent an attempt to ease the loneliness they feel during their time of grieving, since young people because of their relative emotional immaturity are particularly predisposed toward acting out their feelings physically (Noel & Blair, 2003). Based on these findings, the investigators recommended early intervention after the HIV diagnosis is made, counseling services prior to the death, and follow-up over time.

These stigma-related deaths call for special attention to the meaning and attributions made by adolescents in order to help them create a coherent, meaningful perspective and narrative, thus reducing the risk of traumatization (Crenshaw, 2007). There is the risk that the stigma, secrecy, and shame associated with the death will lead to disenfranchised grief (Crenshaw, 2002b; Doka, 1989, 2002), depriving adolescent grievers of the support and facilitation of their grief from the surrounding community and removing any sanction for their grief.

CURRENT STATE OF RESEARCH AND KNOWLEDGE BASE

The field is in need of greatly expanded research into the impact of the deaths of those emotionally close to adolescents, especially traumatic deaths. One review of the current state of research (Caffo, Forresi, & Lievers, 2005) noted that while there is a wide range of studies indicating that traumatized children and adolescents are at high risk for developing a variety of behavioral, psychological, and even neurological problems, these studies are beset by numerous methodological difficulties. These limitations include questions regarding the validity of current criteria for PTSD and comorbidity with conditions such as anxiety and depressive disorders. In addition, these authors pointed out that the studies are often retrospective, use self-report questionnaires, and have limited generalizability. Some studies have considered issues of vulnerability and the role of protective factors, including gender effects and social support, while others do not take the hardiness or resilience of the individual into account.

While it is unlikely that any researcher or clinician in the bereavement field would dispute the need for more carefully designed and controlled studies, it is not clear that the current status of research is as weak as asserted. Further, the critical importance of the issue of meaning for adolescents has not gone unnoticed in the field (Cohen & Mannarino, 2004; Cohen, Mannarino, & Deblinger, 2006; Crenshaw, 2002a, 2007; Davis, Wortman, Lehman, & Silver, 2000; Neimeyer, 2000; Siegel, 1999). Renewed interest in creating meaning, perspective, and coherence stems from the synthesis of attachment theory and neurobiological interpersonal research from the Center for Culture, Brain, and Development at UCLA (Siegel, 1999, 2007). Siegel explained (1999; Siegel & Hartzell, 2003) that attachment theory research has found that adults who have unresolved trauma and grief are more likely to raise children who are not securely attached. In order to resolve early trauma, it is necessary to create a meaningful perspective, a coherent and cohesive narrative of the trauma events or unresolved grief. Thus, finding and creating meaning plays a pivotal role in this critical therapeutic task that affects the health and well-being of future generations.

A promising development in the field is the work of Cohen, Mannarino, and Deblinger (2006) who developed an empirically tested Childhood Traumatic Grief (CTG) protocol that addresses both grief and trauma features and can be used with children and adolescents. Cohen and Mannarino (2004) defined CTG as a condition in which trauma symptoms interfere with the child's ability to negotiate the normal grieving process. The original protocol was designed for a relatively short intervention of 16 sessions that included individual, group, and parent–child therapy components. Recently, an abbreviated 12-session protocol of cognitive-behavioral treatment (CBT) for CTG was introduced and pilot-tested (Cohen, Mannarino, & Staron, 2006).

The program was tested on children 6–17 years of age. The results of the pilot study indicated that children reported significant improvement in CTG, PTSD, depression, and anxiety. Parents reported significant improvements in children's PTSD, internalizing and total behavior problems, and their personal PTSD symptoms. While PTSD significantly improved only during the trauma-focused module of treatment, CTG improved significantly during both trauma- and grief-focused modules of treatment. Furthermore, child satisfaction and parent satisfaction for this treatment protocol were high. While the investigators pointed to the need to further evaluate this CBT-CTG model in randomized, controlled treatment trials, these preliminary findings suggest that the shortened CBT-CTG protocol may be efficacious for this population.

Another hopeful example of grief work with adolescents in a population where a history of loss has often been ignored is the work of Walker and Shaffer (2007) with adolescents in the Indiana correctional system. They described a program called "Growing through Loss" that addresses the core issues of grief and loss instead of the destructive behaviors that brought these youths to the prison system. There is an educational component that teaches adolescents about the stages and manifestations of grief, as well as the opportunity to share their painful experiences with others in an accepting and nonjudgmental setting. The program reports a significant reduction in the symptoms of depression of 88% of the participants.

Anger and rage often are manifestations of unaddressed and buried grief. Because the destructive behavior is often so ugly and hideous, and by no means do the authors condone violence in any form, it often distracts those responsible for the care and containment of youths from adequately treating the core invisible wounds that ultimately lead to the destructive and sometime violent acts. The work of Walker and Shaffer (2007) represents a refreshing exception to this trend.

CLINICAL IMPLICATIONS OF WORKING WITH PROLONGED GRIEF IN ADOLESCENCE

Most researchers and clinical practitioners in the bereavement field recognize that it is an oxymoron to talk about resolving the death of someone with whom one was closely attached. The best that can be realistically hoped for is to help the person reconcile to the death and to gradually resume full participation in life. The loss through death of those closest and most important to us can be considered the ultimate dilemma of human existence along with coming to terms with our own mortality. Unfortunately, the deaths of those we cherish most sometimes come when they can be least afforded: A young child losing a parent, for example, or at the other end of the life spectrum, losing a spouse when one is frail and increasingly dependent on the other. During the time of adolescence, the experience of losing a loved one is compounded by the inherent losses associated with the teenage years: loss of friends as they outgrow one another, loss of elementary school and teachers, loss of one's boyfriend or girlfriend, and loss of the comfort that is tied to dependency on parents at younger ages. These losses converge at a time when life is making extra demands (Jewett, 1982). Yet opportunities for growth are never as great as when adolescents are confronted in a dramatic way with how fragile and precious life is and how every day is a gift to be valued and treasured.

TRAUMATIC GRIEF

Prolonged grief in adolescence is likely to be related to either traumatic or complicated grief. Cohen and Mannarino (2004) defined CTG as a condition in which trauma symptoms interfere with the child's ability to negotiate the normal grieving process. Cohen and Mannarino (2004; Cohen et al., 2006) described an empirically derived treatment model for CTG that addresses both trauma and grief symptoms and includes a parental treatment component as well. An expanded model (Crenshaw, 2007) built on Cohen and Mannarino's evidence-based treatment model was designed to incorporate findings from attachment and interpersonal neurobiological research, in particular, (a) the establishment of a secure attachment within the therapeutic relationship that permits children to face and integrate emotional states that would otherwise be overwhelming and countertherapeutic; (b) honoring the timeless attachment bond between the child and deceased loved one; and (c) developing a coherent narrative, meaning, and perspective.

There are clinical hazards, however, in assuming traumatic grief. While it is often assumed that the death of a parent for preschool children will be traumatic due to the magnitude of the death, it is important to avoid a confirmation bias that leads therapists to look for signs of trauma. With such preconceived notions, signs of trauma will always be found. Rather, therapists should maintain an open mind as the meaning for each person is explored in depth. Some sudden, unexpected deaths by their nature will be assumed to be traumatic, and that may well be the case, but once again this outcome needs to be determined with an open-minded exploration with each individual. As in the case example detailed below of Majid (fictional name), when the death of a parent comes early in life, it is far from a single event. Rather, it triggers a series of life changes that in many cases is experienced as further losses. There is cumulative loss throughout the developmental years related to the sense of deprivation of a vitally needed maternal or paternal presence at the time when the need is most critical.

This wound is aggravated over and over when reminders of their devastating loss trigger an acute grieving episode. Such regrief phenomena occur especially in adolescence when young people have the cognitive and emotional resources to fully appreciate and grieve the significance of the loss. This full appreciation of the loss is a primary reason for the prolonged grief because the adolescent repeatedly experiences the need and longing for the missing parent and startling reminders that the parent is not there. This experience is often accompanied by intense anger, if not rage.

Another important clinical pitfall revolves around the issue of identity. In adolescence the forging of a sense of self, emerging autonomy, and identity is a key developmental task. When adolescents have experienced a traumatic death during the teen years or earlier in their development, a key therapeutic task is to help adolescents avoid crystallizing their identity around the traumatic experience. It is crucial to help them appreciate that they are far more than a bereaved teen, to expand and create a more complex view of themselves that includes unique abilities, talents, and personal qualities. Some of the gifts may be shared in common with their deceased parent or their surviving parent or grandparents, while some gifts will be their own unique talents and assets.

COMPLICATED GRIEF IN ADOLESCENTS

In the grief field there has been a movement toward recognition of a syndrome called complicated grief (CG). According to this view, CG is a syndrome characterized by a maladaptive symptom pattern secondary to a major loss that lasts beyond the normal grieving time. In addition, the symptoms are not fully captured by depression or PTSD, such as prolonged and intense pining and yearning for the deceased (Jacobs, Mazure, & Prigerson, 2000; Lichtenthal, Cruess, & Prigerson, 2004; Prigerson et al., 1999). Recent research has provided empirical support for the incremental validity of the concept of CG that cannot be explained by the combination of PTSD and depression alone (Bonanno et al., 2007).

Recent research has also supported CG as a valid concept in children and adolescents even after controlling for current depression, anxiety, and posttraumatic stress disorder (Melhem, Moritz, Walker, Shear, & Brent, 2007). While more research, particularly of a longitudinal type, is needed, it is likely that many adolescents suffering prolonged grief are suffering from CG.

CLINICAL CONSIDERATIONS WITH ADOLESCENT RAGE

Adolescents suffering prolonged grief often manifest rage when reminders of their devastating loss trigger a grieving episode. This rage is understandable since the major loss they have suffered so early in their lives can never be made up to them. While their anger is legitimate and needs to be validated, it also needs to be rechanneled and redirected into constructive paths, such as fueling their determination to achieve their cherished goals in life, lest the rage becomes a further depriving agent itself. In other words, if adolescents are unable to rechannel or redirect their rage, they can become stuck in a place that sets them up for more deprivation. This repetitive pattern becomes a sad cycle of cumulative loss because the adolescent may be looking for recompense for their harrowing loss—some way this devastating loss can be made up to them, when it never can.

Therapeutically it is crucial to help the teen to (a) accept that the loss can never be made up to them, (b) cancel the harrowing debt, (c) mourn the loss fully, and (d) resume full participation in life. Otherwise, there will be a never ending cycle of experiences that are not satisfying, because they are perceived as "not enough." Adolescents with prolonged grief have a burning sense of "something being owed to them." The best friendships in the world, a relationship with a romantic partner, and relationships with other family members can all be experienced as another increment of "not enough," thus further increasing the sense of deprivation and accompanying rage. This sense of deprivation is a pivotal issue in treating adolescents with prolonged grief who have not adequately reconciled to the loss of a loved one.

CLINICAL CASE EXAMPLE

A therapist first met with Majid, an Iranian-American boy, when he was 6. His mother had died of cancer about a year before. In an early session, the therapist asked Majid and his sister, who was 2 years older, to bring in albums of their favorite pictures of their mother and photos that depicted happy memories of the family together. His sister tried hard to maintain a brave front that was also typical of their mother in dealing with her terminal illness. In a subsequent session, they brought other photographs to share with the therapist that captured happy memories together with their mother. The therapist validated their love for one another so beautifully and poignantly expressed in the pictures.

In a family session that included their father, the therapist used a grief workbook that validated and normalized the range of emotions of grief that the children and their father had expressed. The therapist highlighted the happy memories and love for one another. Majid acknowledged guilt for getting angry with his mother during her long illness but added that he was able to make it up to her.

Majid at the time of this early intervention was so overwhelmed with his feelings that he was unable to go further at the time. His sister, however, was able to do a considerable amount of work in sessions arranged in intervals as needed over the next several years. His sister worked hard on her anger about losing her mother at a time so early in her life when her need for her mother was great.

Majid, however, was not seen again until middle school when he was 14. This is a good example of how work with children in grief needs to follow a developmentally sequenced path as outlined by James (1989). This consideration is particularly true in the case of traumatic grief. Research suggests that when death of a parent occurs in the lives of children preschool age or younger, "the death of a parent has such a devastating effect on the child's sense of personal safety that it is often impossible to say where grief ends and trauma begins" (Lieberman, Compton, Van Horn, & Ippen, 2003, p. 7).

As a teenager Majid now possessed the emotional and cognitive resources to undertake the grief work that he was unable to do at a younger age. Majid immediately impressed the therapist with his deep sensitivity and access to his emotions. He was able to express his sadness freely, sometimes sobbing during his sessions when talking about missing out by growing up without a mother. He also expressed anger that on occasion bordered on rage, when triggered by a reminder of his mother's death. He shared with the therapist, for example, that he became upset when his aunt had a dream about his mother because he has few memories and rarely dreams about her. His anger relates to having missed out on the connection to his mother that could be fostered by memories or even dreams about her. Lacking memories is one of the dear prices of losing a parent so early in life. Although he often engaged in power struggles with his father, he also worried about his father; after all, he was the only parent Majid had left.

Throughout Majid's adolescence, he saw his therapist as the need dictated. He sometimes had acute bouts of depression that were initially unexplained. In further exploration, it was sometime possible to trace the trigger to a reminder of being without his mother. One incident that stood out that invoked both enormous sadness and outrage in Majid occurred on Mother's Day when he, his sister, and father went to a diner for lunch. The waitress, in an inexcusable moment of insensitivity, chided Majid and his sister for leaving their mother at home on Mother's Day. Majid could barely contain his rage and told his therapist that he wanted to scream out, "Don't you think if I had my mother, I would have her here with me on Mother's Day. I would give anything to be with her on Mother's Day." Although meant to be humorous or chiding rather than malicious, remarks such as what the waitress said cause enormous pain to those youngsters who have longed deeply for their parent. This pain arises often in elementary schools when children are instructed by their teachers to make Mother's Day or Father's Day cards, and the child who is without a parent is totally lost, embarrassed, and sometimes mortified that he or she is so different from classmates.

In one session Majid discussed how important the New York Knicks were to him after his mother died. He was very attached to the players on the team, and when they lost he would cry. He felt betrayed when

Patrick Ewing (the Knick's star center) was traded. He now realizes that it was his attempt to fill a big void and vacuum in his life. His sister going away to college was another loss for him. Even though he and his sister had the normal sibling conflicts, they are also close and protective of each other.

Majid's long-term grief was brought to the fore in a dramatic way when his maternal grandfather's health began to deteriorate. He kindly gave permission to reprint the following poignant essay written for his high school English class. In the essay he expresses eloquently his feelings after a visit to his grandfather in a nursing facility.

> I arrived at the airport, my grandmother told me not to be upset if he did not recognize me. I nodded politely, but in my mind I scoffed at the fact that my grandfather would ever forget me. Besides I had seen him six months ago, and although he was not doing great, we could still take walks together. It turned out my grandmother was right; when I arrived at the assisted living center where my grandfather now lived, he did not recognize me, or my sister. He just sat there, helplessly, and observed us as if we were total strangers, barely speaking. And if he did, how could a person not be dead, but "gone"? In this case it was called Parkinson's. When there was an irrelevant mumble, I looked him in the eyes and it just wasn't the same. It seemed as if he had no soul, like God had come and taken him to a better place, but left his body on earth with his heart still beating. Not even the pain of losing my mother to brain tumors at age five hit me as hard as this; probably because I could barely remember her and her struggle. I believe there was no physical pain to match the way I was feeling. How could a man who had taught me so much, and meant so much to me not even know who I was, or remember all the good times we had?
>
> When I looked hard into his eyes, I could tell those memories that burned so vividly in my mind were gone from his. I thought to myself, "How could such a strong, hardworking man, who came over on a boat from Great Britain, and started out cleaning chimneys before working himself all the way up to becoming the owner of an oil company, be reduced to this helpless man?" It didn't matter how it could have happened, because it did happen, and now he remembered nothing of me. Those eyes of his told me he did not remember being out on the tennis court with me, teaching me how to play. He could not see how far I had come with tennis. His eyes also told me he did not remember how much of a difference he had made in my life through the minor things he did for me. He had lost his daughter, my mother, to cancer when I was only five years old. Although I cannot remember my mother, I have the fond memory of my grandfather trying to fill that void by nurturing me. Now, for the first time ever in my life I finally

felt what real devastation was like, and this time there was no grandfather to fill the void with his love.

Even though my grandfather, whom I always looked upon as my superman, has found his kryptonite, and is in his last stages of Parkinson's, his spirit will live on through me. Whether it is through striving to be a successful businessman later in life, or while playing tennis, I will always have my grandfather in my mind because of how much he taught me, and how much he meant to me. At the same time, even though mentally I suffered so much pain from seeing my grandfather in such a poor state, I have learned to be grateful for the times we shared, and not bitter about what has happened to him. His influence on me has been so thorough, although sometimes unintentional. I believe that the desire to make him proud will provide me with the motivation to strive for success throughout my college years and beyond.

DISCUSSION AND CLINICAL IMPLICATIONS

Majid is a remarkable young person, and the depth of his feeling is revealed in this moving account of his visit with his grandfather. Majid was outraged when he received a disappointing grade on this essay because, as he explained, he put his heart and soul into it. His therapist told him that he would have given him an A+.

What Majid was missing was not only his grandfather with whom he had been quite close, but the long-felt intense longing for his mother, his grandfather representing a direct link and connection to his mom. Subsequent to the initial drafts of this chapter, Majid's grandfather died. He called to tell his therapist how proud he was that he was the only one in the family composed enough to be able to speak at the memorial service. This eulogy was a significant milestone in Majid's mind in the long road to reconcile to the death of his mother. He spoke eloquently of his love for his grandfather and his mother, but he did so without being overwhelmed with his grief. It was a watershed moment in his long struggle to emotionally accept these monumental losses and to move forward with his life.

Many adolescents, particularly boys, will lack the ready access to their feelings that Majid demonstrated even early in the therapy process. While adolescent girls typically are more able to identify and articulate their feelings than boys, emotional and verbal expressiveness is not always the case for girls. Research has shown that bereaved girls are more likely than boys to develop internalizing symptoms such as anxiety, depression, and somatic or eating disorders (Raveis, Siegel, & Karus, 1999). Boys facing bereavement show higher levels of overall psychopathology, more aggression, and acting-out behaviors (Dowdney et al., 1999). When adolescents who suffer prolonged grief express it through acting-out behavior, it compounds the underlying pain. Hardy and Laszloffy (2005) described the invisible, emotional wounds that these youths suffer that in extreme cases is sometimes expressed in violent actions. It is not only that these teens are misunderstood by others, but they often do not acknowledge their invisible wounds or their corresponding grief either. In many instances, they do not recognize in themselves the underlying grief that drives their acting-out behavior. Society often responds to these youths with punitive responses, while ignoring the invisible wounds, the unresolved grief, and in some cases untreated trauma.

When adolescents do not acknowledge the losses they have suffered and deny the associated grief, the therapy necessarily needs to gradually bring into the teen's awareness the losses that may have been minimized, trivialized, or devalued, along with the feelings that were disassociated—in some cases, a long time ago. Rage is often a mask for grief that adolescents feel too vulnerable to embrace.

Prolonged grief in adolescents is not always focused on the loss of a key attachment figure or a close friend. In addition to what Hardy and Laszloffy (2005) called tangible losses, such as the death of an important person or loss of a home or family, adolescents can also suffer intangible losses such as loss of hope, dreams, dignity, and vision. The intangible losses may be associated with the death of an important person, or they may be suffered independently from such a tangible loss. Adolescents typically receive less support or even acknowledgement of intangible losses, but for some teens these may be most difficult of all losses to overcome. It may be that the crushing of the spirit of a youth is the most devastating of all losses, and yet the support for grieving such losses is perhaps the most lacking. When the dreams of our youths are destroyed by obstacles and harsh life circumstances too difficult to overcome, the cycle of hopelessness and demoralization can be difficult to reverse. This is the fate of far too many teens who ultimately end up in the juvenile justice system.

Bonime (1989) emphasized that validation of assets in the client is empowering. By contrast, reassurance is of little or no help. Reassurance encourages youths to rely on the strengths of the therapist; validation locates the strengths within the adolescent.

In work with adolescents, in addition to the obvious tangible losses, it is important for therapists to pursue the many forms of intangible losses such as devaluation, marginalization, and discrimination that may be based on class, race, gender, or sexual orientation. Pursuing the intangible as well as the tangible losses that too often are overlooked is central to addressing the hidden grief that far too many young people suffer. Sometimes it is hidden from the teens as well. Pursuing intangible losses can be seen in two different clinical presentations. Some teens will demonstrate cognitive awareness of their tangible, and perhaps even intangible, losses, but the affect will be disassociated and out of awareness. Such teens will talk about the death of a family member with an absence of affect, as if they were reporting the scores of yesterday's baseball game. Other teens will be aware of a deep sadness or depressed mood but be unable to connect the affect to the losses they have suffered. In order to facilitate the therapy process with these youths, it is imperative to work toward integration of the cognitive awareness and the affective experience of these losses.

Adolescents are well known for their ability to hide, disown, or minimize their feelings and problems. One teen who had suffered a traumatic loss when asked what advice she would give therapists working with grieving teens said, "You have to dig deep. Teens know how to hide their feelings and unless you are determined and persist, you may never find out how they truly feel." This same 14-year-old girl who repeatedly told her friends and family that she was "fine," reluctantly confided in her therapist after considerable pursuit of how she really felt, "I feel like I am carrying 100 lbs. on my back."

A mistake that can easily be made by therapists with grieving teens who may be reluctant to discuss their feelings in the first place, is failure to pursue the complexity of their feelings. Bonime (1989) explained that feelings are like chords in music, not single notes. The richness of the inner life of an adolescent is often illuminated by a determined pursuit of the complex, often mixed, perhaps ambivalent feelings they are unlikely to reveal unless the therapist persists. Such exploration, of course, depends on establishing trust and a strong therapeutic alliance that serves as a foundation for all successful therapeutic work.

Therapists should keep in mind that adolescents have repeatedly taught us in our clinical work that as much as they are reluctant to reveal the hurt and pain that accompanies prolonged grief, a part of them wants the therapist not to give up because they have a strong wish to tell their story, to unburden, and to heal. It is a great privilege to hear their stories, to accompany them through the arduous journey of grief, until they have resumed their developmental stride and full engagement with life again, and no longer need the company of the healer.

In addition to pursuing the hidden, often denied grief, it is imperative to also pursue the often overlooked strengths, talents, and resources of grieving adolescents (Crenshaw & Garbarino, 2007). It is a serious mistake for therapists to overemphasize pathology and overlook the assets and talents, as well as the resilient qualities of the adolescent. Expressing interest and curiosity about the talents and interests of grieving youths is often a key factor in helping them resume a fuller participation in life.

The parting with the therapist when the therapeutic journey through grief has concluded can be another loss for the teen and may bring the previous losses into awareness with full force. But with sensitivity to this issue on the part of the therapist, leaving therapy can be a ripe opportunity to address what is therapeutically unfinished with the prior losses. In addition, the ending of the therapeutic relationship can be handled in a collaborative manner with full input from the adolescent, giving them more of a say and control over the ending, something that was usually lacking in the suffering of previous losses. The opportunity to anticipate, process, and plan for the therapeutic ending facilitates this particular parting to serve as an emotionally corrective experience that leads to further growth and consolidates the gains of the therapeutic work on the previous losses.

The ending of such a meaningful, challenging, and emotionally demanding collaborative therapeutic journey often results in growth in both the adolescent and the therapist. Neither will ever be the same again after sharing such a rewarding and meaningful therapeutic endeavor.

REFERENCES

Bonanno, G. A., Neria, Y., Mancini, A., Coifman, K. G., Litz, B., & Insel, B. (2007). Is there more to complicated grief than depression and posttraumatic stress disorder? A test of incremental validity. *Journal of Abnormal Psychology, 116*(2), 342–351.

Bonime, W. (1989). *Collaborative psychoanalysis: Anxiety, depression, dreams, and personality change.* Rutherford, NJ: Fairleigh Dickinson Press.

Caffo, E., Forresi, B., & Lievers, L. S. (2005). Impact, psychological sequelae and management of trauma affecting children and adolescents. *Current Opinion in Psychiatry, 18*(4), 422–428.

Cohen, J., Mannarino, A. P., & Deblinger, E. (2006) *Treating trauma and traumatic grief in children and adolescents.* New York: Guilford.

Cohen, J. A., & Mannarino, A. P. (2004). Treatment of childhood traumatic grief. *Journal of Clinical Child and Adolescent Psychology, 33*(4), 819–831.

Cohen, J. A., Mannarino, A. P., & Staron, V. R. (2006). A pilot study of modified Cognitive-Behavioral Therapy for Childhood Traumatic Grief (CBT-CTG). *Journal of the American Academy of Child & Adolescent Psychiatry, 45*(12), 1465–1473.

Crenshaw, D. A. (2002a). *Bereavement: Counseling the grieving throughout the life cycle.* Eugene, OR: Wipf & Stock Publishers.

Crenshaw, D. A. (2002b). Disenfranchised grief of children. In K. J. Doka (Ed.), *Disenfranchised grief: New directions, challenges, and strategies for practice* (pp. 293–306). Champaign, IL: Research Press.

Crenshaw, D. A. (2006). Neuroscience and trauma treatment: Implications for creative arts therapists. In L. Carey (Ed.), *Expressive and creative arts methods for trauma survivors* (pp. 21–38). London: Jessica Kingsley Publishers.

Crenshaw, D. A. (2007). An interpersonal neurobiological-informed treatment model for childhood traumatic grief. *Omega, Journal of Death and Dying, 54,* 315–332.

Crenshaw, D. A. & Garbarino, J. (2007). The hidden dimensions: Profound sorrow and buried human potential in violent youth. *Journal of Humanistic Psychology, 47,* 160–174.

Davis, C. G., Wortman, C. B., Lehman, D. R., & Silver, R. C. (2000). Searching for meaning in loss: Are clinical assumptions correct? *Death Studies, 24*(6), 497–540.

Dickens, C. (2003). *A tale of two cities* (Reprint). New York: Penguin Classics (Original work published 1859).

Doka, K. J. (Ed.). (1989). *Disenfranchised grief: Recognizing hidden sorrow.* Lexington, MA: Lexington Books.

Doka, K. J. (Ed.). (2002). *Disenfranchised grief: New directions, challenges, and strategies for practice.* Champaign, IL: Research Press.

Dowdney, L., Wilson, R., Maughan, B., Allerton, M., Scholfield, P., & Skuse, D. (1999). Psychological disturbance and service provision in parentally bereaved children: Prospective case-control study. *British Medical Journal, 319,* 354–357.

Ewalt, P. L., & Perkins, L. (1979). The real experience of death among adolescents: An empirical study. *Social Casework, 60*(9), 547–551.

Goenjian, A. K., Walling, D., Steinberg, A. M., Karayan, I., Najarian, L. M., & Pynoos, R. (2005). A prospective study of posttraumatic stress and depressive reactions among treated and untreated adolescents 5 years after a catastrophic disaster. *American Journal of Psychiatry, 162,* 2302–2308.

Hardy, K. V., & Laszloffy, T. A. (2005). *Teens who hurt: Clinical interventions to break the cycle of adolescent violence.* New York: Guilford.

Harrison, L., & Harrington, R. (2001). Adolescents' bereavement experiences: Prevalence, association with depressive symptoms, and use of services. *Journal of Adolescence, 24,* 159–169.

Jacobs, S., Mazure, C., & Prigerson, H. (2000). Diagnostic criteria for complicated grief. *Death Studies, 24,* 185–199.

James, B. (1989). *Creative interventions with abused and traumatized children.* Lexington, MA: Lexington Books.

Jewett, C. L. (1982). *Helping children cope with separation and loss.* Harvard, MA: The Harvard Common Press.

Lichtenthal, W. G., Cruess, D. G., & Prigerson, H. G. (2004). A case for establishing complicated grief as a distinct mental disorder in *DSM–V. Clinical Psychology Review, 24,* 637–662.

Lieberman, A. F., Compton, N. C., Van Horn, P., & Ippen, C. G. (2003). *Losing a parent to death in the early years: Guidelines for the treatment of traumatic bereavement in infancy and early childhood.* Washington, DC: Zero to Three Press.

McCarthy, J. R. (2007). "They all look as if they're coping, but I'm not": The relational power/lessness of "youth" in responding to experiences of bereavement. *Journal of Youth Studies, 10*(3), 285–303.

Melhem, N. M., Moritz, G., Walker, M., Shear, M. K., & Brent, D. (2007). Phenomenology and correlates of complicated grief in children and adolescents. *Journal of the American Academy of Child & Adolescent Psychiatry, 46*(4), 493–499.

Neimeyer, R. A. (2000). Searching for the meaning of meaning: Grief therapy and the process of reconstruction. *Death Studies, 24*(6), 541–558.

Noel, B., & Blair, P. D. (2003). *I wasn't ready to say goodbye: A companion workbook for surviving, coping and healing after the sudden death of a loved one.* Fredonia, WI: Champion Press.

Prigerson, H. G., Shear, M. K., Jacobs, S. C., Reynolds, C. F., Maciejewski, P. K., Davidson, J. R. T., et al. (1999). Consensus criteria for complicated grief: A preliminary empirical test. *British Journal of Psychiatry, 174,* 67–73.

Raveis, V. H., Siegel, K., & Karus, D. (1999). Children's psychological distress following the death of a parent. *Journal of Youth and Adolescence, 28*(2), 165–180.

Rotheram-Borus, M. J., Weiss, R., Alber, S., Lester, P. (2005). Adolescent adjustment before and after HIV-related parental death. *Journal of Consulting and Clinical Psychology, 73*(2), 221–228.

Servaty-Seib, H. L., & Pistole, M. C. (2006). Adolescent grief: Relationship category and emotional closeness. *Omega, Journal of Death and Dying, 54*(2), 147–167.

Siegel, D. J. (1999). *The developing mind: Toward a neurobiology of interpersonal experience.* New York: Guilford.

Siegel, D. J. (2007). *The mindful brain: Reflection and attunement in the cultivation of well-being.* New York: Norton.

Siegel, D. J., & Hartzell, M. (2003). *Parenting from the inside out: How a deeper self-understanding can help you raise children who thrive.* New York: Tarcher.

Walker, P., & Shaffer, M. (2007). Reducing depression among adolescents dealing with grief and loss: A program evaluation report. *Health & Social Work, 32*(1), 67–68.

20

Interventions for Caregivers Suffering From Compassion Fatigue or Burnout

CAROL WOGRIN

Working with the dying and the bereaved is both rewarding and uniquely challenging for professionals. It is gratifying to put energy into work that feels very meaningful. However, work in this field entails engaging with the suffering of others on a regular basis. Without proper attention given to the stressors inherent in this work, professional caregivers are at risk of developing compassion fatigue or burnout. This chapter examines the experience of professionals who care for the dying and bereaved, with particular thought given the to developmental issues of adolescence and the impact these have on the caregiver, as well as effective strategies for the prevention and management of caregiver stress.

SIGNIFICANT DEVELOPMENTAL ISSUES

Adolescence is a time of significant physical, cognitive, emotional, and spiritual growth. Important tasks of adolescence include adjusting to many physical changes; separating from parents; focusing increasingly on relationships with peers; and developing a sense of competence, mastery, and control (Balk & Corr, 1996; Fleming & Balmer, 1996). Adolescents typically cope with an evolving sense of self that is still tentative and is largely comprised of a sense of potentials. They work to develop a self-awareness that includes an inner complexity as well as an ability to relate this multifaceted sense of self to others in a larger social context (Meeks & Bernet, 1990). Their view of themselves in relation to others shifts back and forth between seeing reality as a set situation to which they must mold themselves and viewing it as a malleable medium on which they can project an image of their inner struggles. In addition to their tendency to interact with others as if their projections are the reality they are dealing with, Noppe and Noppe (2004) point out that adolescents enjoy argument for the purpose of exploring their logical abilities. They jump to conclusions to test the reactions of listeners and actively work to contradict or discredit adult positions in order to boost their self-confidence. At the same time, they need to be able to count on adult assistance in critical areas.

The imposition of a life-threatening illness, trauma, or significant loss directly challenges these tasks. An adolescent coping with serious illness and death will both engage in the developmental push for independence and also be thrust back into a more dependent role. Conflicts between remaining dependent and striving for independence can be particularly difficult for families with adolescents receiving palliative care (Maunder, 2004). The ambivalence such adolescents feel over being more dependent on the adults who care for them and the resulting feelings of helplessness can frequently trigger anger at those on whom they depend (Stevens & Dunsmore, 1996; see also chapter 7 in this book). Just as these developmental issues in the context of life-threatening illness will impact adolescents and their relationships, they will, in turn, impact the experience of professional caregivers who are working with them.

Anyone who has worked with ill adolescents who are coping with the demands of treatment protocols has witnessed episodes of conflict as the adolescents struggle with competing needs when making difficult decisions, as well as when negotiating with parents and staff. Considering the tendency of adolescents to project their internal experiences onto those around them and then perceive their projections as external reality, combined with their need for a sense of control and mastery, adolescents will assign some aspects of their experience to others and then battle them. The angst around such difficult experiences so early in life can be particularly challenging to witness and even infuriating at times, especially when caregivers suddenly find themselves being held responsible for positions that are outside their own intent or beliefs.

CAREGIVING AND STRESS

People are drawn to working with death and grief for a variety of personal and professional reasons. Daily, countless medical, mental health, and spiritual care professionals provide care for individuals who are dying, their families and friends, and people who are bereaved. These professionals must negotiate a complex interplay between the needs and expectations of the patients with their own needs and expectations (Arbore, Katz, & Johnson, 2006). The suffering of the people for whom they provide care will be experienced in some degree by the caregivers as well. Professional work centered on the emotional suffering of clients includes not only absorbing information about suffering, but also often absorbing that suffering itself as well (Figley, 1995, 2002a). Further, therapists who have enormous capacity for feeling and expressing empathy—in short, the most effective therapists—are the ones who tend to be at highest risk of being adversely affected by the experience of their clients, as they are the most likely to absorb the pain and traumatization of their clients (Figley, 1995). Providers who do not manage their traumatization are more likely to emotionally distance from their clients in a self-protective stance, which will reduce both the effectiveness of the care they provide and their job satisfaction (Meadors & Lamson, 2008).

Stresses inherent in working with suffering can be either growth enhancing or destructive. Kanter (2007) identified factors that can contribute to negative rather than positive outcomes associated with experiences of stress from working with suffering. These factors include insufficient skills and training to accomplish one's professional objectives, an unrealistic wish to rescue all clients, and cumulative countertransference responses to a caseload of clients with similar difficulties. These factors are pertinent to work with death and grief. Particularly when working with children and adolescents, the wish to rescue them and their families from suffering, and even from death, is a common one, although achieving this outcome is clearly impossible. Also, in settings such as hospice or pediatric palliative care, all clients are coping with similar difficulties that typically accompany facing death, and the risk of cumulative countertransference responses is high.

Working with terminally ill children and adolescents poses its own set of specific stressors. Deaths of young people challenge us in specific ways. Children are supposed to grow up. We are supposed to be able to keep them safe. Adolescents who are turning their attention to their potential and their hopes and dreams for the future are supposed to have the opportunity to step into their dreams and plans. Repeated exposure to dying children and adolescents can erode these expectations or myths of safety that are generally assumed by most people. Many authors have found that staff who work with the dying find it more distressing to work with younger patients, especially patients with whom they identify strongly (Ablett & Jones, 2007; Graham et al., 1996; Maytun, Heiman, & Garwick, 2004; Rourke, 2007). For example, Meadors and Lamson (2008) found that even though children in a pediatric intensive care unit are not the provider's own, often there is an emotional identification if the patient is similar in age, gender, or temperament to one's own child, which adds additional stress.

The majority of physicians and nurses interviewed in one study (Papadatou, Bellali, Papazoglou, & Petraki, 2002) reported that the dying process and death of a child was a source of major distress and difficulty. For these professionals, death triggered a sense of helplessness and powerlessness resulting from their inability to decrease the physical and emotional suffering of patients and families or, even, their inability to prevent the death. Further, professionals providing care at the end of life are both witnesses to and participants in a child's and family's trauma. Professionals are often required to provide painful or upsetting treatments and may be unable to provide full relief from pain. As a result, their complex role in a family's trauma can be distressing, and at times the provider may begin to experience similar levels of traumatization to that of the child or family (Davies et al., 1996; Meadors & Lamson, 2008; Papadatou et al., 2002; Rourke, 2007).

As an adolescent battles with life-threatening illness, the unpredictability of a patient's response to treatment may prompt caregivers or parents to try to reduce uncertainty by pursuing additional diagnostic studies and innovative therapies. At times, however, efforts to extend life may increase the burden on the patient and family. Nurses and other health care professionals may experience frustration and ridicule if they question the treatment plan, suggest that the burden of treatment has exceeded the benefit of sustaining life, or argue that scientific curiosity and efforts to learn have supplanted patient goals (Rushton, 2004).

Central concerns for most adolescents are loss of control and becoming totally dependent on others, helpless and childlike. Adolescents are also typically concerned that they will not have an opportunity to achieve their goals in life (Stevens & Dunsmore, 1996). As illnesses progress and many of these fears become realities, staff are likely to absorb the feelings of the adolescents they care for as they witness these events.

Also, nurses and physicians involved in terminal care have often reported themselves to be at a loss for words, especially when dying children raised questions about their prognosis (Papadatou et al., 2002). Given that one of the fears of ill adolescents is that they will not be told the truth (Stevens & Dunsmore, 1996), it is not hard to imagine that these discussions are sources of stress in and of themselves.

Countertransference issues are important considerations in all therapeutic work. Countertransference can be defined simply as the feelings that a client evokes in the professional care provider. Katz (2006) summarizes useful conceptualizations of countertransference described in the literature, including objective and subjective countertransference. Objective countertransference is the expected reaction to clients, given their situation and presentation. Subjective reactions are those that are rooted in the unique history and experience of the caregiver. Both types are important to acknowledge when working with adolescents.

The intense relationships that often occur between palliative care providers, youngsters, and their families can themselves be sources of stress (Rourke, 2007). Palliative care providers often encounter situations that echo losses in their own lives and reactivate their personal pain and grief, even if only temporarily. At these times, health care providers may actually be responding emotionally as much to their own personal grief as they are to the present reality of the patient and family for whom they are caring. Likewise, parents may also be reacting with strong emotions that are more closely linked psychologically to their own past traumatic experiences than to the objective aspects of the situations. These reactions, the causes of which are invisible to those around them, can seem inappropriate, offensive, and exasperating to health care providers and can thus lead team members to feel abused, angry, powerless, or resentful (Rourke, 2007).

Finally, an additional factor that may increase the stress experienced by those caring for adolescents is the number of stressors that many adolescents are coping with above and beyond those imposed by their normal developmental tasks and the illness. In one study of 360 parentally bereaved youngsters drawn from a community-based sample, almost half of whom were adolescents, the initial criteria of recruiting only youngsters without significant stressors other than parental death had to be revised. Almost half of all those recruited would have been ineligible for the study (Cerel, Fristad, Verducci, Weller, & Weller, 2006). While this study specifically looked at parentally bereaved children and adolescents, it suggests that many adolescents are already coping with complex significant stressors; illness and grief may be added to previously difficult life circumstances. These additional struggles, which can contribute to an adolescent feeling overwhelmed, are likely to evoke feelings of helplessness and powerlessness in the professional care provider, feelings that are already heightened in work with death and grief.

GRIEF IN CAREGIVERS

In addition to grief over losses in their personal lives, caregivers for the dying will also experience grief over the deaths of the patients they care for, with whom they often form close relationships as caring extends over long periods of time. Several studies of professionals caring for terminally ill children (e.g., Kaplan, 2000; Papadatou, 2000; Papadatou et al., 2002) found that, regardless of work or cultural setting, health care professionals need to find ways to experience and express their grief, as well as ways to avoid or repress it. Fluctuating between experiencing and expressing grief, on the one hand, and avoiding or repressing it by moving away from the loss experience, on the other hand, is normal, healthy, and adaptive. It allows health care professionals to grieve without being overwhelmed by the loss experience. Reported grief experiences of physicians and nurses are similar and include crying, sadness, withdrawal, and recurring thoughts of the dying conditions and death of the child. These professionals frequently reported guilt feelings and an active search for philosophic explanations or meaning that would decrease their distress. Both groups often withdrew into themselves as a way of coping. However, physicians saw their grief as a private affair, while nurses identified a need to share experiences with colleagues to find an emotional outlet and receive support.

COMPASSION FATIGUE

Over the past two decades, there has been an evolving understanding of the effect that working with the trauma and suffering of others can have on the caregiver (Figley, 1995; Meadors & Lamson, 2008). Figley (1995) defines the concept of secondary traumatic stress as "the natural consequent behaviors and emotions resulting from knowing about a traumatizing event experienced by a significant other—the stress resulting from helping or wanting to help a traumatized or suffering person" (p. 7). Secondary traumatic stress disorder is a syndrome with symptoms nearly identical to Post Traumatic Stress Disorder, except that symptoms are due to exposure to knowledge about the traumatizing event experienced by another person rather than symptoms that are directly connected to the experience of the person in harm's way (Becvar, 2003). The symptoms that a provider may exhibit include a constellation of reactions that can be separated into three domains: (a) reexperiencing the primary person's traumatic events; (b) avoidance of reminders of the event or the people/places/things involved in the event; and (c) numbing in response to triggers and reminders, along with persistent arousal across psychological, cognitive, and emotional domains (Figley, 2002a, 2002b). When helpers' survival strategies are insufficient to resolve victim stresses, helpers become secondarily stressed by carrying both the maladaptive coping strategies of the victim, with which they identify, and their own complementary maladaptive or insufficient survival strategies (Valent, 2002). These reactions are considered common and even expected for professionals who help others by providing care and empathy (Rourke, 2007). In addition to the stress of witnessing the suffering and traumas of others, professional caregivers will inevitably experience a variety of stressors and traumas in their personal lives. These concurrent stressors will have a cumulative effect on the caregiver and can inhibit many providers in a number of ways from being as effective as they may otherwise be within their profession (Meadors & Lamson, 2008).

Many labels have been applied interchangeably to describe the kinds of psychological consequences experienced by professionals working with people in the wake of traumatic and painful events. These include secondary traumatic stress, vicarious traumatization, compassion stress, and compassion fatigue. Joinson (1992) and Figley (1995) have advocated for the phrase *compassion fatigue* as one that reflects the inevitable experience of the emotional exhaustion that comes from continuous compassion directed toward those in crisis. In keeping with this recommendation, the phrase *compassion fatigue* is used in this chapter.

Signs and symptoms of compassion fatigue follow classic stress patterns. Individuals may find that they forget or lose things more frequently or have a shorter attention span. They may be exhausted and may experience a variety of somatic complaints such as frequent headaches or stomachaches (Becvar, 2003; Figley, 1995; Joinson, 1992). Resistance can be low, resulting in more frequent illnesses. Additionally, signs of compassion fatigue can include anger that is too frequent and intense for the situation, increasing countertransference issues with certain individuals, difficulty separating work from personal life, diminished sense of purpose and enjoyment with career, lowered functioning in nonprofessional settings, loss of hope, and depression.

BURNOUT

In contrast to compassion fatigue, burnout is a state of physical, emotional, and mental exhaustion; depersonalization; and reduced sense of personal accomplishment resulting from long-term involvement in emotionally demanding situations, powerlessness, and inability to achieve work goals, rather than the specific exposure to the trauma and suffering of a client (Maslach, 1982; Pines & Aronson, 1998; Sprang, Clark, & Whitt-Woosley, 2007; Valent, 2002). Along with mental exhaustion, burnout is characterized by psychophysiological arousal symptoms, including sleep disturbance, headaches, irritability, and aggression. Other symptoms include callousness, pessimism, and cynicism, as well as problems in work relationships and performance.

In contrast to compassion fatigue, which has more to do with the personal situation and countertransference responses on the part of the caregiver, burnout tends to be caused by real, external factors (Figley, 1995). The risk of burnout is high when professionals perceive a low level of control over the care they provide, whether that is due to authoritarian supervisors, lack of input into policies that govern a person's job, or being given more responsibility or higher work volume than a person feels able to handle. Burnout can also occur when caregivers are unable to achieve their goals for their patients, due to organizational factors outside their control (Ablett & Jones, 2007; Maslach, 1982). Hospice and palliative care staff, specifically, have been found to experience increased stress when workloads were unrealistic, level of involvement in decision making was low, and social support was not available (Vachon, 2004).

In her study on occupational stress in nurses caring for the terminally ill, Vachon (1987) noted that most of the stress experienced was attributed to the work environment and occupational role rather than the direct work with dying patients and their families. Supporting the finding that it is not the work with dying or suffering patients that contributes to burnout, Liakopoulou and colleagues (2008) found that burnout in pediatric oncology staff was not differentiated from that in staff of other pediatric specialties.

Unlike compassion fatigue, which can develop suddenly and without warning, burnout emerges gradually as a result of emotional exhaustion, and symptoms tend to be greater. At times, symptoms of compassion fatigue that are not attended to can progress to burnout. Likewise, recovery from burnout tends to be slower than recovery from compassion fatigue (Maytun et al., 2004).

One specific situational stressor for nurses who work with dying children is being in a position of following orders that are in conflict with their belief that children should be allowed to die peacefully without unnecessary pain (Davies et al., 1996). Because nurses developed close relationships with the children and/or families, they were profoundly aware of patient's and family's preferences for care. When nurses perceived their input was not considered by physicians in decision making, and they felt they were in a position of inflicting suffering beyond the point of a possible cure or extension of life with reasonable quality, they felt they were acting in ways that were not in the child's best interest. As a result, those nurses suffered significantly in their feelings of powerlessness. These feelings of powerlessness in the system are the types that, over time, contribute to burnout.

AVOIDING AND MANAGING COMPASSION FATIGUE AND BURNOUT

Caregiver grief, compassion fatigue, and burnout all stem from different causes, each with a significant personal and professional interplay. Consequently, when focusing on strategies to manage these different experiences, it is important to evaluate carefully the cause of the distress. Effective strategies must target the cause of the problem. Preventing and ameliorating compassion fatigue and burnout involves both cognitive and behavioral strategies. They can be divided into three primary areas: professional strategies, personal strategies, and organizational strategies.

Professional Strategies

When working in the field of thanatology, times of increased stress for caregivers are inevitable. Crises, losses of all kinds, and deaths are to be expected. Witnessing the suffering of young people is particularly painful, and professionals are often helpless against the cause of their suffering. The development and utilization of peer support and the development and maintenance of good boundaries are important and effective strategies for self-care.

Because many of the stresses occur in our workplaces, it is important to have *social support from peers and colleagues within the workplace.* In part, workplace support is important because it is our colleagues who understand the rewards of the work and the reasons we are in this field. The people who understand the rewards are the ones who best understand the losses and related stress we experience in this context (Davies et al., 1996; Papadatou et al., 2002; Vachon, 2007).

Davies and her colleagues (1996) found that peer support had the greatest influence on nurses' ability to manage their distress. Those who were able to acknowledge their need to express sad emotions, and then seek support and share their struggles with others, were most able to effectively manage their own distress and to provide support to youngsters and their families.

However, few formal supports tend to exist (Kaplan, 2000). To the contrary, there are implicit, yet widely known professional codes of conduct that give strong messages: Don't cry while on duty, be cheerful, do not let your emotions interfere with the tasks that need doing, and do not get emotionally involved with patients and their families (Davies et al., 1996). Some nurses responded to their grief over patients' deaths by physically or emotionally withdrawing. However, while this tactic relieved their distress in the short term, if used as a primary strategy over the long term it prevented nurses from releasing emotions and resolving their distress and resulted in their feeling overwhelmed, guilty, and sad. It also eroded their self-confidence in their judgment and made it more difficult to leave their distress behind them when they left work. These nurses were likely in time to abandon work that involved caring for dying youngsters.

Vachon (2007) stressed the importance of caregivers learning to recognize their feelings associated with grief following the death of a patient and to identify the source of these feelings. Caregivers should question their reactions in terms of whether they reflect normal grief over the loss of someone to whom they were close, or whether their reactions are in any way reflective of overidentification with the person who died, unresolved grief from past losses, or feelings of guilt over care they believed was not optimal given the circumstances. These experiences are best shared with caring and supportive coworkers or the team.

The other important strategy in self-care is the development and maintenance of clear professional boundaries (Pearlman & Saakvitne, 1995; Rourke, 2007). Boundaries can be defined simply as "the edge of appropriate behavior" (Gutheil & Gabbard, 1998, p. 410) or as the lines we draw to help us define our roles and interactions in relationships (Leurquin-Hallett, 1999). Boundaries define and protect the space between the power inherent in our professional positions and the access we have to a client's private information. Clear boundaries serve to create an atmosphere of safety and predictability. They also allow for a therapeutic connection between the practitioner and the client. The rules for appropriate behavior consist of guidelines for contact, including how much, how often, and method; types of information to be shared; physical closeness; and the setting in which the interactions may occur (Martsolf, 2002). There are many factors that help define where this line is appropriately drawn, including professional discipline and the practice setting, such as a facility versus home care or city versus a small rural area (Knapp & Slattery, 2004).

The maintenance of clear professional boundaries serves a protective function, distancing professional care providers from the emotional distress resulting from working with patients who are themselves addressing existential end-of-life issues. This function is particularly apparent when nurses describe forming attachments with patients and when there is overidentification because a particular situation was too "close to home" (Ablett & Jones, 2007). When examining stressors that made things particularly difficult for nurses caring for terminally ill children, by far the most frequently cited issue was being overly involved or crossing professional boundaries (Maytun et al., 2004).

Peteet, Ross, Medeiros, Walsh-Burke, and Rieker (1992) examined relational issues between staff and oncology patients. They found that when boundaries were loosened, staff identified a number of challenges including less objectivity; more difficulty delivering bad news; greater difficulty managing one's own feelings; and greater likelihood of confusing one's own needs with those of the client, making it more difficult to stay focused on the needs of the client and family. When professional boundaries are overstepped, the lines between clients and caregivers are blurred, and, among other problems, the work will take a greater emotional toll.

Rourke (2007) identified three relational complications that can occur when a professional is experiencing compassion fatigue: splitting, the savior versus helper, and detachment. Each of these complications involves difficulties with boundaries. *Splitting* is a relational pattern common to people who have experienced trauma. It involves perceiving one person or subgroup of people as entirely good and helpful, and another person or subgroup as entirely bad and extremely unhelpful. The *savior versus helper* complication involves responding to a family's anxiety and fear in ways that inappropriately join them in their wishes for rescue from the dire circumstances that, in reality, are not open to rescue. Finally, becoming overwhelmed by unrecognized overinvolvement or overidentification can result in *emotional detachment.*

The nature of these relational complications dovetails with adolescent development in ways that can escalate compassion fatigue. The needs of adolescents to separate from parents while also needing more from adults as they cope with the demands of serious illness, combined with their way of projecting their more difficult feelings onto others, make it easy for so-called good guy/bad guy dynamics to develop. These dynamics can occur between the adolescent and parents as well as between different staff members, as some caregivers are perceived as helpful and others not. Fears and vulnerability on the part of the adolescent and family members, combined with the caregiver's own feelings about the young age of the patient as death approaches, can easily tap into wishes on the part of the caregiver to save the child. Finally, if the caregiver identifies in any way with the adolescent, for example, seeing the child as similar to his or her own, the caregiver could become overwhelmed or emotionally detached in order to manage difficult feelings. If the professional is already emotionally fatigued and does not have the energy to remain vigilant to the risks of these relational dynamics, compassion fatigue is likely to develop.

In addition to interpersonal boundaries are boundaries that help to keep a clear line between work and home. Caregivers who are able to exhibit self-assertive behavior, set time limits on their work, maintain a balance, and keep their work life separate from their home life manage their stress much more effectively over time (Ablett & Jones, 2007; Becvar, 2003; Davies et al., 1996; Meadors & Lamson, 2008). Time off work needs to be time to focus on things other than attending to the suffering of others. It must be a time to pay attention to one's own needs and the needs of family and friends. A helpful approach to separating work from home is to use the transition time between work and home to emotionally decompress or shift gears. Techniques such as mental imagery, distraction by activities such as listening to music during the drive home, or physical exercise can be helpful (Welsh, 1999).

Professional caregivers need to develop the skill of engaging empathically with the experiences of those being cared for, and at the same time, not taking on a patient's pain and suffering as one's own. While it is necessary to be open to the suffering when we are with a client in order to do the work well, it is important to be able to separate from that suffering at the end of a session or the end of the workday. Without this skill, it is unlikely that a professional will be able to do the work well over long periods of time.

Personal Strategies

In addition to supports within professional realms, a variety of ways to nourish oneself are needed in order to counterbalance the ways in which the stresses of this type of work can affect a person. Social supports outside of the work world are extremely important because they allow individuals to develop aspects of themselves that are not about caregiving (Figley, 2002a).

Activities and behaviors that support physical, emotional, and spiritual health are critical in preventing or managing compassion fatigue (Becvar, 2003; Holland & Neimeyer, 2005; Joinson, 1992; Meadors & Lamson, 2008). Physical health is supported by regular exercise, good nutrition, and adequate rest. Emotional health may be fostered through activities such as meditation, journaling, personal psychotherapy, and developing good social support systems. Spiritual well-being may be enhanced through spending time in nature, either alone or with others, or through engaging in the religious or spiritual practices of one's choice. Other ways, such as taking vacations, getting regular massages, going on personal retreats, or engaging in relaxing activities such as going to the movies, as well as occasionally indulging in childlike behavior, may also be useful (Davies et al., 1996). Finally, humor can offer tremendous benefits in terms of releasing the effects of stress (Ablett & Jones, 2007; Welsh, 1999).

Organizational Strategies

The organization within which a professional works sets the stage for how stressful the work is and how effectively the provider is able to defuse that stress. It is essential that the larger organization recognizes that pediatric death occurs in large enough numbers to warrant allocating the resources necessary for the job to be done well (Rourke, 2007).

Professionals who care for those coping with life-threatening illness often find themselves working in a health care system in which there is an emphasis on cure, and where death, to varying degrees, represents failure. It is important that there be a broadening of the goals of treatment to include recognition of the value of palliative care on a systems level. The emphasis that is commonly placed on cure-related goals has been identified as a problematic factor that contributes to a heightened sense of helplessness and personal failure when treatment goals become palliative (Rourke, 2007).

Primary factors that offset stress and mitigate against the development of compassion fatigue and burnout depend on finding the work meaningful and thus experiencing a significant level of compassion satisfaction and job satisfaction (Papadatou et al., 2002). In general, caring for dying patients and their families can be a major source of job satisfaction (Grunfeld et al., 2005). It is easy to imagine that for professional caregivers, supporting an adolescent's efforts to maintain as normal a life as possible when living with life-threatening illness, along with providing the necessary support as that youngster faces issues surrounding death, feels very meaningful. Helping such adolescents and their families navigate the stresses and losses, while still maintaining a quality of life where goals and plans are accomplished, generally is gratifying for the professionals involved.

An additional factor that contributes significantly to job satisfaction is role clarity. Professionals who have a clear sense of their role in the provision of care are able to achieve a greater sense of personal achievement and demonstrate less emotional exhaustion and burnout (Liakopoulou et al., 2008). Also, nurses who achieve a good balance between their personal and professional lives and who have good family and peer support report greater job satisfaction (Davies et al., 1996). It is reasonable to expect that this experience would hold true for other disciplines as well.

Training opportunities are important for professionals involved in caring for people who are traumatized and suffering. Specialized training on trauma has been shown to enhance compassion satisfaction and reduce compassion fatigue and burnout (Davies et al., 1996; Figley, 2002a). Keeping in mind the level of trauma that children and adolescents with life-threatening illness and their families are experiencing, and the secondary effects of this trauma on the professional caregivers, ongoing staff education should be an integral component of the support offered to caregivers on the organizational level.

Additionally, organizational efforts to assess and promote the development of systems for staff support are important (Davies et al., 1996; Figley, 2002a; Meadors & Lamson, 2008). Formal training can create opportunities for transitory or ongoing support from colleagues. These experiences serve a protective function against the development of compassion fatigue and burnout. Creating mechanisms for peer support is especially needed by clinicians working in isolated settings. When nurses are unable to share their distress or seek resources, their energy is devoted to maintaining their professional demeanor, and little energy is left to implement the other strategies, such as finding meaning. As a result, little satisfaction is obtained from the experience, and heightened frustration increases distress. An institutional value placed on the development of these resources, including staff support, supervision, and educational training, is fundamental to developing a culture that promotes job satisfaction and an environment that is conducive to the management of the stressors inherent in the work. Further, providing formal institutional support and recognition that compassion fatigue is expected at times when professionals are caring for the dying and their families is essential (Rourke, 2007). Without this support from organizations and institutions, it is too easy overtly or covertly to frame both compassion fatigue and burnout as weaknesses in the individual rather than as hazards in this line of work or as reflective of wider systemic problems.

CONCLUSION

Along with the rewards that come with work in the field of thanatology, there are times when those who care for the dying and bereaved are affected by the suffering of others to a degree that makes it difficult to stay fully engaged. Coping with suffering tends to be most difficult when the caregiver is simultaneously challenged with high stress in his or her personal life or when there are excessive demands and too little support in the workplace. Unaddressed stress can result in the development of compassion fatigue or burnout. Preventing or managing these conditions involves the development of good professional, personal, and organizational strategies. To date, the research on caregiver stress focuses on those who care for adults and, more recently, on children. There is very little that specifically focuses on those who work with adolescents. Considering the developmental issues of adolescence and the impact of those issues on their relationships, the experiences of professionals who care for adolescents needs further research.

REFERENCES

Ablett, J., & Jones, R. (2007). Resilience and well-being in palliative care staff: A qualitative study of hospice nurses' experience of work. *Psycho-Oncology, 16,* 733–744.

Arbore, P., Katz, R. S., & Johnson, T. A. (2006). Suffering and the caring professional. In R. S. Katz & T. A. Johnson (Eds.), *When professionals weep* (pp.13–26). New York: Taylor & Francis.

Balk, D. E., & Corr, C. A. (1996) Adolescents, developmental tasks, and encounters with death and bereavement. In C. A. Corr & D. E. Balk (Eds.), *Handbook of adolescent death and bereavement* (pp. 3–24). New York: Springer Publishing.

Becvar, D. S. (2003). The impact on the family therapist of a focus on death, dying, and bereavement. *Journal of Marital and Family Therapy, 29,* 469–477.

Cerel, J., Fristad, M., Verducci, J., Weller, R., & Weller, E. (2006). Childhood bereavement psychopathology in the 2 years postparental death. *Journal of the American Academy of Child and Adolescent Psychiatry, 45,* 681–691.

Davies, B., Clarke, D., Connaughty, S., Cook, K., MacKenzie, B., McCormick, J., et al. (1996). Caring for dying children: Nurses' experiences. *Pediatric Nursing, 22,* 500–507.

Figley, C. R. (1995). Compassion fatigue as secondary traumatic stress disorder: An overview. In C. R. Figley (Ed.), *Compassion fatigue: Coping with secondary traumatic stress disorder in those who treat the traumatized* (pp. 1–20). New York: Brunner/Mazel.

Figley, C. R. (2002a). Compassion fatigue: Psychotherapists' chronic lack of self care. *Journal of Clinical Social Psychology, 58,* 1433–1441.

Figley, C. R. (2002b). *Treating compassion fatigue.* New York: Brunner-Routledge.

Fleming, S., & Balmer, L. (1996). Bereavement in adolescence. In C. A. Corr & D. E. Balk (Eds.), *Handbook of adolescent death and bereavement* (pp. 139–154). New York: Springer Publishing.

Graham, J., Ramirez, A. J., Cull, A., Finlay, I., Hoy, A., & Richards, M. A. (1996). Job stress and satisfaction among palliative physicians. *Palliative Medicine, 10,* 185–194.

Grunfeld, E., Zitselsberger, L., Coristine, M., Whelan, T., Aspelund, F., & Evans, W. (2005). Job stress and job satisfaction of cancer care workers. *Psycho-Oncology, 14,* 61–69.

Gutheil, T. G., & Gabbard, G. O. (1998). Misuses and misunderstandings of boundary theory in clinical and regulatory settings. *American Journal of Psychiatry, 155,* 409–414.

Holland, J. M., & Neimeyer, R. A. (2005). Reducing the risk of burnout in end-of-life settings: The role of daily spiritual experiences and training. *Palliative and Supportive Care, 3,* 173–181.

Joinson, C. (1992). Coping with compassion fatigue: Taking care of one's self while taking care of others. *Nursing, 22,* 116–121.

Kanter, J. (2007). Compassion fatigue and secondary traumatization: A second look. *Clinical Social Work Journal, 35,* 289–293.

Kaplan, L. (2000). Towards a model of caregiver grief: Nurses' experiences of treating dying children. *Omega, Journal of Death and Dying, 41,* 187–206.

Katz, R. S. (2006). The journey inside: Examining countertransference and its implications for practice in end-of-life. In R. S. Katz & T. A. Johnson (Eds.), *When professionals weep* (pp. 13–26). New York: Taylor & Francis.

Knapp, S. & Slattery, J. (2004). Professional boundaries in nontraditional settings. *Professional Psychology: Research and Practice, 35,* 553–558.

Leurquin-Hallett, L. (1999). Professional boundaries in nephrology nursing practice. *ANNA Journal, 26,* 80–82.

Liakopoulou, M., Panaretaki, I., Papadakis, V., Katsika, A., Sarafidou, J., Lasakari, H., et al. (2008). Burnout, staff support, and coping in pediatric oncology. *Support Care Cancer, 16,* 143–150.

Martsolf, D. S. (2002). Codependency, boundaries, and the professional nurse caring: Understanding similarities and differences. *Orthopedic Nursing, 21,* 61–67.

Maslach, C. (1982). *Burnout: The cost of caring.* Englewood Cliffs, NJ: Prentice-Hall.

Maunder, E. Z. (2004). The challenge of transitional care for young people with life-limiting illness. *British Journal of Nursing, 13,* 594–596.

Maytun, J. C., Heiman, M. B., & Garwick, A. W. (2004). Compassion fatigue and burnout in nurses who work with children with chronic conditions and their families. *Journal of Pediatric Health, 18,* 171–179.

Meadors, P., & Lamson, A. (2008). Compassion fatigue and secondary traumatization: Provider self care on intensive care units for children. *Journal of Pediatric Health Care, 22,* 24–34.

Meeks, J., & Bernet, W. (1990). *The fragile alliance: An orientation to the psychiatric treatment of the adolescent.* Malabar, FL: Robert E. Krieger Publishing Company.

Noppe, I. C., & Noppe, L. D. (2004). Adolescent experiences with death: Letting go of immortality. (Theory and practice.) *Journal of Mental Health Counseling, 26,* 146–166.

Papadatou, D. (2000). A proposed model of health care professionals' grieving process. *Omega, Journal of Death and Dying, 41,* 59–77.

Papadatou, D., Bellali, T., Papazoglou, I., & Petraki, D. (2002). Greek nurse and physician grief as a result of caring for children dying of cancer. *Pediatric Nursing, 28,* 345–353.

Pearlman, L. A., & Saakvitne, K. W. (1995). *Trauma and the therapist: Countertransference and vicarious traumatization in psychotherapy with incest survivors.* New York: W. W. Norton.

Peteet, J. R., Ross, D. M., Medeiros, C., Walsh-Burke, K., & Rieker, P. (1992). Relationships with patients in oncology: Can a patient be a friend. *Psychiatry, 55,* 223–229.

Pines, A., & Aronson, E. (1988). *Career burnout: Causes and cures.* New York: Free Press.

Rourke, M. T. (2007). Compassion fatigue in pediatric palliative care providers. *Pediatric Clinics of North America, 54,* 631–644.

Rushton, C. H. (2004). The other side of caregiving: Caregiver suffering. In B. S. Carter & M. Levetown (Eds.), *Palliative care for infants, children and adolescents* (pp. 220–243). Baltimore: Johns Hopkins University Press.

Sprang, G., Clark, J. J., & Whitt-Woosley, A. (2007). Compassion fatigue, compassion satisfaction, and burnout: Factors impacting a professional's quality of life. *Journal of Loss and Trauma, 12,* 259–280.

Stevens, M. M., & Dunsmore, J. C. (1996). Adolescents who are living with a life-threatening illness. In C. A. Corr & D. E. Balk (Eds.), *Handbook of adolescent death and bereavement* (pp. 107–135). New York: Springer Publishing.

Vachon, M. L. S. (1987). *Occupational stress in the care of the critically ill, the dying, and the bereaved.* Washington, DC: Hemisphere.

Vachon, M. L. S. (2004). The stress of professional caregivers. In D. Doyle, G. Hanks, N. Cherny, & K. Calman (Eds.) *Oxford textbook of palliative care* (3rd ed., pp. 992–1004). New York: Oxford University Press.

Vachon, M. L. S. (2007). Caring for the professional caregivers: Before and after the death. In K. J. Doka (Ed.), *Living with grief: Before and after the death* (pp. 311–330). Washington, DC: Hospice Foundation of America.

Valent, P. (2002). Diagnosis and treatment of helper stresses, traumas, and illnesses. In C. Figley (Ed.), *Treating compassion fatigue* (pp. 17–38). New York: Brunner-Routledge.

Welsh, D. (1999). Caregiving for the caregiver: Strategies for avoiding compassion fatigue. *Journal of Clinical Oncology, 3,* 183–184.

Name Index

Subject Index